A History of Our Time

A HISTORY OF OUR TIME

Readings on Postwar America
SIXTH EDITION

Edited by
William H. Chafe
Harvard Sitkoff
Beth Bailey

New York   Oxford
OXFORD UNIVERSITY PRESS
2003

Oxford University Press

Oxford   New York
Auckland   Bangkok   Buenos Aires   Cape Town   Chennai
Dar es Salaam   Delhi   Hong Kong   Istanbul   Karachi   Kolkata
Kuala Lumpur   Madrid   Melbourne   Mexico City   Mumbai
Nairobi   São Paulo   Shanghai   Taipei   Tokyo   Toronto

Copyright © 1983, 1987, 1991, 1995, 1999, 2003
by Oxford University Press, Inc.

Published by Oxford University Press, Inc.
198 Madison Avenue, New York, New York 10016
http://www.oup-usa.org

Oxford is a registered trademark of Oxford University Press

Library of Congress Cataloging-in-Publication Data

A history of our time : readings on postwar America—6th ed. / edited by William H.
Chafe, Harvard Sitkoff, and Beth Bailey.
     p. cm.
   Includes bibliographical references.
   ISBN 0-19-515105-4 (acid-free paper)
   1. United States—History—1945–   I. Chafe, William Henry. II. Sitkoff, Harvard. III.
Bailey, Beth L., 1957–
E742.H57   2003
973.92—dc21   2002025755

Printing number: 9 8 7 6 5 4 3

Printed in the United States of America
on acid-free paper

For William E. Leuchtenburg
our teacher and friend
with gratitude and affection
    –W.H.C.
    –H.S.

and for Max
    –B.B.

Contents

vii

PART 3: CIVIL RIGHTS AND RACIAL JUSTICE   117

PART 4: STRUGGLES OVER GENDER AND SEXUAL
         LIBERATION   177

PART 5: THE VIETNAM WAR   247

Preface

More than two decades ago, when we first contemplated putting together a collection of documents and essays on U.S. history since 1945, we agreed that our overriding aim was a book that addressed the *real* concerns and needs of the students we knew and taught, one lively and challenging enough to provoke discussions in the dorm room as well as the classroom. That is still our aim. Of course, much has changed in the intervening years, and this sixth edition addresses new matters of interest and new viewpoints on continuing issues of relevance. Beginning with this edition, we are joined by a new editor, Beth Bailey. As always, we have incorporated the suggestions of students and instructors who used earlier editions of *A History of Our Time*. We are grateful for such advice and hope to continue to receive recommendations for future editions.

As in the earlier editions, this book is structured to give students the opportunity to hear different voices of and about the past, to enable them to compare and contrast, and thus to provide a basis for asking critical questions and arriving at independent judgments on major issues. Consequently, each section of the book contains an introduction and headnotes that place the readings in historical perspective and highlight their relevance, documents that provide firsthand, and personal, analyses of postwar issues, and well-written essays that both convey the drama and "humanness" of history and reveal the diversity of themes and interpretations of the recent past. Much, of necessity, has been left out of this brief collection, and we urge those interested to consult the updated Suggestions for Further Reading.

The recent past is not dead; indeed, much of it is not even past. We firmly believe that the history of the last half-century still strongly in-

fluences our lives and that any conscious shaping of the future requires an understanding of this past. To that end, this collection illu-
minates the major political and social developments and events from
the anxieties of the Cold War and McCarthyism to the movements for
political and social change in the 1960s, the American involvement in
the Vietnam War, and the conservative backlash in the 1970s and
1980s. Lastly, it focuses on the challenges facing the United States at
the beginning of the new millennium: recent political struggles and
their legacies; "the new economy"; globalism and the environment;
the significance of race and ethnicity; and the complexity of international affairs in the post–Cold War era. This edition ends with a medi-
tation on September 11 by novelist Don DeLillo.

We hope that this edition of *A History of Our Time* will help readers
better understand America's past and also serve as a guide to some
of the unresolved questions in American life as we face the new
millennium.

Durham, N.C.   W. H. C.
Durham, N.H.   H. S.
Albuquerque, N.M.   B. B.

A History of Our Time

Part 1

THE COLD WAR
ABROAD AND AT HOME

The Cold War literally defined the half-century after World War II, marking a new era in both American and world history. It shaped international relations around the globe and decisively affected the cultural, economic, and political lives of many peoples, particularly Americans. In the United States, the anxieties and tensions associated with its onset helped produce the Second Red Scare—McCarthyism— a wide-ranging anticommunist crusade at home that paralleled the worsening contest between (according to Americans) the Soviet-masterminded worldwide communist conspiracy against peace, democracy, and capitalism, and (according to the Soviets) the militarized, economically aggressive U.S. effort to dominate the globe.

At its root was the transformation of the uneasy wartime collaboration between the Allies fighting Hitler's Germany into the conflict between the United States and the Soviet Union over the nature of the postwar world. Above all else, the Soviet Union demanded secure borders and control over those nations closest to Russia. It sought to refashion eastern Europe in its own image. The United States, however, clearly the strongest nation in the world and wanting to shape a new international system suited to its desires, insisted that the war had been fought for self-determination, territorial integrity, free trade, and traditional Western freedoms. This conflict over priorities and values would come to a head over five critical issues.

The Polish question—the first—symbolized to both sides the primary purpose for which they had fought the war. On three occasions, Western nations had invaded Russia via the Polish corridor. Hence, a Polish government subservient, or at least friendly, to the Soviet Union was Stalin's overriding aim. Conversely, the Western Allies had gone to war with Germany over the matter of self-determination for

1

Poland; and the right of Poland to its own democratically elected government represented, in the purest possible form, a test of the principles of the Atlantic Charter. The second issue revolved around the fate of the future governments for Greece, Romania, and the occupied nations of eastern Europe, again pitting the Soviet Union's fears for its own security and desire to control its neighbors, versus Washington's vision of a postwar world of American-led capitalist democracies. The third involved Germany, splitting the wartime allies over such questions as whether Germany should be deindustrialized, whether it should be permanently divided, and how much it must pay in reparations. Control over atomic energy constituted a fourth point of division. Many Russians believed that the U.S. monopoly over atomic weaponry represented an American effort to intimidate the Soviet Union. The United States, however, refused to relinquish control of its nuclear secrets until the Soviet Union submitted to a comprehensive system of control and inspection by a United Nations agency. The fifth issue, relating to the economic reconstruction of Europe, found the United States and the Soviet Union at loggerheads over the specific issue of rehabilitation loans and the more general conflict between capitalism and socialism.

The historical literature on the Cold War is vast and rapidly changing, especially as historians gain access to government documents and archives previously closed to them. Historical debates over the Cold War have been—and continue to be—hotly contested. Who was responsible for the Cold War? Was it avoidable?

The first selections in Part 1, a historian's analysis and a set of documents from the time, address some of the major reasons for the Cold War and for the U.S. policy of "containment" of the Soviet Union. Historian Thomas G. Paterson describes a postwar world beset by massive physical destruction, political instability, and vacuums of power in regions formerly dominated by Germany and Japan. Rejecting earlier historical interpretations, which were more likely to place responsibility for the Cold War on communist ideology and the actions of Josef Stalin, Paterson blames the worsening Cold War largely on President Harry S. Truman's exaggeration of the Soviet threat.

A set of documents also sheds light on the development of American Cold War policy. Writing from Moscow in early 1946, American diplomat George F. Kennan warned of an expansionist Soviet communist system and proposed policies that might serve to contain it "without recourse to war." President Truman spelled out the larger implications of "containment" for American foreign policy in his 1947 speech to Congress, in which he articulated what came to be known as the Truman Doctrine: The United States would take a stand against the expansion of communism anywhere in the world. The last document in this section, the April 1950 report to the president by the National Security Council (NSC-68), makes clear the massive expansion of U.S. military spending required by a worldwide containment policy and calls for the intensification of intelligence activities.

Reading these selections, students ought to consider such questions as: Was the Cold War inevitable? If so, what made it so? If not, how could it have been avoided? Or, at least, how could its pervasive costs have been minimized? In what areas was compromise possible? What were the sources of American and Soviet policy? Ideology? Economics? Domestic politics? Strategic and geopolitical considerations? What role did misperception play? Would it have made much difference if Roosevelt had lived and remained president until 1949? Or if Stalin had died in 1945? Finally, what light is cast on the onset of the Cold War by its recent dissolution? Compare the crucial determinants of U.S. and Russian foreign policies in 1990 or 2000 with those of 1945.

The second section of Part 1 turns to the domestic impact of the Cold War. Worsening relations with the Soviet Union after World War II provided the context for the growth of what we now call McCarthyism. America's former ally quickly moved to assert control over eastern Europe. Apprehension grew when, before the end of the decade, the Soviet Union exploded its own atomic bomb. Tension escalated when Chinese communists took control of the Chinese mainland in 1949. These anxieties—reasonable ones in a world just beginning recovery from a worldwide conflagration that had killed millions—left the American public receptive to the accusations of demagogues such as Sen. Joseph R. McCarthy.

When Sen. McCarthy asserted to the Women's Republican Club in Wheeling, West Virginia, in February 1950 that he had a list of 205 card-carrying communists in the State Department, he carried to a new height the hysteria already gripping the nation. McCarthy had no such list. Most of his charges were fabrications. He never uncovered a single communist spy. His investigations and exposés did not lead to the successful prosecution of a single person for treasonous or disloyal acts. Yet, the very brashness of his accusations, the abrasiveness of his insinuations, the exaggerated big lie and red smear enabled McCarthy to hold center stage for four years, intimidating the innocent as well as the suspect and destroying numerous careers and lives. In late 1954, the Senate voted 67–22 to censure McCarthy, ending his personal effectiveness; but the larger crusade he had come to symbolize still cast a pall over the land, chilling political debate, and making it virtually impossible for yet another decade for most Americans to support any cause, domestic or international, that could possibly be distorted as sympathetic to socialism or communism.

Two documents illustrate the techniques and impacts of McCarthyism. The first, an excerpt from the House Un-American Activities Committee's 1947 investigation of communism in Hollywood, illustrates the reach of the post–World War II Red Scare and its impact on the lives of Americans. The second, a revised version of Senator McCarthy's Wheeling, West Virginia, speech that he introduced into the 1950 Congressional Record, illustrates his "big lie" tactics as the investigations spread into higher reaches of the U.S. government. Finally, two historians offer powerful evidence, based on newly available documents, that there really *were* communist spies in the American government and atomic weapons programs and that American government officials had certain knowledge of that fact.

Students should consider how newly opened archives complicate our understanding of Cold War anticommunism and its lessons. Historians have generally seen the entire episode as an example of national hysteria or paranoia, in which government officials engaged in a "witch-hunt," or a "search for scapegoats to take the blame" for "America's difficulties in the world," to quote an earlier edition of *A History of Our Time*. How does the proof offered by historians John Haynes and Harvey Klehr challenge that interpretation? Does it in any way alter our understandings of the evils of McCarthyism?

Those questions might lead to others: What was the link between the Cold War and demands for domestic intellectual conformity? To what extent might President Truman and George Kennan have paved the way for McCarthyism by their definition of the stakes in the Cold War? Why would Hollywood be an obvious target for HUAC or for any group attempting to control the sentiments of the nation? Could leaders with actual knowledge of Soviet espionage have prevented the spread of suspicion through the nation and the ruin of innocent lives?

Finally, what are the valid limits of ideological dissent in a democracy? As the nation faces new challenges to civil liberties following an undeniably real incident of terrorism, America's domestic Cold War experience is especially worth pondering.

The Cold War Begins

Thomas G. Paterson

The enormous, and still growing, literature on the causes and origins of the Cold War presents students with an array of conflicting interpretations. Historians disagree on whether the United States or the Soviet Union was most responsible for the conflict, on whether the Cold War could have been avoided, and on which factors were the key determinants: atomic weaponry, domestic politics, economics, geopolitics, ideology, misperception, national security, personality, or . . . . Diplomatic historian Thomas G. Paterson of the University of Connecticut, the author of numerous works on American foreign policy in the Cold War years, argues that President Harry S. Truman pursued unnecessarily provocative policies. A so-called revisionist, influenced by the politics of the 1960s and by the U.S. involvement in the Vietnam War, Paterson rejects the traditional interpretation of most American historians that the Soviet Union was mostly to blame for the Cold War. Instead, in this selection from his Meeting the Communist Threat: Truman to Reagan (1988), *Paterson emphasizes Truman's exaggerated perception of the Soviet threat, and his disproportionate response to it, as the chief initial obstacle to accommodation or compromise between the two postwar superpowers.*

Presidents from Eisenhower to Reagan have exalted Truman for his decisiveness and success in launching the Truman Doctrine, the Marshall Plan, and NATO, and for staring the Soviets down in Berlin during those hair-trigger days of the blockade and airlift. . . . Some historians have gone so far as to claim that Truman saved humankind from World War III. On the other hand, . . . many historians have questioned Truman's penchant for his quick, simple answer, blunt, careless rhetoric, and facile analogies, his moralism that obscured the complexity of causation, his militarization of American foreign policy, his impatience with diplomacy itself, and his exaggeration of the Soviet threat.

Still, there is no denying the man and his contributions. He fashioned policies and doctrines that have guided leaders to this day. He helped initiate the nuclear age with his decisions to annihilate Hiroshima and Nagasaki with atomic bombs and to develop the hydrogen bomb. His reconstruction programs rehabilitated former enemies West Germany and Japan into thriving, industrial giants and close American allies. His administration's search for oil in Arab lands and endorsement of a new Jewish state in Palestine planted the United States in the Middle East as never before. Overall, Truman projected American power onto the world stage with unprecedented activity, expanding American interests worldwide, providing American solutions to problems afflicting countries far distant from the United States, establishing the United States as the pre-eminent nation in the postwar era.

. . . About three months after assuming office, . . . Truman boarded a ship for Europe, there to meet at Potsdam, near Berlin, with . . . Winston Churchill and Josef Stalin. . . . Truman's assertiveness at Potsdam on such issues as Poland and Germany stemmed not only from his forthright personality, but also from his learning that America's scientists had just successfully exploded an atomic bomb which could be used against Japan to end World War II. And more, it might serve as a diplomatic weapon to persuade others to behave according to American precepts. The news of the atomic test's success gave Truman "an entirely new feeling of confidence . . . ," Secretary of War Henry L. Stimson recorded in his diary. . . .

Truman soon became known for what he himself called his "tough method." He crowed about giving Russia's Commissar for Foreign Affairs, V. M. Molotov, a "straight 'one-two to the jaw'" in their first meeting in the White House not long after Roosevelt's death. Yet Secretary Stimson worried about the negative effects of Truman's "brutal frankness," and Ambassador Harriman was skeptical that the President's slam-bang manner worked to America's advantage. Truman's brash, salty style suited his bent for the verbal brawl, but it ill-fit a world of diplomacy demanding quiet deliberation, thoughtful weighing of alternatives, patience, flexibility, and searching analysis of the motives and capabilities of others. If Truman "took 'em for a ride," as he bragged after Potsdam, the dangerous road upon which he raced led to the Cold War. . . .

The United States entered the postwar period, then, with a new, in-experienced, yet bold President who was aware of America's enviable power in a world hobbled by war-wrought devastation and who shared the popular notion of "Red Fascism." . . . Truman's lasting legacy is his tremendous activism in extending American influence on a global scale—his building of an American "empire" or "hege-mony." We can disagree over whether this postwar empire was created reluctantly, defensively, by invitation, or deliberately, by self-interested design. But few will deny that the drive to contain Commu-nism fostered an exceptional, worldwide American expansion that produced empire and ultimately, and ironically, insecurity, for the more the United States expanded and drove in foreign stakes, the more vulnerable it seemed to become—the more exposed it became to a host of challenges from Communists and non-Communists alike.

. . . [The war] bequeathed staggering human tragedy, rubble, and social and political chaos. . . . Europe lost more than 30 mil-lion dead in the Second World War. . . . Everywhere, armies had trampled farms and bombs had crumbled cities. . . .

. . . [E]conomic, social, and hence political "disintegration" char-acterized the postwar international system. The question of how this disintegration could be reversed preoccupied Truman officials. Thinking in the peace and prosperity idiom, they believed that a fail-ure to act would jeopardize American interests, drag the United States into depression and war, spawn totalitarianism and aggression, and permit the rise of Communists and other leftists who were eager to exploit the disorder. . . . [The] formidable task of reconstruc-tion drew the United States and the Soviet Union into conflict, for each had its own model for rebuilding states and each sought to align nations with its foreign policy.

Political turmoil within nations also drew America and Russia into conflict, for each saw gains to be made and losses to be suffered in the outcome of the political battles. Old regime leaders vied with left-ists and other dissidents in state after state. . . . When the United States and the Soviet Union meddled in these politically unstable set-tings in their quest for influence, they collided—often fiercely.

The collapse of old empires also wrenched world affairs and in-vited confrontation between America and Russia. Weakened by the war and unable to sustain colonial armies in the field, the imperialists were forced to give way to nationalists who had long worked for inde-pendence. . . . Decolonization produced a shifting of power within the international system and the emergence of new states whose allegiances both the Americans and Russians avidly sought.

With postwar economies, societies, politics, and empires shattered, President Truman confronted an awesome set of problems that would have bedeviled any leader. He also had impressive responsibilities and opportunities, because the United States had escaped from World War II not only intact but richer and stronger. America's abundant farmlands were spared from the tracks of marching armies, its cities were never leveled by bombs, and its factories remained in place. During the war, America's gross national product skyrocketed and every economic indicator, such as steel production, recorded significant growth. . . . To create the American-oriented world the Truman Administration desired, and to isolate adversaries, the United States issued or withheld loans (giving one to Britain but not to Russia), launched major reconstruction programs like the Marshall Plan . . . and offered technical assistance through the Point Four Program [U.S. aid to Third World countries]. . . . American dollars and votes also dominated the World Bank and International Monetary Fund, transforming them into instruments of American diplomacy.

The United States not only possessed the resources for reconstruction, but also the implements of destruction. The United States had the world's largest Navy, floating in two oceans, the most powerful Air Force, a shrinking yet still formidable Army, and a monopoly of the most frightening weapon of all, the atomic bomb. . . .

Because of America's unusual postwar power, the Truman Administration could expand the United States sphere of influence beyond the Western Hemisphere and also intervene to protect American interests. But this begs a key question: Why did President Truman think it necessary to project American power abroad, to pursue an activist, global foreign policy unprecedented in United States history? The answer has several parts. First, Americans drew lessons from their experience in the 1930s. While indulging in their so-called "isolationism," they had watched economic depression spawn political extremism, which in turn, produced aggression and war. Never again, they vowed. . . . Americans felt compelled to project their power, second, because they feared, in the peace-and-prosperity thinking of the time, economic doom stemming from an economic sickness abroad that might spread to the United States, and from American dependency on overseas supplies of raw materials. To aid Europeans and other peoples would not only help them, but also sustain a high American standard of living and gain political friends. . . .

Strategists spoke of the shrinkage of the globe. . . . Airplanes could travel great distances to deliver bombs. Powerful as it was, then, the United States also appeared vulnerable, especially to air attack. . . . To prevent such an occurrence, American leaders worked to acquire overseas bases in both the Pacific and Atlantic, thereby denying a potential enemy an attack route to the Western Hemisphere. Forward bases would also permit the United States to conduct offensive operations more effectively. . . .

These several explanations for American globalism suggest that the United States would have been an expansionist power whether or not the obstructionist Soviets were lurking about. . . . As the influential National Security Council Paper No. 68 (NSC-68) noted in April 1950, the "overall policy" of the United States was "designed to foster a world environment in which the American system can survive and flourish." This policy "we would probably pursue even if there were no Soviet threat."

Americans, of course, did perceive a Soviet threat. . . . Their harsh Communist dogma and propagandistic slogans were not only monotonous; they also seemed threatening because of their call for world revolution and for the demise of capitalism. . . .

The Soviet Union, moreover, had territorial ambitions. . . . To Truman and his advisers, the Soviets stood as the world's bully, and the very existence of this menacing bear necessitated an activist American foreign policy and an exertion of American power as a "counterforce."

But Truman officials exaggerated the Soviet threat, imagining an adversary that never measured up to the galloping monster so often depicted by alarmist Americans. Even if the Soviets intended to dominate the world, or just Western Europe, they lacked the capabilities to do so. The Soviets had no foreign aid to dispense; outside Russia Communist parties were minorities; [and] the Soviet economy was seriously crippled by the war. . . . The Soviets lacked a modern navy, a strategic air force, the atomic bomb, and air defenses. Their wrecked economy could not support or supply an army in the field for very long, and their technology was antiquated. . . .

Why then did Americans so fear the Soviets? Why did the Central Intelligence Agency, the Joint Chiefs of Staff, and the President exaggerate the Soviet threat? The first explanation is that their intelligence estimates were just that—estimates. The American intelligence community was still in a state of infancy. . . . Truman officials also exaggerated the Soviet threat in order "to extricate the United States from commitments and restraints that were no longer considered desirable." For example, they loudly chastised the Soviets for violating the Yalta agreements; yet Truman and his advisers knew the Yalta provisions were at best vague and open to differing interpretations. . . .

Another reason for the exaggeration: Truman liked things in black and white. . . . Nuances, ambiguities, and counterevidence were often discounted to satisfy the President's preference for the simpler answer or his pre-conceived notions of Soviet aggressiveness. . . . American leaders also exaggerated the Soviet threat because it was useful in galvanizing and unifying American public opinion for an abandonment of recent and still lingering "isolationism" and support for an expansive foreign policy. . . . The military particularly overplayed the Soviet threat in order to persuade Congress to endorse larger defense budgets. . . .

Still another explanation for why Americans exaggerated the Soviet threat is found in their attention since the Bolshevik Revolution of 1917 to the utopian Communist goal of world revolution, confusing goals with actual behavior. . . .

Why dwell on this question of the American exaggeration of the Soviet threat? Because it over-simplified international realities by under-estimating local conditions that might thwart Soviet/Communist successes and by over-estimating the Soviet ability to act. Because it encouraged the Soviets to fear encirclement and to enlarge their military establishment, thereby contributing to a dangerous weapons race. Because it led to indiscriminate globalism. Because it put a damper on diplomacy; American officials were hesitant to negotiate with an opponent variously described as malevolent, deceitful, and inhuman. They especially did not warm to negotiations when some critics were ready to cry that diplomacy, which could produce compromises, was evidence in itself of softness toward communism.

Exaggeration of the threat also led Americans to misinterpret events and in so doing to prompt the Soviets to make decisions contrary to American wishes. For example, the Soviet presence in Eastern Europe, once considered a simple question of the Soviets' building an iron curtain or bloc after the war, is now seen by historians in more complex terms. The Soviets did not seem to have a master plan

for the region and followed different policies in different countries.
. . . The Soviets did not have a firm grip on Eastern Europe before
1948. . . .

American policies were designed to roll the Soviets back. The
United States reconstruction loan policy, encouragement of dissident
groups, and appeal for free elections alarmed Moscow, contributing
to a Soviet push to secure the area. . . .

Another example of the exaggeration of the Soviet threat at work is
found in the Truman Doctrine of 1947. Greece was beset by civil war,
and the British could no longer fund a war against Communist-led in-
surgents who had a considerable non-Communist following. On
March 12, Truman enunciated a universal doctrine: It "must be the
policy of the United States to support free peoples who are resisting
attempted subjugation by armed minorities or by outside pressures."
Although he never mentioned the Soviet Union by name, his juxta-
position of words like "democratic" and "totalitarian" and his references to Eastern Europe made the menace to Greece appear to be
the Soviets. But there was and is no evidence of Soviet involvement in
the Greek civil war. . . .

The story of Truman's foreign policy is basically an accounting of
how the United States, because of is own expansionism and exaggeration of the Soviet threat, became a global power. Truman projected
American power after the Second World War to rehabilitate Western
Europe, secure new allies, guarantee strategic and economic links,
and block Communist or Soviet influence. He firmly implanted the
image of the Soviets as relentless, worldwide transgressors with whom
it is futile to negotiate. Through his exaggeration of the Soviet threat,
Truman made it very likely that the United States would continue to
practice global interventionism years after he left the White House.

The Necessity for Containment (1946)

George F. Kennan

A diplomat in the U.S. Embassy in Moscow and a leading expert on Soviet affairs, George F. Kennan sent a long, eight-thousand-word, secret telegram to the State Department early in 1946 sketching the roots of Soviet policy and warning of serious difficulties with the Soviet Union in the years ahead. Kennan then recommended a long-term, firm policy of resistance by the United States to Soviet expansionism. Known as the containment policy, it became the basis of President Truman's new departure in foreign policy (see "The Truman Doctrine," p. 20). In reading the excerpts from Kennan's telegram that follow, students should note Kennan's view of the methods the Soviet Union was likely to employ to expand its economic and political influence, the principles of Soviet foreign policy, the U.S. interests involved, what the United States has to fear from the Soviets, and the course of action the United States should take.

BASIC FEATURES OF POST WAR SOVIET OUTLOOK, AS PUT FORWARD BY OFFICIAL PROPAGANDA MACHINE, ARE AS FOLLOWS:

(a) USSR still lives in antagonistic "capitalist encirclement" with which in the long run there can be no permanent peaceful coexistence. As stated by Stalin in 1927 to a delegation of American workers:

> In course of further development of international revolution there will emerge two centers of world significance: a socialist center, drawing to itself the countries which tend toward socialism, and a capitalist center, drawing to itself the countries that incline toward capitalism. Battle between these two centers for command of world economy will decide fate of capitalism and of communism in entire world.

Excerpted from U.S. Department of State, *Foreign Relations of the United States, 1946* (Washington, D.C., 1969), 6:697–99, 701–9.

(b) Capitalist world is beset with internal conflicts, inherent in nature of capitalist society. These conflicts are insoluble by means of peaceful compromise. Greatest of them is that between England and US.

(c) Internal conflicts of capitalism inevitably generate wars. Wars thus generated may be of two kinds: intra-capitalist wars between two capitalist states, and wars of intervention against socialist world. Smart capitalists, vainly seeking escape from inner conflicts of capitalism, incline toward latter.

(d) Intervention against USSR, while it would be disastrous to those who undertook it, would cause renewed delay in progress of Soviet socialism and must therefore be forestalled at all costs.

(e) Conflicts between capitalist states, though likewise fraught with danger for USSR, nevertheless hold out great possibilities for advancement of socialist cause, particularly if USSR remains militarily powerful, ideologically monolithic and faithful to its present brilliant leadership.

. . . So much for premises. To what deductions do they lead from standpoint of Soviet policy? To following:

(a) Everything must be done to advance relative strength of USSR as factor in international society. Conversely, no opportunity must be missed to reduce strength and influence, collectively as well as individually, of capitalist powers.

(b) Soviet efforts, and those of Russia's friends abroad, must be directed toward deepening and exploiting of differences and conflicts between capitalist powers. If these eventually deepen into an "imperialist" war, this war must be turned into revolutionary upheavals within the various capitalist countries.

(c) "Democratic-progressive" elements abroad are to be utilized to maximum to bring pressure to bear on capitalist governments along lines agreeable to Soviet interests.

(d) Relentless battle must be waged against socialist and social-democratic leaders abroad. . . .

BACKGROUND OF OUTLOOK

Before examining ramifications of this party line in practice there are certain aspects of it to which I wish to draw attention.

First, it does not represent natural outlook of Russian people. . . .

But party line is binding for outlook and conduct of people who make up apparatus of power—party, secret police and Government—and it is exclusively with these that we have to deal. Second, please note that premises on which this party line is based are for most part simply not true. Experience has shown that peaceful and mutually profitable coexistence of capitalist and socialist states is entirely possible. . . . Nevertheless, all these theses, however baseless and disproven, are being boldly put forward again today. What does this indicate? It indicates that Soviet party line is not based on any objective analysis of situation beyond Russia's borders: that it has, indeed, little to do with conditions outside of Russia; that it arises mainly from basic inner-Russian necessities which existed before recent war and exist today.

At bottom of Kremlin's neurotic view of world affairs is traditional and instinctive Russian sense of insecurity. Originally, this was insecurity of a peaceful agricultural people trying to live on vast exposed plain in neighborhood of fierce nomadic peoples. To this was added, as Russia came into contact with economically advanced West, fear of more competent, more powerful, more highly organized societies in that area. . . . For this reason they have always feared foreign penetration, feared direct contact beteween Western world and their own, feared what would happen if Russians learned truth about world without or if foreigners learned truth about world within. And they have learned to seek security only in patient but deadly struggle for total destruction of rival power, never in compacts and compromises with it. . . .

PROJECTION OF SOVIET OUTLOOK IN PRACTICAL POLICY ON OFFICIAL LEVEL

. . . (a) Internal policy devoted to increasing in every way strength and prestige of Soviet state: intensive military-industrialization; maximum development of armed forces; great displays to impress outsiders; continued secretiveness about internal matters, designed to conceal weaknesses and to keep opponents in dark.

(b) Wherever it is considered timely and promising, efforts will be made to advance official limits of Soviet power. . . .

(c) Russians will participate officially in international organizations where they see opportunity of extending Soviet power or of inhibiting or diluting power of others. . . .

(d) Toward colonial areas and backward or dependent peoples, Soviet policy, even on official plane, will be directed toward weakening of power and influence and contacts of advanced Western nations, on theory that in so far as this policy is successful, there will be created a vacuum which will favor Communist-Soviet penetration. . . .

BASIC SOVET POLICIES ON UNOFFICIAL, OR SUBTERRANEAN PLANE . . .

Agencies utilized for promulgation of policies on this plane are following:

1. Inner central core of Communist Parties in other countries . . . tightly coordinated and directed by Moscow. . . .
2. Rank and file of Communist Parties. . . . no longer even taken into confidence about realities of movement. . . .
3. A wide variety of national associations or bodies which can be dominated or influenced. . . . These include: labor unions, youth leagues, women's organizations, racial societies, religious societies, social organizations, cultural groups, liberal magazines, publishing houses, etc.
4. International organizations which can be similarly penetrated through influence over various national components. Labor, youth and women's organizations are prominent among them. . . .

It may be expected that component parts of this far-flung apparatus will be utilized . . . as follows:

(a) To undermine general political and strategic potential of major western powers. Efforts will be made in such countries to disrupt national self confidence, to hamstring measures of national defense, to increase social and industrial unrest, to stimulate all forms of disunity. . . . Here poor will be set against rich, black against white, young against old, newcomers against established residents, etc.

(b) On unofficial plane particularly violent efforts will be made to weaken power and influence of Western Powers of [*on*] colonial backward, or dependent peoples. On this level, no holds will be barred. . . .

(c) Where individual governments stand in path of Soviet purposes pressure will be brought for their removal from office. . . .

(d) In foreign countries Communists will, as a rule, work toward destruction of all forms of personal independence, economic, political or moral. . . .

(e) Everything possible will be done to set major Western Powers against each other. . . .

(f) In general, all Soviet efforts on unofficial international plane will be negative and destructive in character, designed to tear down sources of strength beyond reach of Soviet control. . . . The Soviet regime is a police regime par excellence, reared in the dim half world of Tsarist police intrigue, accustomed to think primarily in terms of police power. This should never be lost sight of in gauging Soviet motives. . . .

PRACTICAL DEDUCTIONS FROM STANDPOINT OF U S POLICY

In summary, we have here a political force committed fanatically to the belief that with US there can be no permanent *modus vivendi*, that it is desirable and necessary that the internal harmony of our society be disrupted, our traditional way of life be destroyed, the international authority of our state be broken, if Soviet power is to be secure. . . . This is admittedly not a pleasant picture. Problem of how to cope with this force in [*is*] undoubtedly greatest task our diplomacy has ever faced and probably greatest it will ever have to face. . . . I would like to record my conviction that problem is within our power to solve—and that without recourse to any general military conflict. And in support of this conviction there are certain observations of a more encouraging nature I should like to make:

1. Sovet power . . . does not take unnecessary risks. . . . For this reason it can easily withdraw—and usually does—when strong resistance is encountered at any point. Thus, if the adversary has sufficient force and makes clear his readiness to use it, he rarely has to do so. . . .

2. Gauged against Western World as a whole, Soviets are still by far the weaker force. Thus, their success will really depend on degree of cohesion, firmness and vigor which Western World can muster. . . .

3. Success of Soviet system, as form of internal power, is not yet finally proven. . . .

4. All Soviet propaganda beyond Soviet security sphere is basically negative and destructive. It should therefore be relatively easy to combat it by any intelligent and really constructive program.

For these reasons I think we may approach calmly and with good heart problem of how to deal with Russia. . . . [B]y way of conclusion, following comments:

1. Our first step must be to apprehend, and recognize for what it is, the nature of the movement with which we are dealing. . . .

2. We must see that our public is educated to realities of Russian situation. . . .

3. Much depends on health and vigor of our own society. World communism is like malignant parasite which feeds only on diseased tissue. . . .

4. We must formulate and put forward for other nations a much more positive and constructive picture of sort of world we would like to see than we have put forward in past. . . .

5. Finally we must have courage and self-confidence to cling to our own methods and conceptions of human society. After all, the greatest danger that can befall us in coping with this problem of Soviet communism, is that we shall allow ourselves to become like those with whom we are coping.

The Truman Doctrine (1947)

Harry S. Truman

Once President Truman decided on the containment policy advocated by his closest advisors, including Clifford and Acting Secretary of State Dean Acheson, he faced the task of persuading the Congress and the American people that this potentially dangerous and expensive new departure was necessary. Taking the advice of Republican senator Arthur Vandenberg, the president resolved to "scare the hell out of the country." Responding to the immediate crisis brought on by Great Britain's decision that it could no longer afford to assist the governments of Greece and Turkey in their respective struggles against a communist-aided insurgent guerrilla movement and against Soviet pressure for access to the Mediterranean, the president went before the Congress in March 1947 to request $400 million in military assistance to Greece and Turkey. Truman starkly depicted a communist menace that imperiled the world and threatened the United States.

"[I] wished to state, for all the world to know, what the position of the United States was in the face of the new totalitarian challenge," Truman later recalled about his address to Congress. "This was, I believe, the turning point in America's foreign policy, which now declared that wherever aggression, direct or indirect, threatened the peace, the security of the United States was involved." Accordingly, the Truman Doctrine came to mean that the United States had to draw the line against the spread of communism everywhere, and, that in its role of global policeman, the United States faced an almost limitless confrontation with the Soviet Union and any of its allies. The Truman Doctrine, which quickly led to the Marshall Plan and then to the North Atlantic Treaty Organization (NATO), laid the foundation for American foreign policy for much of the next four decades.

From *Public Papers of the Presidents, Harry S Truman, 1947* (Washington, D.C., 1963), pp. 176–80.

19

MR. PRESIDENT, MR. SPEAKER, MEMBERS OF THE CONGRESS OF THE
UNITED STATES:

    . . . The United States had received from the Greek Government
an urgent appeal for financial and economic assistance. Preliminary
reports from the American Economic Mission now in Greece and reports from the American Ambassador in Greece corroborate the
statement of the Greek Government that assistance is imperative if
Greece is to survive as a free nation. . . .
    The very existence of the Greek state is today threatened by the ter-
rorist activities of several thousand armed men, led by Communists,
who defy the government's authority at a number of points, particularly along the northern boundaries. A Commission appointed by the
United Nations Security Council is at present investigating disturbed
conditions in northern Greece and alleged border violations along
the frontier between Greece on the one hand and Albania, Bulgaria,
and Yugoslavia on the other.
    Meanwhile, the Greek Government is unable to cope with the
situation. The Greek army is small and poorly equipped. It needs supplies and equipment if it is to restore authority to the government
throughout Greek territory.
    Greece must have assistance if it is to become a self-supporting and
self-respecting democracy. . . .
    No government is perfect. One of the chief virtues of a democracy,
however, is that its defects are always visible and under democratic
processes can be pointed out and corrected. The government of
Greece is not perfect. Nevertheless it represents 85 percent of the
members of the Greek Parliament who were chosen in an election
last year. Foreign observers, including 692 Americans, considered
this election to be a fair expression of the views of the Greek people.
    The Greek Government has been operating in an atmosphere of
chaos and extremism. It has made mistakes. The extension of aid by
this country does not mean that the United States condones everything that the Greek Government has done or will do. We have condemned in the past, and we condemn now, extremist measures of the
right or the left. We have in the past advised tolerance, and we advise
tolerance now.
    Greece's neighbor, Turkey, also deserves our attention. . . .
    The British Government has informed us that, owing to its own dif-
ficulties, it can no longer extend financial or economic aid to Turkey.

As in the case of Greece, if Turkey is to have the assistance it needs, the United States must supply it. We are the only country able to provide that help.

I am fully aware of the broad implications involved if the United States extends assistance to Greece and Turkey, and I shall discuss these implications with you at this time. One of the primary objectives of the foreign policy of the United States is the creation of conditions in which we and other nations will be able to work out a way of life free from coercion. This was a fundamental issue in the war with Germany and Japan. Our victory was won over countries which sought to impose their will, and their way of life, upon other nations.

To ensure the peaceful development of nations, free from coercion, the United States has taken a leading part in establishing the United Nations. The United Nations is designed to make possible lasting freedom and independence for all its members. We shall not realize our objectives, however, unless we are willing to help free peoples to maintain their free institutions and their national integrity against aggressive movements that seek to impose upon them totalitarian regimes. This is no more than a frank recognition that totalitarian regimes imposed upon free peoples, by direct or indirect aggression, undermine the foundations of international peace and hence the security of the United States.

The peoples of a number of countries of the world have recently had totalitarian regimes forced upon them against their will. The Government of the United States has made frequent protests against coercion and intimidation, in violation of the Yalta agreement, in Poland, Rumania, and Bulgaria. I must also state that in a number of other countries there have been similar developments.

At the present moment in world history nearly every nation must choose between alternative ways of life. The choice is too often not a free one.

One way of life is based upon the will of the majority, and is distinguished by free institutions, representative government, free elections, guarantees of individual liberty, freedom of speech and religion, and freedom from political oppression.

The second way of life is based upon the will of a minority forcibly imposed upon the majority. It relies upon terror and oppression, a controlled press and radio, fixed elections, and the suppression of personal freedoms.

I believe that it must be the policy of the United States to support free peoples who are resisting attempted subjugation by armed minorities or by outside pressures.

I believe that we must assist free peoples to work out their own destinies in their own way.

I believe that our help should be primarily through economic and financial aid which is essential to economic stability and orderly political processes.

The world is not static, and the *status quo* is not sacred. But we cannot allow changes in the *status quo* in violation of the Charter of the United Nations by such methods as coercion, or by such subterfuges as political infiltration. In helping free and independent nations to maintain their freedom, the United States will be giving effect to the principles of the Charter of the United Nations.

It is necessary only to glance at a map to realize that the survival and integrity of the Greek nation are of grave importance in a much wider situation. If Greece should fall under the control of an armed minority, the effect upon its neighbor, Turkey, would be immediate and serious. Confusion and disorder might well spread throughout the entire Middle East.

Moreover, the disappearance of Greece as an independent state would have a profound effect upon those countries in Europe whose peoples are struggling against great difficulties to maintain their freedoms and their independence while they repair the damages of war.

It would be an unspeakable tragedy if these countries, which have struggled so long against overwhelming odds, should lose that victory for which they sacrificed so much. Collapse of free institutions and loss of independence would be disastrous not only for them but for the world. Discouragement and possibly failure would quickly be the lot of neighboring peoples striving to maintain their freedom and independence.

Should we fail to aid Greece and Turkey in this fateful hour, the effect will be far reaching to the West as well as to the East. . . .

NSC-68: A Report to the National Security Council (1950)

Following the detonation of the Soviet Union's first atomic bomb and the communist victory in China in 1949, President Truman asked his advisers for a comprehensive analysis of the course of world affairs and the foreign and military policies of the United States. Largely the work of Secretary of State Dean Acheson, NSC-68 was officially a report to the National Security Council by the Departments of State and Defense in April 1950. It defined the Soviet–American conflict as global in scope and primarily military in nature. Predicting continued, perpetual conflict with international communism, NSC-68 called for a vastly enlarged military budget to counter the Soviet's alleged ambition for global domination. How to sell such an expensive, militaristic policy to a war-weary American people and a budget-minded Congress worried proponents of NSC-68. "We were sweating over it, and then—with regard to NSC-68—thank God Korea came along," recalled one of Dean Acheson's aides. Do you think Russian and/or Chinese actions as of April 1950 justified the tone and recommendations of NSC-68? What were the costs, financially and otherwise, of the "eternal vigilance" called for by NSC-68? What practical alternatives to NSC-68 did President Truman have in 1950? What were the implications of this pivotal report for the wars in Korea and Indochina?

Within the past thirty-five years the world has experienced two global wars of tremendous violence. It has witnessed two revolutions—the Russian and the Chinese—of extreme scope and intensity. It has also seen the collapse of five empires—the Ottoman, the Austro-Hungarian, German, Italian and Japanese—and the drastic decline of two major imperial systems, the British and the French. During the span of one generation, the international distribution of power has

Excerpts from "NSC-68: A Report to the National Security Council," April 14, 1950, from *Foreign Relations of the United States: 1950,* I, pp. 237–92.

been fundamentally altered. For several centuries it had proved impossible for any one nation to gain such preponderant strength that a coalition of other nations could not in time face it with greater strength. The international scene was marked by recurring periods of violence and war, but a system of sovereign and independent states was maintained, over which no state was able to achieve hegemony.

Two complex sets of factors have now basically altered this historical distribution of power. First, the defeat of Germany and Japan and the decline of the British and French Empires have interacted with the development of the United States and the Soviet Union in such a way that power has increasingly gravitated to these two centers. Second, the Soviet Union, unlike previous aspirants to hegemony, is animated by a new fanatic faith, antithetical to our own, and seeks to impose its absolute authority over the rest of the world. Conflict has, therefore, become endemic and is waged, on the part of the Soviet Union, by violent or non-violent methods in accordance with the dictates of expediency. With the development of increasingly terrifying weapons of mass destruction, every individual faces the ever-present possibility of annihilation should the conflict enter the phase of total war.

On the one hand, the people of the world yearn for relief from the anxiety arising from the risk of atomic war. On the other hand, any substantial further extension of the area under the domination of the Kremlin would raise the possibility that no coalition adequate to confront the Kremlin with greater strength could be assembled. It is in this context that this Republic and its citizens in the ascendancy of their strength stand in their deepest peril.

The issues that face us are momentous, involving the fulfillment or destruction not only of this Republic but of civilization itself. They are issues which will not await our deliberations. With conscience and resolution this Government and the people it represents must now take new and fateful decisions. . . . The fundamental design of those who control the Soviet Union and the international communist movement is to retain and solidify their absolute power, first in the Soviet Union and second in the areas now under their control. In the minds of the Soviet leaders, however, achievement of this design requires the dynamic extension of their authority and the ultimate elimination of any effective opposition to their authority.

The design, therefore, calls for the complete subversion or forcible destruction of the machinery of government and structure of society in the countries of the non-Soviet world and their replacement by an apparatus and structure subservient to and controlled from the Kremlin. To that end Soviet efforts are now directed toward the domination of the Eurasian land mass. The United States, as the principal center of power in the non-Soviet world and the bulwark of opposition to Soviet expansion, is the principal enemy whose integrity and vitality must be subverted or destroyed by one means or another if the Kremlin is to achieve its fundamental design.

The Kremlin regards the United States as the only major threat to the achievement of its fundamental design. There is a basic conflict between the idea of freedom under a government of laws, and the idea of slavery under the grim oligarchy of the Kremlin, which has come to a crisis with the polarization of power described in Section I, and the exclusive possession of atomic weapons by the two protagonists. The idea of freedom, moreover, is peculiarly and intolerably subversive of the idea of slavery. But the converse is not true. The implacable purpose of the slave state to eliminate the challenge of freedom has placed the two great powers at opposite poles. It is this fact which gives the present polarization of power the quality of crisis. . . .

Thus unwillingly our free society finds itself mortally challenged by the Soviet system. No other value system is so wholly irreconcilable with ours, so implacable in its purpose to destroy ours, so capable of turning to its own uses the most dangerous and divisive trends in our own society, no other so skillfully and powerfully evokes the elements of irrationality in human nature everywhere, and no other has the support of a great and growing center of military power. . . .

Our overall policy at the present time may be described as one designed to foster a world environment in which the American system can survive and flourish. It therefore rejects the concept of isolation and affirms the necessity of our positive participation in the world community.

This broad intention embraces two subsidiary policies. One is a policy which we would probably pursue even if there were no Soviet threat. It is a policy of attempting to develop a healthy international community. The other is the policy of "containing" the Soviet system. . . .

A more rapid build-up of political, economic, and military strength and thereby of confidence in the free world than is now contemplated is the only course which is consistent with progress toward achieving our fundamental purpose. The frustration of the Kremlin design requires the free world to develop a successfully functioning political and economic system and a vigorous political offensive against the Soviet Union. These, in turn, require an adequate military shield under which they can develop. It is necessary to have the military power to deter, if possible, Soviet expansion, and to defeat, if necessary, aggressive Soviet or Soviet-directed actions of a limited or total character. The potential strength of the free world is great; its ability to develop these military capabilities and its will to resist Soviet expansion will be determined by the wisdom and will with which it undertakes to meet its political and economic problems. . . .

A comprehensive and decisive program to win the peace and frustrate the Kremlin design should be so designed that it can be sustained for as long as necessary to achieve our national objectives. It would probably involve:

1. The development of an adequate political and economic framework for the achievement of our long-range objectives.
2. A substantial increase in expenditures for military purposes adequate to meet the requirements for the tasks listed in Section D-1 [omitted].
3. A substantial increase in military assistance programs, designed to foster cooperative efforts, which will adequately and efficiently meet the requirements of our allies for the tasks referred to in Section D-1-e [omitted].
4. Some increase in economic assistance programs and recognition of the need to continue these programs until their purposes have been accomplished.
5. A concerted attack on the problem of the United States balance of payments, along the lines already approved by the President.
6. Development of programs designed to build and maintain confidence among other peoples in our strength and resolution, and to wage overt psychological warfare calculated to encourage mass defections from Soviet allegiance and to frustrate the Kremlin design in other ways.
7. Intensification of affirmative and timely measures and operations by covert means in the fields of economic warfare and political and psychological warfare with a view to fo-

menting and supporting unrest and revolt in selected strategic satellite countries.
8. Development of internal security and civilian defense programs.
9. Improvement and intensification of intelligence activities.
10. Reduction of Federal expenditures for purposes other than defense and foreign assistance, if necessary by the deferment of certain desirable programs.
11. Increased taxes. . . .

In summary, we must, by means of a rapid and sustained build-up of the political, economic, and military strength of the free world, and by means of an affirmative program intended to wrest the initiative from the Soviet Union, confront it with convincing evidence of the determination and ability of the free world to frustrate the Kremlin design of a world dominated by its will. Such evidence is the only means short of war which eventually may force the Kremlin to abandon its present course of action and to negotiate acceptable agreements on issues of major importance.

The whole success of the proposed program hangs ultimately on recognition by this Government, the American people, and all free peoples, that the cold war is in fact a real war in which the survival of the free world is at stake. Essential prerequisites to success are consultations with Congressional leaders designed to make the program the object of non-partisan legislative support, and a presentation to the public of a full explanation of the facts and implications of the present international situation. The prosecution of the program will require of us all the ingenuity, sacrifice, and unity demanded by the vital importance of the issue and the tenacity to persevere until our national objectives have been attained. . . .

HUAC Investigates
Hollywood (1947)

In the fall of 1947 the House Un-American Activities Committee garnered national attention by investigating the Communist Party's influence within the
motion picture industry. Most of the witnesses, like actors Gary Cooper and
Ronald Reagan, cooperated with the committee, testifying about communist
involvement in the film business and/or assuring HUAC that the movie
colony was overwhelmingly anticommunist. A group of screenwriters and directors known as the "Hollywood Ten," however, refused to answer the committee's questions about their political beliefs and activities. Led by John Howard
Lawson of the Screen Writers Guild, who had on other occasions openly urged
fellow-leftists to present the communist position in their films, the ten current
or past Communist Party members sought to turn the table and put HUAC on
trial for violating their rights of freedom of speech and association. For not di-
vulging their political affiliations, the Hollywood Ten were found guilty of
contempt of Congress and served prison terms. Consequently, the entertainment industry adopted blacklists barring the employment of suspected communists or anyone who failed to cooperate with congressional investigators, and
HUAC, looking for bigger game, began investigating espionage by public officials and atomic scientists.

RONALD REAGAN, TESTIMONY BEFORE THE HOUSE UN-AMERICAN ACTIVITIES COMMITTEE (1947)

Staff members present: Mr. Robert E. Stripling, Chief Investigator;
Messrs. Louis Russell, H. A. Smith, and Robert B. Gatson, Investigators; and Mr. Benjamin Mand, Director of Research.

MR. STRIPLING: When and where were you born, Mr. Reagan?

MR. REAGAN: Tampico, Illinois, February 6, 1911.

Excerpted from House Committee on Un-American Activities, *Hearings
Regarding Communist Infiltration of the Hollywood Motion-Picture Industry*, 80
Congress, 1st Session (Oct. 23, 27, 1947).

MR. STRIPLING: What is your present occupation?

MR. REAGAN: Motion-picture actor. . . .

MR. STRIPLING: Have you ever held any other position in the Screen Actors Guild?

MR. REAGAN: Yes, sir. Just prior to the war I was a member of the board of directors, and just after the war, prior to my being elected president, I was a member of the board of directors.

MR. STRIPLING: As a member of the board of directors, as president of the Screen Actors Guild, and as an active member, have you at any time observed or noted within the organization a clique of either Communists or Fascists who were attempting to exert influence or pressure on the guild?

MR. REAGAN: Well, sir, my testimony must be very similar to that of Mr. [George] Murphy and Mr. [Robert] Montgomery. There has been a small group within the Screen Actors Guild which has consistently opposed the policy of the guild board and officers of the guild, as evidenced by the vote on various issues. That small clique referred to has been suspected of more or less following the tactics that we associate with the Communist Party.

MR. STRIPLING: Would you refer to them as a disruptive influence within the guild?

MR. REAGAN: I would say that at times they have attempted to be a disruptive influence.

MR. STRIPLING: You have no knowledge yourself as to whether or not any of them are members of the Communist Party?

MR. REAGAN: No, sir, I have no investigative force, or anything, and I do not know.

MR. STRIPLING: Has it ever been reported to you that certain members of the guild were Communists?

MR. REAGAN: Yes, sir, I have heard different discussions and some of them tagged as Communists.

MR. STRIPLING: Would you say that this clique has attempted to dominate the guild?

MR. REAGAN: Well, sir, by attempting to put over their own particular views on various issues, I guess you would have to say that our side was attempting to dominate, too, because we were fighting just as hard to put over our views, and I think we were proven correct by the figures—Mr. Murphy gave the figures—and those figures were always approximately the same, an average of ninety per cent or better of the Screen Actors Guild voted in favor of those matters now guild policy.

MR. STRIPLING: Mr. Reagan, there has been testimony to the effect here that numerous Communist-front organizations have been set up in Hollywood. Have you ever been solicited to join any of those organizations or any organization which you considered to be a Communist-front organization?

MR. REAGAN: Well, sir, I have received literature from an organization called the Committee for a Far-Eastern Democratic Policy. I don't know whether it is Communist or not. I only know that I didn't like their views and as a result I didn't want to have anything to do with them.

MR. STRIPLING: Were you ever solicited to sponsor the Joint Anti-Fascist Refugee Committee?

MR. REAGAN: No, sir, I was never solicited to do that, but I found myself misled into being a sponsor on another occasion for a function that was held under the auspices of the Joint Anti-Fascist Refugee Committee.

MR. STRIPLING: Did you knowingly give your name as a sponsor?

MR. REAGAN: Not knowingly. Could I explain what that occasion was?

MR. STRIPLING: Yes, sir.

MR. REAGAN: I was called several weeks ago. There happened to be a financial drive on to raise money to build a badly needed hospital called the All Nations Hospital. I think the purpose of the building is so obvious by the title that it has the support of most of the people of Los Angeles. Certainly of most of the doctors. Some time ago I was called to the telephone. A woman introduced herself by name. I didn't make any particular note of her name, and I couldn't give it now. She told me that there would be a recital held at which Paul Robeson would sing, and she said that all the money for the tickets would go to the hospital, and asked if she could use my name as one of the sponsors. I hesitated for a moment, because I don't think that Mr. Robeson's and my political views coincide at all, and then I thought I was being a little stupid because, I thought, here is an occasion where Mr. Robeson is perhaps appearing as an artist, and certainly the object, raising money, is above any political consideration: it is a hospital supported by everyone. I have contributed money myself. So I felt a little bit as if I had been stuffy for a minute, and I said, "Certainly, you can use my name." I left town for a couple of weeks, and, when I returned, I was handed a newspaper story that said that this recital was held at the Shrine Auditorium in Los Angeles under the auspices of the Joint Anti-Fascist Refugee Committee. The principal speaker was Emil Lustig [Ludwig?], Robert Burman took up a collection, and remnants of the Abraham Lincoln Brigade were paraded on the platform. I did not, in the newspaper story, see one word about the hospital. I called the newspaper and said I am not accustomed to writing to editors but would like to explain my position, and he laughed and said, "You needn't bother, you are about the fiftieth person that has called with the same idea, including most of the legitimate doctors who had also been listed as sponsors of that affair."

MR. STRIPLING: Would you say from your observation that that is typical of the tactics or strategy of the Communists, to solicit and use the names of prominent people to either raise money or gain support?

MR. REAGAN: I think it is in keeping with their tactics, yes, sir.

MR. STRIPLING: Do you think there is anything democratic about those tactics?

MR. REAGAN: I do not, sir.

MR. STRIPLING: As president of the Screen Actors Guild, you are familiar with the jurisdictional strike which has been going on in Hollywood for some time?

MR. REAGAN: Yes, sir.

MR. STRIPLING: Have you ever had any conferences with any of the labor officials regarding this strike?

MR. REAGAN: Yes, sir.

MR. STRIPLING: Do you know whether the Communists have participated in any way in this strike?

MR. REAGAN: Sir, the first time that this word "Communist" was ever injected into any of the meetings concerning the strike was at a meeting in Chicago with Mr. William Hutchinson, president of the carpenters' union, who were on strike at the time. He asked the Screen Actors Guild to submit terms to Mr. [Richard] Walsh, and he told us to tell Mr. Walsh that, if he would give in on these terms, he in turn would run this Sorrell and the other Commies out—I am quoting him—and break it up. I might add that Mr. Walsh and Mr. Sorrell were running the strike for Mr. Hutchinson in Hollywood.

MR. STRIPLING: Mr. Reagan, what is your feeling about what steps should be taken to rid the motion-picture industry of any Communist influences?

MR. REAGAN: Well, sir, ninety-nine per cent of us are pretty well aware of what is going on, and I think, within the bounds of our democratic rights and never once stepping over the rights given us by democracy, we have done a pretty good job in our business of keeping those people's activities curtailed. After all, we must recognize them at present as a political party. On that basis we have exposed their lies when we came across them, we have opposed their propaganda, and I can certainly testify that in the case of the Screen Actors Guild we have been eminently successful in preventing them from, with their usual tactics, trying to run a majority of an organization with a well-organized minority. In opposing those people, the best thing to do is make democracy work. In the Screen Actors Guild we make it work by insuring everyone a vote and by keeping everyone informed. I believe that, as Thomas Jefferson put it, if all the American people know all of the facts they will never make a mistake. Whether the Party should be outlawed, that is a matter for the Government to decide. As a citizen, I would hesitate to see any political party outlawed on the basis of its political ideology. We have spent a hundred and seventy years in this country on the basis that democracy is strong enough to stand up and fight against the inroads of any ideology. However, if it is proven that an organization is an agent of a foreign power, or in any way not a legitimate political party—and I think the Government is capable of proving that—then that is another matter. I happen to be very proud of the industry in which I work; I happen to be very proud of the way in which we conducted the fight. I do not believe the Communists have ever at any time been able to use the motion-picture screen as a sounding board for their philosophy or ideology. . . .

MR. CHAIRMAN: There is one thing that you said that interested me very much. That was the quotation from Jefferson. That is just why this Committee was created by the House of Representatives: to acquaint the American people with the facts. Once the American people are acquainted with the facts there is no question but what the

American people will do the kind of a job that they want done: that is, to make America just as pure as we can possibly make it. We want to thank you very much for coming here today.

MR. REAGAN: Sir, I detest, I abhor their philosophy, but I detest more than that their tactics, which are those of the fifth column, and are dishonest, but at the same time I never as a ctitizen want to see our country become urged, by either fear or resentment of this group, that we ever compromise with any of our democratic principles through that fear or resentment. I still think that democracy can do it.

JOHN HOWARD LAWSON, TESTIMONY BEFORE THE HOUSE UN-AMERICAN ACTIVITIES COMMITTEE (1947)

STRIPLING: What is your occupation, Mr. Lawson?

LAWSON: I am a writer.

STRIPLING: How long have you been a writer?

LAWSON: All my life—at least thirty-five years—my adult life.

STRIPLING: Are you a member of the Screen Writers Guild?

LAWSON: The raising of any question here in regard to membership, political beliefs, or affiliation—

STRIPLING: Mr. Chairman—

LAWSON: Is absolutely beyond the powers of this committee.

STRIPLING: Mr. Chairman—

LAWSON: But—

(The chairman pounding gavel.)

LAWSON: It is a matter of public record that I am a member of the Screen Writers Guild.

STRIPLING: I ask—

[Applause.]

CHAIRMAN: I want to caution the people in the audience: You are the guests of this committee and you will have to maintain order at all times. I do not care for any applause or any demonstrations of one kind or another.

STRIPLING: Now, Mr. Chairman, I am also going to request that you instruct the witness to be responsive to the questions.

CHAIRMAN: I think the witness will be more responsive to the questions.

LAWSON: Mr. Chairman, you permitted—

CHAIRMAN (ponding gavel): Never mind—

LAWSON (continuing): Witnesses in this room to make answers of three or four or five hundred words to questions here.

CHAIRMAN: Mr. Lawson, you will please be responsive to these questions and not continue to try to disrupt these hearings.

LAWSON: I am not on trial here, Mr. Chairman. This committee is on trial here before the American people. Let us get that straight. . . .

STRIPLING: Have you ever held any office in the guild?

LAWSON: The question of whether I have held office is also a question which is beyond the purview of this committee.

(The chairman pounding gavel.)

LAWSON: It is an invasion of the right of association under the Bill of Rights of this country.

CHAIRMAN: Please be responsive to the question. . . .

LAWSON: I wish to frame my own answers to your questions, Mr. Chairman, and I intend to do so.

CHAIRMAN: And you will be responsive to the questions or you will be excused from the witness stand.

STRIPLING: I repeat the question, Mr. Lawson:

Have you ever held any position in the Screen Writers Guild?

LAWSON: I stated that it is outside the purview of the rights of this committee to inquire into any form of association—

CHAIRMAN: The Chair will determine what is in the purview of this committee.

LAWSON: My rights as an American citizen are no less than the responsibilities of this committee of Congress.

CHAIRMAN: Now, you are just making a big scene for yourself and getting all "het up." [Laughter.]

Be responsive to the questioning, just the same as all the witnesses have. You are no different from the rest. . . .

LAWSON: It is absolutely beyond the power of this committee to inquire into my association in any organization.

CHAIRMAN: Mr. Lawson, you will have to stop or you will leave the witness stand. And you will leave the witness stand because you are in contempt. That is why you will leave the witness stand. And if you are just trying to force me to put you in contempt, you won't have to try much harder. You know what has happened to a lot of people that have been in contempt of this committee this year, don't you?

LAWSON: I am glad you have made it perfectly clear that you are going to threaten and intimidate the witnesses, Mr. Chairman.

(The chairman pounding gavel.)

LAWSON: I am an American and I am not at all easy to intimidate, and don't think I am.

(The chairman pounding gavel.) . . .

STRIPLING: Mr. Lawson, are you now, or have you ever been a member of the Communist Party of the United States?

LAWSON: In framing my answer to that question I must emphasize the points that I have raised before. The question of communism is in no way related to this inquiry, which is an attempt to get control of the screen and to invade the basic rights of American citizens in all fields.

McDOWELL: Now, I must object—

STRIPLING: Mr. Chairman—

(The chairman pounding gavel.)

LAWSON: The question here relates not only to the question of my membership in any political organization, but this committee is attempting to establish the right—

(The chairman pounding gavel.)

LAWSON (continuing): Which has been historically denied to any committee of this sort, to invade the rights and privileges and immunity of American citizens, whether they be Protestant, Methodist,

Jewish, or Catholic, whether they be Republicans or Democrats or anything else.

CHAIRMAN (pounding gavel): Mr. Lawson, just quiet down again.

Mr. Lawson, the most pertinent question that we can ask is whether or not you have ever been a member of the Communist Party. Now, do you care to answer that question?

LAWSON: You are using the old technique, which was used in Hitler's Germany in order to create a scare here— . . .

STRIPLING: Mr. Chairman, the witness is not answering the question. . . .

CHAIRMAN (pounding gavel): We are going to get the answer to that question if we have to stay here for a week.

Are you a member of the Communist Party, or have you ever been a member of the Communist Party? . . .

LAWSON: I am framing my answer in the only way in which any American citizen can frame his answer to a question which absolutely invades his rights.

CHAIRMAN: Then you refuse to answer that question; is that correct?

LAWSON: I have told you that I will offer my beliefs, affiliations, and everything else to the American public, and they will know where I stand.

CHAIRMAN (pounding gavel): Excuse the witness—

LAWSON: As they do from what I have written.

CHAIRMAN (pounding gavel): Stand away from the stand—

LAWSON: I have written Americanism for many years, and I shall continue to fight for the Bill of Rights, which you are trying to destroy.

CHAIRMAN: Officers, take this man away from the stand—

[Applause and boos.]

The Internal Communist Menace (1950)

Joseph R. McCarthy

While the debate about the deeper causes of the Second Red Scare continues—whether it was a mass movement rooted in the status resentments of lower-middle-class and working-class Americans or whether it was the result of the actions (and inactions) of both conservative and liberal political elites and interest groups—few historians doubt that Sen. Joseph R. McCarthy did more than any other individual to turn the fear of internal communism into a national hysteria. His name still stirs violent emotions in those who lived through that turbulent period. The words McCarthyism and McCarthyite have become a part of our language.

McCarthy had floundered through four years in the Senate and was desperately searching for a winning reelection issue when he appeared before the Ohio County Women's Republican Club in Wheeling, West Virginia, on February 9, 1950. Following the lead of other Republican politicians, and adding his own hyperbole, McCarthy blamed American reverses in the world not on the Soviet Union but on Democratic traitors. He claimed to have a list of 205 communist spies in Truman's State Department. When later challenged to produce the evidence for his charges, McCarthy changed his accusation to "bad risks" and lowered the number to fifty-seven. The excerpt below is from the revised speech that McCarthy introduced into the Congressional Record on February 20, 1950.

In fact, McCarthy had no list at all. But that did not matter. In an atmosphere charged by the Truman administration's own campaign against subversion, by the communist victory in China and the successful explosion of an A-bomb by the Soviet Union, by the Hiss-Chambers confrontations, and very soon by the arrest of the Rosenbergs as atomic spies and the outbreak of war in Korea, Joe McCarthy had an issue that dominated news headlines and the Republican party had a potent weapon to pummel Democrats.

From the *Congressional Record*, 81 Congress, 2d Session, pp. 1954–57.

Five years after a world war has been won, men's hearts should anticipate a long peace, and men's minds should be free from the heavy
weight that comes with war. But this is not such a period—for this is
not a period of peace. This is a time of the "cold war." This is a time
when all the world is split into two vast, increasingly hostile armed
camps—a time of a great armaments race. . . .

Today we are engaged in a final, all-out battle between communis-
tic atheism and Christianity. The modern champions of communism
have selected this as the time. And, ladies and gentlemen, the chips
are down—they are truly down. . . .

Six years ago, at the time of the first conference to map out
the peace—Dumbarton Oaks—there was within the Soviet orbit
180,000,000 people. Lined up on the antitotalitarian side there were
in the world at that time roughly 1,625,000,000 people. Today, only 6
years later, there are 800,000,000 people under the absolute domination of Soviet Russia—an increase of over 400 percent. On our side,
the figure has shrunk to around 500,000,000. In other words, in less
than 6 years the odds have changed from 9 to 1 in our favor to 8 to 5
against us. This indicates the swiftness of the tempo of Communist
victories and American defeats in the cold war. As one of our outstanding historical figures once said, "When a great democracy is destroyed, it will not be because of enemies from without, but rather because of enemies from within." . . .

The reason why we find ourselves in a position of impotency is not
because our only powerful potential enemy has sent men to invade our
shores, but rather because of the traitorous actions of those who have
been treated so well by this Nation. It has not been the less fortunate or
members of minority groups who have been selling this Nation out,
but rather those who have had all the benefits that the wealthiest
nation on earth has had to offer—the finest homes, the finest college
education, and the finest jobs in Government we can give.

This is glaringly true in the State Department. There the bright
young men who are born with silver spoons in their mouths are the
ones who have been the worst. . . . In my opinion the State Department, which is one of the most important government departments,
is thoroughly infested with Communists.

I have in my hand 57 cases of individuals who would appear to be
either card carrying members or certainly loyal to the Communist
Party, but who nevertheless are still helping to shape our foreign
policy. . . .

I know that you are saying to yourself, "Well, why doesn't the Congress do something about it?" Actually, ladies and gentlemen, one of the important reasons for the graft, the corruption, the dishonesty, the disloyalty, the treason in high Government positions—one of the most important reasons why this continues is a lack of moral uprising on the part of the 140,000,000 American people. In the light of history, however, this is not hard to explain.

It is the result of an emotional hang-over and a temporary moral lapse which follows every war. It is the apathy to evil which people who have been subjected to the tremendous evils of war feel. As the people of the world see mass murder, the destruction of defenseless and innocent people, and all of the crime and lack of morals which go with war, they become numb and apathetic. It has always been thus after war.

However, the morals of our people have not been destroyed. They still exist. This cloak of numbness and apathy has only needed a spark to rekindle them. Happily, this spark has finally been supplied.

As you know, very recently the Secretary of State proclaimed his loyalty to a man guilty of what has always been considered as the most abominable of all crimes—of being a traitor to the people who gave him a position of great trust. The Secretary of State in attempting to justify his continued devotion to the man who sold out the Christian world to the atheistic world, referred to Christ's Sermon on the Mount as a justification and reason therefore, and the reaction of the American people to this would have made the heart of Abraham Lincoln happy.

When this pompous diplomat in striped pants, with a phony British accent, proclaimed to the American people that Christ on the Mount endorsed communism, high treason, and betrayal of a sacred trust, the blasphemy was so great that it awakened the dormant indignation of the American people.

He has lighted the spark which is resulting in a moral uprising and will end only when the whole sorry mess of twisted, warped thinkers are swept from the national scene so that we may have a new birth of national honesty and decency in government.

The Venona Project and Atomic Espionage

John Earl Haynes and Harvey Klehr

Historians' interpretations of the past are shaped by the sources available to them. For that reason, writing about the Cold War has been an especial challenge for historians. Before 1991 and the end of the Cold War, most records of the Soviet Union, for obvious reasons, were not available to U.S. historians. But neither were many of the records of the U.S. government. For reasons of national security, large numbers of important U.S. documents were classified and kept secret from researchers and the American public alike.

Among those classified documents were almost three thousand telegraphic cables between Soviet officials about Soviet spies in the United States. These cables, decrypted in the years following World War II in a project code-named Venona, were among the most closely guarded secrets of the American Cold War until 1995, when the National Security Agency, acting as part of a Clinton administration initiative, began to open these files to historians.

These cables, when read in conjunction with FBI files, congressional hearings, and documents from Soviet archives, proved something long disputed by many historians: There were a large number of spies within the United States passing information to the Soviet Union.

Historians John Earl Haynes and Harvey Klehr are careful to distinguish their history of espionage from McCarthyism and its effects. They see McCarthy as a demagogue and a liar and McCarthyism as a partisan attack by conservative Republicans on the loyalty of the Truman and Roosevelt administrations. But they also make a strong claim: Our understanding of Cold War anticommunism and the domestic Red Scare has been fundamentally warped. The Venona Project, they argue, proves that there was a "fifth column" working inside the United States during the Cold War. Thus, the anti-

communist actions of the U.S. government—such as President Truman's executive order that denied government employment to anyone judged a security risk—were not paranoid repressions of basic freedoms but reasonable attempts to counter a very real threat.

How might the existence of such documents change our interpretations of the Cold War and domestic anticommunism? Was the U.S. government justified in keeping these materials secret at the time?

The Venona Project began because Carter Clarke did not trust Joseph Stalin. Colonel Clarke was chief of the U.S. Army's Special Branch, part of the War Department's Military Intelligence Division, and in 1943 its officers heard vague rumors of secret German-Soviet peace negotiations. With the vivid example of the August 1939 Nazi-Soviet Pact in mind, Clarke feared that a separate peace between Moscow and Berlin would allow Nazi Germany to concentrate its formidable war machine against the United States and Great Britain. Clarke thought he had a way to find out whether such negotiations were under way.

Clarke's Special Branch supervised the Signal Intelligence Service, the Army's elite group of code-breakers and the predecessor of the National Security Agency. In February 1943 Clarke ordered the service to establish a small program to examine ciphered Soviet diplomatic cablegrams. Since the beginning of World War II in 1939, the federal government had collected copies of international cables leaving and entering the United States. If the cipher used in the Soviet cables could be broken, Clarke believed, the private exchanges between Soviet diplomats in the United States and their superiors in Moscow would show whether Stalin was seriously pursuing a separate peace.

The coded Soviet cables, however, proved to be far more difficult to read than Clarke had expected. American code-breakers discovered that the Soviet Union was using a complex two-part ciphering system involving a "one-time pad" code that in theory was unbreakable. The Venona code-breakers, however, combined acute intellectual analysis with painstaking examination of thousands of coded telegraphic cables to spot a Soviet procedural error that opened the cipher to attack. But by the time they had rendered the first messages into readable text in 1946, the war was over and Clarke's initial goal was moot. Nor did the messages show evidence of a Soviet quest for a separate peace. What they did demonstrate, however, stunned American officials. Messages thought to be between Soviet diplomats at the Soviet consulate in New York and the People's Commissariat of Foreign Affairs in Moscow turned out to be cables between professional intelligence field officers and Gen. Pavel Fitin, head of the foreign intelligence directorate of the KGB in Moscow. Espionage, not diplomacy, was the subject of these cables. One of the first cables rendered into coherent text was a 1944 message from KGB officers in New York showing that the Soviet Union had infiltrated America's most secret enterprise, the atomic bomb project.

By 1948 the accumulating evidence from other decoded Venona cables showed that the Soviets had recruited spies in virtually every major American government agency of military or diplomatic importance. American authorities learned that since 1942 the United States had been the target of a Soviet espionage onslaught involving dozens of professional Soviet intelligence officers and hundreds of Americans, many of whom were members of the American Communist Party (CPUSA). The deciphered cables of the Venona Project identify 349 citizens, immigrants, and permanent residents of the United States who had had a covert relationship with Soviet intelligence agencies. Further, American cryptanalysts in the Venona Project deciphered only a fraction of the Soviet intelligence traffic, so it was only logical to conclude that many additional agents were discussed in the thousands of unread messages. Some were identified from other sources, such as defectors' testimony and the confessions of Soviet spies.

The deciphered Venona messages also showed that a disturbing number of high-ranking U.S. government officials consciously maintained a clandestine relationship with Soviet intelligence agencies and had passed extraordinarily sensitive information to the Soviet Union that had seriously damaged American interests. . . .

AMERICANS' UNDERSTANDING OF SOVIET AND COMMUNIST ESPIONAGE

During the early Cold War, in the late 1940s and early 1950s, every few months newspaper headlines trumpeted the exposure of yet another network of Communists who had infiltrated an American laboratory, labor union, or government agency. Americans worried that a

Communist fifth column, more loyal to the Soviet Union than to the United States, had moved into their institutions. By the mid-1950s, following the trials and convictions for espionage-related crimes of Alger Hiss, a senior diplomat, and Julius and Ethel Rosenberg for atomic spying, there was a widespread public consensus on three points: that Soviet espionage was serious, that American Communists assisted the Soviets, and that several senior government officials had betrayed the United States. The deciphered Venona messages provide a solid factual basis for this consensus. But the government did not release the Venona decryptions to the public, and it successfully disguised the source of its information about Soviet espionage. This decision denied the public the incontestable evidence afforded by the messages of the Soviet Union's own spies. Since the information about Soviet espionage and American Communist participation derived largely from the testimony of defectors and a mass of circumstantial evidence, the public's belief in those reports rested on faith in the integrity of government security officials. These sources are inherently more ambiguous that the hard evidence of the Venona messages, and this ambiguity had unfortunate consequences for American politics and Americans' understanding of their own history.

The decision to keep Venona secret from the public, and to restrict knowledge of it even within the government, was made essentially by senior Army officers in consultation with the FBI and the CIA. Aside from the Venona code-breakers, only a limited number of military intelligence officers, FBI agents, and CIA officials knew of the project. The CIA in fact was not made an active partner in Venona until 1952 and did not receive copies of the deciphered messages until 1953. The evidence is not entirely clear, but it appears that Army Chief of Staff Omar Bradley, mindful of the White House's tendency to leak politically sensitive information, decided to deny President Truman direct knowledge of the Venona Project. The president was informed about the substance of the Venona messages as it came to him through FBI and Justice Department memorandums on espionage investigations and CIA reports on intelligence matters. He was not told that much of this information derived from reading Soviet cable traffic. This omission is important because Truman was mistrustful of J. Edgar Hoover, the head of the FBI, and suspected that the reports of Soviet espionage were exaggerated for political purposes. Had he been aware of Venona, and known that Soviet cables confirmed the testimony of Elizabeth Bentley and Whittaker Chambers, it is unlikely that his aides would have considered undertaking a campaign to discredit Bentley and indict Chambers for perjury, or would have allowed themselves to be taken in by the disinformation being spread by the American Communist party and Alger Hiss's partisans that Chambers had at one time been committed to an insane asylum.

There were sensible reasons for the decision to keep Venona a highly compartmentalized secret within the government. In retrospect, however, the negative consequences of this policy are glaring. Had Venona been made public, it is unlikely there would have been a forty-year campaign to prove that the Rosenbergs were innocent. The Venona messages clearly display Julius Rosenberg's role as the leader of a productive ring of Soviet spies. Nor would there have been any basis for doubting his involvement in atomic espionage, because the deciphered messages document his recruitment of his brother-in-law, David Greenglass, as a spy. It is also unlikely, had the messages been made public or even circulated more widely within the government than they did, that Ethel Rosenberg would have been executed. The Venona messages do not throw her guilt in doubt; indeed, they confirm that she was a participant in her husband's espionage and in the recruitment of her brother for atomic espionage. But they suggest that she was essentially an accessory to her husband's activity, having knowledge of it and assisting him but not acting as a principal. Had they been introduced at the Rosenberg trial, the Venona messages would have confirmed Ethel's guilt but also reduced the importance of her role.

Further, the Venona messages, if made public, would have made Julius Rosenberb's execution less likely. When Julius Rosenberg faced trial, only two Soviet atomic spies were known: David Greenglass, whom Rosenberg had recruited and run as a source, and Klaus Fuchs. Fuchs, however, was in England, so Greenglass was the only Soviet atomic spy in the media spotlight in the United States. Greenglass's confession left Julius Rosenberg as the target of public outrage at atomic espionage. That prosecutors would ask for and get the death penalty under those circumstances is not surprising.

In addition to Fuchs and Greenglass, however, the Venona messages identify three other Soviet sources within the Manhattan Project. The messages show that Theodore Hall, a young physicist at Los Alamos, was a far more valuable source than Greenglass, a machinist. Hall withstood FBI interrogation, and the government had no direct evidence of his crimes except the Venona messages, which because of their secrecy could not be used in court; he therefore escaped prosecution. The real identities of the sources Fogel and Quantum are not known, but the information they turned over to the Soviets suggests that Quantum was a scientist of some standing and that Fogel was either a scientist or an engineer. Both were probably more valuable sources than David Greenglass. Had Venona been made public, Greenglass would have shared the stage with three other atomic spies and not just with Fuchs, and all three would have appeared to have done more damage to American security than he. With Greenglass's role diminished, that of his recruiter, Julius Rosenberg, would have been reduced as well. Rosenberg would assuredly have been convicted, but his penalty might well have been life in prison rather than execution.

There were broader consequences, as well, of the decision to keep Venona secret. The overlapping issues of Communists in government, Soviet espionage, and the loyalty of American Communists quickly became a partisan battleground. Led by Republican senator Joseph McCarthy of Wisconsin, some conservatives and partisan Republicans launched a comprehensive attack on the loyalties of the Roosevelt and Truman administrations. Some painted the entire New Deal as a disguised Communist plot and depicted Dean Acheson, Truman's secretary of state, and George C. Marshall, the Army chief of staff under Roosevelt and secretary of state and secretary of defense under Truman, as participants, in Senator McCarthy's words, in "a conspiracy on a scale so immense as to dwarf any previous such venture in the history of man. A conspiracy of infamy so black that, when it is finally exposed, its principals shall be forever deserving of the maledictions of all honest men." There is no basis in Venona for implicating Acheson or Marshall in a Communist conspiracy, but because the deciphered Venona messages were classified and unknown to the public, demagogues such as McCarthy had the opportunity to mix together accurate information about betrayal by men such as Harry White and Alger Hiss with falsehood about Acheson and Marshall that served partisan political goals.

A number of liberals and radicals pointed to the excesses of McCarthy's charges as justification for rejecting the allegations altogether. Anticommunism further lost credibility in the late 1960s, when critics of U.S. involvement in the Vietnam War blamed it for America's ill-fated participation. By the 1980s many commentators, and perhaps most academic historians, had concluded that Soviet espionage had been minor, that few American Communists had assisted the Soviets, and that no high officials had betrayed the United States. Many history texts depicted America in the late 1940s and 1950s as a "nightmare in red" during which Americans were "sweat-drenched in fear" of a figment of their own paranoid imaginations. As for American Communists, they were widely portrayed as having no connection with espionage. One influential book asserted emphatically, "There is no documentation in the public record of a direct connection between the American Communist Party and espionage during the entire postwar period."

Consequently, Communists were depicted as innocent victims of an irrational and oppressive American government. In this sinister but widely accepted portrait of America in the 1940s and 1950s, an idealistic New Dealer (Alger Hiss) was thrown into prison on the perjured testimony of a mentally sick anti-Communist fanatic (Whitaker Chambers), innocent progressives (the Rosenbergs) were sent to the electric chair on trumped-up charges of espionage laced with anti-Semitism, and dozens of blameless civil servants had their careers ruined by the smears of a professional anti-Communist (Elizabeth Bentley). According to this version of events, one government official (Harry White) was killed by a heart attack brought on by Bentley's lies, and another (Laurence Duggan, a senior diplomat) was driven to suicide by more of Chambers's malignant falsehoods. Similarly, in many textbooks President Truman's executive order denying government employment to those who posed security risks, and other laws aimed at espionage and Communist subversion, were and still are described not as having been motivated by a real concern for American security (since the existence of any serious espionage or subversion was denied) but instead as consciously anti-democratic attacks on basic freedoms. As one commentator wrote, "The statute books groaned under several seasons of legislation designed to outlaw dissent."

Despite its central role in the history of American counterintelligence, the Venona Project remained among the most tightly held government secrets. By the time the project shut down, it had decrypted nearly three thousand messages sent between the Soviet Union and its embassies and consulates around the world. Remarkably, although rumors and a few snippets of information about the project had become public in the 1980s, the actual texts and the enormous import of the messages remained secret until 1995. The

U.S. government often has been successful in keeping secrets in the short term, but over a longer period secrets, particularly newsworthy ones, have proven to be very difficult for the government to keep. It is all the more amazing, then, how little got out about the Venona Project in the fifty-three years before it was made public.

Unfortunately, the success of government secrecy in this case has seriously distorted our understanding of post-World War II history. Hundreds of books and thousands of essays on McCarthyism, the federal loyalty security program, Soviet espionage, American communism, and the early Cold War have perpetuated many myths that have given Americans a warped view of the nation's history in the 1930s, 1940s, and 1950s. The information that these messages reveal substantially revises the basis for understanding the early history of the Cold War and of America's concern with Soviet espionage and Communist subversion. . . .

GIVING STALIN THE BOMB

Even before the 1995 release of the Venona cables, several books reported rumors that deciphered Soviet cables had played a critical role in uncovering atomic spies. Not only were the rumors true, but the decryptions exposed several theretofore-unknown Soviet agents responsible for the remarkable success of the USSR's atomic bomb program.

Klaus Fuchs and Harry Gold

The British began their atomic bomb program before the United States, and the Soviets quickly developed a key source within the project. One of the scientists enlisted to work on the British bomb project was a naturalized British subject and brilliant young physicist named Klaus Fuchs. A refugee from Nazi Germany, Fuchs had also been a member of the German Communist party. After he joined the British atomic project in 1941, Fuchs contacted a refugee German Communist leader, Jürgen Kuczynski, and offered to spy for the Soviets. Kuczynski put Fuchs in touch with a contact at the Soviet embassy, and Fuchs was soon reporting the secrets of the British bomb project to the GRU through Ursula Kuczynski (Jürgen's sister). After America entered the war, the British threw their resources into the

U.S. bomb program, whose immense industrial capacities would be more likely to develop a practical atomic weapon swiftly.

Fuchs arrived in the United States in late 1943, part of a contingent of fifteen British scientists augmenting the Manhattan Project. (By this point the KGB had also taken over control of Fuchs from the GRU.) Initially he worked with a Manhattan Project team at Columbia University, which was experimenting with uranium separation through gaseous diffusion.

Uranium in its natural state consists of two isotopes, U-235 and U-238. U-235 is highly radioactive and better suited for achieving an atomic explosion, but it accounts for less than 1 percent of natural uranium. The two isotopes are chemically identical, so their physical separation is difficult and constituted one of the major technical barriers to building an atomic bomb. The Manhattan Project developed several separation methods. One of them, gaseous diffusion, converted solid uranium into gas and then pumped it through a porous screen through which the lighter U-235 isotope would diffuse faster than (and thus be separated from) the heavier U-238. The physics of the procedure was complex, and in that day many scientists thought the process impractical.

After his work on gaseous diffusion, Fuchs was transferred in August 1944 to Los Alamos, the top-secret heart of the U.S. atomic bomb project, to join its theoretical division. He continued working at Los Alamos until mid-1946, when he returned to England as one of the leaders of the once-again-independent British atomic bomb program. He also continued his work as a spy for the Soviet Union.

In late 1948 the FBI turned over to its British counterparts the Venona decryptions and the supporting evidence that Fuchs was a Soviet agent. The British were convinced. In December officers of MI5 began to question Fuchs. Under interrogation, he collapsed quickly and began his confession on January 24, 1950, which led to his trial and conviction on charges of espionage. Released in 1959 after serving nine years of a fourteen-year sentence, Fuchs moved to Communist East Germany, where he became director of a nuclear research institute.

Because he did confess, the Venona cables serve primarily to confirm and enrich the story Fuchs told. They also corroborate the confession of Harry Gold, the American who was the chief link between Fuchs and the KGB. Gold first appears in the Venona cables in 1944 in connection with his work as the liaison with Fuchs. As noted earlier, Gold had been working as an industrial spy for the Soviets for nine years. On the basis of information from Fuchs's confession and on decrypted Venona cables, the FBI confronted Gold in 1950 and found ample evidence in his house of his long work as a Soviet agent. Like Fuchs, Gold easily broke and confessed. He received a thirty-year sentence for his crimes and served sixteen years before receiving a parole in 1966.

A February 1944 New York KGB message told Moscow that Fuchs, who had arrived in the United States in December 1943, and Gold had firmly established their relationship. Fuchs, the cable said, had turned over information about the organization of the U.S. atomic project and work on uranium separation, both gaseous diffusion and an alternative method, electromagnetic separation, developed at the University of California Radiation Laboratory at Berkeley. Other KGB messages report that Fuchs delivered information on the progress of the project and more technical details about gaseous diffusion. The New York KGB was so pleased by the quality of his information that it planned to give Fuchs a $500 bonus.

In August, however, the New York KGB reported that Fuchs had failed to show up for several meetings with Gold. Initially the KGB thought that Fuchs might have returned to Britain, but it sent Gold to see Fuchs's sister, who lived near Boston, and find out what happened to him. Gold learned that Fuchs had been transferred to Los Alamos, where tight security had cut him off from his KGB links. Fuchs was able to phone his sister, however, while on a business trip to Chicago. Informed of Gold's inquires, Fuchs told his sister to tell Gold that when he got leave from Los Alamos at Christmas he would reestablish contact. Once he did, Fuchs continued his espionage, this time from Los Alamos itself.

Fuchs's transfer to Los Alamos increased the range of secrets he turned over to the Soviets. In addition to his long-standing work on uranium separation, he now gained access to work on the development of plutonium as an alternative to uranium U-235 as a bomb fuel and on the implosion mechanism as a way to detonate plutonium.

The Manhattan Project developed two different types of atomic bombs. The first, dropped on Hiroshima, was a pure uranium bomb with a "gun-type" detonator. The second, dropped on Nagasaki, was a plutonium bomb with an implosion detonator. In the first type, a small amount of U-235 is fired down a barrel at tremendous speed to hit another piece of uranium. The collision sets off a fusion chain reaction that produces an atomic explosion. One of the difficulties with this type of atomic bomb is that it depends on the rare U-235 isotope, and the separation methods required the expenditure of tremendous industrial resources.

In the face of the daunting problem of obtaining enough U-235, the Manhattan Project developed an alternative. A team of Berkeley scientists in 1941 used a cyclotron to create (transmute) a new element that did not exist in nature: plutonium. Plutonium, they discovered, was more fissionable than U-235 and could be created in quantity in a nuclear reactor. This greatly reduced (although it did not eliminate) the need for laborious uranium separation.

A practical plutonium bomb, however, required a different method of detonation. Plutonium was so unstable that in a gun-type bomb system plutonium would begin a premature chain reaction before the two pieces of plutonium were fully fused. A premature chain reaction would destroy the rest of the plutonium before it could be affected, thus producing a small nuclear explosion (a "fizzle") rather than a city-destroying blast. The solution worked out was implosion. An explosive sphere is shaped around a central core of plutonium. The sphere is then set off by a system of detonators that essentially allow all parts of the sphere to explode simultaneously. The result is that the core of plutonium is squeezed from all directions at the same time by a uniform force, and simultaneously all parts of the squeezed plutonium core undergo fission.

Fuchs's assignment to the theoretical division at Los Alamos gave him access to information on the plutonium bomb and use of implosion in a detonation device. Given Fuchs's position at Los Alamos, it is no surprise that messages from Moscow KGB show intense interest in Fuchs and his work. Indeed, the messages from Moscow to the New York KGB attest not only that the KGB received the information but also that it quickly turned the information over to Soviet scientists working on an atomic bomb, because Moscow sent technical follow-up questions with instructions that the queries be passed to Fuchs and other Soviet sources inside the Manhattan Project.

Fuchs's confession in Britain led the FBI to Harry Gold in the United States. Gold's confession, in turn, uncovered other Soviet agents. The credibility of Gold's confession has been harshly attacked by those who refuse to believe that there was significant Soviet espionage in the United States. The Venona cables, however, offer independent confirmation of many points Gold made.

Greenglass and the Rosenbergs

Harry Gold's confession did more than corroborate Klaus Fuchs's story. Although most of his trips to New Mexico had been to get material from Fuchs, on one trip he picked up documents from another Soviet source at Los Alamos, whom he described, in the words of his FBI interrogators, as "a soldier, non-commissioned, married, no children (name not recalled.)" Gold's description quickly led the FBI to Sgt. David Greenglass, a machinist working at one of Los Alamos's secret laboratories. Greenglass confessed to espionage and also implicated his wife, Ruth, and his brother-in-law, Julius Rosenberg. Ruth Greenglass also confessed, corroborating David's testimony that Julius Rosenberg had recruited David as a Soviet source. Under further interrogation, the Greenglasses implicated David's sister Ethel (Julius's wife) in espionage. Simultaneously the FBI was comparing the decrypted Venona cables containing their cover names with the confessions of Fuchs, Gold, and the Greenglasses and with the results of their investigative work. Fuchs, it had been determined earlier, had the cover names Rest and Charles, while Harry Gold was known as Goose and Arnold in the Venona traffic. By the latter half of June, the FBI and the NSA had identified the cover names Antenna and Liberal as Julius Rosenberg, Caliber as David Greenglass, and Osa as Ruth Greenglass.

David and Ruth Greenglass were both fervent Communists who had joined the Young Communist League as teenagers. David had ambitions to become a scientist, but the need for a job forced him to drop out of Brooklyn Polytechnic Institute after only one semester. Just a few months after his marriage in late 1942 he was drafted. After he entered the Army, the young soldier's letters to his bride mixed declarations of love and longing with equally ardent profession of loyalty to Marxism-Leninism. One letter declared, "Victory shall be ours and the future is socialism's." Another looked to the end of the war when "we will be together to build—under socialism—our future." In yet another David wrote of his proselytizing for communism among his fellow soldiers: "Darling, we who understand can bring understanding to others because we are in love and have our Marxist outlook." And in a June 1944 letter he reconciled his Communist faith with the violence of the Soviet regime: "Darling, I have been reading a lot of books on the Soviet Union. Dear, I can see how farsighted and intelligent those leaders are. They are really geniuses, everyone of them . . . I have come to a stronger and more resolute faith in and belief in the principles of Socialism and Communism. I believe that every time the Soviet Government used force they did so with pain in their hearts and the belief that what they were doing was to produce good for the greatest number. . . . More power to the Soviet Union and a fruitful and abundant life for their peoples."

At the time David Greenglass wrote this last letter, he was a skilled machinist in an Army ordnance unit that was preparing to go overseas. But he was unexpectedly transferred to work on a secret project. By August he was in Los Alamos and assigned to work in a facility that made models of the high-technology bomb parts being tested by various scientific teams; specifically he worked on models of the implosion detonators being developed for the plutonium bomb.

Through phone calls and letters David let Ruth know something about what he was working on. She, in turn, informed David's older sister, Ethel Rosenberg, and her husband, Julius. Although they did not know the details, both of the Greenglasses were aware that Julius was involved in secret work with concealed Communist engineers who worked in defense plants. Julius immediately understood the importance of the project on which David was working. He quickly reported this to the KGB. A September 1944 cable from the New York KGB states: "Liberal [Rosenberg] recommended the wife of his wife's brother, Ruth Greenglass, with a safe flat in view. She is 21 years old, a Townswoman [U.S. citizen], Gymnast [Young Communist]. Liberal and wife recommend her as an intelligent and clever girl. . . . Ruth learned that her husband was called up by the army but he was not sent to the front. He is a mechanical engineer and is now working at the Enormous [atomic bomb project] plant in Santa Fe, New Mexico."

The Rosenbergs suggested to the Greenglasses that David should put the knowledge he was gaining in the service of the Soviet Union. David worked under secure conditions at Los Alamos, so in the initial approach guarded language was used in phone calls and letters. Nevertheless, in early November 1944 David wrote a letter to Ruth in which he said plainly that he would "most certainly will be glad to be part of the community project that Julius and his friends have in mind" [sic].

Shortly afterward, David got five days of leave, and Ruth prepared to visit him in Santa Fe, the city nearest to the secret Los Alamos facility. She testified that she had dinner with the Rosenbergs just before she left. Julius and Ethel both pushed her to press David to take part in Julius's plan for espionage. According to those who believe the Rosenbergs to be innocent, Ruth's testimony was phony and there had been no such discussion. Among the Venona cables, however, there is a KGB message dated November 14, 1944, and devoted entirely to the work of Julius Rosenberg. Among other matters, it reported that Ruth Greenglass had agreed to assist in "drawing in" David, and that Julius would brief her before she left for New Mexico.

As for Ethel's role, the same September KGB cable that first noted the contact with Ruth Greenglass stated that Ethel had recommended recruitment of her sister-in-law. Both Greenglasses later testified that Ethel was fully aware of Julius's espionage work and assisted him by typing some material. The only other deciphered reference to Ethel in the Venona cables came in November 1944, when the New York KGB responded to a Moscow headquarters inquiry about her: "Information on Liberal's wife. Surname that of her husband, first name Ethel, 29 years old. Married five years. Finished secondary school. A fellow-countryman [CPUSA member] since 1938. Sufficiently well developed politically. Knows about her husband's work and the role of Meter [Joel Barr] and Nil [unidentified agent]. In view of delicate health does not work. Is characterized positively and as a devoted person."

A December 13 KGB cable stated that the New York office had decided to designate Julius Rosenberg as the liaison with the Greenglasses rather than to shift them to another KGB link. A few days later, on December 16, a triumphant New York KGB reported that Ruth had returned from Sante Fe with the news that David had agreed to become a Soviet source and that he anticipated additional leave and would be visiting New York soon. The cable noted that Julius Rosenberg felt technically inadequate to ask the right scientific questions and wanted assistance in debriefing David during his visit. Finally, in a January 1945 Venona cable, the New York KGB reported that while David Greenglass had been on leave in New York, his recruitment had been completed and arrangements for delivery of material made. He had also given an initial report on his implosion detonator work. All this information matches the later testimony of both David and Ruth Greenglass.

The Venona cables greatly assisted the FBI's investigation by providing a documentary basis against which interrogators could check Fuchs's, Gold's, and Greenglass's confessions and the statements made by others. It provided leads for follow-up questions and the tracking down of additional witnesses. Because of the policy decision not to reveal the Venona secret, prosecutors could not use cables as evidence in court. Nonetheless, they provided the FBI and other Justice Department officials with the sure knowledge that they were prosecuting the right people.

Initially, the FBI's investigation gave promise of being a classic case of "rolling up" a network link by link. First Fuchs was identified, and he confessed. His confession led to Gold, Gold's confession led to David Greenglass. Greenglass then confessed, followed swiftly by his wife Ruth. But there it ended. The next link in the chain was Julius Rosenberg, and he refused to admit anything. So did Ethel.

The government charged Julius and Ethel Rosenberg with espionage. They were swiftly convicted, even without use of the deciphered Venona cables. The eyewitness testimony of David and Ruth Greenglass, the eyewitness testimony of Max Elitcher, the corroborative testimony of Harry Gold, and an impressive array of supporting evidence led to a quick conviction. David Greenglass was sentenced to fifteen years in prison. In view of her cooperation and that of her husband, Ruth Greenglass escaped prosecution. Morton Sobell was tried with the Rosenbergs and also refused to confess, but Elitcher's testimony and his flight to Mexico led to Sobell's conviction and to a term of thirty years.

The stonewalling by the Rosenbergs and Sobell took its toll, however, on the ability of the government to prosecute additional members of the Rosenberg network. William Perl was convicted, but only of perjury rather than of espionage. Barr and Sarant secretly fled to the USSR and avoided arrest. Others suffered nothing more than exclusion from employment by the government or by firms doing defense work.

The government asked for and got the death penalty for the Rosenbergs, and they were executed on June 19, 1953. It appears that government authorities, hoping to use the death sentences as leverage to obtain their confessions and roll up other parts of the Soviet espionage apparatus, did not expect to carry out the executions. But the Rosenbergs were Communist true believers and refused to confess.

The deciphered KGB messages of the Venona Project do more than confirm the participation of Fuchs, Greenglass, and Rosenberg in Soviet atomic espionage. They also show that the Soviet Union's intelligence services had at least three additional sources within the Manhattan Project.

Part 2

THE POLITICS OF
THE AFFLUENT SOCIETY

The 1950s and 1960s are generally seen as very different eras in American history. In our stereotypes of decades, the fifties are the era of conformity, of complacent affluence, a time in which the American people turned away from the challenges of the world, moved to the suburbs, bought refrigerators and televisions and cars with massive tailfins.

There is some truth to this stereotype. Under the leadership of President Eisenhower, the first Republican to be elected in twenty years, the nation seemed remarkable for its stability. While not extending New Deal social welfare programs, neither did the Eisenhower administration attempt to reverse them. Rather, his was an administration of consolidation. Following the Great Depression and World War II, as well as the uncertainty of the immediate postwar years, the 1950s did seem an era of peace, prosperity, and stability—despite the Korean War, the continuing Cold War, McCarthyism, and the growth of a movement for African American civil rights. The 1950s were an age of economic prosperity for most Americans. The percentage of young people attending high school jumped dramatically, as did the number attending college. In a time of low unemployment, rising real wages, and readily available consumer goods, a majority of Americans came to see themselves as middle class. Culturally, as well as politically, the fifties were a time of consolidation.

The sixties, in contrast, are our decade of "great dreams." They are perhaps our most controversial decade, as America's politicians and public figures continue to find the roots of all that is good—or bad—about America in the decade of the sixties. When we talk about "The Sixties," we often mean the latter half of the decade, the years covered in Part 6, "Years of Polarization." But the activism and grand visions of the sixties are equally present in the early years. Led by Presidents John F. Kennedy and Lyndon B. Johnson, the nation set forth to alleviate racial discrimination, to combat poverty, and to create a new and improved society. "We can do better," Kennedy had said in 1960. "We will do better," Johnson promised in 1964. In so many ways, the "Fifties" and the "Sixties" seem radically different, one given to complacency, quietude, and stability, the other to activism, challenge, and change.

In fact, the two eras have much in common. The struggles that brought reform in the 1960s were already emerging throughout the "quiet years" of the 1950s. Moreover, the policies and governmental programs of the 1960s built upon the strong foundation of the New Deal; they show continuity as well as new visions. Fundamentally, though, the fifties and the sixties were joined by an underlying set of beliefs, one that historians have attempted to capture in phrases such as "the politics of affluence," or "the liberal consensus." The politics and culture of postwar America were shaped by the belief that improvement is always possible within a fundamentally sound economic and social system, that right-minded and intelligent people can create a healthy, viable social system, that moderation is preferable to extremism, and that an economy committed to growth will provide the basis for eliminating social problems while assuring prosperity for the growing middle class.

In the following mix of historical documents and historians' analyses, this section traces the development of a politics of affluence, from its postwar manifestations through the Great Society. Historian Roland Marchand looks to popular culture and consumer goods to analyze reconfigurations of class in postwar America—a set of changes that will significantly shape the politics of the rest of "the American Century." Turning from culture to politics, historian Stephen Ambrose reconsiders the presidency of Dwight D. Eisenhower—a man once dismissed as bland and bumbling who may in fact, Ambrose argues, deserve much of the credit for the peace and prosperity of the 1950s.

Speeches by President John F. Kennedy and Lyndon B. Johnson—Kennedy's Inaugural Address and Johnson's "Great Society" speech—offer a glimpse of the "politics of affluence" in our national life. Animated by grand visions and a sense of possibility perhaps hard to imagine today, these speeches also show important changes in focus and approach from the Kennedy to the Johnson presidency.

Finally, historian Bruce Schulman discuss the development of American liberalism and evaluates Lyndon Johnson's Great Society.

Many questions are raised by these selections. Why do we tend to think of the 1950s and 1960s as radically different from one another? To what extent are leaders—Eisenhower, Kennedy, Johnson—responsible for the major changes in American life chronicled here? Do their policies owe more to the ongoing Cold War or to the unprecedented affluence of most Americans? What role does a broader set of cultural changes play in shaping the political possibilities of the 1960s? Looking back to the 1960s, how would you evaluate the Great Society? Would such an ambitious program be possible today?

Visions of Classlessness, Quests for Dominion

Roland Marchand

"The great majority of Americans," wrote poet and Librarian of Congress Archibald MacLeish in 1943, "understand very well that this war is not a war only, but an end and a beginning—an end to things known and a beginning of things unknown. . . . We know that whatever the world will be when the war ends, the world will be different."

The United States emerged from World War II the most powerful and prosperous nation on earth. It was a beginning, and a different world—but one shaped by the legacy of war. In this article, historian Roland Marchand looks beyond Cold War politics to examine the legacies of war in the culture of postwar America. Wartime promises of abundance and democracy, prosperity and equality, he argues, ran up against a more complex set of social realities. The resulting tensions were played out, among other places, in American popular culture.

Does Marchand convince you that a more homogenous and national culture developed in the postwar years? If so, how do you account for the great diversity of popular culture that exists today? What role might the development of a more national, homogenous culture have played in the development of, for example, the Great Society (following in Part 2) or the Civil Rights movement (Part 3)?

The constraints and sacrifices of World War II did not prepare Americans to meet the realities of the postwar era with equanimity. Expec-

I am indebted to the students in my fall 1979 undergraduate seminar, and to David Brody, Eckard Toy, and James Lapsley, for their criticism of ideas contained in an initial version of this essay.

tations ran high, despite underlying anxieties about atomic perils and the possibility of a postwar depression. Wartime discourse resonated with acclamations of equality and promises of the coming of a better, technologically wondrous life for all. The common man, idealized in nostalgic imagery, would carve out a future of unobstructed independence. Centralized controls, bureaucratic complexities, diminished autonomy for the individual—these were largely dismissed as the temporary conditions of war. Postwar popular culture reflected these expectations, expressing complacent satisfaction in the realization of some and providing vicarious compensations for the intense disappointment of others.

World War II came closer than any other twentieth-century phenomenon to enacting the drama of the melting pot in the United States, as disparate groups and values seemed to fuse into a composite national culture. Four years of war brought unprecedented national consolidation. Vast wartime migrations—to the armed forces and to war industries and boomtowns—undermined regional loyalties and broadened provincial horizons. Class barriers, and even some of the outward identifying marks of class, seemed to disappear. The nation's dramatists of popular culture, its persuaders and performers, enlisted in the task of uniting the nation behind common assumptions.

The explicitly democratic themes of wartime popular culture promoted unity. Morale-builders stressed the idea of equal sacrifices and personalized the war through such democratic figures as G. I. Joe, Rosie the Riveter, Norman Rockwell's everyman figure in the "Freedom of Speech" poster, and Rockwell's Willie Gillis (the common man as G.I.). The war years also prolonged the modest redistribution of income from rich to poor that had begun during the 1930s. Although this process was to come to a standstill in the late 1940s, Americans emerged from the war confident of a snowballing trend toward economic democratization and a classless culture.

Meanwhile, in what Frank Fox has characterized as "World of Tomorrow" advertising, business interests painted stirring images of the technological future. Wartime research, when applied to consumer products, would bring new power and comfort to the common man in a "thermoplastic, aerodynamic, supersonic, electronic, gadgetonic" postwar world. Popular anticipation of a precise watershed moment—when the war would end and the "future" begin—took on a millennial cast. In style these wartime visions paralleled themes of the General Motors Futurama at the 1939 World's Fair. The message was one of man's technological dominion over nature, of machines as social solutions. Yet another wartime message, infused in advertising and other forms of popular culture, promised that victory would restore a cherished version of the true American way of life, based on the small town, the corner drugstore, and the close-knit family—an image aptly described as "American Pastoral."

Instead, the postwar world brought bureaucratic complexity, cold war insecurity, and a shrunken sense of individual mastery. It produced a technology of atomic peril as well as material comfort. Inspired by the sweeping democratic promises of wartime ideology and a hunger for security and stability, Americans welcomed the notion of classless prosperity. Enticed by expectations of increased power and control, they reacted with dismay as they found themselves slipping into a condition of greater vulnerability and dependency. In response they embraced popular culture reveries that seemed to enhance their sense of personal dominion.

The postwar period saw the emergence of a popular culture more homogeneous than Americans had previously known, as the cold war reinforced the trend toward consolidation. This greater homogeneity also reflected changes in demography, increasingly centralized production of popular culture images and artifacts, and more effective dissemination of popular culture by the media.

One measure of increasing homogeneity was a decline in competition from ethnic cultures. By the time of World War II, unrestricted immigration had been cut off for a full generation. Between 1940 and 1960 the percentage of foreign-born declined from 8.8 percent to 5.4 percent, and the percentage of Americans with at least one parent of foreign birth fell from 17 percent to 13.5 percent. A decline in carriers of ethnic culture such as foreign-language newspapers, theaters, musical organizations, and social halls reflected these demographic changes. Commercial entertainment increasingly outrivaled the attractions of ethnic folk culture and filled the new increments of leisure time. Network radio expanded its nationalizing and homogenizing influence, and radio sets in use increased right up to the advent of an even more powerful agent of common popular culture— television. Between 1940 and 1950 the "big four" popular periodicals, *Life, Reader's Digest, Look,* and *Saturday Evening Post,* increased their combined total circulation by 105 percent. Although some groups did maintain "taste subcultures," more and more Americans read, heard, and saw the same popular fare.

Another measure of homogeneity was the decline of class and regional differences in clothing and recreation. During the late 1940s sales of traditional work clothes fell precipitously, with the production of men's casual pants and shirts rising almost as rapidly. More workers wore casual clothes on the job, and off work men of different classes seemed indistinguishable on the street. *Life* referred matter-of-factly in 1949 to blue jeans as part of a national teenage "uniform." By the 1950s these classless, vaguely "western" progeny of democratic G.I. dungarees had come to symbolize the triumph of denim as an equalizing casual wear for virtually all Americans. Steady increases in the length of paid vacations for workers had also begun to equalize the distribution of formal leisure time. The Bureau of Labor Statistics even argued that by 1950 the earlier, distinctively "working class" patterns of spare-time activities and expenditures had almost disappeared among urban workers.

Signs of a national culture abounded. In the early 1950s, as journalist Russell Lynes remarked, Sears, Roebuck ceased publication of regional catalogs on the grounds that tastes in furniture had become identical throughout the country. *Fortune* reported that tastes in food were "flattening" regionally. Merchandising consultants began to talk about a "standard middle-majority package," a laundry list of home furnishings and other consumer goods that should be marketable to all families. One suburb looked pretty much like another; what Louise Huxtable has characterized as "Pop Architecture" dominated the landscape everywhere. Local bowling palaces, motels, and auto showrooms quickly copied the flash, glitter, and eccentric shapes of Las Vegas's "architecture of the road." Even where franchised chains did not proliferate, the designers of shopping centers and the entrepreneurs of a thousand "miracle miles" created uniform visual imagery.

The leveling of styles was in many ways a leveling *down*—a fact that did not escape the champions of high culture. In their search for the culprits of cultural debasement, they excoriated first the threats to literacy, order, and good taste coming from the comic book industry, and then the affronts to high culture by the new monster, TV. No previous mass medium, not even radio, expanded its audience so explosively as television. Households with TV sets mounted from fewer than one million in 1949 to more than 46 million in 1960, at which point 90 percent of all American homes were consuming TV programming at an average rate of five hours per day. The convenience

of TV and the national standards of performance it set were devastating to provincial commercial entertainment and much of ethnic
culture.

The 1950s would later seem a golden age of diversity and cultural
quality on TV. But, fixing their gaze on Hopalong Cassidy, Milton
Berle, wrestling matches, and formula westerns, contemporary critics
denounced the new medium as an attack on culture and literacy.
With the advance of TV, homogenized franchise operations, and organizational bureaucracy, a major debate erupted among intellectuals over the prospects and perils of mass culture. Even political concerns seemed to fade before the social menace of mass culture. Did a
debased mass culture involve passivity, conformity, and a stifling of
creativity in the audience and a formulaic, manipulative, whatever-
will-sell attitude by the producer? Then TV seemed to its critics to
have unquestionably triumphed as *the* mass culture medium.

Actually, TV probably served more to nationalize and homogenize
than either to uplift or degrade. Television advertising embedded
slogans, brand names, and affective imagery into the national consciousness with a new intensity, creating symbols for a more uniform
national language. Television also helped promote the "common
language" functions of national sports spectatorship. Together with
convenient air travel, TV made attractive the nationalizing of the
professional sports leagues. Minor league baseball declined as did
a multitude of more significant local institutions—ethnic clubs,
local union meetings, local political clubs—contributing, in Martin
Mayer's view, to individual feelings of anomie and powerlessness.

Manufacturers of TV sets fought this negative interpretation of the
social impact of TV. Their ads nostalgically depicted warm family
scenes in which the connective links of the old family circle were restored in the harmony of the family semicircle plus TV. However spe-
cious the implied claims that TV would keep the kids home and the
generations together, TV did serve the momentarily unifying function of making children more frequent participants in (or cospecta-
tors of) their parents' entertainment.

A critical component of the popular culture that TV helped dis-
seminate was "California Culture." Even before the war California
had become the symbol of relaxed, prosperous outdoor living, linked
to a "car culture." . . . The media readily promoted California culture as mobile, changing, comparatively "democratic." It had a "life-
style." The ambience of that life-style was just about everything that

media advertisers liked to associate with their products—an image of the new, the enjoyable, the casual. . . . The imagery of California culture centered around the postwar fad in popular architecture—the California ranch house. A single-story, ground-hugging structure, it was adaptable to split-level form. Picture windows and other expanses of glass accentuated the idea of a free-flowing continuity of space and mood between indoors and out-doors. Population pressure and high costs had imposed limitations on the postwar suburban search for spaciousness. In response the ranch house nurtured illusions of open continuous space and free-dom. This was particularly necessary as the sprawling ranch house (invariably pictured alone with no adjacent neighbors) was pared down to 1,200-square-foot tract dimensions.

Inside, the quest for openness was linked with architectural expres-sions of democracy and "togetherness" (a word coined by *McCall's* in a moment of nostalgia and marketing acumen). In a servantless set-ting the dining room often disappeared, and the door segregating the kitchen gave way to a counter or open vista that allowed the wife to maintain contact with family and guests. A new room appeared—an amalgam of rumpus room and den. Introduced as "the room with-out a name," it quickly gained status as the "family room"—a casual, nurturing, and democratic gathering place for all. Naturally, the new room was where the TV was lodged, to be followed in due course by TV trays and TV dinners.

By 1954 Russell Lynes pronounced the California ranch house "ubiquitous," a national symbol of the increasing unity of tastes of "the relatively poor and the relatively well-to-do," and "the standard new suburban dwelling in the suburbs of New York as of Boston, of Chicago as of . . . Los Angeles." . . .

The California ranch house seemed to epitomize the postwar dream of classlessness and dominion. Everybody, presumably, was moving to the suburbs. Everyone could belong to the modern, demo-cratic version of the "landed gentry." Limitless energy would make possible heated patios, air-conditioners, and countless appliances. A prolonged do-it-yourself craze suggested that husband as well as wife could make the suburban home a fulfilling last refuge for the exer-cise of competence and control. Here the common American might evade international tensions and organizational complexities and thus regain a reassuring sense of individual dominion.

The dream of suburban comfort and microcosmic control was a

striking instance of upper-middle-class myopia. "Everybody" was *not* moving to the suburbs, despite impressions conveyed by Sunday supplements, TV advertisements, and popular sociology. Most housing developments were priced out of the range of those below the median income. The migration that inundated the suburbs came primarily from those among the top 40 percent in family income, especially those of the professional and technological elites who made impressive gains in income after 1945. Moreover, the most highly publicized sociological studies of suburbia focused on areas that were even more affluent than average—thus exaggerating "typical" suburban prosperity. Since writers, academics and advertising executives came from the very segment of society making the most rapid gains, they found it easier to believe everyone was riding the same wave of prosperity. The idea of a consummated classlessness struck them with the force of a revelation.

The celebration of this "classless prosperity" permeated the popular culture that other Americans of the era consumed. Russell Lynes helped popularize the new "obsolescence" of class with his essay "High-brow, Low-brow, Middle-brow" in 1949. *Life* magazine's version carried a striking two-page chart depicting the cultural tastes of Lynes's various "brows" in ten categories ranging from furniture to entertainment. Economic classes were obsolete, Lynes insisted; people now chose their pleasures and consumer goods strictly on the basis of individual taste. Sociologist William Whyte noted the "displacement of the old class criterion" by "the impulse to 'culture' and 'good taste.'" Values were "coming together," he concluded, and the suburbs had become the "second great melting pot."

"The distinction between economic levels in the ownership of tangibles is diminishing," the Bureau of Labor Statistics noted, thus "breaking down the barriers of community and class." Sportswriters celebrated the supposed democratization of golf: "Class lines are eliminated," they argued, "when the nation wears sports clothes." Producers of the big-money TV quiz shows nurtured popular enthusiasm for illusions of equality by creating such folk heroes as the "cop who knew Shakespeare." The sponsor of "The $64,000 Question" explained: "We're trying to show the country that the little people are really very intelligent. . . ." Winners were prototypes of the common man and woman, symbols of democratized intelligence. Advertisers now cast affluent suburban families not only as models of appropriate consumer styles but also as realistic portrayals of *average* Americans. In the 1920s and 1930s, Americans had known that they were seeing explicit models of high society "smartness" in many ads. Now they were encouraged to see the advertising models as mirrors of themselves. Such images and perceptions of classlessness eventually found expression in the language itself. The 1961 *Webster's International Dictionary* acknowledged the existence of a new word not recognized in earlier editions: *life-style*. This new term, which gradually replaced the older phrase "way of life," conveyed nuances of classlessness. The phrase "way of life," had been fully compatible with a recognition of important economic class distinctions. Although people might be described as seeking to *choose* or *achieve* a certain "way of life," they could also easily be thought of as having inherited a particular way of life along with their class standing. But a "life-style" was less likely to seem class-determined or inherited. The word *style* suggested free choice, the uninhibited search for what looked and felt right. It might also connote a particular consumer-consciousness, a notion of choosing among various ensembles or "packages" of goods that represented a style consistency, i.e., that "went well together." Behind the rise of the world *life-style* lay the assumption that increases in real income, the equalizing qualities of new synthetic fabrics and suburban amenities, and the expansion of automobile and appliance ownership had created a totally middle-class society in which all significant differences were simply free expressions of personal tastes.

This vision reflected some real changes in American society. During the 1950s the average income of all families and individuals rose 26 percent in real dollars, and increased installment buying allowed many families to raise their living standard at an even greater rate. Still, as Richard Parker has pointed out, "among those who called themselves middle class, perhaps a majority have always lacked the money to be in fact what they believe they are." It was those of high income, as ever, who consumed the bulk of popular culture products and services—whether sports event admissions, frozen foods, cars, or hi-fi components. And the gains that *were* achieved by median and marginal sectors of the society did not represent gains in relative wealth or power. In fact, those below the top 40 percent remained stationary in their proportion of national income during the 1950s, and all but the wealthiest lost in relative power. Despite the National Advertising Council's puffery about "people's capitalism," corporate assets were more narrowly held in 1960 than in 1945.

Americans appreciated their new material comforts, but many no doubt sensed an erosion of independence and control as large organizations in media, government, and business overshadowed or preempted their spheres of competence and power. It fell to popular culture to exorcise these demons and provide compensating, vicarious adventures in potency and dominion.

Enter the Shmoo and Mike Hammer! Best described as a "snow-white ham with legs," the Shmoo appeared in cartoonist Al Capp's 1948 parable on the quandaries of prosperity. Lured musically into that consumer's paradise, the "Valley of the Shmoon," Capp's hero Li'l Abner recognized the Shmoo as utopia incarnate. The accommodating little creature, so eager to please that it would die of sheer happiness from one hungry look, provided for nearly all material needs. It laid eggs (in cartons) and gave milk (bottled). Broiled, it made the finest steak; roasted, it resembled pork; fried, it came out chicken. And Shmoos reproduced at a remarkable rate.

A national favorite, the Shmoo recapitulated wartime promises. It offered families in Capp's Dogpatch lifelong control over the necessities of life, just as Americans had been led to dream of a technological uptopia. In another sense the Shmoo, endlessly and identically reproduced, conjured up intimations of conformity, of boring and emotionless satiety. So dull was this prospect that Capp eventually had his obliging and well-merchandised progeny commit "Shmooicide." Although the spirit of the Shmoo lived on in such tangible forms as the energy consumption binge, the national credit card, and the Playboy bunny, Capp found its appropriate cartoon replacement in the Kigmy, who loved to be kicked. Americans of the era, Capp implied, sought a target for the release of aggression as keenly as they yearned for the security of the Shmoo.

Mike Hammer's phenomenal success as a popular culture hero seemed to confirm that notion. First appearing in 1947 in Mickey Spillane's *I, the Jury*, detective Mike Hammer rewrote the history of American best-sellers with his escapades of vengeance. His self-righteous vigilantism breathed contempt for established institutions and authorities. He worried that prosperity would make Americans soft and weak. And he banished the specters of impotence and conformity by acting remorselessly and alone:

. . . I killed more people tonight than I have fingers on my hands. I shot them in cold blood and enjoyed every minute of it. . . . They were Commies, Lee. They were red sons-of-bitches who should have died long ago. . . . I just walked into that room with a tommy gun and shot their guts out. They never thought that there were people like me in this country. They figured us all to be soft as horse manure. . . .

For Americans beginning to suffer from a vague closed-in feeling, a restless frustration stemming from Russian threats abroad and the restraints and manipulations of large organizations at home, Mike Hammer represented recovery of a lost dominion. In postwar popular culture the defense of traditional masculinity was difficult to separate from this search for renewed dominion. John Cawelti aptly describes Spillane's "love" scenes as stripteases, many of them unconsummated sexual provocations that led ultimately to "fulfillment in violence." Contempt for women, expressed in frequent violence and sadism by Mike Hammer and in manipulative detachment by such mutant successors as James Bond and the Hugh Hefner Playboy, may have expressed fears of feminine power that went beyond insecure resentment of fancied sexual teasing. Modern society seemed to place "feminine" restraints on man's dominion. In large organizations the executive as well as the worker had to "subdue his personality to another's . . . to act like a good old-fashioned wife." One response in the popular culture was to reassert a compensating image of masculinity that conceded nothing to feminine limitations. . . .

The emphasis on traditional masculinity may have stemmed in part from the fear that increasing leisure would tempt Americans to become soft—perhaps to lose their competitive drive and their will to resist communism. Another part may have arisen from the loss of a sense of achievement and mastery within the workplace and from indignities experienced in lives constrained by the actions of faceless organizations. The increased collective power that had subdued nature with vast highways and massive expenditures of electrical energy did not enhance the power of individuals in their increasingly complex interactions with other people. The traditional gender of the word *mastery* in American culture had been unequivocally male. Fears of powerlessness in the midst of mass society had unsurprisingly triggered ritual efforts to reaffirm the masculine.

Americans of the postwar era also sought solace from anxieties and frustrations by turning their search for dominion inward. Both religion and popular psychology flourished in the postwar era, as did hybrids of the two.

Church membership advanced steadily during the late 1940s and early 1950s until it reached the unprecedented level of 63 percent of all Americans. . . . In the atmosphere of a cold war against "atheistic" communism, religion tended to merge with patriotism. In the mid-1950s Congress sought to formalize the union by adding "under God" to the pledge of allegiance and establishing a prayer room in the Capitol. The physical mobility of the 1940s also enhanced the church's role as social anchor in the midst of social disruption, a place where new residents in a community might make social contacts. Theologian Will Herberg concluded that the three major faiths, Protestantism, Catholicism, and Judaism, had come to serve as a new American "triple melting pot" for third-generation immigrants as ethnic subcultures declined. But Herberg and other religious leaders also worried about the quality of the new "religious awakening." What could one make of an enthusiasm for faith in which 86 percent of all Americans declared the Bible to be the word of God, yet 53 percent could not name a single one of the Gospels? Perhaps the answer lay in a 1957 Gallup poll in which 81 percent affirmed their expectation that "religion can answer all or most of today's problems."

Postwar piety was paralleled by a surge of psychology. The prewar decades had witnessed a considerable popularization of the concepts of psychology and psychiatry, especially among the well-educated. World War II increased popular awareness of applied psychology and its contributions to personnel selection and "adjustment." Familiarity with psychological jargon—neurosis, inferiority complex, schizophrenia, maladjustment—was already widespread. But in the postwar years, psychology became a popular mania. Publishers responded to a thirst for self-analysis with quizzes, how-to-do-it manuals, and psychological advice. A typical issue of *Reader's Digest* contained at least two articles of the "What's Your Personality?" and "Do You Think like a Man or a Woman?" variety. . . . When Lucy set up her "Psychiatric Help—5¢" booth in Charles Schulz's popular "Peanuts" comic strip, it simply marked with mild satire a logical conclusion to the trend toward universal dissemination of popular psychology.

The craze for the psychological explanation did not reflect unequivocal acceptance of psychological techniques. True, psychologists were much in demand to provide explanations of juvenile delinquency, rock 'n' roll music, marriage problems, personal aptitudes, and college panty raids. Even the Kinsey Reports on sexual practices were accepted as useful by a majority of Americans. But the frequency with which psychology and psychoanalysis served as topics for humor attested to deep ambivalence about psychology's "contributions." Although psychology promised a kind of control, an opportunity to reshape one's personality or gain a form of dominion by understanding and manipulating others, it also awakened fears that one might be the *object* rather than the *agent* of manipulation. . . .

Millions of Americans, however, hopefully sought assurance from a fusion of psychology and religion. A major element in postwar popular culture was the "cult of reassurance," promoted most effectively by the Presbyterian minister Norman Vincent Peale. An amalgam of psychology and religion, the cult gained its initial postwar impulse from Rabbi Joshua Liebman's prescriptions for the cure of inner tensions in *Peace of Mind* (1946). Liebman's book topped the best-seller list in 1947 and eventually sold a million copies. Peale advanced the movement's momentum with his best-selling *A Guide to Confident Living* (1949) and then with *The Power of Positive Thinking* (1952), which dominated the nonfiction best-seller charts from 1952 to 1955, soon surpassing two million copies.

Peale employed six psychiatrists and commanded radio and TV audiences in the millions. Although he had initially sought psychological knowledge for personal counseling, "Peale's deep attraction," as Donald Meyer writes, was to mass counseling. The message was simple: people's problems were individual. "Negative thinking," not technology, social forces, or institutional structures, was the cause of feelings of powerlessness and frustration. By using Peale's techniques, each follower could "become a more popular, esteemed, and well-liked individual," gaining new energy and peace of mind. Through psychological self-manipulation, each could gain control over circumstances rather than submitting to them. "Positive thinking" accepted and reinforced the notion of classlessness. It proved another popular culture prescription for the nagging sense of loss of dominion.

A popular culture of reassurance was not everybody's answer to powerlessness. It was true that certain consolidating tendencies—the influences of network television and the common language and repetitious visual landscapes of national advertising, pop architecture and restaurant and motel chains—worked to reinforce the "adjustment" theme of applied psychology. And it was true also that the "packaging" craze in popular culture, from shopping centers to entertainment "worlds" like Disneyland, helped push forward the process of homogenization by offering convenience and relief from individual decision-making. In fact, the whole Disney empire, from the "disney-fication" of children's classics to TV's Mickey Mouse Club and the Davy Crockett craze, strikingly epitomized the trend toward uniformity. But consolidation in popular culture did not advance undisturbed. As regional, ethnic, and visible class divergences began to fade, new fissures appeared. Some pursued the quest for dominion not through adjustment and reassurance but rather through excitement, diversity, and vicarious rebellion.

The most obvious, and to contemporaries the most shocking, new breach in society was an apparently increasing division based on age. Juvenile delinquency had appeared to rise during World War II and afterward. The striking increase in disposable income and free time among teen-agers in the late 1940s stamped adolescence as a social phenomenon rather than simply a stage in individual development. "The brute fact of today," Dr. Robert Linder warned a Los Angeles audience in 1954, "is that our youth is no longer in rebellion but in a condition of downright active and hostile mutiny." In "a profound and terrifying change," youth now acted out its "inner turmoil."

Psychological analyses of juveniles, both delinquent and normal, abounded. The film industry, reacting to the loss of its mass audience to television, began to produce specialized films for minority audiences—one of which was teen-agers. Radio followed the same pattern. Advertisers soon recognized the existence of a massive teenage market. Eugene Gilbert built a large marketing business by providing advertisers with inside information on teen-age consumers. His trick was spectacularly simple: employ teen-agers themselves to quiz other teen-agers about their wants and needs. Eventually *Life* confirmed the discovery of a teen-age market in an article entitled "A New $10 Billion Power: The U.S. Teen-age Consumer." *Life* personalized the story by featuring pictures of the loot accumulated by "the businessman's dream of the ideal teen-ager," Suzie Slattery from (where else?) California.

Attempts by the media to explore the rebellious aspects of the teen-age culture created new fissures in popular culture. In the movie *Rebel without a Cause* (1955), the plot and dialogue comprise a virtual textbook of popular psychology. The police lieutenant is an amateur psychologist; the hero's mother, a castrating female. The father's multiple complexes make him a complete buffoon. The hero's friend is a self-destructive neurotic, abandoned by his parents; and the heroine's father panics at her emerging sexuality and treats her with alternating rage and condescension. *Rebel without a Cause* was a "lesson" movie for parents: be careful and understanding, or this (rebellion) could happen to you. But James Dean's portrayal of the teen-age hero, his most influential acting role, diverted attention to the style and mannerisms of the misunderstood "rebel." Youths made the movie theirs. Vicarious rebels adopted the James Dean image as an expression of contempt for the satiated and challengeless life of middle-aged suburban America.

The evolution of popular music revealed even more vividly the process of disruption, the fraying of social nerves by age conflicts. Before the 1950s producers of popular music had largely ignored age differences, and the songs of adults and teen-agers were the same. As late as 1951 Gallup polls on favorite vocalists showed little variation among age groups. Far more significantly, the pollsters did not record responses for persons under 21. Yet teen-agers were already a major buying public for records, and the average age of purchasers continued to fall during the 1950s. With the rise of the 45 rpm record (cheap, unbreakable, easy to transport and change) and the transformation of radio in the early 1950s, the weight of teen-age preferences tipped the scales toward diversity in this form of popular culture.

Even earlier, fragmentation had begun to appear within the popular music industry. A boycott by radio stations in the early 1940s had broken the monopoly of the "big three" record companies. Radio disc jockeys gained new power, and technological advances meant that production of quality recordings was no longer confined to a handful of studios in New York, Chicago, and Los Angeles. Independent companies, the primary producers of "race" and "hillbilly" music, gained new opportunities. Still, the resulting tremors in the industry were relatively minor. From 1946 to 1953 the six dominant recording companies—Decca, Columbia, Victor, Capitol, MGM, and Mercury—recorded all but 5 of the 163 records that sold over a million copies.

Radio, in reaction to the abrupt abduction of its general audience by TV, cast about for minority tastes to satisfy. One market for subcultural programming was teen-agers. Specialized radio stations now gave them a medium of their own. Some argue that teen-age audiences created "rock 'n' roll." Others explain that TV, that powerful consolidating force in popular culture, was also, inadvertently, the cause of this vehicle of dissent and fragmentation. Both are largely correct; together these two forces set the stage for a popular culture explosion.

By 1953 certain ingredients of rock 'n' roll had been fermenting for several years. Migrations out of the South had increased national familiarity with "hillbilly" and black styles in music. In the late 1940s *Billboard* magazine, the arbiter of pop music, bolstered the respectability of both styles by rechristening the "hillbilly" category as "country and western" and "race music" as "rhythm and blues." Elements of each style began to appear in pop hits. Meanwhile, with the postwar demise of the big bands, the individual singer gained prominence. Frank Sinatra epitomized the trend, winning the adulation of young "bobby-soxers" in the early 1940s and sustaining his popularity by projecting qualities of sincerity and involvement. Meanwhile, country singers Roy Acuff and then Hank Williams won huge followings with their sincere, emotional styles.

Against the backdrop of a pallid, taken-for-granted prosperity and cold war perils about which youth could do little, a thirst arose among the young for forms of popular culture that would permit expressions of highly personalized emotion. Frankie Laine ("Jezebel," "Your Cheatin' Heart," "I Believe") "sold Emotion . . . with a capital E" even more explicitly than did Sinatra. In 1951 Johnnie Ray stirred up a riotous teen-age response and set new standards for emotion and involvement in his popular hit "Cry." Ray, unlike Sinatra, was neither smooth nor controlled. He exposed an emotional vulnerability as he abandoned himself to the song's despair, "quivering, sobbing, crying and finally collapsing on the floor." Here were intimations not only of the impending rock 'n' roll performer as oracle of unconcealed emotion but also of the sensitive hero as victim.

It was in 1953 that Cleveland disc jockey Alan Freed, intrigued by his discovery that white adolescents were increasingly buying "rhythm and blues" records, initiated his "Moondog's Rock and Roll Party," playing records by black singers for a largely white teen-age radio audience. *Billboard* noted Freed's success. Record companies rushed to find white performers to "cover" (copy) up-tempo, heavy beat, rhythm and blues hits. Bill Haley and His Comets made the national pop charts with "Crazy Man Crazy" in 1953. The next year Haley's cover of "Shake, Rattle, and Roll" ranked in the top ten for twelve weeks, followed by an even longer run for "Rock around the Clock," the theme song from the popular film on juvenile delinquency *Blackboard Jungle*. . . .

In 1956 the polarizing assault by rock 'n' roll on popular music (and on American culture generally) culminated. A black original,

Little Richard's strident "Long Tall Sally," outsold Pat Boone's bland cover version. With his frantic movements and raucous shouts, Little Richard, in Charlie Gillett's words, was "coarse, uncultured, and un-controlled, in every way hard for the musical establishment to take." The lines were being drawn largely on the basis of age, although the preference of many white teen-agers for "black" music added another dimension to the rift.

Critics of the new music and of the mixed-up, misunderstood hero decried the new mystique. The tough, self-pitying "sad-bad-boy" fig-ures represented an "apotheosis of the immature." Rock 'n' roll used a "jungle strain" to provoke a "wave of adolescent riot." How could a prosperous, middle-class nation find satisfaction in such moronic lyrics and "quivering adolescents"? *Time* compared rock 'n' roll con-certs to Hitler's mass meetings, and other critics denounced the new music as nauseating and degenerate, an appeal to "vulgarism and animality." Could a consolidating popular culture even begin to bridge the gap suggested by such reactions?

Extreme views would remain irreconcilable. But 1955 elevated to stardom a versatile performer who brought the rock 'n' roll move-ment to a climax yet ultimately helped partially to reconcile rock with mainstream popular culture. Elvis Presley, the "hillbilly cat," as Greil Marcus writes, "deeply absorbed black music, and transformed it. . . ." The style of his early singles was "rockabilly"—"the only style of early rock 'n' roll that proved white boys could do it all—that they could be as strange, as exciting, as scary, and as free as the black men who were suddenly walking America's airwaves. . . ." Even as Elvis moved up to RCA and national fame in 1955 and 1956 with "Heart-break Hotel" and "You Ain't Nuthin' But a Hound Dog," he contin-ued to evoke sexuality, exhibitionism, and a defiance of restraint. Elvis projected emotional involvement; he encompassed the prized qualities of both toughness and vulnerability.

But Elvis not only fulfilled the image of frustrated, sensitive, rebel-lious hero for the new teen-age generation; he was also "hellbent on the mainstream." By the end of the 1950s, he had achieved hits with gospel songs and sentimental ballads. Eventually, one of his best-selling albums was "Blue Hawaii." His style encompassed schmaltz as well as rebellion, Las Vegas as well as Memphis. Along with Pat Boone, Bobby Darin, Bobby Rydell, Paul Anka, Ricky Nelson, and a host of new teen-age crooners, and with the added influence of Dick Clark's "American Bandstand" on TV, Elvis eased rock 'n' roll's way into the mainstream. The aura of challenge and threat in rock was overshadowed by the sentimentalities of teen-age love. By 1960 the popular music industry was fragmented. The venerable and consensus-based "Your Hit Parade" had expired after a period of senility, spurred on by rock 'n' roll. More concerned with the style of performance than with the song itself, the new rock audience was bored by interpretations of hit rock numbers by "Hit Parade" regulars. But, thus far, the fissure created in American popular culture by rock 'n' roll and generational stress had proved to be a crevice rather than a chasm.

Teen culture and rock 'n' roll, however, were not the only signs in the late 1950s of a possible countermarch in popular culture away from homogeneity toward segmentation. In reaction to the severe inroads of TV, movie-makers had sought specialized audiences that included intellectuals as well as teen-agers. Radio had fully adopted specialty programming. Gated, exclusive suburban developments gained in popularity. Portents of a difficult future for the great mass-circulation, general-audience magazines began to appear, as both *Life* and *Saturday Evening Post* lost advertising. Despite the "whitewardly mobile" messages of middle-class black magazines like *Ebony*, inklings could be found in the eventual movement of blacks to a more protective, conserving attitude toward the distinctive qualities of their own culture. On top of everything, enclaves of "beatniks" now flaunted a life-style even more irreconcilable with mainstream popular culture than that associated with rock 'n' roll.

One prospect for popular culture at the end of the 1950s was fragmentation, with increasing specialization in production and participation. But in one significant way, the consolidating process in American popular culture continued to move ahead. The history of modern popular culture is more characteristically an aspect of the history of business than an aspect of the histories of art, literature, music, or architecture. And the business that determined the available choices for *most* popular culture consumers had not been verging toward fragmentation or diversity. The "popular culture establishment"—in the form of CBS, NBC, and ABC, or General Motors, Walt Disney Enterprises, MGM, and *Time-Life*, or the J. Walter Thompson, Young and Rubicam, and other great advertising agencies—certainly wielded a more extensive control over the range of products and images available to the public in 1960 than in 1945. These giants, like most of the small popular culture entrepreneurs, watched the sales figures, the Nielsen ratings, and the audience surveys and produced what would sell itself or sell the sponsor's goods. . . .

Beset by cold war fears and organizational complexities, Americans found solace in a popular culture that provided hopeful visions of an emerging classlessness and vicarious compensations for a hedged-in, manipulated feeling. Popular culture provided the fantasies, evasions, material artifacts, and vicarious experiences through which Americans tried to recapture a sense of dominion.

A Revisionist View of Eisenhower

Stephen E. Ambrose

Although still commonly portrayed by the mass media as an era of easy living, of material abundance and social tranquillity, the 1950s are now depicted by many historians as a far more complex era. There were both prosperity and persistent poverty, the end of the war in Korea and an escalating thermonuclear arms race, civil rights victories and rampant racism, the Baby Boom and the Beat Generation, June Cleaver and Margaret Anderson and also Women Strike for Peace. A major aspect of this fuller, more nuanced picture of the 1950s has been the reevaluation of the Eisenhower presidency (1953–1961). Today's historians, as Stephen Ambrose points out, are more inclined to compare President Eisenhower with his successors rather than with Franklin D. Roosevelt—thus, more positively; and, with the passage of time, these historians have less of a partisan interest in harping on Eisenhower's shortcomings and more of a desire to understand why so many liked Ike. Following the lead of Ambrose and the scholars he cites in this selection, especially Fred Greenstein, many historians have replaced the image of a bumbler who preferred golf to government, a do-nothing who "reigned but did not rule," with a view of a politically skillful Eisenhower actively operating to great effect to keep the peace and maintain stable economic growth. But not all historians agree, and in assessing Eisenhower's record, or that of any president, students need to keep in mind both the failures and the successes, the achievements as well as the problems ignored or denied—and left to worsen for a future generation.

Since Andrew Jackson left the White House in 1837, 33 men have served as president of the United States. Of that number, only four have managed to serve eight consecutive years in the office—Ulysses Grant, Woodrow Wilson, Franklin Roosevelt, and Dwight Eisenhower.

From "The Ike Age: The Revisionist View of Eisenhower" by Stephen E. Ambrose, in *The New Republic* (May 9, 1981). Reprinted by permission of *The New Republic*, © 1981, The New Republic, Inc.

Of these four, only two were also world figures in a field outside politics—Grant and Eisenhower—and only two had a higher reputation and broader popularity when they left office than when they entered—Roosevelt and Eisenhower.

Given this record of success, and the relative failure of Ike's successors, it is no wonder that there is an Eisenhower revival going on. . . . Another major reason for the current Eisenhower boom is nostalgia for the 1950s—a decade of peace with prosperity, a 1.5 percent annual inflation rate, self-sufficiency in oil and other precious goods, balanced budgets, and domestic tranquility. Eisenhower "revisionism," now proceeding at full speed, gives Ike himself much of the credit for these accomplishments.

The reassessment of Eisenhower is based on a multitude of new sources, as well as new perspectives, which have become available only in the past few years. The most important of these is Ike's private diary, which he kept on a haphazard basis from the late 1930s to his death in 1969. Other sources include his extensive private correspondence with his old military and new big business friends, his telephone conversations (which he had taped or summarized by his secretary, who listened in surreptitiously), minutes of meetings of the cabinet and of the National Security Council, and the extensive diary of his press secretary, the late James Hagerty. Study of these documents has changed the predominant scholarly view of Eisenhower from, in the words of the leading revisionist, political scientist Fred Greenstein of Princeton, one of "an aging hero who reigned more than he ruled and who lacked the energy, motivation, and political skill to have a significant impact on events," to a view of Ike as "politically astute and informed, actively engaged in putting his personal stamp on public policy, [who] applied a carefully thought-out conception of leadership to the conduct of his presidency."

The revisionist portrait of Ike contains many new features. Far from being a "part-time" president who preferred the golf course to the Oval Office, he worked an exhausting schedule, reading more and carrying on a wider correspondence than appeared at the time. Instead of the "captive hero" who was a tool of the millionaires in his cabinet, Ike made a major effort to convince the Republican right wing to accept the New Deal reforms, an internationalist foreign policy, and the need to modernize and liberalize the Republican party. Rather than ducking the controversial issue of Joseph McCarthy, Eisenhower strove to discredit the senator. Ike's failure to issue a public endorsement of *Brown v. Topeka* was not based on any fundamental disagreement with the Warren Court's ruling, but rather on his understanding of the separation, the balance, of powers in the U.S. government—he agreed with the decision, it turns out, and was a Warren supporter. Nor was Ike a tongue-tied general of terrible syntax; he was a careful speaker and an excellent writer who confused his audiences only when he wanted to do so.

Most of all, the revisionists give Eisenhower high marks for ending the Korean War, staying out of Vietnam, and keeping the peace elsewhere. They argue that these achievements were neither accidental nor lucky, but rather the result of carefully conceived policies and firm leadership at the top. The revisionists also praise Ike for holding down defense costs, a key factor in restraining inflation while maintaining prosperity.

Altogether, the "new" Ike is an appealing figure, not only for his famous grin and winning personality, but also because he wisely guided us through perilous times.

"The bland leading the bland." So the nightclub comics characterized the Eisenhower administration. Much of the blandness came from Ike's refusal to say, in public, anything negative about his fellow politicians. His lifelong rule was to refuse to discuss personalities. But in the privacy of his diary, parts of which have just been published with an excellent introduction by Robert H. Ferrell (*The Eisenhower Diaries*, W. W. Norton), he could be sarcastic, slashing, and bitter.

In 1953, when Ike was president and his old colleague from the war, Winston Churchill, was prime minister, the two met in Bermuda. Churchill, according to Ike,

> has developed an almost childlike faith that all of the answers to world problems are to be found merely in British-American partnership. . . . He is trying to relive the days of World War II. In those days he had the enjoyable feeling that he and our president were sitting on some rather Olympian platform . . . and directing world affairs. Even if this picture were an accurate one of those days, it would have no application to the present. But it was only partially true, even then, as many of us who . . . had to work out the solutions for nasty local problems are well aware.

That realistic sense of the importance of any one individual, even a Churchill or a Roosevelt, was basic to Eisenhower's thought. Back in 1942, with reference to MacArthur, Ike scribbled in his diary that in modern war, "no one person can be a Napoleon or a Caesar." What was required was teamwork and cooperation. . . .

Ike didn't like "politics," and he positively disliked "politicians." The behind-the-scenes compromises, the swapping of votes for pork-barrel purposes, the willingness to abandon conviction in order to be on the popular side all nearly drove him to distraction. His favorite constitutional reform was to limit congressional terms to two for the Senate and three or four for the House, in order to eliminate the professional politician from American life.

Nor did Ike much like the press. "The members of this group," he wrote in his diary, "are far from being as important as they themselves consider," but he did recognize that "they have a sufficient importance . . . in the eyes of the average Washington officeholder to insure that much government time is consumed in courting favor with them and in dressing up ideas and programs so that they look as saleable as possible." Reporters, Ike wrote, "have little sense of humor and, because of this, they deal in negative criticism rather than in any attempt toward constructive helpfulness." (Murray Kempton, in some ways the first Eisenhower revisionist, recalled how journalists had ridiculed Ike's amiability in the 1950s, while the president actually had intelligently confused and hoodwinked them. Kempton decided that Eisenhower was a cunning politician whose purpose was "never to be seen in what he did.")

The people Ike did like, aside from his millionaire friends, were those men who in his view rose above politics, including Milton Eisenhower, Robert Anderson, and Earl Warren. Of Milton, Ike wrote in 1953, "I believe him to be the most knowledgeable and widely informed of all the people with whom I deal. . . . So far as I am concerned, he is at this moment the most highly qualified man in the United States to be president. This most emphatically makes no exception of me. . . ." Had he not shrunk from exposing Milton to a charge of benefiting from nepotism, Ike would have made his younger brother a member of his cabinet.

In 1966, during an interview in Eisenhower's Gettysburg office, I asked him who was the most intelligent man he had ever met, expecting a long pause while he ran such names as Marshall, Roosevelt, de Gaulle, Churchill, Truman, or Khrushchev through his mind. But Ike never hesitated: "Robert Anderson," he said emphatically. Anderson, a Texan and a Democrat, served Ike in various capacities, including secretary of the navy and secretary of the treasury. Now Ewald reveals for the first time that Eisenhower offered Anderson the second spot on the Republican ticket for 1956 and wanted Anderson to be his successor. Anderson turned down the president because he thought the offer was politically unrealistic.

Which inevitably brings up the subject of Richard Nixon. Eisenhower's relations with Nixon have long been a puzzle. Ike tried to get Nixon to resign during the 1952 campaign, but Nixon saved himself with the Checkers speech. In 1956 Ike attempted to maneuver Nixon off the ticket by offering him a high-level cabinet post, but Nixon dug in his heels and used his connections with the right wing of the party to stay in place. And in 1960, Ike's campaign speeches for Nixon were distinctly unenthusiastic. Still, Eisenhower and Nixon never severed their ties. Ike stuck with Nixon throughout his life. He often remarked that Nixon's defeat by Kennedy was one of his greatest disappointments. And, of course, his grandson married one of Nixon's daughters. Sad to say, neither the diary nor the private correspondence offers any insights into Eisenhower's gut feelings toward Nixon. The relationship between the two men remains a puzzle.

Some writers used to say the same about the Eisenhower–Earl Warren relationship, but thanks to Ike's diary, Ewald's book, and the correspondence, we now have a better understanding of Eisenhower's feelings toward Warren personally, and toward his Court. In December 1955, Jim Hagerty suggested that if Ike could not run for a second term for reasons of health, Warren might make a good nominee. "Not a chance," Ike snapped back, "and I'll tell you why. I know that the Chief Justice is very happy right where he is. He wants to go down in history as a great Chief Justice, and he certainly is becoming one. He is dedicated to the Court and is getting the Court back on its feet and back in respectable standing again."

Eisenhower and Warren were never friends; as Ewald writes, "For more than seven years they sat, each on his eminence, at opposite ends of Pennsylvania Avenue, by far the two most towering figures in Washington, each playing out a noble role, in tragic inevitable estrangement." And he quotes Attorney General Herbert Brownell as saying, "Both Eisenhower and Warren were very reserved men. If you'd try to put your arm around either of them, he'd remember it for sixty days."

Ike had a great deal of difficulty with *Brown v. Topeka*, but more because of his temperament than for any racist reasons. He was always an evolutionist who wanted to move forward through agreement and compromise, not command and force. Ike much preferred consensus to conflict. Yet Ewald argues that he privately recognized the necessity and justice of *Brown v. Topeka*. Even had that not been so, he would have supported the Court, because—as he carefully explained to one of his oldest and closest friends, Sweed Hazlett, in a private letter—"I hold to the basic purpose. There must be respect for the Constitution—which means the Supreme Court's interpretation of the Constitution—or we shall have chaos. This I believe with all my heart—and shall always act accordingly."

Precisely because of that feeling, Eisenhower never made a public declaration of support for the *Brown v. Topeka* decision, despite the pleas of liberals, intellectuals, and many members of the White House staff that he do so. He felt that once the Supreme Court had spoken, the president had no right to second-guess nor any duty to support the decision. The law was the law. That Ike was always ready to uphold the law, he demonstrated decisively when he sent the U.S. Army into Little Rock in 1957 to enforce court-ordered desegregation.

Despite his respect for Warren and the Court, when I asked Eisenhower in 1965 what was his biggest mistake, he replied heatedly, "The appointment of that S.O.B. Earl Warren." Shocked, I replied, "General, I always thought that was your best appointment." "Let's not talk about it," he responded, and we did not. Now that I have seen the flattering and thoughtful references to Warren in the diary, I can only conclude that Eisenhower's anger at Warren was the result of the criminal rights cases of the early 1960s, not the desegregation decisions of the 1950s.

As everyone knows, Ike also refused publicly to condemn Senator McCarthy, again despite the pleas of many of his own people, including his most trusted adviser, Milton. Ike told Milton, "I will not get into a pissing contest with that skunk."

The revisionists now tell us that the president was working behind the scenes, using the "hidden hand" to encourage peaceful desegregation and to censure McCarthy. He helped Attorney General Brownell prepare a brief from the Justice Department for the Court on *Brown v. Topeka* that attacked the constitutionality of segregation in the schools. As for McCarthy, Greenstein writes that Eisenhower,

> working most closely with Press Secretary Hagerty, conducted a virtual day-to-day campaign via the media and congressional allies to end McCarthy's political effectiveness. The overall strategy was to avoid *direct mention* of McCarthy in the president's public statements, lest McCarthy win sympathy as a spunky David battling against the presidential Goliath. Instead Eisenhower systematically condemned the *types* of actions in which McCarthy engaged.

Eisenhower revisionism is full of nostalgia for the 1950s, and it is certainly true that if you were white, male, and middle class or better, it was the best decade of the century. The 1950s saw peace and prosperity, no riots, relatively high employment, a growing GNP, virtually no inflation, no arms race, no great reforms, no great changes, low taxes, little government regulation of industry or commerce, and a president who was trusted and admired. Politics were middle-of-the-road—Eisenhower was the least partisan president of the century. In an essay entitled "Good-By to the 'Fifties—and Good Riddance," historian Eric Goldman called the Eisenhower years possibly "the dullest and dreariest in all our history." After the turmoil of the 1960s and 1970s—war, inflation, riots, higher taxes, an arms race, all accompanied by a startling growth in the size, cost, and scope of the federal government—many Americans may find the dullness and dreariness of the 1950s appealing.

Next to peace, the most appealing fact was the 1.5 percent inflation rate. The revisionists claim that Ike deserved much of the credit for that accomplishment because of his insistence on a balanced budget (which he actually achieved only twice, but he did hold down the deficits). Ike kept down the costs by refusing to expand the New Deal welfare services—to the disgruntlement of the Republican right wing, he was equally firm about refusing to dismantle the New Deal programs—and, far more important, by holding down defense spending.

This was, indeed, Ike's special triumph. He feared that an arms race with the Soviet Union would lead to uncontrollable inflation and eventually bankrupt the United States, without providing any additional security. In Ike's view, the more bombs and missiles we built, the less secure we would be, not just because of the economic impact, but because the more bombs we built, the more the Soviets would build. In short, Ike's fundamental strategy was based on his recogni-

tion that in nuclear warfare, there is no defense and can be no winner. In that situation, one did not need to be superior to the enemy
in order to deter him.

The Democrats, led by Senator John F. Kennedy, criticized Ike for
putting a balanced budget ahead of national defense. They accused
him of allowing a "bomber gap" and, later, a "missile gap" to develop,
and spoke of the need to "get America moving again." Nelson Rockefeller and Richard Nixon added to the hue and cry during the 1960
campaign, when they promised to expand defense spending. But as
long as Eisenhower was president, there was no arms race. Neither
the politicians nor the military-industrial complex could persuade
Eisenhower to spend more money on the military. Inheriting a $50
billion defense budget from Truman, he reduced it to $40 billion and
held it there for the eight years of his tenure.

Holding down defense costs was a long-standing theme of Ike's. As
early as December 1945, just after he replaced George Marshall as
army chief of staff, he jotted in his diary, "I'm astounded and ap-
palled at the size and scope of plans the staff sees as necessary to
maintain our security position now and in the future." And in 1951,
before he became a candidate, he wrote in his diary that if the Congress and military could not be restrained about "this armament business, we will go broke and still have inefficient defenses."

President Eisenhower was unassailable on the subject. As one senator complained, "How in hell can I argue with Ike Eisenhower on a
military matter?" But as Ike wrote in 1956 to his friend Hazlett, "Some
day there is going to be a man sitting in my present chair who has not
been raised in the military services and who will have little understanding of where slashes in their estimates can be made with little or
no damage. If that should happen while we still have the state of tension that now exists in the world, I shudder to think of what could
happen in this country."

One reason why Ike was able to reduce the military in a time of
great tension was his intimate knowledge of the Soviet military situation. From 1956 on, he directed a series of flights by the U-2 spy
plane over the Soviet Union. He had personally taken the lead in getting the U-2 program started, and he kept a tight personal control
over the flights—he gave his approval to the individual flights only
after a thorough briefing on where in the USSR the planes were
going and what the CIA wanted to discover. Here too the revisionists
have shown that the contemporary feeling, especially after Francis

Gary Powers was shot down in 1960, that Ike was not in charge and hardly knew what was going on inside his own government is altogether wrong. He was absolutely in charge, not only of broad policy on the use of the U-2, but of implementing details as well. The major factor in Eisenhower's ability to restrain defense spending was keeping the peace. His record here is clear and impressive— he signed an armistice in Korea less than half a year after taking office, stayed out of Vietnam, and managed to avoid war despite such crisis situations as Hungary and the Suez, Quemoy and Matsu, Berlin and Cuba. The revisionists insist that the credit must go to Ike, and they equally insist that Eisenhower, not Secretary of State John Foster Dulles, was in command of American foreign policy in the 1950s. Dulles, says Greenstein, "was assigned the 'get tough' side of foreign-policy enunciation, thus placating the fervently anti-Communist wing of the Republican party." Ike, meanwhile, appeared to be above the battle, while actually directing it on a day-to-day basis.

"In essence, Eisenhower used Dulles." So writes Robert Divine, one of America's leading diplomatic historians, in his provocative new book, *Eisenhower and the Cold War* (Oxford University Press). Divine concludes that "far from being the do-nothing President of legend, Ike was skillful and active in directing American foreign policy." All the revisionists agree that the contemporary idea that Dulles led Ike by the nose was a myth that Eisenhower himself did the most to encourage. Nevertheless, Eisenhower did have a high opinion of his secretary of state. Divine quotes Ike's comment to Emmet Hughes on Dulles: "There's only one man I know who has seen *more* of the world and talked with more people and *knows* more than he does—and that's me."

The quotation illustrates another often overlooked Eisenhower characteristic—his immense self-confidence. He had worked with some of the great men of the century—Churchill, Roosevelt, Stalin, de Gaulle, Montgomery, and many others—long before he became president. His diary entry for the day after his inauguration speaks to the point: "My first day at the president's desk. Plenty of worries and difficult problems. But such has been my portion for a long time— the result is that this just seems (today) like a continuation of all I've been doing since July 1941—even before that."

Ike's vast experience in war and peace made him confident in crises. People naturally looked to him for leadership. No matter how serious the crisis seemed to be, Ike rarely got flustered. During a war scare in the Formosa Straits in 1955, be wrote in his diary, "I have so often been through these periods of strain that I have become accustomed to the fact that most of the calamities that we anticipate really never occur."

Ike's self-confidence was so great that, Greenstein writes, he had "neither a need nor a desire" to capture headlines. "He employed his skills to achieve his ends by inconspicuous means." In foreign policy, this meant he did not issue strident warnings, did not—in public—threaten Russia or China with specific reprisals for specific actions. Instead, he retained his room for maneuver by deliberately spreading confusion. He did not care if editorial writers criticized him for jumbled syntax; he wanted to keep possible opponents guessing, and he did. For example, when asked at a March 1955 press conference if he would use atomic bombs to defend Quemoy and Matsu, he replied:

> Every war is going to astonish you in the way it occurred, and in the way it is carried out. So that for a man to predict, particularly if he has the responsibility for making the decision, to predict what he is going to use, how he is going to do it, would I think exhibit his ignorance of war; that is what I believe.

As he intended, the Chinese found such statements inscrutable, as they had in Korea two years earlier. When truce talks in Korea reached an impasse in mid-May 1953, Ike put the pressure on the Chinese, hinting to them that the United States might use atomic weapons if a truce could not be arranged, and backing this up by transferring atomic warheads to American bases in Okinawa. The Chinese then accepted a truce. As Divine writes, "Perhaps the best testimony to the shrewdness of the President's policy is the impossibility of telling even now whether or not he was bluffing."

Nearly all observers agree that one of Ike's greatest accomplishments was staying out of Vietnam in the face of intense pressure from his closest advisers to save the French position there or, after July 1954, to go in alone to defeat Ho Chi Minh. Ike was never tempted. As early as March 1951 he wrote in his diary, "I'm convinced that no military victory is possible in that kind of theater." And in a first draft of his memoirs, written in 1963 but not published until 1981 by Ewald, Ike wrote:

> The jungles of Indochina would have swallowed up division after division of United States troops, who, unaccustomed to this kind of war-

fare, would have sustained heavy casualties until they had learned to live in a new environment. Furthermore, the presence of ever more numbers of white men in uniform probably would have aggravated rather than assuaged Asiatic resentments.

That was hardheaded military reasoning by General Eisenhower. But President Eisenhower stayed out of Vietnam as much for moral as for military reasons. When the Joint Chiefs suggested to him in 1954 that the United States use an atomic bomb against the Vietminh around Dien Bien Phu, the president said he would not be a party to using that "terrible thing" against Asians for the second time in less than a decade. And in another previously unpublished draft of his memoirs, he wrote:

> The strongest reason of all for the United States refusal to [intervene] is that fact that among all the powerful nations of the world the United States is the only one with a tradition of anti-colonialism. . . . The standing of the United States as the most powerful of the anti-colonial powers is an asset of incalculable value to the Free World. . . . Thus it is that the moral position of the United States was more to be guarded than the Tonkin Delta, indeed than all of Indochina.

Ike's international outlook, already well known, is highlighted by the new documents. He believed that the bonds that tied Western Europe and the United States together were so tight that the fate of one was the fate of the other. In May 1947, one year before the Marshall Plan, he wrote in his diary, in reference to Western Europe:

> I personally believe that the best thing we could now do would be to post 5 billion to the credit of the secretary of state and tell him to use it to support democratic movements wherever our vital interests indicate. Money should be used to promote possibilities of self-sustaining economies, not merely to prevent immediate starvation.

Ike also anticipated Kennedy's Alliance for Progress. Historian Burton Kaufman, in the narrowest but perhaps most important study reviewed here, *Trade and Aid: Eisenhower's Foreign Economic Policy* (Johns Hopkins University Press), concludes: "Not only did Eisenhower reorient the mutual security program away from military and toward economic assistance, he was also the first president to alter the geographical direction of American foreign aid toward the developing world." After an exhaustive examination, Kaufman also gives Ike high marks for resisting Nelson Rockefeller and others who wanted the president to encourage private investment overseas through tax breaks, while reducing or eliminating all forms of public foreign aid. Kaufman's basic theme is "the transition of a foreign economic program based on the concept of 'trade not aid' when Eisenhower took office to one predicated on the principle of 'trade and aid,' with the emphasis clearly on the flow of public capital abroad, by the time he left the White House."

That Ike himself was in charge of this transition, Kaufman leaves no doubt. That Kaufman likes Ike is equally clear: the foreign aid and trade program, Kaufman writes, "demonstrates the quality and character of Eisenhower's intellect and the cogency and forcefulness of his arguments in defense of administration policy. Finally, it emphasizes Eisenhower's flexibility as president and his capacity to alter his views in response to changing world conditions."

Kaufman, however, is critical of Ike on a number of points. Eisenhower himself, it turns out, could be as hypocritical as the "politicians" he scorned. In his speeches, Ike espoused the principles of free trade with sincerity and conviction; in his actions, he supported a protectionist agricultural policy and made broad concessions to the protectionist forces in Congress. Kaufman reaches the conclusion that "he often retreated on trade and tariff matters; he gave up the struggle with hardly a whimper."

And, as Blanche Wiesen Cook, another of the new Eisenhower scholars (but no revisionist), points out in *The Declassified Eisenhower* (Doubleday), Ike's vision of a peaceful world was based on a sophisticated version of Henry Luce's "American Century." Cook argues that Eisenhower's "blueprint . . . involved a determination to pursue political warfare, psychological warfare, and economic warfare everywhere and at all times." Under Ike's direction, she writes, the CIA and other branches of the government "ended all pretensions about territorial integrity, national sovereignty and international law. Covert operatives were everywhere, and they were active. From bribery to assassination, no activity was unacceptable short of nuclear war."

Cook does stress the importance of Eisenhower's stance against general war and his opposition to an arms race, but insists that these positions have to be placed in context, a context that includes the CIA-inspired and -led governmental overthrows in Iran and Guatemala, covert operations of all types in Vietnam and Eastern Europe, and assassination attempts against political leaders in the Congo and Cuba. Returning to an earlier view of Ike, Cook regards him as a "captive hero," the "chosen instrument" of the leaders of the great multinational corporations "to fight for the world they wanted."

One does not have to accept Cook's "captive hero" view to realize that it may indeed be time, as Kaufman indicates, to blow the whistle on Eisenhower revisionism. Ike had his shortcomings and he suffered serious setbacks. For all his openness to new ideas, he was rigid and dogmatic in his anti-communism. The darker side of Eisenhower's refusal to condemn McCarthy was that Ike himself agreed with the senator on the nature, if not the extent, of the problem, and he shared the senator's goals, if not his methods. After his first year in office, Ike made a list of his major accomplishments to date. Peace in Korea was first, the new defense policy second. Third on the list: "The highest security standards are being insisted upon for those employed in government service," a bland way of saying that under his direction, the Civil Service Commission had fired 2,611 "security risks" and reported that 4,315 other government workers had resigned when they learned they were under investigation. That was the true "hidden hand" at work, and the true difference between Ike and McCarthy—Ike got rid of Communists and fellow travelers (and many liberals) quietly and effectively, while McCarthy, for all his noise, accomplished nothing.

Thus, no matter how thoroughly the revisionists document Ike's opposition to McCarthy personally or his support for Warren, it remains true that his failure to speak out directly on McCarthy encouraged the witch hunters, just as his failure to speak out directly on the *Brown v. Topeka* decision encouraged the segregationists. The old general never admitted that it was impossible for him to be truly above the battle, never seemed to understand that the president is inevitably a part of the battle, so much so that his inaction can have as great an impact as his action.

With McCarthy and *Brown v. Topeka* in mind, there is a sad quality to the following Eisenhower diary passage, written in January 1954, about a number of Republican senators whom Ike was criticizing for being more inclined to trade votes than to provide clear leadership:

> They do not seem to realize when there arrives that moment at which soft speaking should be abandoned and a fight to the end undertaken. Any man who hopes to exercise leadership must be ready to meet this requirement face to face when it arises; unless he is ready to fight when necessary, people will finally begin to ignore him.

One of Ike's greatest disappointments was his failure to liberalize and modernize the Republican party, in order to make it the majority party in the United States. "The Republican party must be known as a progressive organization or it is sunk," he wrote in his diary in November 1954. "I believe this so emphatically that far from appeasing or reasoning with the dyed-in-the-wool reactionary fringe, we should completely ignore it and when necessary, repudiate it." Responding to cries of "impeach Earl Warren," Ike wrote in his diary, "If the Republicans as a body should try to repudiate him, I shall leave the Republican Party and try to organize an intelligent group of independents, however small." He was always threatening to break with the Republican party, or at least rename it; in March 1954, he told Hagerty, "You know, what we ought to do is get a word to put ahead of Republican—something like 'new' or 'modern' or something. We just can't work with fellows like McCarthy, Bricker, Jenner and that bunch."

A favorite revisionist quotation, which is used to show Ike's political astuteness, comes from a 1954 letter to his brother Edgar:

> Should any political party attempt to abolish social security and eliminate labor laws and farm programs, you would not hear of that party again in our political history. There is a tiny splinter group, of course, that believes that you can do these things. Among them are H. L. Hunt, a few other Texas oil millionaires, and an occasional politician and businessman from other areas. Their number is negligible and they are stupid.

Good enough, but a critic would be quick to point out that Ike's "tiny splinter group" managed to play a large role in the nominations of Barry Goldwater, Richard Nixon, and Ronald Reagan. In short, although Ike saw great dangers to the right in the Republican party, he did little to counter the reactionary influence in his own organization. Franklin Roosevelt did a far better job of curbing the left wing in the Democratic party, and generally in building his party, than anything Ike did for the Republicans. . . .

Shortly after Ike left office, a group of leading American historians was asked to rate the presidents. Ike came in near the bottom of the poll. That result was primarily a reflection of how enamored the professors were with FDR and Harry Truman. Today, those same historians would compare Ike with his successors rather than his predecessors and place him in the top ten, if not the top five, of all our presidents. No matter how much one qualifies that record by pointing to this or that shortcoming or failure of the Eisenhower administration, it remains an enviable record. No wonder the people like Ike.

Inaugural Address (1961)

John F. Kennedy

Bareheaded and coatless in the bitter cold of a bright January day, John F. Kennedy, the youngest man ever elected president of the United States, placed his hand on the Bible and swore the oath of office. In his inaugural address, Kennedy offered a grand vision. We remember the inspirational words, "ask not what your country can do for you—ask what you can do for your country." What is too often lost in our collective memories, shaped as they are by the tragedy of a young man cut down before his time, is what he asked us to do for our country. "Pay any price, bear any burden, meet any hardship . . .": Kennedy was summoning Americans to a global mission. His words rang out in warning to America's foes abroad. It was a moment, as Robert Frost wrote in his inaugural poem, "Of young ambition eager to be tried . . . . In any game the nations want to play."

How does this speech express the sense of possibility we associate with Kennedy's presidency? Does it fit best here, in a section on "The Politics of the Affluent Society," or with the previous documents on the Cold War?

VICE PRESIDENT JOHNSON, MR. SPEAKER, MR. CHIEF JUSTICE, PRESIDENT EISENHOWER, VICE PRESIDENT NIXON, PRESIDENT TRUMAN, REVEREND CLERGY, FELLOW CITIZENS:

We observe today not a victory of party but a celebration of freedom—symbolizing an end as well as a beginning—signifying renewal as well as change. For I have sworn before you and Almighty God the same solemn oath our forbears prescribed nearly a century and three-quarters ago.

The world is very different now. For man holds in his mortal hands the power to abolish all forms of human poverty and all forms of human life. And yet the same revolutionary beliefs for which our forebears fought are still at issue around the globe—the belief that the rights of man come not from the generosity of the state but from the hand of God.

We dare not forget today that we are the heirs of that first revolution. Let the word go forth from this time and place, to friend and foe alike, that the torch has been passed to a new generation of Americans—born in this century, tempered by war, disciplined by a hard and bitter peace, proud of our ancient heritage—and unwilling to witness or permit the slow undoing of those human rights to which this nation has always been committed, and to which we are committed today at home and around the world.

Let every nation know, whether it wishes us well or ill, that we shall pay any price, bear any burden, meet any hardship, support any friend, oppose any foe to assure the survival and the success of liberty.

This much we pledge—and more.

To those old allies whose cultural and spiritual origins we share, we pledge the loyalty of faithful friends. United there is little we cannot do in a host of cooperative ventures. Divided there is little we can do—for we dare not meet a powerful challenge at odds and split asunder.

To those new states whom we welcome to the ranks of the free, we pledge our word that one form of colonial control shall not have passed away merely to be replaced by a far more iron tyranny. We shall not always expect to find them supporting our view. But we shall always hope to find them strongly supporting their own freedom—and to remember that, in the past, those who foolishly sought power by riding the back of the tiger ended up inside.

To those people in the huts and villages of half the globe struggling to break the bonds of mass misery, we pledge our best efforts to help them help themselves, for whatever period is required—not because the communists may be doing it, not because we seek their votes, but because it is right. If a free society cannot help the many who are poor, it cannot save the few who are rich.

To our sister republics south of our border, we offer a special pledge—to convert our good words into good deeds—in a new alliance for progress—to assist free men and free governments in casting off the chains of poverty. But this peaceful revolution of hope cannot become the prey of hostile powers. Let all our neighbors know that we shall join with them to oppose aggression or subversion anywhere in the Americas. And let every other power know that this Hemisphere intends to remain the master of its own house.

To that world assembly of sovereign states, the United Nations, our last best hope in an age where the instruments of war have far outpaced the instruments of peace, we renew our pledge of support—

to prevent it from becoming merely a forum for invective—to strengthen its shield of the new and the weak—and to enlarge the area in which its writ may run.

Finally, to those nations who would make themselves our adversary, we offer not a pledge but a request: that both sides begin anew the quest for peace, before the dark powers of destruction unleashed by science engulf all humanity in planned or accidental self-destruction.

We dare not tempt them with weakness. For only when our arms are sufficient beyond doubt can we be certain beyond doubt that they will never be employed.

But neither can two great and powerful groups of nations take comfort from our present course—both sides overburdened by the cost of modern weapons, both rightly alarmed by the steady spread of the deadly atom, yet both racing to alter that uncertain balance of terror that stays the hand of mankind's final war.

So let us begin anew—remembering on both sides that civility is not a sign of weakness, and sincerity is always subject to proof. Let us never negotiate out of fear. But let us never fear to negotiate.

Let both sides explore what problems unite us instead of belaboring those problems which divide us.

Let both sides, for the first time, formulate serious and precise proposals for the inspection and control of arms—and bring the absolute power to destroy other nations under the absolute control of all nations.

Let both sides seek to invoke the wonders of science instead of its terrors. Together let us explore the stars, conquer the deserts, eradicate disease, tap the ocean depths and encourage the arts and commerce.

Let both sides unite to heed in all corners of the earth the command of Isaiah—to "undo the heavy burdens . . . (and) let the oppressed go free."

And if a beachhead of cooperation may push back the jungle of suspicion, let both sides join in creating a new endeavor, not a new balance of power, but a new world of law, where the strong are just and the weak secure and the peace preserved.

All this will not be finished in the first one hundred days. Nor will it be finished in the first one thousand days, nor in the life of this Administration, nor even perhaps in our lifetime on this planet. But let us begin.

In your hands, my fellow citizens, more than mine, will rest the final success or failure of our course. Since this country was founded, each generation of Americans has been summoned to give testimony to its national loyalty. The graves of young Americans who answered the call to service surround the globe.

Now the trumpet summons us again—not as a call to bear arms, though arms we need—not as a call to battle, though embattled we are—but a call to bear the burden of a long twilight struggle, year in and year out, "rejoicing in hope, patient in tribulation"—a struggle against the common enemies of man: tyranny, poverty, disease and war itself.

Can we forge against these enemies a grand and global alliance, North and South, East and West, that can assure a more fruitful life for all mankind? Will you join in that historic effort?

In the long history of the world, only a few generations have been granted the role of defending freedom in its hour of maximum danger. I do not shrink from this responsibility—I welcome it. I do not believe that any of us would exchange places with any other people or any other generation. The energy, the faith, the devotion which we bring to this endeavor will light our country and all who serve it—and the glow from that fire can truly light the world.

And so, my fellow Americans: ask not what your country can do for you—ask what you can do for your country.

My fellow citizens of the world: ask not what America will do for you, but what together we can do for the freedom of man.

Finally, whether you are citizens of America or citizens of the world, ask of us here the same high standards of strength and sacrifice which we ask of you. With a good conscience our only sure reward, with history the final judge of our deeds, let us go forth to lead the land we love, asking His blessing and His help, but knowing that here on earth God's work must truly be our own.

"The Great Society": Remarks at the University of Michigan (1964)

Lyndon B. Johnson

On May 22, 1964, President Lyndon Johnson gave the commencement address at the University of Michigan. Before the audience of young men and women and their families, he unveiled his vision of a "Great Society." Though much less well known than John F. Kennedy's Inaugural Address, Johnson's Great Society speech marks a major turning point in American government and politics. Johnson's legislative agenda (as documented in the next article) was extraordinarily ambitious and would reshape the role of American government. But the larger ideas about the role of government Johnson sets forth here are also significant. Compare this speech to Kennedy's Inaugural Address. How do their visions of the nation's purpose differ?

I have come today from the turmoil of your Capital to the tranquility of your campus to speak about the future of our country. The purpose of protecting the life of our Nation and preserving the liberty of our citizens is to pursue the happiness of our people. Our success in that pursuit is the test of our success as a nation. For a century we labored to settle and to subdue a continent. For half a century, we called upon unbounded invention and untiring industry to create an order of plenty for all our people. The challenge of the next half century is whether we have the wisdom to use that wealth to enrich and elevate our national life, and to advance the quality of our American civilization.

Your imagination, your initiative, and your indignation will determine whether we build a society where progress is the servant of our needs, or a society where old values and new visions are buried under unbridled growth. For in your time we have the opportunity to move

Public Papers of the Presidents of the United States, Lyndon B. Johnson, 1963–64, pp. 704–7.

not only toward the rich society and the powerful society, but upward to the Great Society. The Great Society rests on abundance and liberty for all. It demands an end to poverty and racial injustice, to which we are totally committed in our time. But that is just the beginning. The Great Society is a place where every child can find knowledge to enrich his mind and to enlarge his talents. It is a place where leisure is a welcome chance to build and reflect, not a feared cause of boredom and restlessness. It is a place where the city of man serves not only the needs of the body and the demands of commerce, but the desire for beauty and the hunger for community.

It is a place where man can renew contact with nature. It is a place which honors creation for its own sake and for what it adds to the understanding of the race. It is a place where men are more concerned with the quality of their goals than the quantity of their goods. But most of all, the Great Society is not a safe harbor, a resting place, a final objective, a finished work. It is a challenge constantly renewed, beckoning us toward a destiny where the meaning of our lives matches the marvelous products of our labor.

So I want to talk to you today about three places where we begin to build the Great Society—in our cities, in our countryside, and in our classrooms. Many of you will live to see the day, perhaps 50 years from now, when there will be 400 million Americans; four-fifths of them in urban areas. In the remainder of this century urban population will double, city land will double, and we will have to build homes, highways and facilities equal to all those built since this country was first settled. So in the next 40 years we must rebuild the entire urban United States.

Aristotle said, "Men come together in cities in order to live, but they remain together in order to live the good life."

It is harder and harder to live the good life in American cities today. The catalogue of ills is long: There is the decay of the centers and the despoiling of the suburbs. There is not enough housing for our people or transportation for our traffic. Open land is vanishing and old landmarks are violated. Worst of all, expansion is eroding the precious and time-honored values of community with neighbors and communion with nature. The loss of these values breeds loneliness and boredom and indifference. Our society will never be great until our cities are great. Today the frontier of imagination and innovation is inside those cities, and not beyond their borders. New experiments are already going on. It will be the task of your generation to make the American city a place where future generations will come, not only to live but to live the good life.

I understand that if I stay here tonight I would see that Michigan students are really doing their best to live the good life

This is the place where the Peace Corps was started. It is inspiring to see how all of you, while you are in this country, are trying so hard to live at the level of the people.

A second place where we begin to build the Great Society is in our countryside. We have always prided ourselves on being not only America the strong and America the free, but America the beautiful. Today that beauty is in danger. The water we drink, the food we eat, the very air that we breathe, are threatened with pollution. Our parks are overcrowded. Our seashores overburdened. Green fields and dense forests are disappearing.

A few years ago we were greatly concerned about the Ugly American. Today we must act to prevent an Ugly America.

For once the battle is lost, once our natural splendor is destroyed, it can never be recaptured. And once man can no longer walk with beauty or wonder at nature, his spirit will wither and his sustenance be wasted.

A third place to build the Great Society is in the classrooms of America. There your children's lives will be shaped. Our society will not be great until every young mind is set free to scan the farthest reaches of thought and imagination. We are still far from that goal. Today, eight million adult Americans, more than the entire population of Michigan, have not finished five years of school. Nearly 20 million have not finished 8 years of school. Nearly 54 million, more than one-quarter of all America, have not even finished high school.

Each year more than 100,000 high school graduates, with proven ability, do not enter college because they cannot afford it. And if we cannot educate today's youth, what will we do in 1970 when elementary school enrollment will be 5 million greater than 1960? And high school enrollment will rise by 5 million. College enrollment will increase by more than 3 million. In many places, classrooms are overcrowded and curricula are outdated. Most of our qualified teachers are underpaid, and many of our paid teachers are unqualified. So we must give every child a place to sit and a teacher to learn from. Poverty must not be a bar to learning, and learning must offer an escape from poverty.

But more classrooms and more teachers are not enough. We must seek an educational system which grows in excellence as it grows in size. This means better training for our teachers. It means preparing youth to enjoy their hours of leisure as well as their hours of labor. It means exploring new techniques of teaching, to find new ways to stimulate the love of learning and the capacity for creation.

These are three of the central issues of the Great Society. While our government has many programs directed at those issues, I do not pretend that we have the full answer to those problems. But I do promise this: We are going to assemble the best thought and the broadest knowledge from all over the world to find those answers for America. I intend to establish working groups to prepare a series of White House conferences and meetings on the cities, on natural beauty, on the quality of education, and on other emerging challenges. And from these meetings and from this inspiration and from these studies we will begin to set our course toward the Great Society.

The solution to these problems does not rest on a massive program in Washington, nor can it rely solely on the strained resources of local authority. They require us to create new concepts of cooperation, a creative federalism, between the national Capitol and the leaders of local communities.

Woodrow Wilson once wrote: "Every man sent out from this university should be a man of his nation as well as a man of his time."

Within your lifetime powerful forces, already loosed, will take us toward a way of life beyond the realm of our experience, almost beyond the bounds of our imagination. For better or for worse, your generation has been appointed by history to deal with those problems and to lead America toward a new age. You have the chance never before afforded to any people in any age. You can help build a society where the demands of morality, and the needs of the spirit, can be realized in the life of the Nation. So will you join in the battle to give every citizen the full equality which God enjoins and the law requires, whatever his belief, or race, or the color of his skin? Will you join in the battle to give every citizen an escape from the crushing weight of poverty? Will you join in the battle to make it possible for all nations to live in enduring peace as neighbors and not as mortal enemies? Will you join in the battle to build the Great Society, to prove that our material progress is only the foundation on which we will build a richer life of mind and spirit?

There are those timid souls who say this battle cannot be won, that we are condemned to a soulless wealth. I do not agree. We have the power to shape the civilization that we want. But we need your will, your labor, your hearts, if we are to build that kind of society.

Those who came to this land sought to build more than just a new country. They sought a free world.

So I have come here today to your campus to say that you can make their vision our reality. Let us from this moment begin our work so that in the future men will look back and say: It was then, after a long and weary way, that man turned the exploits of his genius to the full enrichment of his life.

Thank you. Goodbye.

Lyndon B. Johnson and American Liberalism

Bruce J. Schulman

Elevated to the presidency in late 1963 by the assassination of John Kennedy, Lyndon Johnson faced a difficult task. Stepping into the shoes of the nation's slain leader, a man very different from himself, required enormous political savvy. But Johnson turned the challenge to his advantage. As he later explained, his goal was to take a "dead man's program and turn it into a martyr's cause."

Johnson was elected to the presidency in 1964 with 61 percent of the popular vote. He used this mandate to further his ambitious legislative agenda, which he called the Great Society. In the following excerpts from his book, Lyndon B. Johnson and American Liberalism, *historian Bruce Schulman analyzes the Great Society and explains the development of 1960s liberalism. In this portrait of a larger-than-life political figure waging legislative war on the ills of American society, Schulman assesses the successes and failures of the Great Society and, by extension, of American political liberalism in the 1960s.*

In the early years of the twentieth century, T[eddy] R[oosevelt], [Woodrow] Wilson, and the Progressives had initiated a transformation of American liberalism, changing the very meaning of the term. *Liberalism* derived, of course, from a passion for liberty, a concern for freedom. Nineteenth-century liberalism, what historians now term *classical liberalism,* embraced a largely negative view of freedom. Freedom, in this sense, meant only absence of restraint, the ability to do as one pleased without undue encumbrance or regulation. Classical

From Bruce J. Schulman, *Lyndon B. Johnson and American Liberalism* (Bedford Books of St. Martin's Press, 1995). Copyright © 11/94 by Bedford/St. Martin's Press. Reprinted with permission of Bedford/St. Martin's Press. Footnotes have been deleted.

liberals saw government as the gravest threat to freedom and believed that the government that governs least governs best.

The complexity of modern life and the forces unleashed by the industrial revolution called into question this negative definition of liberty. Small, limited government conferred only the most tenuous sort of freedom when it afforded citizens no protection against contaminated meat, adulterated drugs, unsafe factories, and price-gouging monopolists. Encountering these new realities, modern liberals recognized that real freedom required the active protection of an interventionist government. "In the present day," Theodore Roosevelt had explained, "the limitation of governmental power means the enslavement of the people." He and his fellow Progressives envisioned a larger role for government as a referee or police officer, ensuring that the economy and society operated freely and fairly.

Franklin Roosevelt inherited and extended this positive view of freedom. He cemented the alliance between liberalism and activist government that his forebear first forged. When FDR laid out what he described as the four basic freedoms in 1941, he included not only traditional liberties like freedom of speech and freedom of religion, but also freedom from want and freedom from fear. These last freedoms represented guaranteed security against economic depression and foreign aggression, freedoms that only an energetic, vigilant big government could assure. . . .

[In the post–World War II era,] liberalism itself evolved, breaking its New Deal template in three crucial respects. First, postwar liberals developed a new attitude toward business and the economy. Economic policy had always been redistributive—taking advantages from one segment of the population and conferring them on another. . . . New Deal liberals had believed that government needed to restrain the worst excesses of big business, guarantee workers a fair shake, and ensure a minimum American standard of living for the poorest citizens. . . .

The wartime experience seemed to prove the efficacy of a new type of liberal economic policy—a way to improve the lives of ordinary Americans without offending business, to feed the hungry and shelter the homeless without asking the well-off to sacrifice.

This new liberal tool was called Keynesian economics, named for its originator, the British economist John Maynard Keynes. For American liberals after World War II, Keynes's most useful insight was that government could use fiscal policy, its powers of taxing and spending, to stimulate the economy. Washington policymakers learned from Keynes that they could heat up a slowing economy and prevent future depressions. But American Keynesians were not content with averting future downturns; they wanted to use Keynesian economics to ensure continued and continuous economic growth, to make the economic pie bigger and bigger. There would be more for everyone, rich and poor, labor and business. . . .

Second, American liberals developed a new view of the political process after World War II, a new vision of democracy. Public policy had become so complicated and distant that individuals had little knowledge of and less input into the nation's most important decisions. . . . In the 1950s political theorists believed that when the people did mobilize and masses of citizens involved themselves in the political process, they tended to act on vague, irrational principles and emotions, not on informed, sober reflection. The rise of Nazism in Germany had proved that mass participation did not necessarily mean increased democracy. In this setting postwar liberals championed pluralist politics, a view of American democracy as a process of bargaining among groups. . . .

Third, and most important, postwar liberals focused their energies on the struggle against international communism. . . . In fact, the cold war struggle against communism underlay all of these changes in liberal outlook. Constant economic growth distinguished American capitalism from Soviet communism, with its commitment to class conflict. . . . Pluralist politics allowed Americans to contrast American democracy with Soviet dictatorship, to champion pragmatic problem solving over crusading ideology. . . .

LYNDON JOHNSON AND 1960s LIBERALISM

[Following Kennedy's assassination,] Johnson assumed the Kennedy mantle, declaring himself the "dutiful executor" of his predecessor's legacy. He shouldered a heavy burden, for the shock of the assassination instantly elevated Kennedy, an uncertain leader only beginning to establish himself, into an unparalleled martyr, the symbol of all that was grand in the nation. Only 49.7 percent of the electorate had cast their ballots for JFK in 1960, but after the assassination, 65 percent claimed that they had voted for him. Even opponents of the slain president, a national poll revealed, overwhelmingly mourned his death as "the loss of someone close and dear."

Five days after the assassination, Johnson made his first presidential address to the American people. Significantly, he made the speech not from the Oval Office of the White House, but before a joint session of Congress, in the place where he had started his career. Johnson began by expressing the collective grief of the nation but did not content himself with honoring the fallen hero. Committing himself to vigorous action on behalf of the Kennedy agenda, Johnson promised to complete the slain leader's work, and he made it clear that the most immediate tasks were on Capitol Hill. He asked for enactment of the Kennedy tax bill and most emphatically for civil rights legislation: "We have talked long enough in this country about equal rights. We have talked for one hundred years or more. It is time now to write the next chapter, and to write it in the books of law."

President Johnson had reassured the American people with his promise to "continue"; he accepted his duty as custodian of the Kennedy legacy. But he made it clear that his would be no caretaker administration. When one adviser warned him against risking too much prestige and power to implement Kennedy's legislative program, LBJ paused, raised his eyebrows, and replied, "Well, then what the hell's the presidency for?"

Johnson immediately went on what his exhausted assistants called the "two-shift day." Rising at six-thirty, LBJ would work furiously until about two o'clock, when he left the Oval Office and took a walk or a swim. Then he would change into his pajamas for a catnap, usually on the long couch in the private sitting room adjoining his office. At four, he was showered and dressed, ready for a "new day's work." The second shift would end after midnight, sometimes lasting until two in the morning if affairs were especially pressing. . . .

Johnson immediately began placing his own distinctive, earthy stamp on the White House. When special assistant Jack Valenti cluttered up the president's schedule with "brief visits" from prominent citizens, Johnson warned him that there was no such thing as a brief visit. "Hell," LBJ complained, "by the time a man scratches his ass, clears his throat, and tells me how smart he is, we've already wasted fifteen minutes." Occasionally, Johnson would interrupt a high-level meeting for a swimming break; he would lead the assembled staff (and sometimes reporters or guests) down to the White House pool, strip naked, and dive in. He expected others to do the same. When using the bathroom, when showering in the morning, when receiving a massage at night—at all of those intimate and possibly embarrassing moments—he expected staff members to follow him into bedroom and bathroom and continue their conversations as if still in an office. . . .

Even as he stamped the White House as his own, Johnson carefully honored the Kennedy legacy. In contrast to his disconcertingly familiar behavior with his own aides, he remained deeply respectful of JFK's cabinet and top officials. He needed Kennedy's aides, needed the image of continuity; and with very few exceptions, Kennedy's appointees stayed on and served the new president. . . .

With the White House geared up for two shifts and the Kennedy men on board, LBJ prepared to revive the stalled Kennedy agenda. In many ways, the moment perfectly suited Johnson's talents. The shocked and sorrowful country cried out for unity and healing, and Lyndon Johnson had spent his whole life fashioning consensus, bringing bitter rivals to compromise through sheer force of will. The liberal agenda had been formulated; it just needed congressional approval. The assassination placed LBJ—an unparalleled legislative tactician and savvy horse trader—in the White House and allowed him to use the president's tragic death to ram through Johnson's legislative program. Few legislators dared oppose the last, best hope of the martyred Kennedy, especially with Lyndon Johnson twisting their arms. Moreover, 1964 was a time of relative quiet in foreign policy. Despite two small-scale crises in Latin America and the deteriorating situation in Vietnam, Johnson was able to hold the line on international affairs—to continue the Kennedy foreign policies while devoting himself to domestic politics. His first State of the Union Address, delivered on January 8, 1964, dealt almost exclusively with problems and prospects at home—the first State of the Union to do so since the beginning of the cold war.

In that speech, Johnson asked the Congress to "carry forward the plans and programs of John Fitzgerald Kennedy." But it was left to Lyndon Johnson to formulate those plans and to execute them. "Everything I had ever learned in the history books taught me that martyrs have to die for causes," LBJ recalled later. "John Kennedy had died. But his 'cause' was not really clear. That was my job. I had to take the dead man's program and turn it into a martyr's cause. . . ."

No president matched Johnson's skills as chief legislator. Despite the far-reaching and controversial nature of his program, LBJ won congressional approval for 58 percent of his proposals in 1964, 69 percent in 1965, and 56 percent in 1966, compared, for example, with 37 percent for Eisenhower in 1957 and just 27 percent for JFK in 1963. In the early days of LBJ's presidency, Republicans complained about the "Xerox Congress" or the "three-B Congress—bullied, badgered, and brainwashed," but they found themselves powerless against Johnson's legislative juggernaut. When the "Great 89th," the Congress which LBJ swept into office with his 1964 landslide, completed its work in the autumn of 1966, it left behind the most productive law-making record in American history. Lawrence O'Brien, LBJ's chief congressional liaison, and domestic policy chief Joseph Califano proudly produced a summary of the legislative achievements.

The list was staggering. For LBJ not only secured the civil rights, health, education, and welfare measures commonly associated with the Great Society, but a host of other reforms. Less noted than Medicare or the war on poverty, many of these proved to have broader and more durable effects. The Immigration Act of 1965 eliminated the odious quota system which first became law amidst an outburst of racist nativism in the 1920s. The national origins system, as it was called, had severely limited immigration from eastern and southern Europe and all but banned arrivals from Asia. Declaring the limits "incompatible with our basic American tradition," Johnson outlawed ethnic quotas and opened the doors to a steady stream of arrivals from Asia. The act made possible the large migrations of Koreans, Filipinos, Japanese, and Vietnamese to the United States that have contributed so much to the nation's economic and cultural life and so dramatically transformed the nation's western states.

Johnson pressed for restrictions on government wiretapping and surveillance and signed an act granting scholars, investigators, and private citizens access to government files. Although he privately taped many of his own phone conversations and allowed the FBI to continue electronic eavesdropping, Johnson ordered other government agencies to halt bugging and urged the Congress to limit the practice.

LBJ also stepped up government regulation of the environment. He signed major federal initiatives restricting water and air pollution, initiated with Lady Bird's help a national highway beautification program, and added more land to the national wildlife refuges, wilderness, and national park systems than any president of the era. At the end of his administration, the chairman of the National Geographic Society called LBJ "our greatest conservation president."

Johnson had spent a lifetime working to pass laws; for him, the major struggle of political life, the principal task of presidential liberalism, was obtaining congressional approval for a broad-scale liberal program. No other president—not JFK, not even FDR, had done that so well. With a stroke of a pen, he set aside land as wilderness, opened the nation's doors to Asian immigrants, or increased the minimum wage. But, in most cases, signing a law was not enough to produce effective action. Making law was only the first step in making policy—programs needed to be implemented and administered as well as enacted by the Congress. Johnson thought that if he could just plant the seeds for his Great Society, it would slowly but surely grow into a vast, powerful, impregnable oak. But he proved better at planting than at watering and nurturing. As one Johnson-watcher put it, "Pass the bill now, worry about its effects and implementation later—this was the White House strategy. . . . The standard of success was the passage of the law—and not only within the administration, but in the press and among the public. By this standard, the Great Society was on its way to becoming the most successful domestic program in history."

THE NOT-SO-GREAT SOCIETY:
IMPLEMENTING LBJ'S PROGRAM

Unfortunately, the very compromises and concessions needed to prevail on Capitol Hill hampered the programs after they won legislative approval. For example, Title I of the Elementary and Secondary Education Act, the marrow of LBJ's education program, allocated one billion federal dollars in compensatory education funds for poor students. Before Title I, local communities had always controlled and financed education in the United States. Local control not only created vast inequities between wealthier and poorer neighborhoods, but perpetuated them, since without good schools, residents of poor areas were unlikely to break free of poverty.

The Johnson administration designed Title I to end this depressing cycle of ignorance and want. The law's rationale was simple: children from poor families lacked the advantages of their better-off classmates and tended to fall behind academically. Schools could compensate for this problem by devoting more attention and resources to the poor than to the nonpoor; needy students would improve in the classroom and stay in school longer. Better education would eventually translate into higher incomes and break the cycle of poverty.

To pass the bill, however, the Johnson administration needed the support of local school districts, of the educational establishment in place. So the ESEA granted local districts the primary responsibility for conceiving and implementing the compensatory program. In the Senate hearings on the bill, LBJ's nemesis, Robert Kennedy, challenged this provision. He asked whether local schools bore responsibility for the educational deficiencies of the poor in the first place—whether it made sense to trust the very people who created the inequities with the funds to remedy them. LBJ's commissioner of education admitted the potential problem but pledged that local school officials would change their attitudes and work for reform.

Robert Kennedy's fears proved justified. The government allocated money to a district based on the number of poor students enrolled in it, but the districts selected which schools, students, and programs received the funds. Most districts pocketed the money and continued business-as-usual. Fresno, California, used its Title I allocation to buy an educational TV system for all students; Camden, New Jersey, subsidized physical education classes for pupils regardless of income. In fact, a 1977 study revealed that few Title I dollars actually benefited poor students; most of the funds supported programs for the middle class and well-to-do. As historian Allen Matusow explained, "President Johnson always believed that Title I was an anti-poverty program. The local school districts made sure it was not."

Similarly, Johnson compromised on Medicare to win the acquiescence of doctors, on the highway beautification bill to conciliate business interests, and on the food stamp program to satisfy southern planters. By amending Great Society bills, Johnson won over stubborn lawmakers, but in the process he diluted his programs and complicated their execution.

If LBJ had dedicated his insatiable energies to implementing the Great Society, he might have overcome weaknesses in the statutes. But Johnson displayed little interest in administrating the agencies he created. This oversight surprised many of LBJ's closest confidants. As a young congressman, Johnson had seen executive branch officials sabotage FDR's initiatives by delaying and obfuscating the president's orders. In fact, one of LBJ's favorite political stories, an anecdote he repeated over and over again to impress on his staff the need for implementing his directives, concerned a visit to a tiny east Texas town during World War II. Purchasing some gasoline, LBJ handed over the Office of Price Administration (OPA) coupons needed to purchase gasoline under wartime rationing rules. The puzzled attendant looked cockeyed at Johnson and then realized where the strange coupons had come from. "Oh, the O, P and A," he exclaimed. "Well, we didn't put that in down here." Johnson understood that laws alone accomplished little good "if you didn't put 'em in," but he found implementing them easier said than done.

Johnson stinted on administration in part because he concentrated on legislative battles and because the war in Vietnam increasingly dominated his attention. But to a large extent, the problem was built into the nature of the presidency. Executive branch officials, from the lowliest bureaucrat to the president himself, papered over the problems and failures of their agencies. They believed that once Congress heard about miscues or failures, it would cut a program, rather than applaud an honest assessment and let the administration try again. "Of course, I understand the difficulties of bureaucracy," LBJ told an aide when informed of deficiencies in one Great Society program. "But what you don't understand is that the President's real trouble is with the Congress, not the bureaucracy. . . . If we went around beating our breasts and admitting difficulties in our programs, then the Congress would immediately slash all our funds for next year and then where would we be? Better to send in the reports as they are, even knowing the situation is more complicated than it appears, and then work from within to make things better and correct the problems." Constantly jockeying with Congress, LBJ mainly ignored the challenges of "putting in" the Great Society programs.

No component of the Great Society aroused higher expectations in the Congress and the country than the war on poverty; none occasioned so much controversy and disappointment when it was put into effect. In 1964, the newly created Office of Economic Opportunity (OEO) led to a multipronged attack on poverty. Head Start, an early education program for preschoolers, began in 1965. Its objective was to prepare underprivileged children for first grade, equipping them with basic academic and social skills, so that they would perform better in the early grades and be more likely to remain in school. Head

Start ultimately proved a modest success, although during the Johnson years, it registered few results. . . .

The most celebrated and controversial skirmish of the war on poverty involved the Community Action Program (CAP). Attacking persistent urban poverty head on, CAP encouraged poor neighborhoods to form their own community action agencies. These agencies would mobilize all parts of the community "to promote fundamental change in the interests of the poor." As OEO chief Sargent Shriver testified before the Congress, the War on Poverty aimed not only at individuals: "It embraces entire neighborhoods, communities, cities, and states. It is an attempt to change institutions as well as people. It must deal with the culture of poverty as well as the individual victims."

Shriver's remarks revealed a new understanding of poverty, especially of the hard-core poor in inner cities, that was taking shape in the Johnson administration during the mid-1960s. Policymakers gradually developed a conception of a "culture of poverty" in the nation's slum communities. Adherents of this view no longer conceived of the urban poor as "rich people without money," essentially like everyone else but lacking resources, skills, and job opportunities. Instead they argued that the hard-core poor possessed a distinctive cultural profile, a way of life passed on from generation to generation, characterized by unstable families, high rates of illegitimacy, low levels of voting and political participation, poor self-esteem, and traumatic childhood experiences. For some liberal policymakers, like LBJ himself, the new concept of a culture of poverty barely altered their outlook; it merely offered an additional rationale for concerted federal effort to ameliorate conditions in the nation's inner cities. For other, more radical observers, it proved that traditional transfer programs must give way to community action projects that actively empowered the poor and involved them in managing their own communities.

The CAP staff contained many people of that more aggressive stripe—young idealists committed as much to stirring up the poor as to helping them. Initially, LBJ paid them little attention. Johnson gave Sargent Shriver one, and only one, piece of advice: "Keep out crooks, communists, and cocksuckers."

Allowed so much free rein, the Community Action Program not only financed neighborhood development projects, but also insisted on including the poor in designing and running local programs.

Convinced that the urban poor needed power as well as resources to transform their communities, CAP administrators wanted the needy to form, in the words of the program's Community Action workbook, "autonomous and self-managed organizations which are competent to exert political influence on behalf of their own self-interest." Unlike federal aid to education, which granted power and money to local school boards, community action would circumvent municipal officials and local elites, directly empowering and funding the poor to rebuild their own neighborhoods. For that reason, inserted into the Economic Opportunity Act was the so-called maximum feasible participation doctrine, a clause requiring that community action agencies be developed, conducted, and administered with the maximum feasible participation of residents of the area—including the poor.

The "maximum feasible participation" directive set up an irreconcilable conflict between national and local authorities. The federalist character of the American political system—the strange division of powers among federal, state, and local governments—has always offered local actors an unusually large bag of tricks for frustrating national policy. This obstructionism was peculiarly in evidence during the War on Poverty. City governments resented the strictures and proceeded to ignore them. They designed community action projects without representatives of the impoverished communities, with little attention to the special needs of blighted neighborhoods. But the OEO meant business: it rejected these plans, held up the funds, and sent city leaders back to the drawing board. It forced them to include minorities and poor people on the boards of their community agencies and to devise projects more responsive to the problems of slum neighborhoods. The conflicts took LBJ and his top aides by surprise. Neither the Congress nor the president seemed to understand the full implications of the maximum feasible participation clause. Congress, which approved the doctrine, certainly opposed any such disruptive influences on local power structures. And President Johnson acceded to it because he feared southern whites might otherwise freeze blacks out of the program. Johnson never envisioned that the overwhelmingly Democratic mayors of northern cities would rage against a program funneling federal dollars into their towns.

The Community Action Program quickly became a political liability. Bowing to the complaints from mayors and other local officials, the Johnson administration retreated. Shriver reined in the idealists on his staff and community action agencies returned to the control of city officials concerned mainly with white middle-class constituencies. When the program came up for renewal in 1967, its ambitious agenda had vanished. Sniffing the pork barrel, ravenous mayors had become its biggest supporters.

Certainly, LBJ bore a great deal of responsibility for CAP's failure; he did not run a tight ship. But the gravest problem of CAP and of the Great Society in general was what one administration official called "a tendency to oversell and underperform." Johnson launched new programs with extravagant claims, but he put up neither the monetary muscle not the clear administrative strategy to put them through.

Domestic policy chief Joseph Califano reflected on the administrative failures of the Great Society in similar terms: "Johnson's extravagant rhetoric announcing new programs belied the modest funds he requested to begin them." Johnson thus alienated both conservatives who "believed that he was hiding his real intentions just to get a foot in the door" and liberals who thought "he wasn't asking for enough to smash the door open."

ASSESSING THE GREAT SOCIETY

Since the 1960s, many voices have debated the success of the Great Society and the reasons for its shortcomings. For thirty years, Johnson's program has remained the standard of liberal public policy in the United States, in both indictments and defenses of modern American liberalism.

Johnson himself took pride in his record. In his memoirs, Johnson pointed to the steep drop in the number of people living below the official poverty line during his term in office, a drop caused by the expanding wartime economy as well as the social programs of the Great Society. "We started something in motion with the attack on poverty," LBJ insisted. "Its effects were felt in education, law, medicine, and social welfare, in business and industry, in civil and philanthropic life, and in religion. . . . Of course, we had not lifted everyone out of poverty," Johnson conceded. "There would be setbacks and frustrations and disappointments ahead. But no one would ever again be able to ignore the poverty in our midst, and I believe that is enough to assure the final outcome and to change the way of life for millions of our fellow human beings."

Johnson's poverty warriors shared their chief's assessment. Joseph Califano claimed that Johnson "converted the hopes and aspirations of all kinds of Americans into a political force that brought out much of the good in each of us. . . . Whatever historians of the Great Society say twenty years later, they must admit that we tried, and I believe they will conclude that America is a better place because we did." Other liberals agreed that the Great Society moved the nation in the right direction but complained that Johnson did not move fast or far enough, did not give programs enough time, and did not allocate enough money.

Conservatives, on the other hand, viewed the Great Society as big government run amok—too much intervention, too much waste, and too much bureaucratic red tape. Writing in 1968, conservative commentator Ernest Van Den Haag denounced the "welfare mess" as a "wasteful hodgepodge" of programs which only trapped and humiliated the poor. During the 1970s and 1980s, this conservative critique of the Great Society gained political force. Nearly two decades after LBJ launched his program, Ronald Reagan used the Great Society as a whipping boy for his resurgent conservative platform. The first annual report of Reagan's Council of Economic Advisers, published in January 1982, listed "reducing the role of the Federal Government in all its dimensions" as Reagan's top priority and blamed all the nation's woes on government "meddling." The report rejected "paternalism" in welfare policies, suggesting that antipoverty programs only aggravated the distress of the needy and trapped them in a cycle of poverty and dependence.

Indeed, Reaganite calls for dismantling the welfare system rested on arguments that Great Society programs had actually harmed the impoverished—encouraging illegitimacy, welfare dependence, and hopelessness. "With the coming of the Great Society," President Reagan declared in 1982, "government began eating away at the underpinnings of the private enterprise system. The big taxers and big spenders in the Congress had started a binge that would slowly change the nature of our society and, even worse, it threatened the character of our people. . . . By the time the full weight of Great Society programs was felt, economic progress for America's poor had come to a tragic halt."

During the 1960s, however, the principal critique of the Great Society came not from conservatives, but from radicals, from the student New Left, the Black Power movement, and various social protest groups. Ultimately, Johnsonian liberalism proved too timid to challenge the powers that be. Johnson could not, would not, see that the interests of rich and poor, business and labor, must sometimes collide; he could not win everyone's cooperation without compromising the effectiveness of his programs.

In 1971, in retirement at the LBJ ranch, Johnson reflected bitterly on the fate of his beloved Great Society. "I figured when my legislative program passed the Congress," he told Doris Kearns, "that the Great Society had the chance to grow into a beautiful woman. And I figured her growth and development would be as natural and inevitable as any small child's. . . . And when she grew up, I figured she'd be so big and beautiful that the American people couldn't help but fall in love with her, and once they did, they'd want to keep her around forever, making her a permanent part of American life, more permanent even than the New Deal." Instead, he saw his successor Richard Nixon starving his program to death: "She's getting thinner and uglier all the time; now her bones are beginning to stick out and her wrinkles are beginning to show. Soon she'll be so ugly that the American people will refuse to look at her; they'll stick her in a closet to hide her away and there she'll die. And when she dies, I, too, will die."

Poignant words, but deceptive ones, for it was Lyndon Johnson himself, more than his aides or opponents or successors, who neglected the Great Society and stunted its growth. Early in his presidency, LBJ made two political mistakes, two fateful errors that ultimately stifled his beloved "child." First, he underestimated the expense of the two-front war in Vietnam. Deciding that he had no choice but to escalate the war in Southeast Asia, Johnson determined to pursue the war and the Great Society simultaneously. Strongly in his mind remained the examples of Woodrow Wilson and FDR who had abandoned domestic reform to lead the nation into war. Johnson believed he could protect the Great Society only by downplaying the expense of his two-front war; he covered up the costs of the Asian struggle, economized on every domestic program, and delayed a tax increase as long as possible. This strategy failed. Eventually, he had to scale back the Great Society to fight the war that took up more and more of his time and energy. "That bitch of a war," Johnson later admitted, "killed the lady I really loved—the Great Society."

Second, he did not anticipate the insidious political current that would further undermine LBJ's liberal program—racial backlash.

Even though Great Society programs mainly benefited middle-class whites—aid to education, Medicare, farm subsidies, expanded Social Security—Johnson spoke repeatedly and passionately about eradicating poverty. The special attention to the poor, combined with the ongoing civil rights revolution, convinced many Americans that Johnson and his fellow liberals lavished too many benefits on African Americans and other racial minorities. This perception stirred up simmering racial antagonisms, a backlash against civil rights and the poverty war which stoked white discontent against liberal government. As one of Johnson's cabinet members warned in 1966, "Many people think the Great Society programs are mainly designed to help the very poor and they don't believe that this Administration has much interest in the middle-class, middle income family. There must be a way to make these people see that every American has an enormous stake in what we're doing."

Johnson feared the white backlash; he worried particularly about losing the backbone of the liberal coalition, the blue-collar, white ethnics of the northeast and midwest who had provided electoral support for every Democratic president since FDR. The Civil Rights Act of 1964 had already sacrificed the votes of white southerners. Now the heart of the New Deal coalition complained about Johnson's poverty program and the intensifying demands of African Americans for power and equality. These constituencies had supported the early civil rights movement—what they saw as largely southern battles for legal equality. When African Americans turned their eyes toward informal discrimination in northern cities and the federal courts began to order the integration of schools in the North, however, the fears and hatreds of people who had voted for FDR, JFK, and LBJ exploded. Liberalism's electoral base began melting in the heat and fury of those racial confrontations.

Part 3

CIVIL RIGHTS AND RACIAL JUSTICE

No domestic development has been more important to postwar American society than the struggle for racial equality. That struggle had a long history. During the three-quarters of a century after the end of Reconstruction, little had occurred to improve the status of African Americans. The vast majority of blacks lived in the South, were denied the right to vote, suffered the overt and covert consequences of segregation, experienced dire poverty, and were subject— at virtually every moment—to the threat of physical intimidation and violence. Yet throughout that time, African Americans had fought back, using their own institutions, resources, and energies to build the best schools, churches, and homes that they could for their children and themselves.

The modern civil rights struggle received its major impetus from three sources: the New Deal, World War II, and the long and finally successful campaign of the National Association for the Advancement of Colored People (NAACP) to overturn the legal sanction for segregation, accomplished in 1954 with the Supreme Court's unanimous ruling in *Brown v. Board of Education* that segregation was inherently unconstitutional.

During the 1930s and 1940s, hundreds of thousands of African Americans left the rural South to migrate to cities within the South, and, especially during World War II, began to take new jobs in the North and West. The number of blacks in labor unions doubled, some economic improvements occurred, and in the North especially, there was the opportunity for some political participation. Eleanor Roosevelt had encouraged her husband, Franklin, to do more to address problems of racial oppression, and in coalition with similar-minded allies in the New Deal, had succeeded in making some differ-

117

ences in administration attitudes toward civil rights. On the other hand, throughout the New Deal and World War II, policies of indifference, hostility, and racism continued largely to predominate. During the war, African American soldiers were not allowed to fight beside white soldiers, black blood supplies were segregated from white blood supplies, and black soldiers in Jim Crow southern training camps were subject to brutal white racism. Together, the New Deal and World War II brought some progress, yet in a context of continued and pervasive discrimination. The combination spurred black anger and frustration, helping to galvanize a new mood of protest. NAACP memberships shot up 1,000 percent during World War II, the black press insistently waged a "Double V" campaign—victory against Nazism abroad *and* racism at home—and a new awareness developed of the linkage between the struggle of African Americans for freedom in the United States, and of colored peoples around the globe for freedom from colonialism.

In the face of ever growing black militancy, liberal Democrats and Republicans began to pay more attention to the issue of civil rights. President Harry Truman established a civil rights commission which called for desegregation of the armed services and greater protection of voting rights; President Dwight Eisenhower proceeded to desegregate Washington, D.C., in response to the *Brown* decision; and the State Department started to use black entertainers—Louis Armstrong and Dizzy Gillespie—as "cultural" ambassadors for the United States abroad. But in general, support was more rhetorical than substantive. Eisenhower refused to endorse the *Brown* decision or promote compliance with it in southern states; the Congress responded slowly and hesitantly to civil rights initiatives; and the State Department had to be dragged into supporting self-determination in Africa. And throughout much of the white South, resolve grew. Integration would not be forced upon southern states by an interventionist federal government.

By the 1960s, it was evident that only when blacks forced white institutions into action could any substantive change be anticipated. The mass of Montgomery blacks had to boycott the city's buses for 381 days in 1955–56 before that city—and the courts—finally agreed to desegregate public transportation there; in 1960, four black college students in Greensboro, North Carolina, had to "sit-in" at a local Woolworth's—and galvanize thousands of others in support—before local merchants agreed to provide the same equal service at the lunch counter that they provided at other counters. By now, it was clear that black Americans would not tolerate any further delay. Within two months of the Greensboro sit-ins, similar demonstrations had erupted in fifty-four cities in nine different states. The Civil Rights movement headed by Martin Luther King, Jr., and the Student Non-Violent Coordinating Committee (SNCC) had taken off. There would be no turning back.

Spurred by the example of the African American Civil Rights movement, and in reaction to long histories of oppression and discrimination of their own, Mexican Americans and Native Americans also engaged in struggles for social justice. The movements that developed were not wholly new; members of both groups had fought for their rights over the preceding decades. But the mass movements that emerged in the late 1960s and early 1970s were very much influenced by the trajectory of the African American movement, and shaped by the increasing polarization of American life.

There are two general interpretations of developments in race relations since World War II. One emphasizes the importance of external and impersonal factors such as migration, economic progress, shifts in governmental policies, and the emergence of an environment more conducive toward racial justice. Clearly, these preconditions are important to social change. Here, however, while portraying some of the external factors, we focus more on the second interpretation, that which emphasizes the collective demands of African Americans themselves for change. Facing massive resistance in the South, governmental reluctance to take action, and the ambivalence of many northern whites, many black Americans chose to follow the axiom of the black abolitionist Frederick Douglass: "Power concedes nothing without demand. It never has and it never will."

The selections included here provide a framework for thinking about the origins, development, and tactics of these movements for civil rights and racial justice. Excerpts from the Supreme Court's 1954 *Brown v. Board of Education* ruling demonstrate what sort of reasoning led portions of the U.S. government to change position on issues of race. "The Southern Manifesto," adopted by 101 members of Congress in response to the *Brown* decision, illustrates how southern opponents of integration argued—and understood—their position. Building upon the questions about the role of leaders addressed in the previous section, Vincent Harding offers both a personal and historical judgment of Martin Luther King, Jr.'s role in the movement.

Turning from leadership to the grassroots, Anne Moody's account of a lunch counter sit-in reminds us how much of the movement's power lay in the bravery and commitment of countless individuals, most of whose names will never be known. The development of demands for "Black Power" rather than civil rights is represented by the 1966 platform statement of the Black Panther Party. This document should be contrasted with Bayard Rustin's 1965 argument in favor of a black-white progressive alliance.

The final section of Part 3 turns from the African American movement to other movements for racial justice. Historian F. Arturo Rosales analyzes the development of *El Movimiento* through the story of the 1968 East Los Angeles high school "blow out." And in a 1969 proclamation, "Indians of All Nations" announce the occupation of Alcatraz Island, an action that helped to launch a mass movement for "Red Power."

Given the continuity of race as a shaping force in America, students may wish to think through a series of questions on the civil rights struggle and movements for racial justice. Why did this movement emerge to such prominence only in the 1950s and 1960s? In which ways did the Civil Rights movement succeed, and in which ways did it fail? What are the legacies of the turn toward cultural nationalism in Black Power, Brown Power, and Red Power movements? How important are the very different specific histories of Native Americans, African Americans, and Mexican Americans or Chicanos in shaping their ongoing movements? What are the relative merits of coalition (either Rustin's vision of a black-white coalition or a coalition of what came to be called collectively "people of color") versus strategies of separatism and self-help?

Brown v. Board of Education (1954)

Supreme Court of the United States

In the years following World War II, racially segregated schools were the norm in the United States. In much of the nation the segregation was de facto, *the result of residential segregation and economic inequality that was created, in large part, by racial prejudice and discrimination. But in twenty states—most of them in the South—school segregation was* de jure, *or by law. Although the National Association for the Advancement of Colored People (NAACP) had used the courts to challenge "Jim Crow" laws since the 1930's, arguing that legal segregation violated the "equal protection" clause of the Fourteenth Amendment, the challenges foundered upon the precedent created by* Plessy v. Ferguson. *This 1896 Supreme Court decision established a doctrine of "separate but equal": segregation of public facilities by race was not in violation of the Fourteenth Amendment so long as the facilities were equal in quality. In fact, the public schools designated for "Negroes" were rarely equal to those for whites. In the most extreme cases, they lacked everything from textbooks to indoor plumbing. But the NAACP was not seeking better enforcement of the "separate but equal" principle; instead it sought the "right" cases with which to challenge school segregation in the Supreme Court.*

Such a case emerged in Topeka, Kansas, in 1951. Oliver Brown, father of a third grader named Linda, sought the help of the NAACP to challenge the restriction that forced his small daughter to travel a great distance to a "black" elementary school even though the "white" school was within walking distance of her home. The U.S. District Court heard Oliver Brown's case against the Topeka Board of Education in June 1951. NAACP lawyers argued that segregated schools were inherently unequal; the Board of Education lawyers argued that segregated schools prepared students for life in a segregated society. While the District Court agreed with the NAACP expert witnesses that segregation had a detrimental effect on black children, it was not willing to overturn Plessy. *The NAACP and Oliver Brown appealed to the Supreme Court.*

The case that came before the Supreme Court in December 1952 as Brown

From *Brown v. Board of Education,* 347 U.S. 483 (1954).

v. Board of Education *was actually a combination of appeals, with school desegregation cases from Delaware, South Carolina, and Virginia joining the one from Kansas. Almost a year and one-half passed between oral arguments and the Supreme Court ruling, in part because Chief Justice Warren wanted nothing less than a unanimous decision in such a highly charged case.*

In reading this document, pay attention to the logic employed in rejecting the doctrine of "separate but equal" for education. Why, nine years after the end of World War II and in the midst of the Cold War, might Chief Justice Warren focus on "the importance of education to our democratic society"?

MR. CHIEF JUSTICE WARREN delivered the opinion of the Court.

These cases come to us from the States of Kansas, South Carolina, Virginia and Delaware. They are premised on different facts and different local conditions, but a common legal question justifies their consideration together in this consolidated opinion.

In each of the cases, minors of the Negro race, through their legal representatives, seek the aid of the courts in obtaining admission to the public schools of their community on a nonsegregated basis. In each instance, they had been denied admission to schools attended by white children under laws requiring or permitting segregation according to race. This segregation was alleged to deprive the plaintiffs of the equal protection of the laws under the Fourteenth Amendment. In each of the cases other than the Delaware case, a three-judge federal district court denied relief to the plaintiffs on the so-called "separate but equal" doctrine announced by this Court in *Plessy v. Ferguson*, 163 U.S. 537 [1896]. Under that doctrine, equality of treatment is accorded when the races are provided substantially equal facilities, even though these facilities be separate. In the Delaware case, the Supreme Court of Delaware adhered to that doctrine, but ordered that the plaintiffs be admitted to the white schools because of their superiority to the Negro schools.

The plaintiffs contend that segregated public schools are not "equal" and cannot be made "equal" and that hence they are deprived of the equal protection of the laws. Because of the obvious importance of the question presented, the Court took jurisdiction. Argument was heard in the 1952 Term, and reargument was heard this Term on certain questions propounded by the Court.

Reargument was largely devoted to the circumstances surrounding the adoption of the Fourteenth Amendment in 1868. It covered exhaustively consideration of the Amendment in Congress, ratification by the states, then existing practices in racial segregation, and the views of proponents and opponents of the Amendment. This discussion and our own investigation convince us that, although these sources cast some light, it is not enough to resolve the problem with which we are faced. At best, they are inconclusive. The most avid proponents of the post-War Amendments undoubtedly intended them to remove all legal distinctions among "all persons born or naturalized in the United States." Their opponents, just as certainly, were antagonistic to both the letter and the spirit of the Amendments and wished them to have the most limited effect. What others in Congress and the state legislatures had in mind cannot be determined with any degree of certainty.

An additional reason for the inconclusive nature of the Amendment's history, with respect to segregated schools, is the status of public education at that time. In the South, the movement toward free common schools, supported by general taxation, had not yet taken hold. Education of white children was largely in the hands of private groups. Education of Negroes was almost nonexistent, and practically all of the race were illiterate. In fact, any education of Negroes was forbidden by law in some states. Today, in contrast, many Negroes have achieved outstanding success in the arts and sciences as well as in the business and professional world. It is true that public school education at the time of the Amendment had advanced further in the North, but the effect of the Amendment on Northern States was generally ignored in the congressional debates. Even in the North, the conditions of public education did not approximate those existing today. The curriculum was usually rudimentary; upgraded schools were common in rural areas; the school term was but three months a year in many states; and compulsory school attendance was virtually unknown. As a consequence, it is not surprising that there should be so little in the history of the Fourteenth Amendment relating to its intended effect on public education. . . .

In approaching this problem, we cannot turn the clock back to 1868 when the Amendment was adopted, or even to 1896 when *Plessy v. Ferguson* was written. We must consider public education in the light of its full development and its present place in American life throughout the Nation. Only in this way can it be determined if segregation in public schools deprives these plaintiffs of the equal protection of the laws.

Today, education is perhaps the most important function of state and local governments. Compulsory school attendance laws and the great expenditures for education both demonstrate our recognition of the importance of education to our democratic society. It is required in the performance of our most basic public responsibilities, even service in the armed forces. It is the very foundation of good citizenship. Today it is a principal instrument in awakening the child to cultural values, in preparing him for later professional training, and in helping him to adjust normally to his environment. In these days, it is doubtful that any child may reasonably be expected to succeed in life if he is denied the opportunity of an education. Such an opportunity where the state has undertaken to provide it, is a right which must be made available to all on equal terms.

We come then to the question presented: Does segregation of children in public schools solely on the basis of race, even though the physical facilities and other "tangible" factors may be equal, deprive the children of the minority group of equal educational opportunities? We believe that it does. . . .

To separate them from others of similar age and qualifications solely because of their race generates a feeling of inferiority as to their status in the community that may affect their hearts and minds in a way unlikely ever to be undone. The effect of this separation on their educational opportunities was well stated by a finding in the Kansas case by a court which nevertheless felt compelled to rule against the Negro plaintiffs:

> Segregation of white and colored children in public schools has a detrimental effect upon the colored children. The impact is greater when it has the sanction of the law; for the policy of separating the races is usually interpreted as denoting the inferiority of the negro group. A sense of inferiority affects the motivation of a child to learn. Segregation with the sanction of law, therefore, has a tendency to [retard] the educational and mental development of negro children and to deprive them of some of the benefits they would receive in a racial[ly] integrated school system.

Whatever may have been the extent of psychological knowledge at the time of *Plessy v. Ferguson*, this finding is amply supported by modern authority. Any language in *Plessy v. Ferguson* contrary to this finding is rejected.

We conclude that in the field of public education the doctrine of "separate but equal" has no place. Separate educational facilities are inherently unequal. Therefore, we hold that the plaintiffs and others similarly situated for whom the actions have been brought are, by reason of the segregation complained of, deprived of the equal protection of the laws guaranteed by the Fourteenth Amendment. . . .

Declaration of Constitutional Principles: The Southern Manifesto (1956)

Signed by 101 members of the U.S. Congress

Even though the experience of World War II had done much to draw the distinct regions of the United States into a more powerful national culture, most white southerners still saw the South as a distinct region, with habits and customs that "outsiders" could not understand. Chief among these "customs" was racial segregation. For white southerners, steeped in a culture of racism and still suspicious of "Yankees" almost one hundred years after the end of the "War between the States," it was relatively easy to see the Brown *decision and all subsequent federal actions related to it as illegitimate interference in problems that northern judges and politicians could not possibly understand. White supremacy was couched in constitutional arguments about States' Rights and the limits of federal power, and much of the white South began a campaign of massive resistance to Court-ordered integration.*

Communities throughout the South responded differently to the integration order, and much depended upon local leadership, both white and black. In many places nothing changed; in others black schoolchildren faced jeering mobs, racist taunting, and even violence. Polls showed that 80 percent of white southerners opposed school integration. In a vacuum of leadership from President Eisenhower, Congressional Democrats from the eleven southern states mobilized, issuing "The Southern Manifesto," which was signed by 101 senators and representatives.

While this section focuses on the actions of African Americans in demanding change, it is also important to understand the arena of national politics in which those attempting to change the nation's laws had to maneuver. How does the existence of the "solid South," both Democratic and anti-integration, limit political options on the national level?

From the *Congressional Record*, 84th Congress, 2d Session, March 12, 1956, pp. 4460–61, 4515–16.

The unwarranted decision of the Supreme Court in the public school cases is now bearing the fruit always produced when men substitute naked power for established law.

The Founding Fathers gave us a Constitution of checks and balances because they realized the inescapable lesson of history that no man or group of men can be safely entrusted with unlimited power. They framed this Constitution with its provisions for change by amendment in order to secure the fundamentals of government against the dangers of temporary popular passion or the personal predilections of public office holders.

We regard the decision of the Supreme Court in the school cases as a clear abuse of judicial power. It climaxes a trend in the federal judiciary undertaking to legislate, in derogation of the authority of Congress, and to encroach upon the reserved rights of the States and the people.

The original Constitution does not mention education. Neither does the Fourteenth Amendment nor any other Amendment. The debates preceding the submission of the Fourteenth Amendment clearly show that there was no intent that it should affect the systems of education maintained by the States.

The very Congress which proposed the Amendment subsequently provided for segregated schools in the District of Columbia.

ESTABLISHED SEGREGATED SCHOOLS

When the Amendment was adopted in 1868, there were 37 States of the Union. Every one of the 26 States that had any substantial racial differences among its people either approved the operation of segregated schools already in existence or subsequently established such schools by action of the same lawmaking body which considered the Fourteenth Amendment.

As admitted by the Supreme Court in the public school case (*Brown v. Board of Education*), the doctrine of separate but equal schools "apparently originated in *Roberts v. City of Boston* . . . (1849), upholding school segregation against attack as being violative of a State constitutional guarantee of equality." This constitutional doctrine began in the North—not in the South, and it was followed not only in Massachusetts, but in Connecticut, New York, Illinois, Indiana, Michigan, Minnesota, New Jersey, Ohio, Pennsylvania and other northern States until they, exercising their rights as States through the constitutional process of local self-government, changed their school systems.

In the case of *Plessy v. Ferguson* in 1896 the Supreme Court expressly declared that under the Fourteenth Amendment no person was denied any of his rights if the States provided separate but equal public facilities. This decision has been followed in many other cases. It is notable that the Supreme Court, speaking through Chief Justice Taft, a former President of the United States, unanimously declared in 1927 in *Lum v. Rice* that the "separate but equal" principle is ". . . within the discretion of the State in regulating its public schools and does not conflict with the Fourteenth Amendment."

This interpretation, restated time and again, became a part of the life of the people of many of the States and confirmed their habits, customs, traditions and way of life. It is founded on elemental humanity and common sense, for parents should not be deprived by government of the right to direct the lives and education of their own children.

NO LEGAL BASIS

Though there has been no constitutional amendment or Act of Congress changing this established legal principle, almost a century old, the Supreme Court of the United States, with no legal basis for such action, undertook to exercise their naked judicial power and substituted their personal political and social ideas for the established law of the land.

This unwarranted exercise of power by the Court, contrary to the Constitution, is creating chaos and confusion in the States principally affected. It is destroying the amicable relations between the white and Negro races that have been created through 90 years of patient effort by the good people of both races. It has planted hatred and suspicion where there has been heretofore friendship and understanding.

Without regard to the consent of the governed, outside agitators are threatening immediate and revolutionary changes in our public school system. If done, this is certain to destroy the system of public education in some of the States.

With the gravest concern for the explosive and dangerous condition created by this decision and inflamed by outside meddlers:

We reaffirm our reliance on the Constitution as the fundamental law of the land.

We decry the Supreme Court's encroachments on rights reserved to the States and to the people, contrary to established law and to the Constitution.

COMMEND MOTIVES

We commend the motives of those States which have declared the intention to resist forced integration by any lawful means.

We appeal to the States and people who are not directly affected by these decisions to consider the constitutional principles involved against the time when they too, on issues vital to them, may be the victims of judicial encroachment.

Even though we constitute a minority in the present Congress, we have full faith that a majority of the American people believe in the dual system of government which has enabled us to achieve our greatness and will in time demand that the reserved rights of the States and of the people be made secure against judicial usurpation.

We pledge ourselves to use all lawful means to bring about a reversal of this decision which is contrary to the Constitution and to prevent the use of force in its implementation.

In this trying period, as we all seek to right this wrong, we appeal to our people not to be provoked by the agitators and troublemakers invading our States and to scrupulously refrain from disorder and lawless acts.

So Much History, So Much Future: Martin Luther King, Jr., and the Second Coming of America

Vincent Harding

Catapulted into national prominence by the Montgomery bus boycott of 1955–56, Martin Luther King, Jr., became the foremost symbol and spokesman for the direct action phase of the civil rights struggle that produced the Civil Rights Act of 1964 and the Voter Registration Act of 1965. With extraordinary eloquence and charisma, King communicated the essence of the black demand for freedom to white America, even as he inspired and mobilized African Americans to join that struggle. King's articulation of nonviolence as a philosophical principle, and his reliance on the Christian doctrine of unconditional love as the starting point for his leadership, helped to make acceptable to millions of white Americans a program of change that, by previous standards of action, seemed revolutionary. At the same time, King was always in danger of not proceeding far enough or fast enough to satisfy his African American supporters.

In this article, Vincent Harding offers a personal, as well as historical, assessment of King's journey as he sought both to respond to those who prodded him to take a more radical path, and to address the realities of white political power. With sensitivity and passion, Harding helps us to gain an inner sense of King's own struggle, and a greater awareness of what King's life meant to the values and direction of American society.

I met Martin King in 1958, twenty years ago this month, and for the ten years of his life that we knew each other he was for me, to me, a brother, comrade, neighbor, and friend. From 1961 to the time of his death he regularly encouraged me to carry out the role I had chosen for myself as one who was both an engaged participant in the movement, and at the same time a committed historian and critical analyst of its development, as one who worked at the vortex of the struggle and yet remained outside of the official structures of the main civil rights organizations. . . . I come then as Martin's friend, his brother, as one who is crazy enough still to find myself talking to him on occasion, sometimes shouting his name—along with Malcolm's, along with Fannie Lou's, along with Clarence Jordan's and Tom Merton's and Ruby Doris Smith's. (Many of these names you don't know, and if you are to get an education at this university—or any other—you must demand to know them.)

The second thing I need to indicate is probably already implicit in my first comment. In 1961, three years after first having met King, I came south from Chicago with Rosemarie Harding, my wife and comrade, to work full-time in the freedom struggle. I do not hesitate to proclaim that I am biased towards that struggle and its participants. Indeed, at the same time I seek to understand and record its past, I am totally committed to work actively towards the creation of its next, still unclear stages of development. And I expect always to maintain that partisan bias in favor of a new, more humane American society, in favor of freedom for all the men, women, and children who seek new beginnings, new opportunities to break the shackles of the many external and internal oppressive realities that still bind so many of us down to lives that are less than our best, most human selves. . . . Within that context, it is clear that we shall understand the role Martin King played in the movement only as we understand that he was at once created by the movement and a creator of some of its major thrusts. He made much history, but in doing so he was aided, limited, and defined by the struggle that was mounting all around him, making him.

This dialectic, the dynamic, ecstatic, often agonized interplay between Martin and the movement may be illustrated in many ways, at many points, but we shall choose five developments to illustrate briefly the relationship between the man and the movement and to comment on its nature and its strengths and weaknesses. Those reference points are Montgomery, Alabama, in 1955–1956; Albany, Georgia, in 1961–1962; Birmingham, Alabama, and Washington, D.C., in 1963; Mississippi and Chicago in 1966, and the fateful, desperate road from Riverside Church, New York, on April 4, 1967, to Memphis, Tennessee, on April 4, 1968.

Let us begin at Montgomery, where black folks took the U.S. Supreme Court more seriously than the court took itself, firmly grasped the *Brown* decision, intuitively recognized its many broader implications, and began immediately to press it far beyond the limited arena of the segregated school systems. Even before he arrived in Montgomery as the new pastor of the prestigious, black middle-class dominated Dexter Avenue Baptist Church, Martin King had entered the dialectic. He was a child of one of those comfortable Atlanta black bourgeoisie, church-dominating families; but nothing could insulate him against the reality of his people's existence in the South, in America. Nothing could blind him to the fact that ever since World War II a new phase of our freedom struggle had been mounted against rugged, often savage opposition, and he knew that what we were doing, largely through the courts at first, and through early, dangerous attempts at voter registration, was somehow tied to the anti-colonial struggles being waged across the world.

Then, just a bit more than a year after he had been in Montgomery, not long after he had completed his doctoral dissertation for Boston University, while thoughts of a relatively easy life as part-pastor and part-academic danced in his head, a strong, gentle woman named Rosa Parks refused to do the usual, agonized black dance on a segregated Montgomery bus. As a result, she was arrested, and a new time was opened in the struggle . . . the new time was building on the efforts and the people of the time before, and King was initially pressed into the role by a small group of genuine local leaders who had proven themselves in the past, and in a real sense he was later anointed by the larger masses of the Montgomery black people to be the public representative of their struggle. Even then no one fully realized that the new time had really begun to come, that it was possible now to make more history than they had ever made before in Montgomery, Alabama.

Before examining that particular [moment], it will probably be helpful to remind ourselves that at the outset of the Montgomery struggle the black folk of the city established their boycott of the segregated buses for very simple goals. They did not initially demand an end to bus segregation. Indeed, as late as April 1956, four months after the beginning of the boycott, King was articulating three objectives which assured continued segregation. The three goals were:

1. More courteous treatment of black passengers.
2. Seating on a first-come, first-served basis, but with blacks continuing the current practice of filling up from the rear of the bus forward, while whites filled in from the front towards the back.
3. Hiring of black bus drivers on predominantly black lines.

That was all. That was all they asked at first, and they did not march, sit-in, or fill up the jails—they just refused to ride the buses. That was all. It seems so simple now, but it was a great step then, and it was the local context in which King began.

In the weekly mass meetings that developed as a series of increasingly politicized, religious revival sessions, King set out to put forward his evolving philosophy of Christian nonviolence. At first, it was defined primarily as a refusal to react violently to the violence of whites, as a willingness to return love for hatred, and a conviction that their action was not only constitutional but within the will of God—therefore also within the onward, righteous flow of history. So, at the first mass meeting on December 5, 1955, in his exhortation to the fearful, courageous, wondering, determined people, King said, "We are not wrong in what we are doing. If we are wrong, the Supreme Court of this nation is wrong. If we are wrong, the Constitution of the United States is wrong. If we are wrong, God Almighty is wrong. If we are wrong, Jesus of Nazareth was merely a Utopian dreamer who never came down to earth." Then he closed with one of his typically rousing and inspiring perorations: "When the history books are written in the future, somebody will have to say, 'There lived a race of people, a black people, fleecy locks and black complexion, but a people who had the marvelous courage to stand up for their rights and thereby they injected a new meaning into the being of history and of civilization.' And we are going to do that."

From that auspicious beginning, one of King's major roles was interpreter, inspirer, the prophet who saw the significance, the larger meaning of what was happening in the immediate movement. He learned that role, grew into it, made important errors in it, but it was his. . . .

So the young pastor, moving into his twenty-seventh year, had

found a black community ready to take certain initial risks on behalf
of a limited vision of its rights and a new determination to establish
its dignity. Beginning where they were, he took the people's courage
and lifted it to the highest possible level, called upon them to see
themselves as far more than black men and women of Montgomery
Alabama, striving for decent treatment on a bus. Instead he pressed
them forward, urging them to claim their roles as actors in a great
cosmic drama, one in which they were at once in unity with the best
teachings of American democracy, with the winds of universal social
change, and at the same time walking faithfully within the unchang-
ing will of God. . . . So, by the time the boycott had successfully
ended in December 1956, by the time blacks were free to sit wherever
they chose on the city buses, the possibility of an entire community of
black men and women in the South taking large risks on the basis of
conscience, justice, and a belief in the will of God had begun to be established. Those men and women and children of Montgomery, with
their leader-spokesman, had made it possible for others to go beyond
them and make even more history, create an even greater future.

Yet, once the Montgomery bus boycott had ended, King was without
the base of direct mass action that he needed for the fullest, continuing development of his own role. . . . On the last day of November
1959, Martin King announced his decision to move to Atlanta by February 1, 1960. Then he said, "The time has come for a bold, broad advance of the Southern campaign for equality . . . a full scale assault
will be made upon discrimination and segregation in all forms. We
must train our youth and adult leaders in the techniques of social
change through nonviolent resistance. We must employ new methods of struggle involving the masses of the people."

Clearly, King was speaking to himself, to the moving black community, and to the white and nonwhite world all around. Then, only two
months after the announcement, on the very day of the planned
move, almost as if by orchestrated agreement, an explosive response
to King's vision came from the very "youth" he had hoped to train.
They were not waiting for that training, and when the student sit-in
movement erupted, beginning in February 1960, in Greensboro,
North Carolina, it drove immediately towards the center of King's
life, transforming it in ways that he had likely not quite anticipated.
That was, of course, appropriate. For these neatly dressed, amazingly
disciplined black young men and women, who with a few white allies

began the new phase of the movement, were not only the products of the on-going school desegregation struggles of the South, they were really the children of Martin Luther King. In spite of many mixed feelings about him, they saw him as hero and model. But as is so often the case in such situations, they also went beyond him, creating what he could not create on his own, establishing the basis for the South-wide movement of massive, direct nonviolent confrontation with the segregated public facilities of the section which King had just announced. . . . They truly believed that through the power of their organized, disciplined, confrontative, nonviolent struggle, they were to be the builders of "the beloved community" in America, the harbingers of the new society Martin King had so continually evoked. Black and white together, they believed and they struggled, taking into their own flesh and spirit many of the hardest blows of white hatred and fear. . . .

But because we often create more history than we realize, because we often give birth to children that we do not understand and cannot control, it was not until the development of the Albany movement that Martin King was really able to catch up with the newest, rapid, explosive expansion of his people's struggle. What happened in this southwestern Georgia community from the fall of 1961 through the summer of 1962 was critical to the development of his role in the movement. Having moved from Montgomery to Atlanta in 1959, having developed no similar nonviolent mass action base in Atlanta, but sensing the new moment of history and its needs, King now became a kind of roving leader, responding to calls from the local movements that were springing up in hundreds of communities all over the South. . . . When in December 1961, the Albany movement invited King to come and help them, new patterns in his role began to be clear.

One of his major functions was admittedly to help inspire the local populace to greater efforts, for by now King had begun to be idolized by large sections of the black community, a development fraught with great pitfalls, of course, both for the idol and his idolizers. Nevertheless, King was their national leader, the acknowledged symbol of their struggle. And he was a great exhorter in every sense of the word. In addition, his presence was now considered a guarantee of national and even international media attention. Moreover, because Martin had begun since Montgomery to establish certain ambivalent contacts and significant influence with "liberal" white forces, especially in the religious, educational, and labor union communities, he began to be seen as the one person who could mobilize the "people of good will" (as he called them) from across the nation to come help in the struggle of local southern communities. Even more important in the minds of some persons was the fact that King seemed to have access to the Kennedy White House and its great potential power. Of course, it also came to be understood that Martin would lead marches and go to jail, and that his own organization, SCLC, with its rapidly growing staff, would provide experienced aid to those who might be new in the ways of nonviolent struggle. Albany actually was the first real testing ground for this developing role of King, the visiting leader/symbol, and SCLC, the black church-based organization, in the new phase of the southern movement.

In many ways, as one might have expected, the first experiment was an ambivalent one. In Albany, King was able with the local movement leaders to test what was essentially a new strategy, one forced upon them by the powerful thrust of the freedom movement. Rather than focusing on a single issue, such as bus desegregation, they decided to make multiple demands for changes toward racial and economic justice in their city. The internal force of the people's rush towards justice, their sense that the new time was indeed upon them, their growing understanding of the wider significance of their movement and the stubborn recalcitrance and evasiveness of the white leadership— all these pushed the black freedom fighters out of the churches, out of the train and bus stations, out of the dime stores, out into the streets.

In this motion, King was a crucial element, constantly in dynamic interaction with the force of its thrust. Through his words, his actions, and the very fact of his presence, Martin served as a great inspiration to the movement of the local black community, especially in the early weeks of their activity. Hundreds of persons for the first time in southern freedom movement history volunteered for acts of direct action civil disobedience right out on the streets—which meant certain jailing in some of the most notorious and dangerous jails of Georgia. Out from the church mass meetings they marched, singing "We Shall Overcome," "Ain't Gonna Let Nobody Turn Me 'Round," and "This Little Light of Mine." They went to jail, singing, "I'm gonna let it shine." They sang and prayed in jail, "Paul and Silas locked in jail had nobody to go their bail, keep your eye on the prize, hold on." In the dirty jails where the memories of blood from older times were still present, they were threatened for singing and praying, and they kept on singing and praying. . . . "Over my head I see freedom in the air. There must be a God somewhere." Indeed out of the Albany jails came one of the most dynamic cultural forces of the southern movement, the SNCC freedom singers, carrying the songs of the movement across the nation and over the world, songs which were bought at a great price. "Woke up this morning with my mind stayed on Freedom." . . .

But there were major problems as well. The Albany movement had not really jelled as an organization before they called on King. Thus, there were both understandable confusions in its goals and in his role. On the one hand, their sense of the need for nonviolent struggle was constantly being strained by the rush of their own motion and the violence they were meeting. On the other hand there was a temptation to see King, to encourage him to see himself as a savior—too often a peripatetic savior, one who had to leave town at various points to keep speaking and fund-raising engagements elsewhere. This created real difficulties, especially for a leader who was not essentially a day-to-day strategist in the first place. In addition, there were understandable hard feelings among the SNCC forces—who were often brilliant, brave, and sometimes foolhardy strategists. These young people were often resentful when, after their initial, lonely, and often dangerous weeks of local organizing, Martin King would arrive on the scene, trailing a coterie of supporters and a crowd of media persons behind him, and the hard, dangerous spade-work of these young freedom soldiers would tend largely to be forgotten in the aura of *Martin Luther King*. Moreover, King's leadership style, which was also SCLC's style, derived largely from the semiautocratic world of the black Baptist church, and it simply grated against the spirits of the young people from SNCC. For they were working out their own forms of sometimes anarchistic-appearing participatory democracy. . . .

Nevertheless, two final words must be spoken about Albany. First it is to King's credit that he recognized many of the problems that were built into his own new role and tried to deal with some of them, but the role of a roving leader in the midst of a mass movement spread over such a massive area, often under the glare of television cameras, was fraught with deep and intrinsic difficulties. These were especially dangerous when added to the tendency to sycophancy and adulation that was building in some of the people around him, and the tendency to psychic murder that was built into the media of mass television. Second, in spite of the mistakes of King, SCLC, SNCC, the NAACP, CORE, and the Albany movement itself, Albany and its black and white people were changed and have been changed in profound, significant ways. There is no way that the black community will ever be pushed back to 1961; there is no way that white Albany will ever be the same again. But the question blacks now ask, as we must all ask, as Martin asked, is, where do we go from here?

In 1963, for King and SCLC, the geographic answer to that question was Birmingham, Alabama. But as we all knew, Birmingham, like Mississippi, was much more than a physical place. It had a bloody reputation, it was a frightening name. It was pronounced by some as "Bombingham" because of the violence whites had consistently brought against any black movements towards justice and equal rights there. And every black person in this country likely knew someone who had been run out of, beaten or killed in Birmingham, Alabama. But the Reverend Fred Shuttlesworth had not been run out, though he had been beaten more than once and almost killed, at one point with national television cameras running. It was largely at Shuttlesworth's insistence that King and SCLC came to Birmingham in the spring of 1963. . . .

By the time that King himself began to lead demonstrations—a week after they began—he was faced with the reality that a very volatile situation was at hand, the most difficult he had ever faced. Birmingham was "bigger and badder" than either Albany or Montgomery, and whites were not the only bad dudes in that town. So certain powerful contradictions began to surface. On the one hand, the "Commandments" handed out to demonstrators began, "Meditate daily on the teachings and life of Jesus," and included such additional admonitions as "walk and talk in the manner of love for God is love. . . . Refrain from violence of fist, tongue or heart." But at the same time, Jim Bevel and other staff members were confiscating a good number of knives and other weapons from some of the brothers who had come prepared for other ways of walking and talking. Obviously, then, the tensions were there, felt more sharply, drawn more clearly than ever before. . . .

These young people of Birmingham and others like them had a powerful effect on Martin King, on the shaping of his role, on the history he was making. He saw the great forces of energy and power, black power, stored up within them, and he knew where it could lead. He realized that now they were at least potentially the children of Malcolm X as well, and he was not unmoved by that recognition. He saw them take on the dogs and the firehoses with courageous anger, and he knew that anger was not easily controlled. So his rationale for nonviolence began to expand to account for such young men and women in Birmingham and everywhere, began to account for Malcolm and the Nation of Islam and other, even more radical and revolutionary voices abroad in the land. Now it was not simply a weapon of love. As he explained it to an increasingly perplexed white world, nonviolence was also a defense against black retaliatory violence. More explicitly than ever before, King was forced to face the stormy potential of the black young people around him, and what they meant for his own sense of the future. When forcibly given a time to rest and think in the Birmingham jail, these children, spawned out of his own body, were clearly on his mind as he wrote his famous letter. Speaking of the American blacks he said,

Consciously and unconsciously, [the Negro] has been swept in by what the Germans call the Zeitgeist, and with his black brothers of Africa, and his brown and yellow brothers of Asia, South America, and the Caribbean, he is moving with a sense of cosmic urgency toward the promised land of racial justice. Recognizing this vital urge that has engulfed the Negro community, one should readily understand public demonstrations. The Negro has many pent-up resentments and latent frustrations. He has to get them out. So let him march some times; let him have his prayer pilgrimages to the city hall; understand why he must have sit-ins and freedom rides. If his repressed emotions do not come out in these nonviolent ways, they will come out in ominous expressions of violence. This is not a threat; it is a fact of history.

From that point onward, King increasingly found himself caught between the rising rage, nationalistic fervor, and questioning of nonviolence in the black community, and the fear of the white community that would seek to hold down all those black energies, to break them up, at worst to destroy them. So while Birmingham represented the largest number of blacks ever engaged in massive direct civil disobedient action up to then, and while the agreement worked out with the city was considered a victory of sorts, King's role was clearly undergoing transition again. Forces were now at work that had long been kept in check; . . .

In a sense, Montgomery was a long, long time ago. Seen from the late spring of 1963, the bus boycott was now a time of quiet, gentle protest compared with the massive action sweeping across the South, challenging the old regime, eliciting some of its most brutal responses. This new massive direction-action pressed King more fully into another role—that of chief movement emissary to the White House. John Kennedy, who had said in January 1963, that civil rights action was not among his highest priorities, was forced to change his priorities by the whirlwind of the black movement. So White House conferences with King and others, by phone and in person, became almost *de rigueur.* But some persons soon learned—King later than some, earlier than others—that conferences with presidents may do more to divert the force of a movement than to fuel and inspire it, especially if that is one of the intentions of the president. . . . As a result, King became, partly unwarily, a tool for defusing a powerful current in a critical struggle for the future of the movement.

This is what I mean: for more than two years before Birmingham, Martin and others had talked about the development of a trained, disciplined nonviolent army that would become the spearhead for a national movement of powerful, disruptive nonviolent civil disobedience, from coast to coast. . . .

During the Birmingham demonstrations the group pressing for the development of such a nonviolent army proposed that its first action be aimed at Washington, D.C., to shut down the activities of the city until adequate civil rights legislation of many kinds was passed. Without going into the details of the transformation, it is enough to say that King allowed himself to be convinced by other more moderate black and white leaders of the civil rights coalition that such a move would be exceedingly unwise. They were convinced and were probably right that it would lose friends and anger many "neutrals" in the white community. It would certainly lose the president's supposed support for civil rights legislation specifically and racial justice generally. So, instead of a disciplined, nonviolent force—largely from the southern testing grounds—descending on Washington for an extended campaign of disruptive civil disobedience, the summer of 1963 produced the one-day, unthreatening March on Washington for Jobs and Freedom. As a result, King passed up an opportunity possibly to transform his role in the struggle, to transform the struggle itself, losing perhaps more than we can ever know. And it was not until the fiery, bloody summers of 1964–1967 had passed that he was eventually forced by the movement of his people and the larger forces of history back to the idea of an organized, national non-violent revolutionary force. By then it would be too late—at least for that time. . . .

The issues which had been simmering, roiling the waters of the movement for a long time—sometimes pressed audaciously to the surface in the recent speeches of Adam Clayton Powell, Jr., the issues of power, the issues of racial pride, solidarity, and nationalism that had poured out anew in the North after the assassination of Malcolm X, El Hajj Malik El Shabazz; the issue of black control over the organizations of our struggle; the issue of the role of whites in the struggle; the issue of the need for black "liberation" as opposed to "integration," raised to a new level by the introduction of Frantz Fanon's *Wretched of the Earth* into the reading experience of many of the SNCC members; the concomitant rising discussion of black "revolution" as opposed to finding a place in the American status quo; the issue of the relationship between the black middle class and the masses of poor blacks, South and North; the issue of the need for the development of black leadership; the issue of sexual relations between white women and black men—all these exciting, frightening, dangerously explosive matters and many more leaped out in a compressed code from the lips of Willie Ricks of SNCC and they found their national identity in Stokely Carmichael, twenty-four-year-old veteran of the freedom rides, of the Black Panther party in Lowndes County, Alabama, of Greenwood, Mississippi. (Always remember that Stokely at his best was no dilettante. But, like the rest of us, he was not always at his best.) *Black Power! Black Power!* Black Power had officially begun its time: June 1966, on the road from Memphis to Jackson, cities of our music and our martyrs. . . .

At many points in the fall and winter of 1966–1967, after another summer of urban rebellions, as the fierce debate over Black Power raged, as he recognized the essential failure of his heroic/quixotic foray into Chicago, as the war in Vietnam continued to expand, as white anger mounted and black criticism of his positions grew more strident, King seemed at times like a great, courageous, but deeply perplexed captain, trying desperately to control a ship that was being rocked by mutinies from within and raging storms from without.

Yet, the truth of that perilous time was even more difficult. For by then there was no longer any one entity—even symbolically speaking—which could be called the Black Freedom movement and which Martin could really lead. Indeed, the very internal power of the movement that he had done so much to create and focus, that had shaped and molded him, had now broken out in many new directions, reviving, inspiring a plethora of older black—and white—traditions. . . .

It was impossible for King—or any other single individual—to understand, much less command all the tendencies now set loose in the black communities of the land. (Of course, he knew that he was being falsely identified as an "Uncle Tom" by many northern black rhetoricians of revolution who had never once risked their lives as King had done so many times in the cause of his people's freedom.) At the same time, Martin was trying to understand where the real, critical centers of power lay in American society, trying to understand how he could tackle the powerful forces that supported war, racism, poverty, and the internal subversion of the freedom movement's many parts.

No easy task. Still King seemed convinced that he would be unfaithful to the history he had already made with others, untrue to his forebears and his children in the struggle for justice, unless he followed what appeared to be the logic of the movement. For him, that logic, that history, that sense of integrity pressed him toward a more radical challenge than he had ever mounted before, one that would leave him more naked to his enemies than ever before. . . .

First, King decided to try to respond fully to the unspeakable agony, the terrible crime of Vietnam, defying all his critics and many of his friends, from the White House to members of his own organization and his own family. On April 4, 1967, at Riverside Church in New York City, the struggling leader-searcher addressed a major meeting sponsored by Clergy and Laymen Concerned about Vietnam. Near the beginning of his vibrant presentation, King admitted that he had not spoken clearly and early enough, but vowed that he would never make that mistake again. Justifying the connection he saw among the struggles for equal rights and economic justice in America and the demand for an end to American military involvement in Vietnam, King placed them all within the context of his commission as a minister of Jesus Christ and a Nobel Peace Prize laureate. Unflinchingly, he identified America as the essential aggressor in the war and called his nation "the greatest purveyor of violence in the world." . . .

Soon he turned from Riverside Church to forge the second prong of his militant challenge to white American power. In the summer of 1967, after two of the decade's most deadly urban uprisings—in Newark and Detroit—had stunned the nation, after a national Black Power convention had done much to stamp that variously defined slogan in the minds of black folk everywhere, King announced his plans for a major attack on America's internal structures of inequality and injustice. . . .

It was a version of the nonviolent army again, now surfacing at a far more volatile, confused, and dangerous moment in the nation's history and in King's own career. . . . By the end of 1967, King and his staff had again decided to focus this potentially revolutionary challenge in Washington, D.C., fully aware of the ugly, angry, and unreceptive mood at work in the White House and elsewhere.

At his radical best, King was determined to press the logic of his position, the movement of his people's history. Having attacked the nation's antiliberationist overseas actions, he now intended to move on the heart of the government, demanding a response to the suffering of its own semicolonized peoples. (Nor was King paving a way of welcome for his move by saying late in 1967: "I am not sad that black Americans are rebelling; this was not only inevitable but eminently desirable. Without this magnificent ferment among Negroes, the old evasions and procrastinations would have continued indefinitely." He was not paving a way, but he was indicating his own way, his own movement in the vortex of "this magnificent ferment.")

Martin was trying to be on time, trying to be faithful, trying to go forward, to create whatever openings toward the future that he could. Jamming his life against the advice of many of his black and white movement supporters, defying the angry warnings of Lyndon Johnson, King searched for his new role, for the new role of his people. In an America that seemed at times on the edge of armed racial warfare, an America increasingly torn over the Vietnam war, an America unresponsive to the deepest needs of its own people, especially its poor—in the midst of this history King was desperately searching for the connections with his past, for the openings to his and our future.

By December 1967, Martin had at least temporarily taken his new powerful and dangerous position. In a series of broadcasts for Canadian public radio, he said, "Negroes . . . must not only formulate a program; they must fashion new tactics which do not count on government goodwill." Instead he said the new tactics must be those which are forceful enough *"to compel unwilling authorities to yield to the mandates of justice."* But here at the end, at the beginning of the end, in his last major published document, King was not talking about blacks alone. The movement had grown; there was no way to "overcome" without taking on much more than we have ever taken on before. Thus he said,

> The dispossessed of this nation—the poor, both white and Negro—live in a cruelly unjust society. *They must organize a revolution against that injustice,* not against the lives of the persons who are their fellow citizens, but against the structures through which the society is refusing to take means which have been called for, and which are at hand, to lift the load of poverty.

Martin King was talking about a nonviolent revolution in America, to transform the entire society on behalf of its poorest people, for the sake of us all. Martin King was moving towards an experiment with truth and power, and he was calling for three thousand persons to join him for three months of intensive training to begin that revolution at the seat of America's political power, Washington, D.C. Martin King was shaping a new role for himself, leader of a nonviolent revolutionary army/movement, one which he also saw connecting with the oppressed peoples of other nations. . . .

Perhaps Martin King had seen and felt more than he was able to accomplish. Perhaps he could not ever be ready for this new role. Perhaps in the violent climate of America, it was impossible to be ready for such a campaign of revolutionary, nonviolent civil disobedience without an organization that was fully prepared for all the dangers, all the opportunities, and all the long, hard, preparatory work. SCLC was not that organization. Nevertheless, ready or not, King appeared to be trying to get ready—facing toward Washington, D.C.

But first there were garbage collectors to help in Memphis, and there were powerful forces at every level of American society who were determined that Martin Luther King would never be ready for the kind of revolution he had now announced. As a result, Martin never made it to Washington, never found out if he was ready or not. . . .

This man who grew from a spokesperson for his people's search for simple dignity in a medium-sized southern city to become a giant symbol of the search for justice across the globe—this man, with all his weaknesses, all his flaws, all his blindspots and all of his creative, courageous greatness, made all the history he could make. Perhaps of even more importance to us here and now, we are able to see that he helped force open the way to the possibility of a new vision, a second coming of America, an America in which justice, compassion, and humanity prevail. . . .

King helped create the possibility that all of us might break beyond our own individual and group interests and catch a vision of a new America, create a vision of a new common good in a new future which will serve us all. He saw that our needs were economic *and* spiritual, political *and* moral, social *and* personal, and as the end, the beginning approached, he was groping his way towards a new integration—one that had very little to do with the legalities of *Brown v. The Board of Education*.

But in the midst of this struggle, this groping, this searching, King learned some things, and the message he left was the message he had learned, the message he had been given by the earlier generations of our freedom-striving people: Freedom is a constant struggle. The message he left was that a new America cannot be created without an even more difficult, radical, and dangerous struggle than we have known up to now. The message he left is that black people can no longer make any separate peace with America, that our needs are the needs of other millions of Americans, that the entire society must be challenged with the force of revolutionary change in all its political, economic, social, and psychic structures.

A Lunch-Counter Sit-In in Jackson, Mississippi (1968)

Anne Moody

The leadership of Martin Luther King, Jr., was critically important to the Civil Rights movement. His eloquence mobilized support throughout the nation and the principles of nonviolence he espoused shaped the movement for almost a decade. Yet the struggle for civil rights was fought, most importantly, at the grassroots level—by the thousands of people who boycotted the buses in Montgomery, who marched in Selma or Chicago, who registered voters in Mississippi and picketed stores and sat-in at lunch counters.

Anne Moody was one of these people. A young woman from a poor share-cropper family in rural Mississippi, Moody became involved in the Civil Rights movement when she attended Tougaloo College. Here, she describes sitting-in at a Woolworth's lunch counter in Jackson, Mississippi, in 1963. This brief, matter-of-fact account captures many of the key elements of the movement in the South: the role of local police and of the media; the complex relations with supportive whites; the purposeful contrast between the respectability of the African Americans who asked to be served and the vulgarity of the white mobs who attacked them. It also shows the bravery of those who, like Anne Moody, risked their lives in the movement.

I had become very friendly with my social science professor, John Salter, who was in charge of NAACP activities on campus. All during the year, while the NAACP conducted a boycott of the downtown stores in Jackson, I had been one of Salter's most faithful canvassers and church speakers. During the last week of school, he told me that sit-in demonstrations were about to start in Jackson and that he wanted me to be the spokesman for a team that would sit-in at Woolworth's lunch counter. The two other demonstrators would be classmates of mine, Memphis and Pearlena. Pearlena was a dedicated NAACP worker, but Memphis had not been very involved in the Movement on campus. It seemed that the organization had had a rough time finding students who were in a position to go to jail. I had nothing to lose one way or the other. Around ten o'clock the morning of the demonstrations, NAACP headquarters alerted the news services. As a result, the police department was also informed, but neither the policemen nor the newsmen knew exactly where or when the demonstrations would start. They stationed themselves along Capitol Street and waited.

To divert attention from the sit-in at Woolworth's, the picketing started at J. C. Penney's a good fifteen minutes before. The pickets were allowed to walk up and down in front of the store three or four times before they were arrested. At exactly 11 A.M., Pearlena, Memphis, and I entered Woolworth's from the rear entrance. We separated as soon as we stepped into the store, and made small purchases from various counters. Pearlena had given Memphis her watch. He was to let us know when it was 11:14. At 11:14 we were to join him near the lunch counter and at exactly 11:15 we were to take seats at it.

Seconds before 11:15 we were occupying three seats at the previously segregated Woolworth's lunch counter. In the beginning the waitresses seemed to ignore us, as if they really didn't know what was going on. Our waitress walked past us a couple of times before she noticed we had started to write our own orders down and realized we wanted service. She asked us what we wanted. We began to read to her from our order slips. She told us that we would be served at the back counter, which was for Negroes.

"We would like to be served here," I said.

The waitress started to repeat what she had said, then stopped in the middle of the sentence. She turned the lights out behind the counter, and she and the other waitresses almost ran to the back of the store, deserting all their white customers. I guess they thought that violence would start immediately after the whites at the counter realized what was going on. There were five or six other people at the counter. A couple of them just got up and walked away. A girl sitting next to me finished her banana split before leaving. A middle-aged white woman who had not yet been served rose from her seat and came over to us. "I'd like to stay here with you," she said, "but my husband is waiting."

The newsmen came in just as she was leaving. They must have discovered what was going on shortly after some of the people began to leave the store. One of the newsmen ran behind the woman who spoke to us and asked her to identify herself. She refused to give her name, but said she was a native of Vicksburg and a former resident of California. When asked why she had said what she had said to us, she replied, "I am in sympathy with the Negro movement." By this time a crowd of cameramen and reporters had gathered around us taking pictures and asking questions, such as Where were we from? Why did we sit-in? What organization sponsored it? Were we students? From what school? How were we classified?

I told them that we were all students at Tougaloo College, that we were represented by no particular organization, and that we planned to stay there even after the store closed. "All we want is service," was my reply to one of them. After they had finished probing for about twenty minutes, they were almost ready to leave.

At noon, students from a nearby white high school started pouring in to Woolworth's. When they first saw us they were sort of surprised. They didn't know how to react. A few started to heckle and the newsmen became interested again. Then the white students started chanting all kinds of anti-Negro slogans. We were called a little bit of everything. The rest of the seats except the three we were occupying had been roped off to prevent others from sitting down. A couple of the boys took one end of the rope and made it into a hangman's noose. Several attempts were made to put it around our necks. The crowds grew as more students and adults came in for lunch.

We kept our eyes straight forward and did not look at the crowd except for occasional glances to see what was going on. All of a sudden I saw a face I remembered—the drunkard from the bus station sit-in. My eyes lingered on him just long enough for us to recognize each other. Today he was drunk too, so I don't think he remembered where he had seen me before. He took out a knife, opened it, put it in his pocket, and then began to pace the floor. At this point, I told Memphis and Pearlena what was going on. Memphis suggested that we pray. We bowed our heads, and all hell broke loose. A man rushed forward, threw Memphis from his seat, and slapped my face. Then another man who worked in the store threw me against an adjoining counter.

Down on my knees on the floor, I saw Memphis lying near the lunch counter with blood running out of the corners of his mouth. As he tried to protect his face, the man who'd thrown him down kept kicking him against the head. If he had worn hard-soled shoes instead of sneakers, the first kick probably would have killed Memphis. Finally a man dressed in plain clothes identified himself as a police officer and arrested Memphis and his attacker.

Pearlena had been thrown to the floor. She and I got back on our stools after Memphis was arrested. There were some white Tougaloo teachers in the crowd. They asked Pearlena and me if we wanted to leave. They said that things were getting too rough. We didn't know what to do. While we were trying to make up our minds, we were joined by Joan Trumpauer. Now there were three of us and we were integrated. The crowd began to chant, "Communists, Communists, Communists." Some old man in the crowd ordered the students to take us off the stools.

"Which one should I get first?" a big husky boy said.

"That white nigger," the old man said.

The boy lifted Joan from the counter by her waist and carried her out of the store. Simultaneously, I was snatched from my stool by two high school students. I was dragged about thirty feet toward the door by my hair when someone made them turn me loose. As I was getting up off the floor, I saw Joan coming back inside. We started back to the center of the counter to join Pearlena. Lois Chaffee, a white Tougaloo faculty member, was now sitting next to her. So Joan and I just climbed across the rope at the front end of the counter and sat down. There were now four of us, two whites and two Negroes, all women. The mob started smearing us with ketchup, mustard, sugar, pies, and everything on the counter. Soon Joan and I were joined by John Salter, but the moment he sat down he was hit on the jaw with what appeared to be brass knuckles. Blood gushed from his face and someone threw salt into the open wound. Ed King, Tougaloo's chaplain, rushed to him.

At the other end of the counter, Lois and Pearlena were joined by George Raymond, a CORE field worker and a student from Jackson State College. Then a Negro high school boy sat down next to me. The mob took spray paint from the counter and sprayed it on the new demonstrators. The high school student had on a white shirt; the word "nigger" was written on his back with red spray paint.

We sat there for three hours taking a beating when the manager decided to close the store because the mob had begun to go wild with stuff from other counters. He begged and begged everyone to leave. But even after fifteen minutes of begging, no one budged. They

would not leave until we did. Then Dr. Beittel, the president of Tougaloo College, came running in. He said he had just heard what was
happening.

About ninety policemen were standing outside the store; they had
been watching the whole thing through the windows, but had not
come in to stop the mob or do anything. President Beittel went outside and asked Captain Ray to come and escort us out. The captain
refused, stating the manager had to invite him in before he could
enter the premises, so Dr. Beittel himself brought us out. He had told
the police that they had better protect us after we were outside the
store. When we got outside, the policemen formed a single line that
blocked the mob from us. However, they were allowed to throw at us
everything they had collected. Within ten minutes, we were picked
up by Reverend King in his station wagon and taken to the NAACP
headquarters on Lynch Street.

After the sit-in, all I could think of was how sick Mississippi whites
were. They believed so much in the segregated Southern way of life,
they would kill to preserve it. I sat there in the NAACP office and
thought of how many times they had killed when this way of life was
threatened. I knew that the killing had just begun. "Many more will
die before it is over with," I thought. Before the sit-in, I had always
hated the whites in Mississippi. Now I knew it was impossible for me
to hate sickness. The whites had a disease, an incurable disease in its
final stage. What were our chances against such a disease? I thought
of the students, the young Negroes who had just begun to protest, as
young interns. When these young interns got older, I thought, they
would be the best doctors in the world for social problems.

From Protest to Politics (1965)

Bayard Rustin

A longtime advocate of nonviolent protest, Bayard Rustin took part in a 1947 effort to desegregate interstate bus facilities in the South, became a principal advisor to Martin Luther King, Jr., during the Montgomery bus boycott, and played a major role in organizing the 1963 March on Washington. By the mid-1960s, however, his path had diverged sharply from that of the more militant black protest leaders. He believed that the realization of true equality for African Americans depended on their remaining part of the broad liberal coalition that had given Lyndon Johnson his landslide victory in 1964. And he feared that black campaigns of disruptive civil disobedience and militant criticism of white leaders would only alienate necessary allies in the labor movement, Congress, and the White House. In the following selection, a 1965 plea for African Americans to turn from protest to politics, Rustin prophesied that despite civil rights victories, the plight of many African Americans would worsen unless a black-and-white progressive force transformed the nation's most fundamental social, economic, and political institutions.

The decade spanned by the 1954 Supreme Court decision on school desegregation and the Civil Rights Act of 1964 will undoubtedly be recorded as the period in which the legal foundations of racism in America were destroyed. To be sure, pockets of resistance remain; but it would be hard to quarrel with the assertion that the elaborate legal structure of segregation and discrimination, particularly in relation to public accommodations, has virtually collapsed. On the other hand, without making light of the human sacrifices involved in the direct-action tactics (sit-ins, freedom rides, and the rest) that were so instrumental to this achievement, we must recognize that in desegregating public accommodations, we affected institutions which are relatively peripheral both to the American socioeconomic order and to the fundamental conditions of life of the Negro people. In a highly industrialized, twentieth-century civilization we hit Jim Crow precisely where it was most anachronistic, dispensable, and vulnerable—in hotels, lunch counters, terminals, libraries, swimming pools, and the like. For in these forms, Jim Crow does impede the flow of commerce in the broadest sense: it is a nuisance in a society on the move (and on the make). Not surprisingly, therefore, it was the most mobility-conscious and relatively liberated groups in the Negro community—lower-middle-class college students—who launched the attack that brought down this imposing but hollow structure.

The term "classical" appears especially apt for this phase of the civil rights movement. But in the few years that have passed since the first flush of sit-ins, several developments have taken place that have complicated matters enormously. One is the shifting focus of the movement in the South, symbolized by Birmingham; another is the spread of the revolution to the North; and the third, common to the other two, is the expansion of the movement's base in the Negro community. To attempt to disentangle these three strands is to do violence to reality. David Danzig's perceptive article, "The Meaning of Negro Strategy," correctly saw in the Birmingham events the victory of the concept of collective struggle over individual achievement as the road to Negro freedom. And Birmingham remains the unmatched symbol of grass-roots protest involving all strata of the black community. It was also in this most industrialized of Southern cities that the single-issue demands of the movement's classical stage gave way to the "package deal." No longer were Negroes satisfied with integrating lunch counters. They now sought advances in employment, housing, school integration, police protection, and so forth.

Thus, the movement in the South began to attack areas of discrimination which were not so remote from the Northern experience as were Jim Crow lunch counters. At the same time, the interrelationship of these apparently distinct areas became increasingly evident. What is the value of winning access to public accommodations for those who lack money to use them? The minute the movement faced this question, it was compelled to expand its vision beyond race relations to economic relations, including the role of education in modern society. And what also became clear is that all these interrelated problems, by their very nature, are not soluble by private, voluntary efforts but require government action—or politics. Already Southern demonstrators had recognized that the most effective way to strike at the police brutality they suffered from was by getting rid of the local sheriff—and that meant political action, which in turn meant, and still means, political action within the Democratic party where the only meaningful primary contests in the South are fought.

And so, in Mississippi, thanks largely to the leadership of Bob Moses, a turn toward political action has been taken. More than voter registration is involved here. A conscious bid for political power is being made, and in the course of that effort a tactical shift is being effected: direct-action techniques are being subordinated to a strategy calling for the building of community institutions or power bases. Clearly, the implications of this shift reach far beyond Mississippi. What began as a protest movement is being challenged to translate itself into a political movement. Is this the right course? And if it is, can the transformation be accomplished?

The very decade which has witnessed the decline of legal Jim Crow has also seen the rise of de facto segregation in our most fundamental socioeconomic institutions. More Negroes are unemployed today than in 1954, and the unemployment gap between the races is wider. The median income of Negroes has dropped from 57 percent to 54 percent of that of whites. A higher percentage of Negro workers is now concentrated in jobs vulnerable to automation than was the case ten years ago. More Negroes attend de facto segregated schools today than when the Supreme Court handed down its famous decision; while school integration proceeds at a snail's pace in the South, the number of Northern schools with an excessive proportion of minority youth proliferates. And behind this is the continuing growth of racial slums, spreading over our central cities and trapping Negro youth in a milieu which, whatever its legal definition, sows an unimaginable demoralization. Again, legal niceties aside, a resident of a racial ghetto lives in segregated housing, and more Negroes fall into this category than ever before.

These are the facts of life which generate frustration in the Negro community and challenge the civil rights movement. At issue, after all, is not *civil rights*, strictly speaking, but social and economic conditions. Last summer's riots were not race riots; they were outbursts of class aggression in a society where class and color definitions are converging disastrously. How can the (perhaps misnamed) civil rights movement deal with this problem?

Before trying to answer, let me first insist that the task of the movement is vastly complicated by the failure of many whites of good will to understand the nature of our problem. There is a widespread assumption that the removal of artificial racial barriers should result in the automatic integration of the Negro into all aspects of American life. This myth is fostered by facile analogies with the experience of various ethnic immigrant groups, particularly the Jews. But the analogies with the Jews do not hold for three simple but profound reasons. First, Jews have a long history as a literate people, a resource which has afforded them opportunities to advance in the academic and professional worlds, to achieve intellectual status even in the midst of economic hardship, and to evolve sustaining value systems in the context of ghetto life. Negroes, for the greater part of their presence in this country, were forbidden by law to read or write. Second, Jews have a long history of family stability, the importance of which in terms of aspiration and self-image is obvious. The Negro family structure was totally destroyed by slavery and with it the possibility of cultural transmission (the right of Negroes to marry and rear children is barely a century old). Third, Jews are white and have the *option* of relinquishing their cultural-religious identity, intermarrying, passing, etc. Negroes, or at least the overwhelming majority of them, do not have this option. There is also a fourth vulgar reason. If the Jewish and Negro communities are not comparable in terms of education, family structure, and color, it is also true that their respective economic roles bear little resemblance.

This matter of economic role brings us to the greater problem—the fact that we are moving into an era in which the natural functioning of the market does not by itself ensure every man with will and ambition a place in the productive process. The immigrant who came to this country during the late nineteenth and early twentieth centuries entered a society which was expanding territorially and or economically. It was then possible to start at the bottom, as an unskilled or semiskilled worker, and move up the ladder, acquiring new skills along the way. Especially was this true when industrial unionism was burgeoning, giving new dignity and higher wages to organized workers. Today the situation has changed. We are not expanding territorially, the western frontier is settled, labor organizing has leveled off, our rate of economic growth has been stagnant for a decade. And we are in the midst of a technological revolution which is altering the fundamental structure of the labor force, destroying unskilled and semiskilled jobs—jobs in which Negroes are disproportionately concentrated.

Whatever the pace of this technological revolution may be, the *direction* is clear: the lower rungs of the economic ladder are being lopped off. This means that an individual will no longer be able to start at the bottom and work his way up; he will have to start in the middle or on top, and hold on tight. It will not even be enough to have certain specific skills, for many skilled jobs are also vulnerable to automation. A broad educational background, permitting vocational adaptability and flexibility, seems more imperative than ever. We live in a society where, as Secretary of Labor Willard Wirtz puts it, machines have the equivalent of a high school diploma. Yet the average educational attainment of American Negroes is 8.2 years.

Negroes, of course, are not the only people being affected by these developments. It is reported that there are now 50 percent fewer unskilled and semiskilled jobs than there are high school dropouts. Almost one-third of the 26 million young people entering the labor market in the 1960s will be dropouts. But the percentage of Negro dropouts nationally is 57 percent, and in New York City, among Negroes 25 years of age or over, it is 68 percent. They are without a future.

To what extent can the kind of self-help campaign recently prescribed by Eric Hoffer in the *New York Times Magazine* cope with such a situation? I would advise those who think that self-help is the answer to familiarize themselves with the long history of such efforts in the Negro community, and to consider why so many foundered on the shoals of ghetto life. It goes without saying that any effort to combat demoralization and apathy is desirable, but we must understand that demoralization in the Negro community is largely a common sense response to an objective reality. Negro youths have no need of statistics to perceive, fairly accurately, what their odds are in American society. Indeed, from the point of view of motivation, some of the healthiest Negro youngsters I know are juvenile delinquents: vigorously pursuing the American Dream of material acquisition and status, yet finding the conventional means of attaining it blocked off, they do not yield to defeatism but resort to illegal (and often ingenious) methods. They are not alien to American culture: They are, in Gunnar Myrdal's phrase, "exaggerated Americans." To want a Cadillac is not un-American; to push a cart in the garment center is. If Negroes are to be persuaded that the conventional path (school, work, etc.) is superior, we had better provide evidence which is now sorely lacking. It is a double cruelty to harangue Negro youth about education and training when we do not know what jobs will be available for them. When a Negro youth can reasonably foresee a future free of slums, when the prospect of gainful employment is realistic, we will see motivation and self-help in abundant enough quantities.

Meanwhile, there is an ironic similarity between the self-help advocated by many liberals and the doctrines of the Black Muslims. Professional sociologists, psychiatrists, and social workers have expressed amazement at the Muslims' success in transforming prostitutes and dope addicts into respectable citizens. But every prostitute the Muslims convert to a model of Calvinist virtue is replaced in the ghetto with two more. Dedicated as they are to the maintenance of the ghetto, the Muslims are powerless to affect substantial moral reform. So too with every other group or program which is not aimed at the destruction of slums, their causes and effects. Self-help efforts, directly or indirectly, must be geared to mobilizing people into power units capable of effecting social change. That is, their goal must be genuine self-help, not merely self-improvement. Obviously, where self-improvement activities succeed in imparting to their participants a feeling of some control over their environment, those involved may find their appetites for change whetted; they may move into the political arena.

Let me sum up what I have thus far been trying to say: the civil rights movement is evolving from a protest movement into a full-fledged *social movement*—an evolution calling its very name into question. It is now concerned not merely with removing the barriers to full *opportunity* but with achieving the fact of *equality*. From sit-ins and freedom rides we have gone into rent strikes, boycotts, community organization, and political action. As a consequence of this natural evolution, the Negro today finds himself stymied by obstacles of far greater magnitude than the legal barriers he was attacking before: automation, urban decay, de facto school segregation. These are problems which, while conditioned by Jim Crow, do not vanish upon its demise. They are more deeply rooted in our socioeconomic order; they are the result of the total society's failure to meet not only the Negro's needs, but human needs generally.

These propositions have won increasing recognition and acceptance, but with a curious twist. They have formed the common premise of two apparently contradictory lines of thought which simultaneously nourish and antagonize each other. On the one hand, there is the reasoning of the *New York Times* moderate who says that the problems are so enormous and complicated that Negro militancy is a futile irritation, and that the need is for "intelligent moderation." Thus, during the first New York school boycott, the *Times* editorialized that Negro demands, while abstractly just, would necessitate massive reforms, the funds for which could not realistically be anticipated; therefore the just demands were also foolish demands and would only antagonize white people. Moderates of this stripe are often correct in perceiving the difficulty or impossibility of racial progress in the context of present social and economic policies. But they accept the context as fixed. They ignore (or perhaps see all too well) the potentialities inherent in linking Negro demands to broader pressures for radical revision of existing policies. They apparently see nothing strange in the fact that in the last twenty-five years we have spent nearly a trillion dollars fighting or preparing for wars, yet throw up our hands before the need for overhauling our schools, clearing the slums, and really abolishing poverty. My quarrel with these moderates is that they do not even envision radical changes; their admonitions of moderation are, for all practical purposes, admonitions to the Negro to adjust to the status quo, and are therefore immoral.

The more effectively the moderates argue their case, the more they convince Negroes that American society will not or cannot be reorganized for full racial equality. Michael Harrington has said that a successful war on poverty might well require the expenditure of $100 billion. Where, the Negro wonders, are the forces now in motion to compel such a commitment? If the voices of the moderates were raised in an insistence upon a reallocation of national resources at levels that could not be confused with tokenism (that is, if the moderates stopped being moderates), Negroes would have greater grounds for hope. Meanwhile, the Negro movement cannot escape a sense of isolation.

It is precisely this sense of isolation that gives rise to the second line of thought I want to examine—the tendency within the civil rights movement which, despite its militancy, pursues what I call a "no-win" policy. Sharing with many moderates a recognition of the magnitude of the obstacles to freedom, spokesmen for this tendency survey the American scene and find no forces prepared to move toward radical solutions. From this they conclude that the only viable strategy is shock; above all, the hypocrisy of white liberals must be exposed. These spokesmen are often described as the radicals of the movement, but they are really its moralists. They seek to change white hearts—by traumatizing them. Frequently abetted by white self-flagellants, they may gleefully applaud (though not really agreeing with) Malcolm X because, while they admit he has no program, they think he can frighten white people into doing the right thing. To believe this, of course, you must be convinced, even if unconsciously, that at the core of the white man's heart lies a buried affection for Negroes—a proposition one may be permitted to doubt. But in any case, hearts are not relevant to the issue; neither racial affinities nor racial hostilities are rooted there. It is institutions—social, political, and economic institutions—which are the ultimate molders of collective sentiments. Let these institutions be reconstructed *today*, and let the ineluctable gradualism of history govern the formation of a new psychology.

My quarrel with the "no-win" tendency in the civil rights movement (and the reason I have so designated it) parallels my quarrel with the moderates outside the movement. As the latter lack the vision or will for fundamental change, the former lack a realistic strategy for achieving it. For such a strategy they substitute militancy. But militancy is a matter of posture and volume and not of effect.

I believe that the Negro's struggle for equality in America is essentially revolutionary. While most Negroes—in their hearts—unquestionably seek only to enjoy the fruits of American society as it now exists, their quest cannot *objectively* be satisfied within the framework of existing political and economic relations. The young Negro who would demonstrate his way into the labor market may be motivated by a thoroughly bourgeois ambition and thoroughly "capitalist" considerations, but he will end up having to favor a great expansion of the public sector of the economy. At any rate, that is the position the movement will be forced to take as it looks at the number of jobs being generated by the private economy, and if it is to remain true to the masses of Negroes. . . .

It will be—it has been—argued that these by-products of the Negro struggle are not revolutionary. But the term revolutionary, as I am using it, does not connote violence; it refers to the qualitative transformation of fundamental institutions, more or less rapidly, to the point where the social and economic structure which they comprised can no longer be said to be the same. The Negro struggle has hardly run its course; and it will not stop moving until it has been utterly defeated or won substantial equality. But I fail to see how the movement can be victorious in the absence of radical programs for full employment, abolition of slums, the reconstruction of our educational system, new definitions of work and leisure. Adding up the cost of such programs, we can only conclude that we are talking about a refashioning of our political economy. It has been estimated, for example, that the price of replacing New York City's slums with public housing would be $17 billion. Again, a multibillion dollar federal public works program, dwarfing the currently proposed $2 billion program, is required to reabsorb unskilled and semiskilled workers into the labor market—and this must be done if Negro workers in these categories are to be employed. "Preferential treatment" cannot help them.

I am not trying here to delineate a total program, only to suggest the scope of economic reforms which are most immediately related to the plight of the Negro community. One could speculate on their political implications—whether, for example, they do not indicate the obsolescence of state government and the superiority of regional structures as viable units of planning. Such speculations aside, it is clear that Negro needs cannot be satisfied unless we go beyond what has so far been placed on the agenda. How are these radical objectives to be achieved? The answer is simple, deceptively so: *through political power.* . . .

Neither that [the civil rights] movement nor the country's twenty million black people can win political power alone. We need allies. The future of the Negro struggle depends on whether the contradictions of this society can be resolved by a coalition of progressive forces which becomes the *effective* political majority in the United States. I speak of the coalition which staged the March on Washington, passed the Civil Rights Act, and laid the basis for the Johnson landslide—Negroes, trade unionists, liberals, and religious groups. . . .

The task of molding a political movement out of the March on Washington coalition is not simple, but no alternatives have been advanced. We need to choose our allies on the basis of common political objectives. It has become fashionable in some no-win Negro circles to decry the white liberal as the main enemy (his hypocrisy is what sustains racism); by virtue of this reverse recitation of the reactionary's litany (liberalism leads to socialism, which leads to Communism) the Negro is left in majestic isolation, except for a tiny band of fervent white initiates. But the objective fact is that *Eastland* and *Goldwater* are the main enemies—they and the opponents of civil rights, of the war on poverty, of Medicare, of social security, of federal aid to education, of unions, and so forth. The labor movement, despite its obvious faults, has been the largest single organized force in this country pushing for progressive social legislation. And where the Negro-labor-liberal axis is weak, as in the farm belt, it was the religious groups that were most influential in rallying support for the Civil Rights Bill.

The durability of the coalition was interestingly tested during the election. I do not believe that the Johnson landslide proved the "white backlash" to be a myth. It proved, rather, that economic interests are more fundamental than prejudice: the backlashers decided that loss of social security was, after all, too high a price to pay for a slap at the Negro. This lesson was a valuable first step in re-educating such people, and it must be kept alive, for the civil rights movement will be advanced only to the degree that social and economic welfare gets to be inextricably entangled with civil rights. . . .

The role of the civil rights movement in the reorganization of American political life is programmatic as well as strategic. We are challenged now to broaden our social vision, to develop functional programs with concrete objectives. We need to propose alternatives to technological unemployment, urban decay, and the rest. We need to be calling for public works and training, for national economic planning, for federal aid to education, for attractive public housing— all this on a sufficiently massive scale to make a difference. We need to protest the notion that our integration into American life, so long delayed, must now proceed in an atmosphere of competitive scarcity instead of in the security of abundance which technology makes possible. We cannot claim to have answers to all the complex problems of modern society. That is too much to ask of a movement still battling barbarism in Mississippi. But we can agitate the right questions by probing at the contradictions which still stand in the way of the "Great Society." The questions having been asked, motion must begin in the larger society, for there is a limit to what Negroes can do alone.

What We Want, What We Believe (1966)

Black Panther Party

The Civil Rights movement began in the 1950s with goals of integration and assimilation. Its most visible leader, Martin Luther King, Jr., called upon doctrines of brotherly love and adopted tactics of nonviolent protest. It was not long, however, before other voices challenged that vision. Nation of Islam spokesman Malcolm X espoused black nationalism and racial separatism, urging African Americans to take control of their communities and to fight white racism "by any means necessary." After his assassination in 1965 Malcolm X came to symbolize militant defiance and racial pride, inspiring those who would move from demands for civil rights to demands for Black Power.

By mid-1965, many of the young people who filled the ranks of major civil rights organizations such as CORE (Congress of Racial Equality) and SNCC (Student Nonviolent Coordinating Committee) had become frustrated with the slow pace of change and angered by the white violence they faced. Both SNCC and CORE had decisively rejected the goal of integration and the tactic of nonviolence by mid-decade, but the turning point came in Greenwood, Mississippi, in 1966. Stokely Carmichael, the fiery young head of SNCC, fresh from his twenty-seventh jailing, shouted to the angry crowd of SNCC and CORE workers waiting for his release: "We been saying freedom for six years and we ain't got nothin'. What we gonna start saying now is Black Power!"

Black Power meant different things to different people, but one of the groups that developed the philosophy the most fully was the Black Panther Party. Organized in Oakland, California, in 1966 by Bobby Seale and Huey P. Newton, the Black Panthers constructed an ideology rooted in self-defense against racist aggression and police brutality. The media-savvy Panthers appeared in public dressed in berets and leather jackets, brandishing an impressive array of weaponry. Claiming that African Americans constituted an oppressed colony within a white oppressor nation, they attempted to create a militant,

Black Panther Party Platform and Program, October 1966.

*community-based organization to address the problems of urban blacks outside
the South.*

*Compare the civil rights message of Martin Luther King, Jr. (as described by
Vincent Harding), to the Black Panthers' statement below, and then compare
both to the previous article by Bayard Rustin. How do you explain the differences in their viewpoints? Why might different segments of the black population find different approaches compelling? How might you account for the
shift from integrationist to separatist sentiments in the African American community in the mid-1960s?*

1. We want freedom. We want power to determine the destiny of our
Black Community.

We believe that black people will not be free until we are able to
determine our destiny.

2. We want full employment for our people.

We believe that the federal government is responsible and obli-
gated to give every man employment or a guaranteed income. We believe that if the white American businessmen will not give full employment, then the means of production should be taken from the
businessmen and placed in the community so that the people of the
community can organize and employ all of its people and give a high
standard of living.

3. We want an end to the robbery by the CAPITALIST of our Black
Community.

We believe that this racist government has robbed us and now we
are demanding the overdue debt of forty acres and two mules. Forty
acres and two mules was promised 100 years ago as restitution for
slave labor and mass murder of black people. We will accept the payment in currency which will be distributed to our many communities.
The Germans are now aiding the Jews in Israel for the genocide of
the Jewish people. The Germans murdered six million Jews. The
American racist has taken part in the slaughter of over fifty million
black people; therefore, we feel that this is a modest demand that we
make.

4. We want decent housing, fit for shelter of human beings.

We believe that if the white landlords will not give decent housing
to our black community, then the housing and the land should be
made into cooperatives so that our community, with government-aid,
can build and make decent housing for its people.

5. We want education for our people that exposes the true nature of this decadent American society. We want education that teaches us our true history and our role in the present-day society.

We believe in an educational system that will give to our people a knowledge of self. If a man does not have knowledge of himself and his position in society and the world, then he has little chance to relate to anything else.

6. We want all black men to be exempt from military service.

We believe that Black people should not be forced to fight in the military service to defend a racist government that does not protect us. We will not fight and kill other people of color in the world who, like black people, are being victimized by the white racist government of America. We will protect ourselves from the force and violence of the racist police and the racist military, by whatever means necessary.

7. We want an immediate end to POLICE BRUTALITY and MURDER of black people.

We believe we can end police brutality in our black community by organizing black self-defense groups that are dedicated to defending our black community from racist police oppression and brutality. The Second Amendment to the Constitution of the United States gives a right to bear arms. We therefore believe that all black people should arm themselves for self-defense.

8. We want freedom for all black men held in federal, state, county and city prisons and jails.

We believe that all black people should be released from the many jails and prisons because they have not received a fair and impartial trial.

9. We want all black people when brought to trial to be tried in court by a jury of their peer group or people from their black communities, as defined by the Constitution of the United States.

We believe that the courts should follow the United States Constitution so that black people will receive fair trials. The 14th Amendment of the U.S. Constitution gives a man a right to be tried by his peer group. A peer is a person from a similar economic, social, religious, geographical, environmental, historical, and racial background. To do this the court will be forced to select a jury from the black community from which the black defendant came. We have been, and are being tried by all-white juries that have no understanding of the "average reasoning man" of the black community.

10. We want land, bread, housing, education, clothing, justice, and peace. And as our major political objective, a United Nations–supervised plebiscite to be held throughout the black colony in which only black colonial subjects will be allowed to participate, for the purpose of determining the will of black people as to their national destiny.

When, in the course of human events, it becomes necessary for one people to dissolve the political bands which have connected them with another, and to assume, among the powers of the earth, the separate and equal station to which the laws of nature and nature's God entitle them, a decent respect to the opinions of mankind requires that they should declare the causes which impel them to the separation.

We hold these truths to be self-evident, that all men are created equal; that they are endowed by their Creator with certain unalienable rights; that among these are life, liberty, and the pursuit of happiness. That, to secure these rights, governments are instituted among men, deriving their just powers from the consent of the governed; that, whenever any form of government becomes destructive of these ends, it is the right of the people to alter or to abolish it, and to institute a new government, laying its foundation on such principles, and organizing its powers in such form, as to them shall seem most likely to effect their safety and happiness. Prudence, indeed, will dictate that governments long established should not be changed for light and transient causes; and, accordingly, all experience hath shown, that mankind are more disposed to suffer, while evils are sufferable, than to right themselves by abolishing the forms to which they are accustomed. But, when a long train of abuses and usurpations, pursuing invariably the same object, evinces a design to reduce them under absolute despotism, it is their right, it is their duty, to throw off such government, and to provide new guards for their future security.

Chicano!

F. Arturo Rosales

El Movimiento, *the Chicano movement that emerged in the mid-1960s, sought social justice for Mexican Americans. In that way it was similar to the African American Civil Rights movement. From its beginnings, however,* el Movimiento *was heavily influenced by ideas of cultural nationalism. The major statement produced by the movement,* El Plan Espiritual de Aztlán, *condemned the "brutal 'Gringo' invasion of our territories" and declared "the Independence of our Mestizo Nation."*

Increasingly, young Mexican American activists claimed for themselves the term Chicano, *barrio slang associated with* pachucos, *the hip, rebellious, and sometimes criminal young men who symbolized a world that "respectable" Mexican Americans adamantly rejected. The most militant of these young people rejected a Mexican-American, hyphenated identity. As they explained in* El Plan de Aztlán, *the Mexican American "lacks respect for his culture and ethnic heritage . . . [and] seeks assimilation as a way out of his 'degraded' social status." In contrast, they believed, their own* chicanismo, *or ethnic pride, made meaningful political action possible. Chicano activists did not seek assimilation; they sought the liberation of "la Raza."*

Historian F. Arturo Rosales chronicles an early event in the development of the Chicano movement, the East Los Angeles high school walkout of 1968. His story of the birth of "Brown Power" demonstrates once again the importance of grassroots protest in bringing about social change. But he, more than any of the other authors in this section, focuses on the large-scale structural factors underlying the movements for racial equality.

At the end of the 1950s Mexican American attempts to end the educational neglect affecting their people seemed to be making headway. No Mexicans were segregated by *de jure* methods anywhere in the

From F. Arturo Rosales, *Chicano!* (Arte Publico Press, 1997). Excerpts of the work by F. Arturo Rosales are reprinted with permission from the publisher of *Chicano! The History of the Mexican American Civil Rights Movement* (Houston: Arte Publico Press–University of Houston, 1997).

country—not even in Texas, where as recently as the previous decade
school authorities had segregation codes for Mexican children. Certainly by the 1960s more U.S. Mexicans than ever were entering the
work force with a high school education or were attending college.
Despite these advances, the perception of inadequate education
served as one of the most crucial forces motivating the 1960s Chicano
Movement. Why was this so at this time when conditions were seemingly improving?

In large cities like Los Angeles, an underlying and partial explanation for this is that whites and a small number of minority families
had abandoned the inner cities for the suburbs (white flight), leaving
minorities behind. Except in border communities or in towns with
large, long-standing Mexican populations such as Santa Fe, San Antonio or Tucson, Mexicans lived in mixed neighborhoods in the larger
southwestern cities. In the 1950s this ethnic heterogeneity started
changing and, by the 1960s the shift resulted in the division of metropolitan areas—with whites living in more affluent peripheries and
the minorities in the central cities. Black ghettos and Mexican barrios
were now islands in a complex of freeways, tacky industrial parks,
auto repair shops, sporting complexes, small office buildings and expanded airport areas. The large Asian communities that are in inner
cities now had not yet emerged except in California. And even there,
they were not as large as today.

In cities like Los Angeles, Denver, Phoenix, San Jose and Houston,
large-scale de facto school segregation of Mexicans and Blacks took
hold as never before. Before, their populations were rarely large
enough to dominate elementary, middle-, and high-school enroll-
ments, as they did by the 1960s and thereafter. Moreover, with white
flight, educational funding was diverted to institutions in the suburbs
at the expense of urban core schools, which by now were stigmatized
as minority institutions.

In addition, the creation of new and better-paying jobs took place
mainly in the suburbs, a factor compounding the inner-city woes.
With whites gone, law-enforcement attitudes toward inner-city residents became uniformly less tolerant and, too often, police and
media overreacted to minority crime. All in all, tension and resentment were on the rise. Their increasing ghettoization made Chicanos
feel betrayed by the American Dream. The optimism that in the U.S.
anything was possible, proclaimed so often by the Mexican American

generation, came into question. This generation had chased an all-American status, but the real white society, it seemed, had left them behind in the barrios, perceiving them simply as "Mexicans."

As a result, like Blacks, many Mexicans gave up on the dream and became more conscious of their own lost identity. Thus, as Chicano intellectuals reconciled themselves to remaining Mexican, they formulated a catharsis to build a positive self-image. But where to start? In their haste to Americanize, their predecessors (Mexican Americans) had seemingly misplaced Mexican identity—not just the leaders and intellectuals but regular folks who did not speak Spanish to their kids and had named them Brenda and Mark, a sign that they wanted their children to Americanize.

It is no small wonder that an impassioned searching for roots—in *lo mexicano*—dominated the beginning of the Chicano Movement. Incipient issues discussed by fledgling Chicanos revolved around cultural nationalism. Mainly Chicanos in institutions of higher education, with access to information about the state of their communities, were stimulated to treat these themes. Then, the degree to which they influenced the folks back in the community was in proportion to the distance of barrios from their universities.

NASCENT YOUTH RUMBLINGS

The first major rumblings of the Chicano youth movement were heard in California in 1967. . . . That year at California college campuses, a social revolution of sorts affected the first large contingent of Chicano Movement participants. Throughout the decade of the 1960s, more Mexican Americans attended college than ever before; they formed part of the college-age population created by the baby boom. A sheer weight of numbers put them on campus. In addition, the Educational Opportunity Programs (EOP), funded by President Johnson's War on Poverty, recruited thousands of Mexican Americans throughout the Southwest, but more so in California. Arizona State University did not make EOP available until 1969, for example. The Vietnam-era GI Bill, instituted in 1966, also brought many Chicanos to campuses. A large number of new student organizations started appearing in the mid-1960s, with an orientation only slightly different from that of the 1940s Mexican American Movement. But the Mexican American student enrollment grew at the precise moment when colleges were radicalizing. . . .

Young *Chicanismo* showed the most vital signs of growth in Southern California. At the end of 1967, thirty-five Mexican American student organizations existed with almost two thousand members. The following year, according to Professor Juan Gómez-Quiñones, thousands more participated as the organizations multiplied to about fifty. By 1968 they were making a greater commitment to confrontationist strategy—white radicals and Black civil rights activists were in the throes of adopting these tactics as well. . . .

LOS ANGELES WALKOUTS: SHOCK WAVES THROUGH THE COMMUNITY

The key event that ushered in the *movimiento* in Los Angeles, and to a great degree elsewhere, was the East Los Angeles high-school walkout. But this action cannot be separated from the student movement. Because college organizations joined a combination of nonstudent activists to organize the protest, it is likely that college student mobilization served as a necessary precursor to the events.

On March 1, 1968, three hundred high-school students walked out of their Friday morning classes upon discovering that Wilson High School Principal Donald Skinner had canceled production of "Barefoot in the Park" because it "was an inappropriate play to be showing the student body." The cancellation was only a surface reason for the walkout. Underneath, discontent and anger stemming from more profound issues had been brewing in the predominantly Mexican American school. This resentment became evident at other schools as well. On Monday, Lincoln High students walked out. On Tuesday, two thousand students evacuated Garfield High School, another predominantly Mexican American high school. By Wednesday, the walkouts, or blowouts, as the students called them, had extended to Roosevelt High School. Some forty-five hundred students marched out of classes that day. In the ensuing two days, thousands of Mexican American students reported to school only to trek out the front doors once inside the buildings. By Friday, more than fifteen thousand students had left their classes throughout the Los Angeles area.

Chicano youths used the walkouts to dramatize what they considered the abysmally poor educational conditions affecting their schools. But the walkout organizers were not the first Mexican Americans to take a critical view of the educational system. It had certainly been a major issue among Mexican American civil rights leaders for at least four decades. In this case, however, the planners were all young people, many not yet out of their teens; none was over thirty, except Lincoln High School teacher Sal Castro.

In themselves, the events were significant because they affected so many schools, students, teachers, and parents. But more crucial was that the publicity created by the walkouts reminded the Mexican-origin community throughout the U.S. to examine educational conditions in their own communities. The sight of high-school kids on picket lines, carrying placards emblazoned with "Chicano Power!" "¡Viva la Raza!" and "Viva la Revolución," prompted a *Los Angeles Times* reporter to dub the walkouts as "The Birth of Brown Power"— this was an accurate prognosis.

The genesis of these events is found at Camp Hess Kramer, a four-hundred-acre spread in the rolling hills just east of Malibu. Significantly, here too were the elements that linked previous Mexican American politics and their ideological orientation to Los Angeles *Chicanismo*. In April 1966 in an effort to tackle Mexican American youth issues such as gangs, school dropout rates, and access to college education, the Los Angeles County Human Relations Council invited adults in community leadership positions to meet with about two hundred teenagers from various backgrounds in roundtable discussions.

The next year, many of the same young people attended a follow-up meeting at the camp. As one of them, David Sánchez, began to stand out, adult camp organizers decided to mentor his progress. Since age fifteen, Sánchez had worked as a youth counselor for the Social Training Center at the Episcopalian Church of the Epiphany under Father John Luce. The Episcopal priest introduced Sánchez to one of Los Angeles's busiest political activists of the time, Richard Alatorre, then a staff member of the Los Angeles Community Services Program, an associate of the NAACP Legal Defense Fund and a Democratic Party activist. Alatorre's connections earned Sánchez a place on the Mayor's Youth Council, which elected him chairman. . . .

By his own admission, Sánchez was clean-cut and not a *cholo* (street tough). When he was chairperson, no inkling existed as to the future of this precocious teenager, except that he might be headed for a successful college career. But most young, Mexican American males growing up in East Los Angeles, regardless of their orientation eventually butted heads with policemen. At one point, Sánchez had been "slapped around by the police," an experience that convinced him that police brutality was a community problem. When he tried to bring up the issue to the youth council, it was ignored because the adult politicians did not wish to air the problem.

In Los Angeles, most Mexican boys his age worked in grocery stores, movie theaters, and car-washes to make spending money. Richard Alatorre, however, obtained for Sánchez a winter job with the Boy's Club while Father Luce used him as youth counselor in the summer under the auspices of Volunteers In Service to America (VISTA). In the summer of 1967, at age seventeen, Sánchez wrote a successful proposal to the Southern California Council of Churches for funding to start the Piranya coffee house—envisioned as a teenager hangout to keep them out of trouble. The grant provided rent and other expenses for one year, enough time for a social revolution to emerge. Sánchez recruited Vickie Castro, Ralph Ramírez and other friends from Camp Hess Kramer, and they formed the Young Citizens for Community Action (YCCA). The Piranya became the headquarters of the YCCA. This upward-bound, clean-cut youthful group became the foundation of one of the most militant, sometimes violence-prone, Chicano organizations in the country: the Brown Berets.

Initially the group worked within the system, but the social ferment which characterized East Los Angeles during this time radicalized the YCCA. Eleazar Risco, for example, a Cuban acculturated to Mexicans (he spoke Spanish with a Mexican accent), began publishing *La Raza*, a tabloid specializing in exposing police brutality and educational inadequacies, issues that resonated among East Los Angeles Mexican Americans.

The crudely printed, passionately written, if not-too-well-researched, *La Raza*, which Risco regularly left at the Piranya clubhouse, excited the young patrons who read not only about police brutality, but also blistering attacks on the school system. This latter issue was close to a group more interested in college than gang life. . . .

But *La Raza* also appealed to the *cholo* (street tough) element of East Los Angeles. Risco and his helpers shaped the tabloid's content to appeal to this marginalized element, chronicling *la vida loca* (the crazy life), as life in LA's mean streets was known. Police bashing was particularly attractive to this group. To their delight, the first issue of *La Raza* led off with a banner headline attacking Los Angeles Police Department (LAPD) Chief Thomas Redding, "*Jefe Placa, tu abuela en mole*" (Fuzz Chief, your grandmother in chili sauce)." But the LAPD and the Sheriff's Department, noting the critical police stance of persons connected with Father Luce's operation, harassed Piranya club members by enforcing a curfew law for teenagers. David Sánchez's sister, for instance, was detained because she was in the coffee house after 10 P.M. The group decided to protest. For many YCCA members who picketed the sheriff's substation located across the street, it was their first militant act. Not all of the coffee house members agreed with the gradual radicalization of the group, however, and many walked out as a consequence.

About this time, Carlos Montes, who also played a crucial role in the rise of the Brown Berets, entered the scene. As a student at East Los Angeles City College, he had obtained a job as a teen post director for the Lincoln Heights area. This was a federal program sponsored by Father Luce's center and the CSO that Tony Ríos, César Chávez's former boss, ran out of Los Angeles. The YCCA members spent a great deal of time at the Church of the Epiphany, and soon Montes blended in with them. At Father Luce's center, Montes also met the passionate Risco, who produced *La Raza* in the church basement.

While it is difficult to trace the idea of the walkouts to any one group or individual, it is certain that Camp Hess Kramer veterans, some who became Brown Berets, were the core planners. But certainly many activists participated from other groups. . . . They devoted numerous hours to discussing educational inadequacies and how they could be changed. Perhaps influenced by the Black cultural movement, they all agreed that education of Mexican Americans lacked cultural relevancy.

Soon the planners favored the idea of a walkout as a means of dramatizing their issues. They then printed propaganda broadsides designed to persuade students to abandon their classes. Their activities became so overt that weeks before the strike, students, teachers, and administrators knew about the impending walkout. In fact, one month before the incident, teachers openly debated the issue and started taking sides. Meanwhile, Chicano newspapers *La Raza, Inside Eastside* and *The Chicano Student* helped fuel the passions of students and boycott supporters by spreading an "awareness" among students and non-students alike. A few days before the walkouts, for example, *La Raza* blasted the shortcomings of the school system and encouraged students to leave their classes. . . .

The college students and Brown Berets must have possessed a precise rationale as to why the walkouts were necessary. But only a few of the ten thousand high-school students who participated in the boycott were as politicized; they did not have the same ideological motives for their action. As John Ortiz, one of the college leaders, indicated,

> It was happening at Berkeley . . . the media reported strikes occurring throughout the country. So many kids got caught in the climate of protest, they were products of their time. Others felt it was the right thing to do. And others because they wanted to "party."

This motivation would be true in other Chicano student activities, whatever their character. But in the same statement, Ortiz explains the outcome for the uncommitted who just followed the crowd:

> But one thing is for sure; as the strike intensified and people were getting arrested, the students became politically aware. The events politicized the students. And that's why they walked out of their classes!

Mexican American teachers antagonistic to the protest came under much criticism. . . . But such tension reflected a general split in the Los Angeles Mexican community, a fissure symbolized to some degree by those who used the term *Chicano* as a self-identifier and those who did not.

The rift over involvement in the movement existed within families as well. Joe Razo, co-editor of *La Raza*, recalled an incident during the walkouts:

> I saw a man over in one of the East L.A. parks slapping his daughter around because she had walked out . . . she was crying but still arguing with him about the necessity for fighting for some of her rights and for changing the curriculum. . . . I still remember this vividly. . . . It was a family that at least a man had the interest enough to get involved with his kid. . . . there were going to be a lot of long discussions in that family . . . as to why she walked out of school. . . . It was not a matter "of it's nice and sunny, I think I'll go to the park." They were political. They really knew what they were fighting for.

Proclamation (1969)

Indians of All Tribes

In November 1969, a small group of activists from the American Indian Movement (AIM) occupied Alcatraz Island, the former site of Alcatraz prison in San Francisco Bay. By the end of the month almost four hundred Native Americans had taken up residency on Alcatraz. In their "Proclamation," the occupiers, calling themselves "Indians of All Tribes," claimed Alcatraz for all American Indians and offered to sell it back to the government for twenty-four dollars' worth of glass beads and some red cloth—a reference to the legendary "sale" of Manhattan Island to European settlers almost three centuries before. The Proclamation's initial pointed sarcasm gives way in the second half of the document to thoughtful proposals for establishing a variety of Indian institutes on Alcatraz Island. The government adopted a hands-off policy and attempted to outwait the activists. Finally, in June 1971, U.S. marshals and FBI agents removed the remaining fifteen occupiers from Alcatraz.

The occupation of Alcatraz was a major watershed in the development of American Indian activism. Before Alcatraz, protest tended to be tribally based and concerned with specific, local issues. Alcatraz signaled the consolidation of a "pan-Indian" approach to activism, as members of different tribes and nations placed their "Indian" identity over significant differences in cultural practices and beliefs, tribal organization, and geography. Though the Alcatraz occupation did not succeed in reclaiming Alcatraz Island for native peoples, it drew national attention to the broken promises and flawed policies of the federal government and inspired participants and supporters to a revitalized sense of purpose.

The movement that consolidated in the wake of the Alcatraz occupation was clearly influenced by the African American movements that preceded it; that is evident even in the use of the slogan, "Red Power." But it is useful to consider the similarities and differences between the two movements. How does this "Proclamation" by Indians of All Tribes differ from the Black Panthers' Platform? How much do the different histories of African Americans and Native Americans shape their respective movements, and how much are they shaped by the era in which they both emerged?

173

PROCLAMATION:

To the Great White Father and All His People:

We, the native Americans, re-claim the land known as Alcatraz Island in the name of all American Indians by right of discovery.

We wish to be fair and honorable in our dealings with the Caucasian inhabitants of this land, and hereby offer the following treaty:

We will purchase said Alcatraz Island for twenty-four dollars ($24) in glass beads and red cloth, a precedent set by the white man's purchase of a similar island about 300 years ago. We know that $24 in trade goods for these 16 acres is more than was paid when Manhattan Island was sold, but we know that land values have risen over the years. Our offer of $1.24 per acre is greater than the 47 cents per acre the white men are now paying the California Indians for their land.

We will give to the inhabitants of this island a portion of that land for their own, to be held in trust by the American Indian Government—for as long as the sun shall rise and the rivers go down to the sea—to be administered by the Bureau of Caucasian Affairs (BCA). We will further guide the inhabitants in the proper way of living. We will offer them our religion, our education, our life-ways, in order to help them achieve our level of civilization and thus raise them and all their white brothers up from their savage and unhappy state. We offer this treaty in good faith and wish to be fair and honorable in our dealings with all white men.

We feel that this so-called Alcatraz Island is more than suitable for an Indian Reservation, as determined by the white man's own standards. By this we mean that this place resembles most Indian reservations, in that:

1. It is isolated from modern facilities, and without adequate means of transportation.
2. It has no fresh running water.
3. It has inadequate sanitation facilities.
4. There are no oil or mineral rights.
5. There is no industry so unemployment is great.
6. There are no health care facilities.
7. The soil is rocky and non-productive; and the land does not support game.
8. There are no educational facilities.
9. The population has always exceeded the land base.

10.   The population has always been held as prisoners and
      kept dependent upon others.

Further, it would be fitting and symbolic that ships from all over
the world, entering the Golden Gate, would first see Indian land, and
thus be reminded of the true history of this nation. This tiny island
would be a symbol of the great lands once ruled by free and noble
Indians.

USE TO BE MADE OF ALCATRAZ ISLAND

What use will be made of this land?

Since the San Francisco Indian Center burned down, there is no
place for Indians to assemble and carry on our tribal life here in the
white man's city. Therefore, we plan to develop on this island several
Indian institutes:

1. A Center for Native American Studies will be developed which
will train our young people in the best of our native cultural arts and
sciences, as well as educate them to the skills and knowledge relevant
to improve the lives and spirits of all Indian peoples. Attached to this
center will be traveling universities, managed by Indians, which will
go to the Indian Reservations in order to learn the traditional values
from the people, which are now absent in the Caucasian higher educational system.

2. An American Indian Spiritual center will be developed which
will practice our ancient tribal religious ceremonies and medicine.
Our cultural arts will be featured and our young people trained in
music, dance, and medicine.

3. An Indian center of Ecology will be built which will train and
support our young people in scientific research and practice in order
to restore our lands and waters to their pure and natural state. We
will seek to de-pollute the air and the water of the Bay Area. We will
seek to restore fish and animal life, and to revitalize sea life which has
been threatened by the white man's way. Facilities will be developed
to desalt sea water for human use.

4. A Great Indian Training School will be developed to teach our
peoples how to make a living in the world, improve our standards of
living, and end hunger and unemployment among all our peoples.
This training school will include a center for Indian arts and crafts,

and an Indian Restaurant serving native foods and training Indians in culinary arts. This center will display Indian arts and offer the Indian foods of all tribes to the public, so they all may know of the beauty and spirit of the traditional Indian ways.

5. Some of the present buildings will be taken over to develop an American Indian Museum, which will depict our native foods and other cultural contributions we have given to all the world. Another part of the Museum will present some of the things the white man has given to the Indians, in return for the land and the life he took: disease, alcohol, poverty, and cultural decimation (as symbolized by old tin cans, barbed wire, rubber tires, plastic containers, etc.). Part of the museum will remain a dungeon, to symbolize both Indian captives who were incarcerated for challenging white authority, and those who were imprisoned on reservations. The Museum will show the noble and the tragic events of Indian history, including the broken treaties, the documentary of the Trail of Tears, the Massacre of Wounded Knee, as well as the victory over Yellow-Hair Custer and his army.

In the name of all Indians, therefore, we re-claim this island for Indian nations, for all these reasons. We feel this claim is just and proper, and that this land should rightfully be granted to us for as long as the rivers shall run and the sun shall shine.

SIGNED,
INDIANS OF ALL TRIBES
November 1969
San Francisco, California

Part 4

STRUGGLES OVER GENDER AND SEXUAL LIBERATION

In a manner similar to the impact of race, gender has served as a primary determinant of power and opportunity in America. To this day, whether one is born male or female has as much to do with shaping one's life possibilities as almost any other factor. It determines the clothes we wear, the emotions we are taught to cultivate, the jobs we are told we should aspire to, the power we exercise—even our sense of who we are and what we are about. Through most of American history, cultural norms prescribed that women should be the tenders of the hearth, rearers of children, and the moral, spiritual guardians of the family. Men, by contrast, were to be assertive, dominant, in control, the major source of power, influence, and income. Even though frequently these norms were not implemented in reality, they remained decisive forces in the culture at large.

Particularly for white women of the middle and upper classes, the norms defined as off-limits any active involvement in the world outside the home except in volunteer organizations. Those women who worked for money prior to 1940 were primarily single, young, and poor. It was virtually unheard of for a married, middle-class white woman to have a job or to pursue a career. For her to do so would be a repudiation of her natural role and a negative reflection on her husband's ability to provide for her. In a culture that defined success for a woman as marriage and motherhood, any deviation from that role marked failure.

World War II played a pivotal role in generating the conditions for significant change in women's roles, just as it created new opportunities for African Americans. Given the urgency of defeating fascism, the government and all its propaganda mechanisms suddenly sanctioned work for women, including wives and mothers. Millions of women took jobs, and under the press of military necessity, older definitions of women's "proper" place were set aside, at least for the moment. On the other hand—as with African Americans—discrimination continued. Woman were paid less than men, they were barred from executive positions, and despite wartime necessity, the government failed to provide or support day care centers in numbers adequate to meet the needs of working parents.

After the war, a kind of cultural schizophrenia occurred. On the one hand, many of the advances that had occurred were reversed. What Betty Friedan labeled the "Feminine Mystique" became once more a pervasive cultural force, pushing women to return to the home and aspire to fulfillment through suburban domesticity. "The independent woman is a contradiction in terms," declared one best-selling treatise. On the other hand, employment figures for women continued to increase—especially after an initial dip immediately after the war; in addition, more and more middle-class and married women were taking jobs in order to make it possible for families to aspire to better lives.

At least partly because of such changes, a revitalized feminism became possible in the late 1960s, exposing the contradiction between traditional definitions of women's place and the new frequency with which women were assuming active economic, political, and social roles outside the home. Questioning most of the traditional definitions of masculinity and femininity, the women's liberation movement became one of the most significant forces of social change in the 1960s and 1970s.

As with the Civil Rights movement, the revival of social protest reflected a combination of external and impersonal changes—such as those triggered by World War II—and the emergence of new insurgent voices among women themselves. At the same time, the women's movement was never as unified as the early Civil Rights movement, neither in goals, tactics, or leadership, nor in its definition of what was wrong with American society.

The first section of Part 4 focuses on the women's movement. In the following pages, historian Jane Sherron De Hart analyzes the emergence and development of the "second wave" of U.S. feminism in the 1960s and '70s, emphasizing its diversity. Two documents illustrate the broad range of 1960s and early 1970s feminism: "New York Radical Women" critiqued the "Degrading Mindless-Boob-Girlie Symbol" of the Miss America Pageant in language that seems quite distant from the careful arguments of the National Organization for Women (as described by De Hart). And Chicana activist Enriqueta Longeaux Vasquez expressed the doubts of many black and Chicana women about the women's liberation movement in a piece titled "¡Soy Chicana Primero!"

While black and Chicana women critiqued the assumptions of what many saw as a white, middle-class movement insensitive to their concerns and experiences, a great many other women simply rejected feminism altogether. Feminism seemed a threat to their ways of life, especially in its varied critiques of traditional gender roles. The Equal Rights Amendment became a rallying point for antifeminists, including many women, under the leadership of conservative spokeswoman Phyllis Schlafly. In her 1972 article, "What's Wrong with 'Equal Rights' for Women," she argued that feminism was antifamily, and that the ERA would destroy the privileges and preferential rights enjoyed by American women. This argument seemed convincing to many, especially in light of the highly visible, radical critiques of the family offered by some feminists at the time and in the context of social changes exemplified by the Supreme Court's 1973 *Roe v. Wade* decision (included here), which guaranteed women's right to choice in the matter of reproductive freedom.

Closely associated with the movements for women's liberation, in the minds of feminists and antifeminists alike, were issues of sexual behavior and sexuality. A powerful statement from the time, Martha Shelley's 1970 article "Gay Is Good," illustrates the ways in which Gay Liberation embodied a larger critique of American society and of traditional gender roles. Finally, historian Beth Bailey writes about the origins of sexual revolution(s), emphasizing, like De Hart on the women's movement, the diversity of what was often seen as a single "movement."

Among the questions raised by these readings are: Why did it take until the middle of the 1960s for a women's liberation movement to develop? Given the diversity in women's experience evident here, was there any way for a women's movement to encompass that diversity and meet all needs? How closely related are issues of gender equality and sexual liberation? Why, as so many Americans rejected—and continue to reject—feminism, have American women's lives and opportunities changed so dramatically since the 1950s?

The Creation of a Feminist Consciousness

Jane Sherron De Hart

The mainstream African American Civil Rights movement began as a call for equality and full access to American society. By the late 1960s, many African Americans called instead for Black Power, and the Chicano and American Indian movements similarly embraced cultural nationalism, rejecting the culture of the dominant white society.

The women's movement that emerged in the 1960s in many ways mirrors that divide. Some women sought equal rights in the existing society; others sought the radical transformation of American life. There was little unity in the feminism of the 1960s and 1970s.

Historian Jane Sherron De Hart traces the various origins of 1960s feminism, showing its variety and its resilience. Analyzing two broadly defined groups, one seeking "women's rights" and the other seeking "women's liberation," she shows how each contributed to the transformation of American society. This piece ends on a note of triumph, with the 1977 International Women's Year Conference in Houston. In reading De Hart's analysis and the selections that follow, consider the question: Was the women's movement the most successful social movement of the postwar era?

Mainstream feminism emerged as a mass movement in the 1960s as different groups and a new generation acquired a feminist consciousness. In the vanguard were educated, middle-class women whose diverse experiences had sharpened their sensitivity to the fundamental inequality between the sexes at a time when America had been thrust into the throes of self-examination by a movement for racial equality. Some were young veterans of the civil rights movement and the New

Left, steeped in a commitment to equality and the techniques of protest. Others were young professionals increasingly aware of their secondary status. Still others were older women who in their long careers as professionals or as activists had used organizations such as the American Civil Liberties Union (ACLU), the Young Women's Christian Association (YWCA) and the United Auto Workers (UAW) to fight sex-based discrimination. Included, too, were those whose outwardly conformist lives belied an intense awareness of the malaise of domesticity and the untenably narrow boundaries of their prescribed roles. To explore how they came self-consciously to appraise women's condition as one demanding collective action is to explore the process of radicalization that helped to create a new feminist movement.

In its early state, a major component of that movement consisted of two different groups—women's rights advocates and women's liberationists. Although the differences between the two groups began to blur as the movement matured, initial distinctions were sharp. Women's rights advocates were likely to have been older, to have had professional training or work experience, to have been more inclined to form or join organized feminist groups. Reform oriented, these organizations used traditional pressure group tactics to achieve changes in laws and public policy that would guarantee women equal rights. Emphasis on "rights" meant extending to women in life outside the home the same "rights" men had, granting them the same options, privileges, and responsibilities that men enjoyed. There was little suggestion initially of personal or cultural transformation.

Women's liberationists were younger women, less highly educated, whose ideology and political style, shaped in the dissent and violence of the 1960s, led them to look at women's predicament differently. Instead of relying upon traditional organizational structure and lobbying techniques, they developed a new style of politics. Instead of limiting their goals to changes in public policy, they embraced a transformation in private, domestic life as well. They sought liberation from ways of thinking and behaving that they believed stunted or distorted women's growth and kept them subordinate to men. Through the extension of their own personal liberation they hoped to remake the male world, changing it as they had changed themselves. For women's liberationists as for women's rights advocates, however, the first step toward becoming feminists demanded a clear statement of women's position in society, one that called attention to the gap between the egalitarian ideal and the actual position of women in American culture. There also had to be a call to action from women themselves, *for* women, *with* women, *through* women. Redefining themselves, they had to make being a woman a political fact; and, as they did so, they had to live with the radical implications of what could only be called a rebirth.

THE MAKING OF LIBERAL FEMINISTS: WOMEN'S RIGHTS ADVOCATES

For some women, the process of radicalization began with the appointment of a Presidential Commission on the Status of Women in 1961. Presidents, Democrat and Republican, customarily discharged their political debt to female members of the electorate, especially to those who had loyally served the party, by appointing a few token women, usually party stalwarts, to highly visible posts. John Kennedy was no exception. He was, however, convinced by Esther Peterson, the highest-ranking woman in his administration, that the vast majority of women would be better served if he also appointed a commission charged with investigating obstacles to the full participation of women in society. Peterson, who was assistant secretary of labor and head of the Women's Bureau, believed that the report of such a commission could sensitize the public to barriers to equality just as her own experience as a labor organizer had sensitized her to the particular problems confronting women workers. Citizens thus informed could then be mobilized on behalf of governmental efforts at reform. Accordingly, the commission was appointed with Eleanor Roosevelt serving as chair until her death a year later. Its report, *American Women* (1963), was conservative in tone, acknowledging the importance of women's traditional roles within the home and the progress they had made in a "free democratic society." Acknowledging also that women were an underutilized resource that the nation could ill afford to ignore, the report provided extensive documentation of discriminatory practices in government, education, and employment, along with substantial recommendations for change. Governors, replicating Kennedy's move, appointed state commissions on the status of women. In these commissions hundreds of men and women encountered further evidence of the economic, social, and legal disabilities that encumbered the nation's "second sex." For some, the statistics were old news; for others, they were a revelation.

Aroused by growing evidence of "the enormity of our problem," members of state commissions gathered in Washington in 1966 for the Third National Conference of the Commissions on the Status of Women. Individuals who were coming to know and rely on one another as they pooled their growing knowledge of widespread inequities, they were a network in the making. They were also women who wanted something done. This time they encountered a situation that transformed at least some of those present into activists in a new movement for women's equality. The catalyst proved to be a struggle involving Representative Martha Griffiths and the Equal Employment Opportunity Commission (EEOC), the federal agency in charge of implementing the Civil Rights Act of 1964.

Despite the fact that the law proscribed discrimination on the basis of sex as well as race, the commission refused to take seriously the problem of sexual discrimination. The first executive director of EEOC, believing that "sex" had been injected into the bill by opponents seeking to block its passage, regarded the sex provision as a "fluke" best ignored. Representative Griffiths from Michigan thought otherwise. The inclusion of sex discrimination, while used by civil rights opponents to sabotage the bill, had been initiated by the venerable and elitist National Woman's Party. Support was also strong among women in the House whom Griffiths had mobilized. While liberals had initially objected, fearing that so encumbering a bill would prevent passage of much-needed legislation on behalf of racial equality, Griffiths had prevailed. Without the sex provision, she had reminded her colleagues, the Civil Rights Act would give black women advantages that white women were denied. A racist appeal that revealed the exclusivity of Griffiths's vision of sisterhood, it had worked. Once the bill passed she was determined to see the new law enforced in its entirety. When EEOC failed to do so, she lambasted the agency for its inaction in a biting speech delivered on the House floor only days before the Conference of the Commissions on the Status of Women met.

Griffiths's concern was shared by a group of women working within EEOC. Echoing an argument made the year before by a black trade unionist in the Women's Bureau, they insisted that the agency could be made to take gender-related discrimination more seriously if women had a civil rights organization as adept at applying pressure on their behalf as was the National Association for the Advancement of Colored People (NAACP) on behalf of blacks. Initially the idea was rejected. Conference participants most upset by EEOC's inaction decided instead to propose a resolution urging the agency to treat sexual discrimination with the same seriousness it applied to racial discrimination. When the resolution was ruled inappropriate by conference leaders, they were forced to reconsider. After a whispered conversation over lunch they concluded the time for discussion of the status of women was over. It was time for action. Before the day was out twenty-eight women had paid five dollars each to join the National Organization for Women (NOW), including author Betty Friedan, who happened to be in Washington at the time of the conference.

Friedan's presence in Washington was auspicious; her involvement in NOW, virtually inevitable. The author of a brilliant polemic published in 1963, she not only labeled the resurgent domestic ideology of recent decades but exposed the groups perpetuating it. Editors of women's magazines, advertising experts, Freudian psychologists, social scientists, and educators—all, according to Friedan, contributed to a romanticization of domesticity she termed "the feminine mystique." The result, she charged, was the infantilization of intelligent women and the transformation of the suburban home into a "comfortable concentration camp." Harsh words, they rang true to those who found the creativity of homemaking and the joys of motherhood vastly exaggerated. Sales of the book ultimately zoomed past the million mark.

By articulating heretofore inarticulated grievances, *The Feminine Mystique* had advanced a process initiated by more dispassionate investigations of women's status and the discriminatory practices which made that status inferior. That process was the collective expression of discontent. It is not surprising that the voices initially heard were those of women who were overwhelmingly white, educated, and middle or upper-middle class. College women who regarded themselves the equals of male classmates by virtue of intellect and training were, as Jo Freeman points out, more likely to develop expectations they saw realized by their male peers but not, in most cases, by themselves. The frustrations were even greater for women with professional training. The very fact that many had sought advanced training in fields not traditionally "female" meant that they were less likely to find in traditional gender roles the identity and self-esteem such roles provided other women. Moreover, when measuring themselves against fellow professionals who happened to be men, the greater rewards enjoyed by their white male counterparts seemed especially galling. Privileged though they were, such women *felt* more deprived in many cases than did those women who were in reality less privileged. By 1966 this sense of deprivation had been sufficiently articulated and shared and the networks of like-minded women sufficiently developed so that collective discontent could be translated into collective action. The formation of NOW signaled a feminist resurgence. The three hundred men and women who gathered in October for the organizational meeting of NOW included mainly professionals, some of them veterans of commissions on the status of women as well as a few feminist union activists, notably Dorothy Haener. Adopting bylaws and a statement of purpose, they elected officers, naming Friedan president. Her conviction that intelligent women needed purposeful, generative work of their own was reflected in NOW's statement of purpose, which attacked "the traditional assumption that a woman has to choose between marriage and motherhood on the one hand and serious participation in industry or the professions on the other." Determined that women should be allowed to develop their full potential as human beings, the organization's goal was to bring them into "full participation in the mainstream of American society NOW, exercising all the privileges and responsibilities thereof in truly equal partnership with men." To that end NOW developed a Bill of Rights, adopted at its 1967 meeting, that exhorted Congress to pass an equal rights amendment to the Constitution, called on EEOC to enforce antidiscrimination legislation, and urged federal and state legislators to guarantee equal and unsegregated education. To ensure women control over their reproductive lives, these new feminists called for removal of penal codes denying women contraceptive information and devices as well as safe, legal abortions. To ease the double burden of working mothers, they urged legislation that would ensure maternity leaves without jeopardizing job security or seniority, permit tax deductions for child care expenses, and create public, inexpensive day care centers. To improve the lot of poor women, they urged reform of the welfare system and equality with respect to benefits, including job-training programs.

Not content simply to call for change, NOW leaders, following the lead of equality advocates within the labor movement, worked to make it happen. Using persuasion, pressure, and even litigation, they, with other newly formed women's rights groups such as the Women's Equity Action League (WEAL), launched a massive attack on sex discrimination. By the end of the 1960s NOW members had filed legal suits against newspapers listing jobs under the headings "Help Wanted: Male" and "Help Wanted: Female," successfully arguing that such headings discouraged women from applying for jobs they were perfectly capable of doing. Building on efforts begun in the Kennedy administration such as the passage of the Equal Pay Act, they pressured the federal government to intensify its commitment to equal opportunity. They urged congressmen and labor leaders to persuade the Department of Labor to include women in its guidelines designed to encourage the hiring and promotion of blacks in firms holding contracts with the federal government. They persuaded the Federal Communications Commission to open up new opportunities for women in broadcasting. Tackling the campus as well as the marketplace, WEAL filed suit against more than three hundred colleges and universities, ultimately securing millions of dollars in salary raises for women faculty members who had been victims of discrimination. To ensure that women receive the same pay men received for doing the same work, these new feminists lobbied for passage of a new Equal Employment Opportunity Act that would enable EEOC to fight discrimination more effectively.

NOW also scrutinized the discriminatory practices of financial institutions, persuading them to issue credit to single women and to married women in their own—not their husband's—name. WEAL, in turn, filed charges against banks and other lending institutions that refused to grant mortgages to single women, or in the case of married couples, refused to take into account the wife's earnings in evaluating the couple's eligibility for a mortgage. Colleges and universities that discriminated against female students in their sports programs came under fire, as did fellowship programs that failed to give adequate consideration to female applicants.

While NOW and WEAL attacked barriers in industry and education, the National Women's Political Caucus (NWPC) focused on government and politics. Formed in 1971, the caucus was initiated by Friedan, New York congresswomen Bella Abzug and Shirley Chisholm—both outspoken champions of women's rights—and Gloria Steinem, soon to become founding editor of the new mass-circulation feminist magazine *Ms.* Abzug, a lawyer and veteran activist for peace and civil rights, and Chisholm, the first black woman elected to

Congress, were especially concerned about the small numbers of women in government. Accordingly the caucus concentrated on getting women elected and appointed to public office while also rallying support for issues such as the Equal Rights Amendment. Meanwhile, women in the professions, aware of their small numbers and inferior status, began to organize as well. Physicians, lawyers, and university professors fought for equal opportunity in the meetings of such overwhelmingly male groups as the American Medical Association, the American Association of University Professors, and the American Historical Association. Union women also mobilized. In 1974, three thousand women from fifty-eight unions attended the founding convention of the Coalition of Labor Union Women (CLUW), resolving to fight for equality in the workplace and within organized labor.

Collectively such protests served notice that more women were becoming radicalized. The particular combination of events that transformed these women into feminists varied with the individual. A southern legislator, describing the process that brought home the reality of her own second-class citizenship, wrote:

> As a State Senator, I succeeded in getting Mississippi women the right to sit on juries (1968); the opposition's arguments were appalling. When women began hiring me in order to get credit, I became upset at the discrimination I saw. After I was divorced in 1970, I was initially denied a home loan. The effect was one of the worst traumas I've suffered. Denial of a home loan to one who was both a professional and a member of the legislature brought things to a head.

Although the number of women who understood what it meant to be the "second sex" were still only a tiny minority, they were nonetheless a minority whose energy, talents, and experience enabled them to work for changes necessary to ensure equal rights. And they were gaining important allies in liberal organizations. The American Civil Liberties Union (ACLU) was a case in point. Best known for its defense of civil liberties, the ACLU put its considerable resources behind a newly created Women's Rights Project, headed by Ruth Bader Ginsberg, then a professor at Columbia School of Law. Her task was to devise a litigation strategy designed to persuade the Supreme Court (of which she is now a member) that gender discrimination in the law was unconstitutional. Since even the liberal Warren Court had been unable to move beyond judicial paternalism and gender stereotypes, the challenge was formidable. But Ginsberg had "high hopes for significant change," as, no doubt, did strategically placed feminists in trade unions, foundations, and other organizations whose support helped legitimate this fledgling movement.

THE MAKING OF RADICAL FEMINISTS:
WOMEN'S LIBERATIONISTS

The process of radicalization that transformed some individuals into liberal feminists occurred simultaneously—but in different fashion and with somewhat different results—among a younger generation of women who were also predominantly white and middle class. Many of them veterans of either the civil rights movement or of the New Left, these were the activists who would initially become identified as women's liberationists. Differing in perspective as well as style, they would ultimately push many of their older counterparts beyond the demand for equal rights to recognition that true emancipation would require a far-reaching transformation of society and culture.

The experiences awakening in this 1960s generation a feminist consciousness have been superbly described by Sara Evans in her book, *Personal Politics.* "Freedom, equality, love and hope," the possibility of new human relationships, the importance of participatory democracy—letting the people decide—were, as Evans points out, part of an egalitarian ideology shared by both the southern-based Student Nonviolent Coordinating Committee (SNCC) in its struggle for racial equality and the Students for Democratic Society (SDS) in its efforts to mobilize an interracial organization of the urban poor in northern ghettos. Membership in both organizations—"the movement"—thus reinforced commitment to these ideals among the women who joined. In order to translate ideals into reality, however, young, college-age women who had left the shelter of middle-class families for the hard and dangerous work of transforming society found themselves doing things that they would never have thought possible. Amidst the racial strife of the South, they joined picket lines, created freedom schools, and canvassed for voter registration among blacks, often enduring arrest and jailing. SDS women from affluent suburbs entered decaying tenements and were surrounded by the grim realities of the ghetto. They trudged door-to-door in an effort to reach women whose struggle to survive made many understandably suspicious of intruding strangers. In the process, not only did these young activists achieve a heightened sense of self-worth and autonomy, they also learned the skills of movement building and the nuts and bolts of organizing.

Particularly important was the problem of getting people, long passive, to act on their own behalf. SDS women began by encouraging ghetto women to come together to talk about their problems. This sharing of experiences, they believed, would lead these women to recognize not only that their problems were common but that solutions required changes in the system. In the process of organizing, the organizers also learned. They began to understand the meaning of oppression and the valor required of those who fought it. They found new role models, Evans suggests, in extraordinary southern black women whose courage seemed never to waver in the face of violence and in those welfare mothers of the North who confronted welfare bureaucrat and slum lord after years of passivity.

But if being in the movement brought a new understanding of equality, it also brought new problems. Men who were committed to equality for one group were not necessarily committed to equality for another group. Women in SNCC, as in SDS, found themselves frequently relegated to domestic chores and treated as sex objects, denied most leadership positions, and refused a key voice in the formulation of policy. Moreover, the sexual freedom that had been theirs as part of the cultural revolution taking place in the 1960s soon began to feel more like sexual exploitation as they saw their role in the movement spelled out in the draft resister's slogan: "Girls Say Yes to Guys Who Say No." Efforts to change the situation were firmly rebuffed. When SNCC leader Stokely Carmichael joked that the only "position for women in SNCC is prone," he encapsulated views which, while not his own, reflected all too accurately the feelings of males in the New Left as well as many in SNCC.

By 1967 the tensions had become so intense that white women left the movement to organize on behalf of their own "liberation." Black women, whose own tradition of feminism was venerable, stayed. Fully aware of the double jeopardy involved in being both black and female, many would embrace varieties of feminism that reflected their own problems and priorities. In the meantime, however, racial equality remained their top concern.

The women who left did not leave empty-handed. As radicals, they were impatient with liberalism, critical of capitalism, and profoundly suspicious of authority. Accustomed to challenging prevailing ideas and practices, they had acquired a language of protest, an organizing tactic, and a deep-seated conviction that the personal was political. How that legacy would shape this burgeoning new feminist movement became evident as small women's liberation groups began springing up spontaneously in major cities and university communities across the nation.

STRUCTURE, LEADERSHIP, AND CONSCIOUSNESS-RAISING

Initially, at least, the two branches of mainstream feminism seemed almost to be two different movements, so unlike were they in structure and style. Linked only by newsletters, notices in underground newspapers, and networks of friends, women's liberation groups rejected both traditional organizational structure and leadership. Unlike NOW and the other women's rights groups associated with liberal feminism, they had no central headquarters, no elected officers, no bylaws. There was no legislative agenda and little of the activism that transformed the more politically astute women's rights leaders into skilled lobbyists and tacticians. Instead this younger generation of feminists, organizing new groups wherever they found themselves, concentrated on a kind of personal politics rooted in movement days. Looking back on male-dominated meetings in which, however informal the gathering, a few highly verbal, aggressive men invariably controlled debate and dictated strategy and left less articulate and assertive women effectively excluded, they recalled the technique they had used in organizing the poor. They remembered how they had encouraged those women to talk among themselves until the personal became political, that is, until problems which, at first glance, seemed to be personal were finally understood to be social in cause—rooted in society rather than in the individual—and political in solution. Applying this same process in their own informal "rap groups," women's liberationists developed the technique of "consciousness-raising." Adopted by women's rights groups such as local chapters of NOW, consciousness-raising sessions became one of the most important innovations of mainstream feminism.

The immediate task of the consciousness-raising session was to bring together in a caring, supportive, noncompetitive setting women accustomed to relating most intimately not with other women but with men—husbands, lovers, "friends." As these women talked among themselves, exchanging confidences, reassessing old options, and mentally exploring new ones, a sense of shared problems began to emerge. The women themselves gradually gained greater understanding of how profoundly their lives had been shaped by the constraints of culture. Personal experience with those constraints merged with intellectual awareness of women's inferior status and the factors that made it so. By the same token, new understanding of problems generated new determination to resolve them. Anger, aggression, and frustration formerly turned inward in unconscious self-hatred began to be directed outward, becoming transformed into new energy directed toward constructive goals. If society and culture had defined who women were through their unconscious internalization of tradition, they could reverse the process, and, by redefining themselves, redefine society and culture. Or, to put it another way, if woman was a *social construct*—the product not so much of biology, but of what people in a particular society and culture believed to be the implications of biology—then women themselves would re-create the construct. At work was a process of discovery so radicalizing that the individuals undergoing it ultimately emerged in a very real sense as different people. Now feminists, these were women with a different understanding of reality—a new "consciousness," a new sense of "sisterhood," and a new commitment to change.

Consciousness-raising was an invigorating and sometimes frightening experience. As one young woman wrote, "This whole movement is the most exhilarating thing of my life. The last eight months have been a personal revolution. Nonetheless, I recognize there is dynamite in this and I'm scared shitless." "Scared" or not, such women could no longer be contained. Veterans of one rap group fanned out, creating others, often with arresting names such as Cell 16, the Furies, Redstockings, or simply Radical Women.

Since consciousness-raising groups functioned best when the group was homogeneous, women of color and lesbians sometimes felt unwelcome. Nonetheless, groups mushroomed, providing the movement with increased numbers and added momentum, as did the formation of black, Chicana, and Asian-American organizations. For the minority-group women, being feminists took special courage because it meant facing accusations of having deserted the liberation struggles of their own racial and ethnic communities. Whatever their background, women's liberationists were faced with an additional challenge, articulating theoretically as well as personally what "oppression," "sexism," and "liberation" really meant: in short, developing a feminist ideology.

TOWARD A FEMINIST IDEOLOGY: OPPRESSION, SEXISM, AND CHANGE

To explain the significance of the discovery that woman is a *social construct* and that subordination was built into that construct was no simple process. The concept itself was complex. Moreover, women's rights advocates who were essentially pragmatic were more interested in practical results than in theoretical explanations. Even among women's liberationists who were far more theoretically oriented and ideologically fractious, intellectual perspectives reflected differences in politics, experience, temperament, style, and sexual preference. Manifestos, position papers, and books began to pile up as liberationists searched for the historical origins of female oppression. Those whose primary loyalty was still to the New Left—soon dubbed "politicos"—attributed women's oppression to capitalism. Others, who would come to be known as socialist-feminists, insisted that both male supremacy and capitalism were responsible for women's subordination and that feminists must be allied with, but apart from, the left. Still other liberationists argued that male supremacy, not class or race, was the more fundamental and universal form of oppression and that women as a group constituted an oppressed class. Known as radical feminists, their emphasis on the primacy of gender would prevail, although it would be ultimately challenged by feminists of color, who insisted on multiple forms of oppression. In the meantime, however, radical feminists' identification of the family as the basic unit in the system of oppression led to new debates among radical feminists themselves. If marriage as an intersexual alliance divided women, leading them to identity with the oppressor from whom they derived economic advantages rather than each other, ought marriage to be abolished? If so, what new structure should take its place? Pushing the logic of this position, lesbian feminists argued that the ultimate rejection of male domination required not just the rejection of marriage, but the rejection of sexual intimacy with men. Heterosexuality, they insisted, was at the very core of patriarchy. Other feminists disagreed. Family, while a source of gender hierarchy, could also be a site of support. Moreover, collective struggle against male supremacy did not mean rejecting the men with whom one was intimately connected; the challenge ought to be to make them allies.

Other radical feminists, seeking to desexualize lesbianism, argued that sexual behavior—who one slept with—was less important than being "woman identified." They pointed to sex-based role differentiation as a source of oppression, arguing that work and family roles should be restructured in ways that would encourage greater mutuality and fulfillment for both sexes. Others argued that personality—men and women's psychic identity—were also overly differentiated by sex. Only by merging role and personality characteristics of both sexes within each individual could androgynous men and women be developed and real liberation achieved.

Given the great variety of perspectives and positions even among women's liberationists alone, it is impossible to talk about a feminist ideology to which all those who identified with the women's movement subscribed. The ascendancy of radical feminism among women's liberationists in the early 1970s and the eventual embrace of many of their insights by liberal feminists, however, does make it possible to talk about a common conceptual framework shared by mainstream feminists. Most believed that *gender hierarchy* is a primary factor essential to any understanding of why women *as a group* suffer from an unequal distribution of power and resources in a society. They agreed that men have been the dominant sex and that women as a group are subordinate. While not all mainstream feminists were comfortable talking about a *system* of oppression or even using the word "oppression," they were quick to list the many areas where inequities were—and still are—evident.

At the top of the list was the economy. Men, they agreed, are more likely to be economically independent than women because the latter work within the home where their labor has no monetary value and/or outside the home in sex-segregated jobs for wages too meager to ensure economic self-sufficiency. Society and culture also provided numerous examples of the higher status, greater options, and greater power conferred upon men by virtue of their sex. Just as traditional male roles provide access to power and independence, whereas female roles do not, so, feminists pointed out, masculine values define what attributes are admired and rewarded. The very fact that strength, competence, independence, and rationality are considered masculine values, that they are more highly regarded by both sexes, *and* that they constitute the standard by which mental health is judged these new feminists found revealing indeed. The problem, they insisted, is not simply that the qualities themselves, intrinsically neither "male" or "female," are the product of gender socialization. It is the preference, conscious and unconscious, for whatever society regards as "masculine" that is so persistent and so objectionable—a preference feminists termed *sexism*.

Sexism, they believed, is persistent, pervasive, and powerful. It is internalized by women as well as men. It is most dramatically evident in the programmed-to-please women who search for happiness through submissiveness to men and in the men who use their power to limit women's options and keep them dependent. It is also evident in a more subtle fashion among women who emulate male models and values, refusing to see those aspects of women's lives that are positive and life-affirming, and among men who are unaware of the unconscious sexism permeating their attitudes and actions. Internalized in individuals, sexism is also embedded in institutions—the family, the education system, the media, the economy, politics, law, organized religion, language, and sexual morality.

Given the pervasiveness of sexism, many feminists saw no possibility for real equality short of transformation not only of individuals but also of social institutions and cultural values. Even what was once seen as the relatively simple demand of women's rights advocates for equal pay for equal work no longer looked so simple. What seemed to be a matter of obtaining equal rights *within* the existing system in reality demanded changes that *transform* the system. Involved was:

> a reevaluation of women as workers, of women as mothers, of mothers as workers, of work as suitable for one gender and not for the other. The demand implies equal opportunity and thus equal responsibilities. It implies a childhood in which girls are rewarded for competence, risk taking, achievement, competitiveness and independence—just like boys. Equal pay for equal work means a revision in our expectations about women as equal workers and it involves the institutional arrangements to make them so.

"There is nothing small here," a feminist scholar observed. And indeed there was not.

FEMINISM IN ACTION

How feminists chose to enact their new commitment varied. For some the changes consisted largely of private actions—relationships renewed, careers resumed. Others, preferring public statements, used flamboyant methods to dramatize their newfound understanding of the subtle ways in which society defined and thereby confined women. As part of the confrontational politics of the 1960s, radical feminists picketed the 1968 Miss America contest, protesting the commercialization of beauty and our national preoccupation with bust size and "congeniality" rather than brain power and character. (In the process they were dubbed "bra burners," despite the fact that no bras were burned.) Activists pushed their way into all-male bars and restaurants as a way of forcing recognition of how these bastions of male exclusivity were themselves statements about "man's world/woman's place." They sat in at the offices of *Ladies' Home Journal* and *Newsweek* protesting the ways in which the media's depiction of women perpetuated old stereotypes at the expense of new realities. Others focused on abortion, mindful that mishandled illegal abortions claimed the lives of an estimated ten thousand women each year. Organizing "speakouts," they talked publicly about their own humiliating and dangerous encounters with the netherworld of abortion, thereby transforming this heretofore taboo and explosive subject into a matter of public debate and an issue of women's rights. Feminist lawyers, no less convinced that forcing a woman to bear a child against her will was a violation of her fundamental rights, used their legal skills to advance the cause of abortion law repeal in the courts.

Still other feminists chose to work for social change in a different fashion. They created nonsexist day care centers, wrote and published nonsexist children's books, monitored sex stereotyping in textbooks, lobbied for women's studies programs in high schools and colleges, and founded women's health clinics. They formed rape crisis centers so that rape victims could be treated by caring females; they agitated for more informed, sympathetic treatment on the part of hospital staffs, the police, and the courts. They created shelters for battered women, insisting that physical abuse was not a private family matter but a social problem requiring a public response. Feminist scholars used their talents to recover and interpret women's experience, opening new areas for research and in the process furthering change.

Feminist legislators, especially black Congresswoman Shirley Chisholm, sponsored legislation to extended minimum wage coverage to domestic workers. Other lawmakers sponsored bills, not always successful, to help housewives to secure some form of economic recognition for work performed, to enable women workers to obtain insurance that would give them the same degree of economic security afforded male coworkers, and to protect them from violence, which is the most blatant form of male oppression.

Trade union feminists, concerned with their dual identity as women and as wage workers, struggled to keep the needs of working women in the forefront. Black feminists, by their own admission "the most pressed down of us all," focused on issues of special concern to many minority women: media depictions of black women, racially coded credit policies, public housing, household workers' rights, and welfare and prison reform. Their sisters on the left in the Third World Women's Alliance, convinced that imperialism as well as sexism, racism, and classism oppressed women, organized demonstrations of solidarity with the women of Cuba and Vietnam. Actions, like voices, differed. Such diversity, however, was basic to the movement.

FEMINISM: THE PUBLIC IMPACT

In a society in which the media create instant awareness of social change, feminism burst upon the public consciousness with all the understated visibility of a fireworks display on the Fourth of July. The more radical elements of the movement, with their talk of test tube conception, the slavery of marriage, and the downfall of capitalism, might be dismissed out of hand. But it was hard to ignore 50,000 women parading down New York's Fifth Avenue, the presence of *Ms.* magazine on newsstands, feminist books on the best-seller lists, women in hard hats on construction jobs, or the government-mandated affirmative action programs that put them there. It was harder still to ignore the publicity that accompanied the appointment of women to the Carter cabinet, the enrollment of coeds in the nation's military academies, and the ordination of women to the ministry. A Harris poll of December 1975 reported that 63 percent of the women interviewed favored most changes designed to improve the status of women, although some were quick to insist that they were not "women's libbers." Black women, recognizing that equality is indivisi-

ble, viewed feminism even more positively than did their white counterparts, although the feminists among them preferred their own
organizations.

Evidence of changing views was everywhere. The list of organizations lined up in support of ratification of the Equal Rights Amendment included not only such avowedly feminist groups as NOW,
WEAL, and NWPC as well as longtime supporters such as the National Woman's Party and the National Federation of Business and
Professional Women's Clubs, but also well-established women's organizations such as the General Federation of Women's Clubs, the
American Association of University Women, the League of Women
Voters, the National Council of Jewish Women, the National Council
of Negro Women, and the YWCA.

Even more potent evidence that feminism had "arrived" was the
1977 International Women's Year Conference in Houston. Before
more than two thousand delegates from every state and territory in
the United States and twenty thousand guests, three First Ladies—
Lady Bird Johnson, Betty Ford, and Rosalynn Carter—endorsed the
Equal Rights Amendment and the goals of the Houston Conference,
their hands holding a lighted torch carried by women runners from
Seneca Falls where, in 1848, the famous Declaration of Sentiments
had been adopted. Confessing that she once thought the women's
movement belonged more to her daughters than to herself, Lady
Bird Johnson added, "I have come to know that it belongs to women
of all ages." Such an admission, like the presence of these three
women on the platform, proclaimed a message about feminists that
was boldly printed on balloons throughout the convention hall: "We
Are Everywhere."

No More Miss America (1968)

Robin Morgan and New York Radical Women

On September 7, 1968, Miss Kansas (Debra Dene Barnes) walked down the runway in swimsuit and high heels. She was crowned America's beauty queen as Bert Parks sang, "There she is, Miss America." Outside, about two hundred women picketed. They crowned a sheep Miss America (just as the Yippies had nominated a pig for president at Democratic National Convention protests in Chicago the previous month). They threw what they called "instruments of torture"—high heels, girdles, bras, false eyelashes, and curlers—into a large "Freedom Trashcan." Women carried signs: "Miss America Sells It," and "Miss America Is a Big Falsie."

The protesters had originally intended to burn the contents of the Freedom Trashcan. Atlantic City Police, however, were concerned that the wooden boardwalk might catch fire. No bras were burned that day, but shortly thereafter the mainstream press began to refer to bra-burnings when describing the movement for women's liberation. In part, the idea that women were burning their bras connected their protests to the draft card burnings by young men. It also added a titillating element to news stories about the women's liberation movement. By reducing the demands of radical women from social justice to sexual freedom alone, such accounts marginalized and trivialized their message.

In "No More Miss America," the organizers of the protest explained their goals. Why, when women faced so many obstacles in contemporary American society, did they choose to protest a beauty pageant? Why might that be an effective strategy? After the protest, some participants felt that they had made a mistake by seeming to target the contestants. "Miss America and all beautiful women came off as our enemies instead of as our sisters who suffer with us," one wrote. This document begins by inviting a broad range of women's groups to join the protest. Is this statement (and the protest that followed) truly inclusive? How well did the Radical Women reach out to their "sisters"?

On September 7th in Atlantic City, the Annual Miss America Pageant will again crown "your ideal." But this year, reality will liberate the contest auction-block in the guise of "genyooine" de-plasticized, breathing women. Women's Liberation Groups, black women, high-school and college women, women's peace groups, women's welfare and social-work groups, women's job-equality groups, pro–birth control and pro-abortion groups—women of every political persuasion—all are invited to join us in a day-long boardwalk-theater event, starting at 1:00 P.M. on the Boardwalk in front of Atlantic City's Convention Hall. We will protest the image of Miss America, an image that oppresses women in every area in which it purports to represent us. There will be: Picket Lines; Guerrilla Theater; Leafleting; Lobbying Visits to the contestants urging our sisters to reject the Pageant Farce and join us; a huge Freedom Trash Can (into which we will throw bras, girdles, curlers, false eyelashes, wigs, and representative issues of *Cosmopolitan, Ladies' Home Journal, Family Circle,* etc.—bring any such woman-garbage you have around the house); we will also announce a Boycott of all those commercial products related to the Pageant, and the day will end with a Women's Liberation rally at midnight when Miss America is crowned on live television. Lots of other surprises are being planned (come and add your own!) but we do not plan heavy disruptive tactics and so do not expect a bad police scene. It should be a groovy day on the Boardwalk in the sun with our sisters. In case of arrests, however, we plan to reject all male authority and demand to be busted by policewomen only. (In Atlantic City, women cops are not permitted to make arrests—dig that!)

Male chauvinist-reactionaries on this issue had best stay away, nor are male liberals welcome in the demonstrations. But sympathetic men can donate money as well as cars and drivers.

Male reporters will be refused interviews. We reject patronizing reportage. *Only newswomen will be recognized.*

THE TEN POINTS

We Protest:

1. *The Degrading Mindless-Boob-Girlie Symbol.* The Pageant contestants epitomize the roles we are all forced to play as women. The parade down the runway blares the metaphor of the 4-H Club county fair, where the nervous animals are judged for teeth, fleece, etc., and

where the best "specimen" gets the blue ribbon. So are women in our society forced daily to compete for male approval, enslaved by ludicrous "beauty" standards we ourselves are conditioned to take seriously.

2. *Racism with Roses.* Since its inception in 1921, the Pageant has not had one Black finalist, and this has not been for a lack of test-case contestants. There has never been a Puerto Rican, Alaskan, Hawaiian, or Mexican-American winner. Nor has there ever been a *true* Miss America—an American Indian.

3. *Miss America as Military Death Mascot.* The highlight of her reign each year is a cheerleader-tour of American troops abroad—last year she went to Vietnam to pep-talk our husbands, fathers, sons, and boyfriends into dying and killing with a better spirit. She personifies the "unstained patriotic American womanhood our boys are fighting for." The Living Bra and the Dead Soldier. We refuse to be used as Mascots for Murder.

4. *The Consumer Con-Game.* Miss America is a walking commercial for the Pageant's sponsors. Wind her up and she plugs your product on promotion tours and TV—all in an "honest, objective" endorsement. What a shill.

5. *Competition Rigged and Unrigged.* We deplore the encouragement of an American myth that oppresses men as well as women: the win-or-you're-worthless competitive disease. The "beauty contest" creates only one winner to be "used" and forty-nine losers who are "useless."

6. *The Woman as Pop Culture Obsolescent Theme.* Spindle, mutilate, and then discard tomorrow. What is so ignored as last year's Miss America? This only reflects the gospel of our society, according to Saint Male: women must be young, juicy, malleable—hence age discrimination and the cult of youth. And we women are brainwashed into believing this ourselves!

7. *The Unbeatable Madonna-Whore Combination.* Miss America and Playboy's centerfold are sisters over the skin. To win approval, we must be both sexy and wholesome, delicate but able to cope, demure yet titillatingly bitchy. Deviation of any sort brings, we are told, disaster: "You won't get a man!!"

8. *The Irrelevant Crown on the Throne of Mediocrity.* Miss America represents what women are supposed to be: unoffensive, bland, apolitical. If you are tall, short, over or under what weight The Man prescribes you should be, forget it. Personality, articulateness, intel-

ligence, commitment—unwise. Conformity is the key to the crown—
and, by extension, to success in our society.

    9. *Miss America as Dream Equivalent To*—? In this reputedly democ-
ratic society, where every little boy supposedly can grow up to be
President, what can every little girl hope to grow to be? Miss America.
That's where it's at. Real power to control our own lives is restricted
to men, while women get patronizing pseudo-power, an ermine cloak
and a bunch of flowers; men are judged by their actions, women by
their appearance.

    10. *Miss America as Big Sister Watching You.* The Pageant exercises
Thought Control, attempts to scar the Image onto our minds, to further make women oppressed and men oppressors; to enslave us all
the more in high-heeled, low-status roles; to inculcate false values in
young girls; to use women as beasts of buying; to seduce us to prostitute ourselves before our own oppression.

NO MORE MISS AMERICA

¡Soy Chicana Primero! (1971)

Enriqueta Longeaux Vasquez

*When the contemporary "second wave" feminist movement began, many of its
proponents argued that women shared "bonds of sisterhood" across race and
class lines. This position presumed that the common experience of being born
female in a patriarchal social structure transcended in importance and impact the very dissimilar experiences that divided women of different classes
and races or ethnicities. All too often, however, it was the experience of white,
college-educated women that was being used as a basis for generalization.
Controversy over this issue became a critical dividing point in the feminist
movement. Was gender in fact a more important source of opposition than
class or race? Did the mainstream feminist movement deny the validity of the
experiences of women of color, working-class women, or lesbians?*

*Women of color, especially, faced hard questions. Were women who em-
braced feminism betraying their brothers in the Black Power or Chicano movements, as some male leaders charged? Was feminism simply a divisive force
within the larger and more important struggle for racial justice? Were the
sources of women's oppression only external (white supremacy; capitalism), or
did they exist within African American and Chicano/a culture as well?*

*Like African American women, Chicanas struggled with these questions.
The cultural nationalism of the early Chicano movement glorified the traditional, family-oriented, and subordinate woman as a cornerstone of Chicanismo, and that made the issue of feminism particularly difficult. Was it sexist
oppression, or was it a central part of the culture around which the movement
was built? Feminism did grow strong within* el movimiento, *as Chicanas debated these issues and wrote platform statements of their own. But not all
women declared themselves feminists first. In the following article, Enriqueta
Longeaux Vasquez makes a powerful claim: "¡Soy Chicana Primero!", but at
the same time gives voice to the ambivalence and confusion many women felt
in this tumultuous and difficult time. How does Vasquez answer the question*

From *El Cuaderno*, Vol. 1, No. 2, 1971: pp. 17–22. Copyright © 1997. From
Chicana Feminist Thought, edited by Alma M. Garcia. Reproduced by permission of Routledge, Inc., part of the Taylor & Francis group.

above? How does her vision of "la familia de la Raza" differ from the goals of white radical and liberal feminists that appear in earlier documents in this section?

The Chicana today is becoming very serious and observant. On one hand she watches and evaluates the white women's liberation movement and on the other hand she hears the echoes of the "Chicano" movement, "Viva La Raza," the radical raps and rhetoric. For some it becomes fashionable, while for many of us it becomes survival itself. Some of our own Chicanas may be attracted to the white woman's liberation movement, but we really don't feel comfortable there. We want to be a Chicana *primero*, we want to walk hand in hand with the Chicano brothers, with our children, our *viejitos* [elders], our Familia de La Raza.

Then too we hear the whisper that if you are a radical Chicana you lose some of your femininity as a woman. And we question this as we look at the world struggles and know that this accusation as to femininity doesn't make sense. After all, we have seen the Vietnamese woman fight for survival with a gun in one hand and a child sucking on her breast on the other arm. She is certainly feminine. Our own people that fought in the revolution [Mexican Revolution of 1910] were brave and beautiful, even more human because of the struggles we fought for.

So we begin to see what our people are up against as we take very seriously our responsibility to our people, and to our children; as we sense the raging battle for cultural survival. We know that this means we have hardships to endure and we wish to strengthen our endurance in order that we may further strengthen the endurance of our coming generations. Nuestros hijos [our children] that are here and those that are yet to come. Our people would often say when they saw a strong spirited woman, *vienen de buen barro* (she comes from a good clay). Thus we now must make our children strong with the realization that they too, "vienen de buen barro."

When we discuss the Chicana, we have to be informed and know how to relate to the white women's liberation movement in order to come up with some of our own answers. This requires a basic analysis, not just a lot of static. Looking at the issues of the women's lib movement it is easy to relate to the struggle itself as a struggle. We can understand this because the Raza people are no newcomers to struggles, we can sympathize with many basic struggles. However, it is not our business as Chicanas to identify with the white women's liberation movement as a home base for working for our people. We couldn't lead our people there, could we? Remember Raza is our home ground and family and we have strong basic issues and grievances as *a people*.

In looking at women's lib we see issues that are relevant to that materialistic, competitive society of the Gringo. This society is only able to function through the sharpening of wits and development of the human instinct of rivalry. For this same dominant society and mentality to arrive at a point where there is now a white women's liberation movement is *dangerous* and *cruel* in that social structure has reached the point of fracture and competition of the male and female. This competitive thought pattern can lead to the conclusion that the man is the enemy and thus create conflict of the sexes.

Now we, Raza, are a colonized people (we have been a colony of New Spain, we have been Mexico, and have only a veneer of U.S. of A. rule—since 1848, just 100 years) and an oppressed people. We must have a clearer vision of our plight and certainly we can not blame our men for oppression of the woman. Our men are not the power structure that oppresses us as a whole. We know who stole our lands: we know who discriminates against us; we know who came in (our parents still remember), threw out our Spanish books and brought in new, fresh-written history books and we know who wrote those books for us to read. In other words, we know where we hurt and why. And even more important, we can not afford to fight within and among ourselves anymore, much less male pitted against female.

When our man is beaten down by society, in employment, housing or whatever, he should no longer come home and beat his wife and family; and when the woman doesn't have all she needs at home or she perhaps has a family to raise alone, she should not turn around and hate her husband or men for it. Both the man and the woman have to realize where we hurt, we have to figure out why we hurt and why these things are happening to us. And more important, through all of these sufferings and tests we have to receive and share strength from each other and together fight the social system that is destroying us and our families, that is eating away at us, little by little. And we have to build a social system of our own.

One of the greatest strengths of Raza is that of our understanding and obedience to nature and its balance and creation. This same awareness makes us realize that there can't be total fulfillment without the other. Life requires both in order for it to go on, to reproduce. This same basic need of each other is the total fulfillment of beauty in its most creative form. Now the reason that we discuss this is that we must also think of life generally, without the BAD and TABOO connotation that has been placed on our basic human functions. We can not allow negative attitudes in regard to our physical capacities, because when we allow this kind of control on ourselves, we are allowing ourselves to be castrated, controlled, and destroyed at our very basic, essential level. This can affect generations to come.

In working for our people, a woman becomes more and more capable; this Raza woman gains confidence, pride and strength and this strength is both personal and as a people. She gains independence, security, and more human strength because she is working in a familiar area, one in which she puts her *corazón* [heart] and love. When a man sees this kind of spirit and strength, the Chicana may be misunderstood as having lost her femininity. A man may misinterpret this and feel it as a threat. But he, too, must stop and evaluate this. He should not react against her because this is a great source of strength for him, for her, for our children, for the Familia de La Raza. This is the kind of spirit and strength that builds and holds firm La Familia de La Raza. This is love, my Raza; we can not compete with "el barro" that has held us firm for so long. This is total *respect* and equality in loving ourselves, our men, our elders, our children. It is this force that has allowed us to endure through the centuries and it is the strength that carries on the struggle of our people, the demand for justice.

With this kind of strength, how can we possibly question the femininity of the Chicana? Femininity is something more than the outer shell . . . stereotyping of women seems like a materialistic attitude. That kind of judgment should not be placed on our women.

Many Raza women relate to the earth [*La Tierra*]—we have worked in the fields, as migrants and campesinos. We are not afraid of the sweet smell of sweat from our bodies . . . our mother wearing coveralls with knee patches, thinning beets . . . who would dare to say this woman is not feminine?

The Chicana must not choose white woman's liberation. . . . To be a Chicana **PRIMERO** (first), to stand by her people, will make her stronger for the struggle and endurance of her people. The Raza movement needs "La Chicana" very, very much. Today we face a time of commitment, LA FAMILIA DE LA RAZA needs her for the building of our *nación* de Aztlán [our nation of Aztlán].

What's Wrong with "Equal Rights" for Women? (1972)

Phyllis Schlafly

By an overwhelming margin, Congress passed the Equal Rights Amendment (ERA) in early 1972 and submitted it to the states for ratification. Within a year thirty states had voted in support of adding the amendment to the Constitution. Then Phyllis Schlafly organized a "STOP ERA" campaign. Schlafly, mother of six children, believed that feminism was antifamily, antimarriage, and antichildren. But she was not simply a housewife who reacted against a threat to her chosen way of life. Schlafly was a lawyer with degrees from Harvard and Washington Universities who had risen to prominence in conservative circles after writing the bestselling book, A Choice Not an Echo, *in support of Barry Goldwater's 1964 presidential candidacy.*

To fight the ERA, Schlafly put together a coalition of fundamentalist and orthodox religious leaders, conservative businessmen, radical right groups, and a growing number of women who considered themselves antifeminist. Believing that the women's movement had gone too far, these women saw feminism as an enemy responsible for fostering sexual permissiveness, homosexuality, abortion, moral relativism, and what they called "secular humanism." They feared that the ERA would destroy the "special place" of women in the home, force them to fight in combat, and mandate unisex toilets. Because of their efforts, the deadline for ratifying the ERA passed in June 1982 with the amendment still three states short of adoption.

In "What's Wrong with 'Equal Rights' for Women?" Schlafly sets forth her case against the Equal Rights Amendment and the feminist movement. To whom might such an argument appeal, and why? Think about Jane Sherron De Hart's analysis and the radical feminist statement, "No More Miss America," as you read Schlafly's argument. Could feminists have attracted conservative women to their cause by using less inflammatory language and

From *Phyllis Schlafly Report* 5, no. 7 (February 1972). Reprinted by permission of the author.

showing more sensitivity to differences among American women, or were the
interests and goals of the two groups just too different?

Of all the classes of people who ever lived, the American woman is
the most privileged. We have the most rights and rewards, and the
fewest duties. Our unique status is the result of a fortunate combination of circumstances.

1. We have the immense good fortune to live in a civilization
which respects the family as the basic unit of society. This respect is
part and parcel of our laws and our customs. It is based on the fact of
life—which no legislation or agitation can erase—that women have
babies and men don't.

If you don't like this fundamental difference, you will have to take
up your complaint with God because He created us this way. The
fact that women, not men, have babies is not the fault of selfish
and domineering men, or of the establishment, or of any clique of
conspirators who want to oppress women. It's simply the way God
made us.

Our Judeo-Christian civilization has developed the law and custom
that, since women must bear the physical consequences of the sex
act, men must be required to bear the *other* consequences and pay in
other ways. These laws and customs decree that a man must carry his
share by physical protection and financial support of his children and
of the woman who bears his children, and also by a code of behavior
which benefits and protects both the woman and the children.

THE GREATEST ACHIEVEMENT OF WOMEN'S RIGHTS

This is accomplished by the institution of the family. Our respect for
the family as the basic unit of society, which is ingrained in the laws
and customs of our Judeo-Christian civilization, is the greatest single
achievement in the entire history of women's rights. It assures a
woman the most precious and important right of all—the right to
keep her own baby and to be supported and protected in the enjoy-
ment of watching her baby grow and develop.

The institution of the family is advantageous for women for many
reasons. After all, what do we want out of life? To love and be loved?
Mankind has not discovered a better nest for a lifetime of reciprocal

love. A sense of achievement? A man may search 30 to 40 years for accomplishment in his profession. A woman can enjoy real achievement when she is young—by having a baby. She can have the satisfaction of doing a job well—and being recognized for it.

Do we want financial security? We are fortunate to have the great legacy of Moses, the Ten Commandments, especially this one: "Honor thy father and thy mother that thy days may be long upon the land." Children are a woman's best social security—her best guarantee of social benefits such as old age pension, unemployment compensation, workman's compensation, and sick leave. The family gives a woman the physical, financial, and emotional security of the home—for all her life.

THE FINANCIAL BENEFITS OF CHIVALRY

2. The second reason why American women are a privileged group is that we are the beneficiaries of a tradition of special respect for women which dates from the Christian Age of Chivalry. The honor and respect paid to Mary, the Mother of Christ, resulted in all women, in effect, being put on a pedestal.

This respect for women is not just the lip service that politicians pay to "God, Motherhood, and the Flag." It is not—as some youthful agitators seem to think—just a matter of opening doors for women, seeing that they are seated first, carrying their bundles, and helping them in and out of automobiles. Such good manners are merely the superficial evidences of a total attitude toward women which expresses itself in many more tangible ways, such as money.

In other civilizations, such as the African and the American Indian, the men strut around wearing feathers and beads and hunting and fishing (great sport for men!), while the women do all the hard, tiresome drudgery including the tilling of the soil (if any is done), the hewing of wood, the making of fires, the carrying of water, as well as the cooking, sewing and caring for babies.

This is not the American way because we were lucky enough to inherit the traditions of the Age of Chivalry. In America, a man's first significant purchase is a diamond for his bride, and the largest financial investment of his life is a home for her to live in. American husbands work hours of overtime to buy a fur piece or other finery to keep their wives in fashion, and to pay premiums on their life insurance policies to provide for her comfort when she is a widow (benefits in which he can never share).

In the states which follow the English common law, a wife has a dower right in her husband's real estate which he cannot take away from her during life or by his will. A man cannot dispose of his real estate without his wife's signature. Any sale is subject to her 1/3 interest.

Women fare even better in the states which follow the Spanish and French community-property laws, such as California, Arizona, Texas and Louisiana. The basic philosophy of the Spanish/French law is that a wife's work in the home is just as valuable as a husband's work at his job. Therefore, in community-property states, a wife owns one-half of all the property and income her husband earns during their marriage, and he cannot take it away from her.

In Illinois, as a result of agitation by "equal rights" fanatics, the real-estate dower laws were repealed as of January 1, 1972. This means that in Illinois a husband can now sell the family home, spend the money on his girl friend or gamble it away, and his faithful wife of 30 years can no longer stop him. "Equal rights" fanatics have also deprived women in Illinois and in some other states of most of their basic common-law rights to recover damages for breach of promise to marry, seduction, criminal conversation, and alienation of affections.

THE REAL LIBERATION OF WOMEN

3. The third reason why American women are so well off is that the great American free enterprise system has produced remarkable inventors who have lifted the backbreaking "women's work" from our shoulders.

In other countries and in other eras, it was truly said that "Man may work from sun to sun, but woman's work is never done." Other women have labored every waking hour—preparing food on wood-burning stoves, making flour, baking bread in stone ovens, spinning yarn, making clothes, making soap, doing the laundry by hand, heating irons, making candles for light and fires for warmth, and trying to nurse their babies through illnesses without medical care.

The real liberation of women from the backbreaking drudgery of centuries is the American free enterprise system which stimulated inventive geniuses to pursue their talents—and we all reap the profits.

The great heroes of women's liberation are not the straggly-haired women on television talk shows and picket lines, but Thomas Edison who brought the miracle of electricity to our homes to give light and to run all those labor-saving devices—the equivalent, perhaps, of a half-dozen household servants for every middle-class American woman. Or Elias Howe who gave us the sewing machine which resulted in such an abundance of readymade clothing. Or Clarence Birdseye who invented the process for freezing foods. Or Henry Ford, who mass-produced the automobile so that it is within the price-range of every American, man or woman.

A major occupation of women in other countries is doing their daily shopping for food, which requires carrying their own containers and standing in line at dozens of small shops. They buy only small portions because they can't carry very much and have no refrigerator or freezer to keep a surplus anyway. Our American free enterprise system has given us the gigantic food and packaging industry and beautiful supermarkets, which provide an endless variety of foods, prepackaged for easy carrying and a minimum of waiting. In America, women have the freedom from the slavery of standing in line for daily food.

Thus, household duties have been reduced to only a few hours a day, leaving the American woman with plenty of time to moonlight. She can take a full or part-time paying job, or she can indulge to her heart's content in a tremendous selection of interesting educational or cultural or homemaking activities.

THE FRAUD OF THE EQUAL RIGHTS AMENDMENT

In the last couple of years, a noisy movement has sprung up agitating for "women's rights." Suddenly, everywhere we are afflicted with aggressive females on television talk shows yapping about how mistreated American women are, suggesting that marriage has put us in some kind of "slavery," that housework is menial and degrading, and—perish the thought—that women are discriminated against. New "women's liberation" organizations are popping up, agitating and demonstrating, serving demands on public officials, getting wide press coverage always, and purporting to speak for some 100,000,000 American women.

It's time to set the record straight. The claim that American women are downtrodden and unfairly treated is the fraud of the century. The truth is that American women never had it so good. Why should we lower ourselves to "equal rights" when we already have the status of special privilege?

The proposed Equal Rights Amendment states: "Equality of rights under the law shall not be denied or abridged by the United States or by any state on account of sex." So what's wrong with that? Well, here are a few examples of what's wrong with it.

This Amendment will absolutely and positively make women subject to the draft. Why any woman would support such a ridiculous and un-American proposal as this is beyond comprehension. Why any Congressman who had any regard for his wife, sister, or daughter would support such a proposition is just as hard to understand. Foxholes are bad enough for men, but they certainly are *not* the place for women—and we should reject any proposal which would put them there in the name of "equal rights."

It is amusing to watch the semantic chicanery of the advocates of the Equal Rights Amendment when confronted with this issue of the draft. They evade, they sidestep, they try to muddy up the issue, but they cannot deny that the Equal Rights Amendment will positively make women subject to the draft. Congresswoman Margaret Heckler's answer to this question was, Don't worry, it will take two years for the Equal Rights Amendment to go into effect, and we can rely on President Nixon to end the Vietnam War before then!

Literature distributed by Equal Rights Amendment supporters confirms that "under the Amendment a draft law which applied to men would apply also to women." The Equal Rights literature argues that this would be good for women so they can achieve their "equal rights" in securing veterans' benefits.

Another bad effect of the Equal Rights Amendment is that it will abolish a woman's right to child support and alimony, and substitute what the women's libbers think is a more "equal" policy, that "such decisions should be within the discretion of the Court and should be made on the economic situation and need of the parties in the case."

Under present American laws, the man is *always* required to support his wife and each child he caused to be brought into the world. Why should women abandon these good laws—by trading them for something so nebulous and uncertain as the "discretion of the Court"?

The law now requires a husband to support his wife as best as his financial situation permits, but a wife is not required to support her husband (unless he is about to become a public charge). A husband cannot demand that his wife go to work to help pay for family expenses. He has the duty of financial support under our laws and customs. Why should we abandon these mandatory wife-support and child-support laws so that a wife would have an "equal" obligation to take a job?

By law and custom in America, in case of divorce, the mother always is given custody of her children unless there is overwhelming evidence of mistreatment, neglect or bad character. This is our special privilege because of the high rank that is placed on motherhood in our society. Do women really want to give up this special privilege and lower themselves to "equal rights," so that the mother gets one child and the father gets the other? I think not. . . .

WHAT "WOMEN'S LIB" REALLY MEANS

Many women are under the mistaken impression that "women's lib" means more job employment opportunities for women, equal pay for equal work, appointments of women to high positions, admitting more women to medical schools, and other desirable objectives which all women favor. We all support these purposes, as well as any necessary legislation which would bring them about.

But all this is only a sweet syrup which covers the deadly poison masquerading as "women's lib." The women's libbers are radicals who are waging a total assault on the family, on marriage, and on children. Don't take my word for it—read their own literature and prove to yourself what these characters are trying to do.

The most pretentious of the women's liberation magazines is called *Ms.*, and subtitled "The New Magazine for Women," with Gloria Steinem listed as president and secretary.

Reading the Spring 1972 issue of *Ms.* gives a good understanding of women's lib, and the people who promote it. It is anti-family, anti-children, and pro-abortion. It is a series of sharp-tongued, high-pitched whining complaints by unmarried women. They view the home as a prison, and the wife and mother as a slave. To these women's libbers, marriage means dirty dishes and dirty laundry. One article lauds a woman's refusal to carry up the family laundry as "an act of extreme courage." Another tells how satisfying it is to be a lesbian.

The women's libbers don't understand that most women want to be wife, mother and homemaker—and are happy in that role. The women's libbers actively resent the mother who stays at home with her children and likes it that way. The principal purpose of *Ms.*'s shrill tirade is to sow seeds of discontent among happy, married women so that *all* women can be unhappy in some new sisterhood of frustrated togetherness.

Obviously intrigued by the 170 clauses of exemptions from marital duties given to Jackie Kennedy, and the special burdens imposed on Aristotle Onassis, in the pre-marriage contract they signed, *Ms.* recommends two women's lib marriage contracts. The "utopian marriage contract" has a clause on "sexual rights and freedoms" which approves "arrangements such as having Tuesdays off from one another," and the husband giving "his consent to abortion in advance."

The "Shulmans' marriage agreement" includes such petty provisions as "wife strips beds, husband remakes them," and "Husband does dishes on Tuesday, Thursday and Sunday. Wife does Monday, Wednesday and Saturday, Friday is split . . ." If the baby cries in the night, the chore of "handling" the baby is assigned as follows: "Husband does Tuesday, Thursday and Sunday. Wife does Monday, Wednesday and Saturday, Friday is split . . ." Presumably, if the baby cries for his mother on Tuesday night, he would be informed that the marriage contract prohibits her from answering.

Of course, it is possible, in such a loveless home, that the baby would never call for his mother at all.

Who put up the money to launch this 130-page slick-paper assault on the family and motherhood? A count of the advertisements in *Ms.* shows that the principal financial backer is the liquor industry. There are 26 liquor ads in this one initial issue. Of these, 13 are expensive full-page color ads, as opposed to only 18 full-page ads from all other sources combined, most of which are in the cheaper black-and-white.

Another women's lib magazine, called *Women*, tells the American woman that she is a prisoner in the "solitary confinement" and "isolation" of marriage. The magazine promises that it will provide women with "escape from isolation . . . release from boredom," and that it will "break the barriers . . . that separate wife, mistress and secretary . . . heterosexual women and homosexual women."

These women's libbers do, indeed, intend to "break the barriers" of the Ten Commandments, and the sanctity of the family. It hasn't occurred to them that a woman's best "escape from isolation and boredom" is—not a magazine subscription to boost her "stifled ego"—but a husband and children who love her.

The first issue of *Women* contains 68 pages of such proposals as "The BITCH Manifesto," which promotes the line that "Bitch is Beautiful and that we have nothing to lose. Nothing whatsoever." Another article promotes an organization called W.I.T.C.H. (Women's International Terrorist Conspiracy from Hell), "an action arm of Women's Liberation."

In intellectual circles, a New York University professor named Warren T. Farrell has provided the rationale for why men should support women's lib. When his speech to the American Political Science Association Convention is stripped of its egghead verbiage, his argument is that men should eagerly look forward to the day when they can enjoy free sex and not have to pay for it. The husband will no longer be "saddled with the tremendous guilt feelings" when he leaves his wife with nothing after she has given him her best years. If a husband loses his job, he will no longer feel compelled to take any job to support his family. A husband can go "out with the boys" to have a drink without feeling guilty. Alimony will be eliminated.

WOMEN'S LIBBERS DO *NOT* SPEAK FOR US

The "women's lib" movement is *not* an honest effort to secure better jobs for women who want or need to work outside the home. This is just the superficial sweet-talk to win broad support for a radical "movement." Women's lib is a total assault on the role of the American woman as wife and mother, and on the family as the basic unit of society.

Women's libbers are trying to make wives and mothers unhappy with their career, make them feel that they are "second-class citizens" and "abject slaves." Women's libbers are promoting free sex instead of the "slavery" of marriage. They are promoting Federal "day-care centers" for babies instead of homes. They are promoting abortions instead of families.

Why should we trade in our special privileges and honored status for the alleged advantage of working in an office or assembly line? Most women would rather cuddle a baby than a typewriter or factory machine. Most women find that it is easier to get along with a husband than a foreman or office manager. Offices and factories require many more menial and repetitive chores than washing dishes and ironing shirts.

Women's libbers do *not* speak for the majority of American women. American women do *not* want to be liberated from husbands and children. We do *not* want to trade our birthright of the special privileges of American women—for the mess of pottage called the Equal Rights Amendment.

Modern technology and opportunity have not discovered any nobler or more satisfying or more creative career for a woman than marriage and motherhood. The wonderful advantage that American women have is that we can have all the rewards of that number-one career, and still moonlight with a second one to suit our intellectual, cultural, or financial tastes or needs.

And why should the men acquiesce in a system which gives preferential rights and lighter duties to women? In return, the men get the pearl of great price: a happy home, a faithful wife, and children they adore.

If the women's libbers want to reject marriage and motherhood, it's a free country and that is their choice. But let's not permit these women's libbers to get away with pretending to speak for the rest of us. Let's not permit this tiny minority to degrade the role that most women prefer. Let's not let these women's libbers deprive wives and mothers of the rights we now possess.

Tell your Senators NOW that you want them to vote NO on the Equal Rights Amendment. Tell your television and radio stations that you want equal time to present the case FOR marriage and motherhood.

Roe v. Wade (1973)

Justice Harry A. Blackmun

Few Supreme Court decisions have provoked more emotional response or societal polarization than that which ensued after the judges handed down their 7–2 ruling in Roe v. Wade *(1973). The decision held that women had an absolute right to choose an abortion through the first trimester (months one through three) of their pregnancies. Pointing out that state laws prohibiting abortions were a relatively late creation (in the second half of the nineteenth century), the majority opinion, written by Nixon appointee Justice Harry Blackmun, concluded that there was no evidence that the founders of the country meant to include unborn fetuses in their constitutional definition of "personhood." Whether or not human life began at conception or at some undefined later point, the majority reasoned, was a religious question, not a legal certitude. In that circumstance, the judges decided, a woman's right to privacy in controlling her own reproductive life took priority, at least until the health and viability of the fetus gave the state a legitimate right to intervene. The dissenting judges, on the other hand, argued that such reasoning valued "the convenience, whim or caprice of the putative mother more than the life or potential life of the fetus."*

In the years since 1973, disputes over this decision have animated profound—and intense—political debate. The Roman Catholic Church hierarchy has adamantly opposed the pro-choice position (although many Roman Catholic parishioners disagree with the church); antifeminists and the "new right" have used a "pro-life" position to rally support for their political agenda. The Supreme Court itself has modified its position several times, permitting a series of state regulations to limit the right to abortion; yet at the beginning of the new millennium, the core of the Roe v. Wade *decision remained intact. The brief decision that follows concisely summarizes the issues, even as it raises far more questions than it answers.*

MR. JUSTICE [HARRY A.] BLACKMUN DELIVERED THE OPINION OF THE COURT. . . .

We forthwith acknowledge our awareness of the sensitive and emotional nature of the abortion controversy, of the vigorous opposing views, even among physicians, and of the deep and seemingly absolute convictions that the subject inspires. One's philosophy, one's experiences, one's exposure to the raw edges of human existence, one's religious training, one's attitudes toward life and family and their values, and the moral standards one establishes and seeks to observe, are all likely to influence and to color one's thinking and conclusions about abortion. . . .

The Texas statutes that concern us here are Arts. 1191–1194 and 1196 of the State's Penal Code. These make it a crime to "procure an abortion," as therein defined, or to attempt one, except with respect to "an abortion procured or attempted by medical advice for the purpose of saving the life of the mother." Similar statutes are in existence in a majority of the States. . . .

Jane Roe, a single woman who was residing in Dallas County, Texas, instituted this federal action in March 1970 against the District Attorney of the county. She sought a declaratory judgment that the Texas criminal abortion statutes were unconstitutional on their face, and an injunction restraining the defendant from enforcing the statutes.

Roe alleged that she was unmarried and pregnant; that she wished to terminate her pregnancy by an abortion "performed by a competent, licensed physician, under safe, clinical conditions"; that she was unable to get a "legal" abortion in Texas because her life did not appear to be threatened by the continuation of her pregnancy; and that she could not afford to travel to another jurisdiction in order to secure a legal abortion under safe conditions. She claimed that the Texas statutes were unconstitutionally vague and that they abridged her right of personal privacy, protected by the First, Fourth, Fifth, Ninth, and Fourteenth Amendments. By an amendment to her complaint Roe purported to sue "on behalf of herself and all other women" similarly situated. . . .

The principal thrust of appellant's attack on the Texas statutes is that they improperly invade a right, said to be possessed by the pregnant woman, to choose to terminate her pregnancy. Appellant would discover this right in the concept of personal "liberty" embodied in the Fourteenth Amendment's Due Process Clause; or in personal, marital, familial, and sexual privacy said to be protected by the Bill of

Rights . . . or among those rights reserved to the people by the Ninth Amendment, . . .

It perhaps is not generally appreciated that the restrictive criminal abortion laws in effect in a majority of States today are of relatively recent vintage. Those laws, generally proscribing abortion or its attempt at any time during pregnancy except when necessary to preserve the pregnant woman's life, are not of ancient or even of common-law origin. Instead, they derive from statutory changes effected, for the most part, in the latter half of the nineteenth century. . . . It is undisputed that at common law, abortion performed *before* "quickening"—the first recognizable movement of the fetus *in utero,* appearing usually from the sixteenth to the eighteenth week of pregnancy—was not an indictable offense. . . . In this country, the law in effect in all but a few States until mid-nineteenth century was the pre-existing English common law. . . .

Gradually, in the middle and late nineteenth century the quickening distinction disappeared from the statutory law of most States and the degree of the offense and the penalties were increased. By the end of the 1950s, a large majority of the jurisdictions banned abortion, however and whenever performed, unless done to save or preserve the life of the mother. . . .

It is thus apparent that at common law, at the time of the adoption of our Constitution, and throughout the major portion of the nineteenth century, abortion was viewed with less disfavor than under most American statutes currently in effect. Phrasing it another way, a woman enjoyed a substantially broader right to terminate a pregnancy than she does in most States today. At least with respect to the early stage of pregnancy, and very possibly without such a limitation, the opportunity to make this choice was present in this country well into the nineteenth century. Even later, the law continued for some time to treat less punitively an abortion procured in early pregnancy. . . .

The Constitution does not explicitly mention any right of privacy. In a line of decisions, however, . . . the Court has recognized that a right of personal privacy, or a guarantee of certain areas or zones of privacy, does exist under the Constitution. . . . This right of privacy, whether it be founded in the Fourteenth Amendment's concept of personal liberty and restrictions upon state action, as we feel it is, or, as the District Court determined, in the Ninth Amendment's reservation of rights to the people, is broad enough to encompass a woman's decision whether or not to terminate her pregnancy. . . .

We . . . conclude that the right of personal privacy includes the abortion decision, but that this right is not unqualified and must be considered against important state interest in regulation. . . .

In view of all this, we do not agree that, by adopting one theory of life, Texas may override the rights of the pregnant woman that are at stake. We repeat, however, that the State does have an important and legitimate interest in preserving and protecting the health of the pregnant woman, whether she be a resident of the State or a nonresident who seeks medical consultation and treatment there, and that it has still *another* important and legitimate interest in protecting the potentiality of human life. These interests are separate and distinct. Each grows in substantiality as the woman approaches term and, at a point during pregnancy, each becomes "compelling."

With respect to the State's important and legitimate interest in the health of the mother, the "compelling" point, in the light of present medical knowledge, is at approximately the end of the first trimester. This is so because of the now-established medical fact . . . that until the end of the first trimester mortality in abortion may be less than mortality in normal childbirth. It follows that, from and after this point, a State may regulate the abortion procedure to the extent that the regulation reasonably relates to the preservation and protection of maternal health. . . .

This means, on the other hand, that, for the period of pregnancy prior to this "compelling" point, the attending physician, in consultation with his patient, is free to determine, without regulation by the State, that, in his medical judgment, the patient's pregnancy should be terminated. If that decision is reached, the judgment may be effectuated by an abortion free of interference by the State.

With respect to the State's important and legitimate interest in potential life, the "compelling" point is at viability. This is so because the fetus then presumably has the capability of meaningful life outside the mother's womb. State regulation protective of fetal life after viability thus has both logical and biological justifications. If the State is interested in protecting fetal life after viability, it may go so far as to proscribe abortion during that period, except when it is necessary to preserve the life or health of the mother.

Measured against these standards, Art. 1196 of the Texas Penal Code, in restricting legal abortions to those "procured or attempted by medical advice for the purpose of saving the life of the mother," sweeps too broadly. The statute makes no distinction between abortions performed early in pregnancy and those performed later, and it limits to a single reason, "saving" the mother's life, the legal justification for the procedure. The statute, therefore, cannot survive the constitutional attack made upon it here.

Gay Is Good (1970)

Martha Shelley

The Gay Liberation movement had its symbolic beginning on June 27, 1969, when New York police raided the Stonewall Inn, a gay bar in Greenwich Village. The New York State Liquor Authority regulation that no bar could have more than three homosexual patrons at a given time gave police the authority to raid bars frequented by homosexuals, and patrons of these bars risked arrest. This time, however, the police met unexpected resistance. As the Village Voice *described the scene in language that suggests the prejudices of the time, "Limp wrists were forgotten. Beer cans and bottles were heaved at the windows and a rain of coins descended on the cops. . . ." The next day, the slogan "Gay Power" appeared on walls throughout the neighborhood, and that night gay men and women filled the streets, chanting "Gay Power."*

Well before Stonewall, gay men and lesbians had created vibrant, if often secret, communities. "Homophile" organizations worked to end discrimination against homosexuals—but kept membership lists confidential. Though the Kinsey Report had suggested that approximately 10 percent of American men were homosexual, there were very few openly gay men and women in the United States. Even the suspicion of homosexuality carried the risk of expulsion from university, loss of job, and social ostracism. While gay men and lesbians arguably had much to gain by "coming out of the closet," they also had much to lose. Building a social movement in this situation was a challenge: unlike Black Americans or women, who were (usually) easily identified as such whether or not they wished to be, gay men and lesbians had to choose to be so identified.

The Gay Liberation movement that emerged in the summer of 1969, though not the first movement for the rights of homosexuals, was fundamentally a creation of the 1960s. It grew in part from the social changes that contemporaries called "the sexual revolution," and was shaped by struggles and victories of the Civil Rights and Black Power movements and by the tactics of protest developed in the latter half of the 1960s. Unlike the homophile movement, which sought assimilation and "tolerance," the Gay Liberation movement proclaimed "Gay

Reprinted by permission of the author.

*Power" and sought the transformation of society. By 1973 there were almost
eight hundred openly gay organizations in the United States.*

Martha Shelley wrote the following article for the underground paper The
Rat *in 1970. The title came from an editor at the paper; she said later that she
would have made a stronger, angrier, statement in her title. Notice how fundamental the critique of "traditional" gender roles is to Shelley's call to revolution. Keep this article in mind when reading Part 6: How does the concept of
"liberation" link the radical social movements of the 1960s and early 1970s?*

Look out, straights. Here comes the Gay Liberation Front, springing
up like warts all over the bland face of Amerika, causing shudders of
indigestion in the delicately balanced bowels of the movement. Here
come the gays, marching with six-foot banners to Washington and
embarrassing the liberals, taking over Mayor Alioto's office, staining
the good names of War Resister's League and Women's Liberation by
refusing to pass for straight anymore.

We've got chapters in New York, San Francisco, San Jose, Los Angeles, Minneapolis, Philadelphia, Wisconsin, Detroit, and I hear maybe
even in Dallas. We're gonna make our own revolution because we're
sick of revolutionary posters which depict straight he-man types and
earth mothers, with guns and babies. We're sick of the Panthers
lumping us together with the capitalists in their term of universal
contempt—"faggot."

And I am personally sick of liberals who say they don't care who
sleeps with whom, it's what you do outside of bed that counts. This is
what homosexuals have been trying to get straights to understand for
years. Well, it's too late for liberalism. Because what I do outside of
bed may have nothing to do with what I do inside—but my consciousness is branded, is permeated with homosexuality. For years I have
been branded with your label for me. The result is that when I am
among gays or in bed with another woman, I am a person, not a lesbian. When I am observable to the straight world, I become gay. You
are my litmus paper.

We want something more now, something more than the tolerance
you never gave us. But to understand that, you must understand who
we are.

We are the extrusions of your unconscious mind—your worst fears
made flesh. From the beautiful boys at Cherry Grove to the aging
queers in the uptown bars, the taxi-driving dykes to the lesbian fash-

ion models, the hookers (male and female) on 42nd Street, the leather lovers . . . and the very ordinary very un-lurid gays . . . we are the sort of people everyone was taught to despise—and now we are shaking off the chains of self-hatred and marching on your citadels of repression.

Liberalism isn't good enough for us. And we are just beginning to discover it. Your friendly smile of acceptance—from the safe position of heterosexuality—isn't enough. As long as you cherish that secret belief that you are a little better because you sleep with the opposite sex, you are still asleep in your cradle and we will be the nightmare that awakens you.

We are women and men who, from the time of our earliest memories, have been in revolt against the sex-role structure and nuclear family structure. The roles we have played amongst ourselves, the self-deceit, the compromises and the subterfuges—these have never totally obscured the fact that we exist outside the traditional structure—and our existence threatens it.

Understand this—that the worst part of being a homosexual is having to keep it secret. Not the occasional murders by police or teenage queer-beaters, not the loss of jobs or expulsion from schools or dishonorable discharges—but the daily knowledge that what you are is so awful that it cannot be revealed. The violence against us is sporadic. Most of us are not affected. But the internal violence of being made to carry—or choosing to carry—the load of your straight society's unconscious guilt—this is what tears us apart, what makes us want to stand up in the offices, in the factories and schools and shout out our true identities.

We were rebels from our earliest days—somewhere, maybe just about the time we started to go to school, we rejected straight society—unconsciously. Then, later, society rejected us, as we came into full bloom. The homosexuals who hide, who play it straight or pretend that the issue of homosexuality is unimportant, are only hiding the truth from themselves. They are trying to become part of a society that they rejected instinctively when they were five years old, to pretend that it is the result of heredity, or a bad mother, or anything but a gut reaction of nausea against the roles forced on us.

If you are homosexual, and you get tired of waiting around for the liberals to repeal the sodomy laws, and begin to dig yourself—and get angry—you are on your way to being a radical. Get in touch with the reasons that made you reject straight society as a kid (remembering my own revulsion against the vacant women drifting in and out of supermarkets, vowing never to live like them) and realize that you were right. Straight roles stink.

And you straights—look down the street, at the person whose sex is not readily apparent. Are you uneasy? Or are you made more uneasy by the stereotype gay, the flaming faggot or diesel dyke? Or most uneasy by the friend you thought was straight—and isn't? We want you to be uneasy, be a little less comfortable in your straight roles. And to make you uneasy, we behave outrageously—even though we pay a heavy price for it—and our outrageous behavior comes out of our rage.

But what is strange to you is natural to us. Let me illustrate. The Gay Liberation Front (GLF) "liberates" a gay bar for the evening. We come in. The people already there are seated quietly at the bar. Two or three couples are dancing. It's a down place. And the GLF takes over. Men dance with men, women with women, men with women, everyone in circles. No roles. You ever see that at a straight party? Not men with men—this is particularly verboten. No, and you're not likely to, while the gays in the movement are still passing for straight in order to keep up the good names of their organizations or to keep up the pretense that they are acceptable—and to have to get out of the organization they worked so hard for.

True, some gays play the same role games among themselves that straights do. Isn't every minority group fucked over by the values of the majority culture? But the really important thing about being gay is that you are forced to notice how much sex role differentiation is pure artifice, is nothing but a game.

Once I dressed up for an American Civil Liberties Union benefit. I wore a black lace dress, heels, elaborate hairdo and makeup. And felt like—a drag queen. Not like a woman—I am a woman every day of my life—but like the ultimate in artifice, a woman posing as a drag queen.

The roles are beginning to wear thin. The makeup is cracking. The roles—breadwinner, little wife, screaming fag, bulldyke, James Bond—are the cardboard characters we are always trying to fit into, as if being human and spontaneous were so horrible that we each have to pick on a character out of a third rate novel and try to cut ourselves down to its size. And you cut off your homosexuality—and we cut off our heterosexuality.

Back to the main difference between us. We gays are separate from you—we are alien. You have managed to drive your own homosexuality down under the skin of your mind—and to drive us down and out into the gutter of self-contempt. We, ever since we became aware of being gay, have each day been forced to internalize the labels: "I am a pervert, a dyke, a fag, etc." And the days pass, until we look at you out of our homosexual bodies, bodies that have become synonymous and consubstantial with homosexuality, bodies that are no longer bodies but labels; and sometimes we wish we were like you, sometimes we wonder how you can stand yourselves.

It's difficult for me to understand how you can dig each other as human beings—in a man-woman relationship—how you can relate to each other in spite of your sex roles. It must be awfully difficult to talk to each other, when the woman is trained to repress what the man is trained to express, and vice-versa. Do straight men and women talk to each other? Or does the man talk and the woman nod approvingly? Is love possible between heterosexuals; or is it all a case of women posing as nymphs, earth mothers, sex objects, what-have-you, and men writing the poetry of romantic illusions to these walking stereotypes?

I tell you, the function of a homosexual is to make you uneasy.

And now I will tell you what we want, we radical homosexuals: not for you to tolerate us, or to accept us, but to understand us. And this you can do only by becoming one of us. We want to reach the homosexuals entombed in you, to liberate our brothers and sisters, locked in the prisons of your skulls.

We want you to understand what it is to be our kind of outcast—but also to understand our kind of love, to hunger for your own sex. Because unless you understand this, you will continue to look at us with uncomprehending eyes, fake liberal smiles; you will be incapable of loving us.

We will never go straight until you go gay. As long as you divide yourselves, we will be divided from you—separated by a mirror trick of your mind. We will no longer allow you to drop us—or the homosexuals in yourselves—into the reject bin; labelled sick, childish or perverted. And because we will not wait, your awakening may be a rude and bloody one. It's your choice. You will never be rid of us, because we reproduce ourselves out of your bodies—and out of your minds. We are one with you.

Sexual Revolution(s)

Beth Bailey

It is hard for contemporary college students to imagine what life was like for students in the early 1960s. Women were subject to rigid curfew systems called parietals—but men weren't. Despite the existence of The Pill, very few doctors would prescribe it to unmarried girls or women. Abortion was illegal. A woman who had "premarital" sex was, in the eyes of much of American society, "ruined." Homosexual sex was grounds for expulsion. A great deal has changed. Is that evidence of a revolution?

In "Sexual Revolution(s)," historian Beth Bailey argues that the answer to that question depends upon how one defines "revolution." Focusing on the early years of "revolution" in the 1960s, she argues that there was no single sexual revolution, but rather a set of complicated and contradictory movements that people at the time called "the" sexual revolution. Do you agree with her argument that the most modest strand of the "revolution" was probably the most revolutionary? After reading both this article and the previous pieces on women's liberation, why do you think that so many Americans conflated women's liberation and sexual revolution? What, if anything, do the two broad movements have in common? And after reading the previous document, "Gay Is Good," consider whether the Gay Liberation movement that began in 1969 owed more to the movements for women's liberation or to the sexual revolution of the 1960s.

In 1957 America's favorite TV couple, the safely married Ricky and Lucy Ricardo, slept in twin beds. Having beds at all was probably progressive—as late as 1962 June and Ward Cleaver did not even have a bedroom. Elvis's pelvis was censored in each of his three appearances on the "Ed Sullivan Show" in 1956, leaving his oddly disembodied upper torso and head thrashing about on the TV screen. But the sensuality in his eyes, his lips, his lyrics was unmistakable, and his genitals were all the more important in their absence. There was, likewise, no mistaking Mick Jagger's meaning when he grimaced ostentatiously and sang "Let's spend some *time* together" on "Ed Sullivan" in 1967. Much of the audience knew that the line was really "Let's spend the night together," and the rest quickly got the idea. The viewing public could see absence and hear silence—and therein lay the seeds of the sexual revolution.

What we call the sexual revolution grew from these tensions between public and private—not only from tensions manifest in public culture, but also from tensions between private behaviors and the public rules and ideologies that were meant to govern behavior. By the 1950s the gulf between private acts and public norms was often quite wide—and the distance was crucial. People had sex outside of marriage, but very, very few acknowledged that publicly. A woman who married the only man with whom she had had premarital sex still worried years later: "I was afraid someone might have learned that we had intercourse before marriage and I'd be disgraced." The consequences, however, were not just psychological. Young women (and sometimes men) discovered to be having premarital sex were routinely expelled from school or college; gay men risked jail for engaging in consensual sex. There were real penalties for sexual misconduct, and while many deviated from the sexual orthodoxy of the day, all but a few did so furtively, careful not to get "caught."

Few episodes demonstrate the tensions between the public and private dimensions of sexuality in midcentury America better than the furor that surrounded the publication of the studies of sexual behavior collectively referred to as the "Kinsey Reports." . . .

Much of the reaction to Kinsey hinge[d] on the distance between the "overt" and the "covert." People were shocked to learn how many men and women were doing what they were not supposed to be doing. Kinsey found that 50 percent of the women in his sample had had premarital sex (even though between 80 percent and 89 percent of his sample disapproved of premarital sex on "moral grounds"), that 61 percent of college-educated men and 84 percent of men who had completed only high school had had premarital sex, that over one-third of the married women in the sample had "engaged in petting" with more than ten different men, that approximately half of the married couples had engaged in "oral stimulation" of both male and female genitalia, and that at least 37 percent of American men had had "some homosexual experience" during their lifetimes. . . .

Looking back to the century's midpoint, it is clear that the coherence of (to use Kinsey's terms) covert and overt sexual cultures was strained beyond repair. The sexual revolution of the 1960s emerged from these tensions, and to that extent it was not revolutionary, but evolutionary. As much as anything else, we see the overt coming to terms with the covert. But the revision of revolution to evolution would miss a crucial point. It is not historians who have labeled these changes "the sexual revolution"—it was people at the time, those who participated and those who watched. And they called it that before much of what we would see as revolutionary really emerged—before gay liberation and the women's movement and Alex Comfort's *The Joy of Sex* (1972) and "promiscuity" and singles' bars. The term was in general use by 1963—earlier than one might expect.

To make any sense of the sexual revolution, we have to pay attention to the label people gave it. Revolutions, for good or ill, are moments of danger. It matters that a metaphor of revolution gave structure to the myriad of changes taking place in American society. The changes in sexual mores and behaviors could as easily have been cast as evolutionary—but they were not.

Looking back, the question of whether or not the sexual revolution was revolutionary is not easy to answer; it partly depends on one's political (defined broadly) position. Part of the trouble, though, is that the sexual revolution was not one movement. It was instead a set of movements, movements that were closely linked, even intertwined, but which often made uneasy bedfellows. Here I hope to do some untangling, laying out three of the most important strands of the sexual revolution and showing their historical origins, continuities, and disruptions.

The first strand, which transcended youth, might be cast as both evolutionary and revolutionary. Throughout the twentieth century, picking up speed in the 1920s, the 1940s, and the 1960s, we have seen a sexualization of America's culture. Sexual images have become more and more a part of public life, and sex—or more accurately, the representation of sex—is used to great effect in a marketplace that offers Americans fulfillment through consumption. Although the blatancy of today's sexual images would be shocking to someone transported from an earlier era, such representations developed gradually and generally did not challenge more "traditional" understandings of sex and of men's and women's respective roles in sex or in society.

The second strand was the most modest in aspect but perhaps the most revolutionary in implication. In the 1960s and early 1970s an increasing number of young people began to live together "without benefit of matrimony," as the phrase went at the time. While sex was usually a part of the relationship (and probably a more important part than most people acknowledged), few called on concepts of "free love" or "pleasure" but instead used words like "honesty," "commitment," and "family." Many of the young people who lived together could have passed for young marrieds and in that sense were pursuing fairly traditional arrangements. At the same time, self-consciously or not, they challenged the tattered remnants of a Victorian epistemological and ideological system that still, in the early 1960s, fundamentally structured the public sexual mores of the American middle class.

The third strand was more self-consciously revolutionary, as sex was *actively claimed* by young people and used not only for pleasure but also for power in a new form of cultural politics that shook the nation. As those who threw themselves into the "youth revolution" (a label that did not stick) knew so well, the struggle for America's future would take place not in the structure of electoral politics, but on the battlefield of cultural meaning. Sex was an incendiary tool of a revolution that was more than political. But not even the cultural revolutionaries agreed on goals, or on the role and meaning of sex in the revolution.

These last two strands had to do primarily with young people, and that is significant. The changes that took place in America's sexual mores and behaviors in the sixties were *experienced* and *defined* as revolutionary in large part because they were so closely tied to youth. The nation's young, according to common wisdom and the mass media, were in revolt. Of course, the sexual revolution was not limited to youth, and sex was only one part of the revolutionary claims of youth. Still, it was the intersection of sex and youth that signaled danger. And the fact that these were often middle-class youths, the ones reared in a culture of respectability (told that a single sexual misstep could jeopardize their bright futures), made their frontal challenges to sexual mores all the more inexplicable and alarming. . . .

By focusing on the 1960s, we lose much of the "sexual revolution." In many ways, the most important decade of that revolution was the

1970s, when the "strands" of the 1960s joined with gay liberation, the women's movement, and powerful assertions of the importance of cultural differences in America. Yet, by concentrating on the early years of the sexual revolution, we see its tangled roots—the sexual ideologies and behaviors that gave it birth. We can also understand how little had been resolved—even begun—by the end of the 1960s.

BEFORE THE REVOLUTION: YOUTH AND SEX

Like many of the protest movements that challenged American tranquility in the sixties, the sexual revolution developed within the protected space and intensified atmosphere of the college campus. . . .

The media had a field day when the president of Vassar College, Sarah Blanding, said unequivocally that if a student wished to engage in premarital sex, she must withdraw from the college. The oft-quoted student reply to her dictum chilled the hearts of middle-class parents throughout the country: "If Vassar is to become the Poughkeepsie Victorian Seminary for young Virgins, then the change of policy had better be made explicit in admissions catalogs."

Such challenges to authority and to conventional morality were reported to eager audiences around the nation. None of this, of course, was new. National audiences had been scandalized by the panty raid epidemic of the early 1950s; the antics and petting parties of college youth had provided sensational fodder for hungry journalists in the 1920s. The parents—and grandparents—of these young people had chipped away at the system of sexual controls themselves. But they had not directly and publicly denied the very foundations of sexual morality. With few exceptions, they had evaded the controls and circumvented the rules, climbing into dorm rooms through open windows, signing out to the library and going to motels, carefully maintaining virginity in the technical sense while engaging in every caress known to married couples. The evasions often succeeded, but that does not mean that the controls had no effect. On the contrary, they had a great impact on the ways people experienced sex.

There were, in fact, two major systems of sexual control, one structural and one ideological. These systems worked to reinforce one another, but they affected the lives of those they touched differently.

The structural system was the more practical of the two but probably the less successful. It worked by limiting opportunities for the unmarried to have intercourse. Parents of teenagers set curfews and promoted double dating, hoping that by preventing privacy they would limit sexual exploration. Colleges, acting in loco parentis, used several tactics: visitation hours, parietals, security patrols, and restrictions on students' use of cars. . . .

Throughout the 1950s, the structural controls became increasingly complex; by the early 1960s they were so elaborate as to be ludicrous. At the University of Michigan in 1962, the student handbook devoted nine of its fifteen pages to rules for women. . . . Penalties at Michigan (an institutional version of "grounding") began when a student had eleven "late minutes"—but the late minutes could be acquired one at a time throughout the semester. . . .

The myriad of rules, as anyone who lived through this period well knows, did not prevent sexual relations between students so much as they structured the times and places and ways that students could have sexual contact. Students said extended good-nights on the porches of houses, they petted in dormitory lounges while struggling to keep three feet on the floor and clothing in some semblance of order, and they had intercourse in cars, keeping an eye out for police patrols. What could be done after eleven could be done before eleven, and sex need not occur behind a closed door and in a bed— but this set of rules had a profound impact on the *ways* college students and many young people living in their parents' homes *experienced* sex.

The overelaboration of rules, in itself, offers evidence that the controls were beleaguered. Nonetheless, the rules were rarely challenged frontally and thus they offered some illusion of control. This system of rules, in all its inconsistency, arbitrariness, and blindness, helped to preserve the distinction between public and private, the coexistence of overt and covert, that defines midcentury American sexuality.

The ideological system of controls was more pervasive than the structured system and probably more effective. This system centered on ideas of difference: men and women were fundamentally different creatures, with different roles and interests in sex. Whether one adopted a psychoanalytic or an essentialist approach, whether one looked to scholarly or popular analysis, the final conclusion pointed to *difference*. In sex (as in life), women were the limit setters and men the aggressors. . . .

Women did in fact have a different and more imperative interest in controlling sex than men, for women could become pregnant. Few doctors would fit an unmarried woman with a diaphragm, though one might get by in the anonymity of a city with a cheap "gold" ring from a drugstore or by pretending to be preparing for an impending honeymoon. . . .

Women who were too "free" with sexual favors could lose value and even threaten their marriageability. . . . While a girl was expected to "pet to be popular," girls and women who went "too far" risked their futures. Advice books and columns from the 1940s and 1950s linked girls' and womens' "value" to their "virtue," arguing in explicitly economic terms that "free" kisses destroyed a woman's value in the dating system: "The boys find her easy to afford. She doesn't put a high value on herself." The exchange was even clearer in the marriage market. In chilling language, a teen adviser asked: "Who wants second hand goods?" . . .

For most middle-class youth in the postwar era, sex involved a series of skirmishes that centered around lines and boundaries: kissing, necking, petting above the waist, petting below the waist, petting through clothes, petting under clothes, mild petting, heavy petting. The progression of sexual intimacy had emerged as a highly ordered system. Each act constituted a stage, ordered in a strict hierarchy (first base, second base, and so forth), with vaginal penetration as the ultimate step. But in their attempts to preserve technical virginity, many young people engaged in sexual behaviors that, in the sexual hierarchy of the larger culture, should have been more forbidden than vaginal intercourse. One woman remembers: "We went pretty far, very far; everything but intercourse. But it was very frustrating. . . . Sex was out of the question. I had it in my mind that I was going to be a virgin. So I came up with oral sex. . . . I thought I invented it."

Many young men and women acted in defiance of the rules, but that does not make the rules irrelevant. The same physical act can have very different meanings depending on its emotional and social/cultural contexts. For America's large middle class and for all those who aspired to "respectability" in the prerevolutionary twentieth century, sex was overwhelmingly secret or furtive. Sex was a set of acts with high stakes and possibly serious consequences, acts that emphasized and reinforced the different roles of men and women in American society. We do not know how each person felt about his or her private acts, but we do know that few were willing or able to publicly reject the system of sexual controls.

The members of the generation that would be labeled "the sixties" were revolutionary in that they called fundamental principles of sexual morality and control into question. The system of controls they had inherited and lived within was based on a set of presumptions rooted in the previous century. In an evolving set of arguments and actions (which never became thoroughly coherent or unified), they rejected a system of sexual controls organized around concepts of difference and hierarchy. . . .

REVOLUTIONARIES

All those who rejected the sexual mores of the postwar era did not reject the fundamental premises that gave them shape. *Playboy* magazine played an enormously important (if symbolic) role in the sexual revolution, or at least in preparing the ground for the sexual revolution. *Playboy* was a men's magazine in the tradition of *Esquire* (for which its founder had worked briefly) but laid claim to a revolutionary stance partly by replacing *Esquire*'s airbrushed drawings with airbrushed flesh.

Begun by Hugh Hefner in 1953 with an initial print run of 70,000, *Playboy* passed the one million circulation mark in three years. By the mid-1960s Hefner had amassed a fortune of $100 million, including a lasciviously appointed forty-eight-room mansion staffed by thirty Playboy "bunnies" ("fuck like bunnies" is a phrase we have largely left behind, but most people at the time caught the allusion). Playboy clubs, also staffed by large-breasted and long-legged women in bunny ears and cottontails, flourished throughout the country. Though *Playboy* offered quality writing and advice for those aspiring to sophistication, the greatest selling point of the magazine was undoubtedly its illustrations.

Playboy, however, offered more than masturbatory opportunities. Between the pages of coyly arranged female bodies—more, inscribed in the coyly arranged female bodies—flourished a strong and relatively coherent ideology. Hefner called it a philosophy and wrote quite a few articles expounding it (a philosophy professor in North Carolina took it seriously enough to describe his course as "philosophy from Socrates to Hefner").

Hefner saw his naked women as "a symbol of disobedience, a triumph of sexuality, an end of Puritanism." He saw his magazine as an attack on "our ferocious anti-sexuality, our dark antieroticism." But his thrust toward pleasure and light was not to be undertaken in partnership. The Playboy philosophy, according to Hefner, had less to do with sex and more to do with sex roles. American society increasingly "blurred distinctions between the sexes . . . not only in business, but in such diverse realms as household chores, leisure activities, smoking and drinking habits, clothing styles, upswinging homosexuality and the sex-obliterating aspects of togetherness," concluded the "Playboy Panel" in June 1962. In Part 19 of his extended essay on the Playboy philosophy, Hefner wrote: "PLAYBOY stresses a strongly heterosexual concept of society—in which the separate roles of men and women are clearly defined and compatible."

Read without context, Hefner's call does not necessarily preclude sex as a common interest between men and women. He is certainly advocating heterosexual sex. But the models of sex offered are not partnerships. Ever innovative in marketing and design, *Playboy* offered in one issue a special "coloring book" section. A page featuring three excessively voluptuous women was captioned: "Make one of the girls a blonde. Make one of the girls a brunette. Make one of the girls a redhead. It does not matter which is which. The girls' haircolors are interchangeable. So are the girls."

Sex, in the Playboy mode, was a contest—not of wills, in the model of the male seducer and the virtuous female, but of exploitative intent, as in the playboy and the would-be wife. In *Playboy*'s world, women were out to ensnare men, to entangle them in a web of responsibility and obligation (not the least of which was financial). Barbara Ehrenreich has convincingly argued that *Playboy* was an integral part of a male-initiated revolution in sex roles, for it advocated that men reject burdensome responsibility (mainly in the shape of wives) for lives of pleasure through consumption. Sex, of course, was part of this pleasurable universe. In *Playboy*, sex was located in the realm of consumption, and women were interchangeable objects, mute, making no demands, each airbrushed beauty supplanted by the next month's model.

It was not only to men that sexual freedom was sold through exploitative visions. When Helen Gurley Brown revitalized the traditional women's magazine that was *Cosmopolitan* in 1965, she compared her magazine to *Playboy*—and *Cosmo* did celebrate the pleasure of single womanhood and "sexual and material consumerism." But before Brown ran *Cosmo*, she had made her contribution to the sexual revolution with *Sex and the Single Girl*, published in May 1962. By April 1963, 150,000 hard-cover copies had been sold, garnering Brown much media attention and a syndicated newspaper column, "Woman Alone."

The claim of *Sex and the Single Girl* was, quite simply, "nice, single girls *do*." Brown's radical message to a society in which twenty-three-year-olds were called old maids was that singleness is good. Marriage, she insisted, should not be an immediate goal. The Single Girl sounds like the Playboy's dream, but she was more likely a nightmare revisited. Marriage, Brown advised, is "insurance for the worst years of your life. During the best years you don't need a husband." But she quickly amended that statement: "You do need a man every step of the way, and they are often cheaper emotionally and more fun by the dozen."

That fun explicitly included sex, and on the woman's terms. But Brown's celebration of the joys of single life still posed men and women as adversaries. "She need never be bored with one man per lifetime," she enthused. "Her choice of partners is endless and they seek *her*. . . . Her married friends refer to her pursuers as wolves, but actually many of them turn out to be lambs—to be shorn and worn by her."

Brown's celebration of the single "girl" actually began with a success story—her own. "I married for the first time at thirty-seven. I got the man I wanted," begins *Sex and the Single Girl*. Brown's description of that union is instructive: "David is a motion picture producer, forty-four, brainy, charming and sexy. He was sought after by many a Hollywood starlet as well as some less flamboyant but more deadly types. And *I* got him! We have two Mercedes-Benzes, one hundred acres of virgin forest near San Francisco, a Mediterranean house overlooking the Pacific, a full-time maid and a good life."

While Brown believes "her body wants to" is a sufficient reason for a woman to have an "affair," she is not positing identical interests of men and women in sex. Instead, she asserts the validity of women's interests—interests that include Mercedes-Benzes, full-time maids, lunch ("Anyone can take you to lunch. How bored can you be for an hour?"), vacations, and vicuna coats. But by offering a female version of the Playboy ethic, she greatly strengthened its message.

Unlike the youths who called for honesty, who sought to blur the boundaries between male and female, *Playboy* and *Cosmo* offered a vision of sexual freedom based on difference and deceit, but within a shared universe of an intensely competitive market economy. They were revolutionary in their claiming of sex as a legitimate pleasure and in the directness they brought to portraying sex as an arena for struggle and exploitation that could be enjoined by men and women alike (though in different ways and to different ends). Without this strand, the sexual revolution would have looked very different. In many ways *Playboy* was a necessary condition for "revolution," for it linked sex to the emerging culture of consumption and the rites of the marketplace. As it fed into the sexual reconfigurations of the sixties, *Playboy* helped make sex more—or less—than a rite of youth.

In the revolutionary spring of 1968, *Life* magazine looked from the student protests at Columbia across the street to Barnard College: "A sexual anthropologist of some future century, analyzing the pill, the drive-in, the works of Harold Robbins, the Tween-Bra and all the other artifacts of the American Sexual Revolution, may consider the case of Linda LeClair and her boyfriend, Peter Behr, as a moment in which the morality of an era changed."

The LeClair affair, as it was heralded in newspaper headlines and syndicated columns around the country, was indeed such a moment. Linda LeClair and Peter Behr were accidental revolutionaries, but as *Life* not so kindly noted, "history will often have its little joke. And so it was this spring when it found as its symbol of this revolution a champion as staunch, as bold and as unalluring as Linda LeClair." The significance of the moment is not to be found in the actions of LeClair and Behr, who certainly lacked revolutionary glamour despite all the headlines about "Free Love," but in the contest over the meaning of those actions.

The facts of the case were simple. On 4 March 1968 the *New York Times* ran an article called "An Arrangement: Living Together for Convenience, Security, Sex." (The piece ran full-page width; below it appeared articles on "How to Duck the Hemline Issue" and "A Cook's Guide to the Shallot.") An "arrangement," the author informs us, was one of the current euphemisms for what was otherwise known as "shacking up" or, more innocuously, "living together." The article, which offers a fairly sympathetic portrait of several unmarried student couples who lived together in New York City, features an interview with a Barnard sophomore, "Susan," who lived with her boyfriend "Peter" in an off-campus apartment. Though Barnard had strict housing regulations and parietals (the curfew was midnight on weekends and ten o'clock on weeknights, and students were meant to live either at home or in Barnard housing), Susan had received permission to live off campus by accepting a job listed through Barnard's employment office as a "live-in maid." The job had, in fact, been listed by a young married woman who was a good friend of "Susan's."

Not surprisingly, the feature article caught the attention of Barnard administrators, who had little trouble identifying "Susan" as Linda LeClair. LeClair was brought before the Judiciary Council—not for her sexual conduct, but for lying to Barnard about her housing arrangements. Her choice of roommate was certainly an issue; if she had been found to be living alone or, as one Barnard student confessed to the *Times*, with a female cat, she would not have been headline-worthy.

Linda, however, was versed in campus politics, and she and Peter owned a mimeograph machine. She played it both ways, appearing for her hearings in a demure, knee-length pastel dress and churning out pamphlets on what she and Peter called "A Victorian Drama." She and Peter distributed a survey on campus, garnering three hundred replies, most of which admitted to some violation of Barnard's parietals or housing regulations. Sixty women were willing to go public and signed forms that read: "I am a student of Barnard College and I have violated the Barnard Housing Regulations. . . . In the interest of fairness I request that an investigation be made of my disobedience."

Two hundred and fifty students and faculty members attended LeClair's hearing, which was closed to all but members of the college community. Her defense was a civil rights argument: colleges had no right to regulate nonacademic behavior of adult students, and housing rules discriminated on the basis of sex (Columbia men had no such regulations). After deliberating for five hours, the faculty-student judiciary committee found LeClair guilty of defying college regulations; but it also called for reform of the existing housing policy. The punishment they recommended for LeClair was a sort of black humor to anyone who had been to college: they barred her from the Barnard cafeteria.

Linda LeClair had not done anything especially unusual, as several letters from alumnae to Barnard's president, Martha Peterson, testified. But her case was a symbol of change, and it tells us much about how people understood the incident. The president's office received over two hundred telephone calls (most demanding LeClair's expulsion) and over one hundred letters; editorials ran in newspapers, large and small, throughout the country. Some of the letters were vehement in their condemnation of LeClair and of the college. Francis Beamen of Needham, Massachusetts, suggested that Barnard should be renamed "BARNYARD"; Charles Orsinger wrote (on good quality letterhead), "If you let Linda stay in college, I can finally prove to my wife with a front page news story about that bunch of glorified whores going to eastern colleges." An unsigned letter began: "SUBJECT: Barnard College—and the kow-tow to female 'students' who practice prostitution, PUBLICLY!"

Though the term "alley cat" cropped up more than once, a majority of the letters were thoughtful attempts to come to terms with the changing morality of America's youth. Many were from parents who understood the symbolic import of the case. Overwhelmingly, those who did not simply rant about "whoredom" structured their comments around concepts of public and private. The word *flaunt* appeared over and over in the letters to President Peterson. Linda was "flaunting her sneering attitude"; Linda and Peter were "openly flaunting their disregard of moral codes"; they were "openly flaunting rules of civilized society." Mrs. Bruce Bromley, Jr., wrote her first such letter on a public issue to recommend, "Do not let Miss LeClair attend Barnard as long as she flaunts immortality in your face." David Abrahamson, M.D., identifying himself as a former Columbia faculty member, offered "any help in this difficult case." He advised President Peterson, "Undoubtedly the girl's behavior must be regarded as exhibitionism, as her tendency is to be in the limelight which clearly indicates some emotional disturbance or upset."

The public-private question *was* the issue in this case—the letter writers were correct. Most were willing to acknowledge that "mistakes" can happen; many were willing to allow for some "discreet" sex among the unmarried young. But Linda LeClair *claimed* the right to determine her own "private" life; she rejected the private-public dichotomy *as it was framed around sex*, casting her case as an issue of individual rights versus institutional authority.

But public response to the case is interesting in another way. When a woman wrote President Peterson that "it is time for these young people to put sex back in its proper place, instead of something to be flaunted" and William F. Buckley condemned the "delinquency of this pathetic little girl, so gluttonous for sex and publicity," they were not listening. Sex was not what Linda and Peter talked about. Sex was not mentioned. Security was, and "family." "Peter is my family," said Linda. "It's a very united married type of relationship—it's the most important one in each of our lives. And our lives are very much intertwined."

Of course they had sex. They were young and in love, and their peer culture accepted sex within such relationships. But what they claimed was partnership—a partnership that obviated the larger culture's insistence on the difference between men and women. The letters suggesting that young women would "welcome a strong rule against living with men to protect them against doing that" made no sense in LeClair's universe. When she claimed that Barnard's rules were discriminatory because Columbia men had no such rules, that "Barnard College was founded on the principle of equality between women and men," and asked, "If women are able, intelligent people, why must we be supervised and curfewed?" she was denying that men and women had different interests and needs. Just as the private-public dichotomy was a cornerstone of sexual control in the postwar era, the much-touted differences between men and women were a crucial part of the system.

Many people in the 1960s and 1970s struggled with questions of equality and difference in sophisticated and hard-thought ways. Neither Peter Behr nor Linda LeClair was especially gifted in that respect. What they argued was commonplace to them—a natural language and set of assumptions that nonetheless had revolutionary implications. It is when a set of assumptions becomes natural and unself-conscious, when a language appears in the private comments of a wide variety of people that it is worth taking seriously. The unity of interests that Behr and LeClair called upon as they obviated the male-female dichotomy was not restricted to students in the progressive institutions on either coast.

In 1969 the administration at the University of Kansas (KU), a state institution dependent on a conservative, though populist, legislature for its funding, attempted to establish a coed dormitory for some of its scholarship students. KU had tried coed living as an experiment in the 1964 summer session and found students well satisfied, though some complained that it was awkward to go downstairs to the candy machines with one's hair in curlers. Curlers were out of fashion by 1969, and the administration moved forward with caution.

A survey on attitudes toward coed housing was given to those who lived in the scholarship halls, and the answers of the men survive.

The results of the survey go against conventional wisdom about the provinces. Only one man (of the 124 responses recorded) said his parents objected to the arrangement ("Pending further discussion," he noted). But what is most striking is the language in which the men supported and opposed the plan. "As a stereotypical answer," one man wrote, "I already am able to do all the roleplaying socially I need, and see communication now as an ultimate goal." A sophomore who listed his classification as both "soph." and "4-F I Hope" responded: "I believe that the segregation of the sexes is unnatural. I would like to associate with women on a basis other than dating roles. This tradition of segregation is discriminatory and promotes inequality of mankind." One man thought coed living would make the hall "more homey." Another said it would be "more humane." Many used the word "natural." The most eloquent of the sophomores wrote: "[It would] allow them to meet and interact with one another in a situation relatively free of sexual overtones; that is, the participating individuals would be free to encounter one another as human beings, rather than having to play the traditional stereotyped male and female roles. I feel that coed living is the only feasible way to allow people to escape this stereotypical role behavior."

The student-generated proposal that went forward in December 1970 stressed these (as they defined them) "philosophical" justifications. The system "would NOT be an arrangement for increased boy-meets-girl contact or for convenience in finding dates," the committee insisted. Instead, coed living would "contribute to the development of each resident as a full human being." Though "interpersonal relationships based on friendship and cooperative efforts rather than on the male/female roles we usually play in dating situations" students would try to develop "a human concern that transcends membership in one or the other sex."

While the students disavowed "'boy-meets-girl' contact" as motivation, no one seriously believed that sex was going to disappear. The most cogently stated argument against the plan came from a young man who insisted: "[You] can't ignore the sexual overtones involved in coed living; after all, sex is the basic motivation for your plan. (I didn't say lust, I said sex)." Yet the language in which they framed their proposal was significant: they called for relationships (including sexual) based on a common humanity.

Like Peter Behr and Linda LeClair, these students at the University of Kansas were attempting to redefine both sex and sex roles. Sex should not be negotiated through the dichotomous pairings of male and female, public and private. Instead, they attempted to formulate and articulate a new standard that looked to a model of "togetherness" undreamed of and likely undesired by their parents. The *Life* magazine issue with which this section began characterized the "sexual revolution" as "dull." "Love still makes the world go square," the author concluded, for the revolutionaries he interviewed subscribed to a philosophy "less indebted to Playboy than Peanuts, in which sex is not so much a pleasure as a warm puppy." To his amusement, one "California girl" told him: "Besides being my lover, Bob is my best friend in all the world," and a young man insisted, "We are not sleeping together, we are living together."

For those to whom *Playboy* promised revolution, this attitude was undoubtedly tame. And in the context of the cultural revolution taking place among America's youth, and documented in titillating detail by magazines such as *Life*, these were modest revolutionaries indeed, seeming almost already out of step with their generation. But the issue, to these "dull" revolutionaries, as to their more flamboyant brothers and sisters, was larger than sex. They understood that the line between public and private had utility; that the personal was political.

1967, The Summer of Love

It was a "holy pilgrimage," according to the Council for a Summer of Love. In the streets of Haight-Ashbury, thousands and thousands of "pilgrims" acted out a street theater of costumed fantasy, drugs and music and sex that was unimaginable in the neat suburban streets of their earlier youth. Visionaries and revolutionaries had preceded the deluge; few of them drowned. Others did. But the tide flowed in with vague countercultural yearnings, drawn by the pop hit "San Francisco (Be Sure to Wear Flowers in Your Hair)" and its promise of a "love-in," by the pictures in *Life* magazine or in *Look* magazine or in *Time* magazine, by the proclamations of the underground press that San Francisco would be "the love-guerilla training school for drop-outs from mainstream America . . . where the new world, a human world of the 21st century is being constructed." Here sexual freedom would be explored; not cohabitation, not "arrangements," not "living together" in ways that looked a lot like marriage except for the lack of a piece of paper that symbolized the sanction of the state. Sex in the Haight was revolutionary.

In neat suburban houses on neat suburban streets, people came to imagine this new world, helped by television and by the color pictures in glossy-paper magazines (a joke in the Haight told of "bead-wearing *Look* reporters interviewing bead-wearing *Life* reporters"). Everyone knew that these pilgrims represented a tiny fraction of America's young, but the images reverberated. America felt itself in revolution. . . .

Youth culture and counterculture were not synonymous, and for many the culture itself was more a matter of life-style than revolutionary intent. But the strands flowed together in the chaos of the age, and the few and the marginal provided archetypes that were read into the youth culture by an American public that did not see the lines of division. "Hippies, yippies, flippies," said Mayor Richard Daley of Chicago. "Free Love," screamed the headlines about Barnard's Linda LeClair.

But even the truly revolutionary youths were not unified, no more on the subject of sex than on anything else. Members of the New Left, revolutionary but rarely countercultural, had sex but did not talk about it all the time. They consigned sex to a relatively "private" sphere. Denizens of Haight-Ashbury lived a Dionysian sexuality, most looking nowhere but to immediate pleasure. Some political-cultural revolutionaries, however, claimed sex and used it for the revolution. They capitalized on the sexual chaos and fears of the nation, attempting to use sex to politicize youth and to challenge "Amerika."

In March 1968 the *Sun*, a Detroit people's paper put out by a "community of artists and lovers" (most notably John Sinclair of the rock group MC5), declared a "Total Assault on the Culture." Sinclair, in his "editorial statement," disavowed any prescriptive intent but informed his readers: "We *have* found that there are three essential human activities of the greatest importance to all persons, and that people are well and healthy in proportion to their involvement in these activities: rock and roll, dope, and fucking in the streets. . . . We suggest the three in combination, all the time." . . .

Sinclair was not alone in his paean to copulation. Other countercultural seekers believed that they had to remake love and reclaim sex to create community. These few struggled, with varying degrees of honesty and sincerity, over the significance of sex in the beloved community.

For others, sex was less a philosophy than a weapon. In the spring of 1968, the revolutionary potential of sex also suffused the claims of the Yippies as they struggled to stage a "Festival of Life" to counter the "Death Convention" in Chicago. "How can you separate politics and sex?" Jerry Rubin asked with indignation after the fact. Yippies lived by that creed. Sex was a double-edged sword, to be played two ways. Sex was a lure to youth; it was part of their attempt to tap the youth market, to "sell a revolutionary consciousness." It was also a challenge, "flaunted in the face" (as it were) of America.

The first Yippie manifesto, released in January 1968, summoned the tribes to Chicago. It played well in the underground press, with its promise of "50,000 of us dancing in the streets, throbbing with amplifiers and harmony . . . making love in the parks." Sex was a politics of pleasure, a politics of abundance that made sense to young middle-class whites who had been raised in the world without limits that was postwar America.

Sex was also incendiary, and the Yippies knew that well. It guaranteed attention. Thus the "top secret" plans for the convention that Abbie Hoffman mimeographed and distributed to the press promised a barbecue and lovemaking by the lake, followed by "Pin the Tail on the Donkey," "Pin the Rubber on the Pope," and "other normal and healthy games." Grandstanding before a crowd of Chicago reporters, the Yippies presented a city official with an official document wrapped in a *Playboy* centerfold inscribed, "To Dick with love, the Yippies." The *Playboy* centerfold in the Yippies' hands was an awkward nexus between the old and the new sexuality. As a symbolic act, it did not proffer freedom so much as challenge authority. It was a sign of disrespect—to Mayor Richard Daley and to straight America.

While America was full of young people sporting long hair and beads, the committed revolutionaries (of cultural stripe) were few in number and marginal at best. It is telling that the LeClair affair could still be a scandal in a nation that had weathered the Summer of Love. But the lines were blurred in sixties America. One might ask with Todd Gitlin, "What was marginal anymore, where was the mainstream anyway?" when the Beatles were singing, "Why Don't We Do It in the Road?"

CONCLUSION

The battles of the sexual revolution were hard fought, its victories ambiguous, its outcome still unclear. What we call the sexual revolution was an amalgam of movements that flowed together in an unsettled era. They were often at odds with one another, rarely well thought out, and usually without a clear agenda.

The sexual revolution was built on equal measures of hypocrisy and honesty, equality and exploitation. Indeed, the individual strands contain mixed motivations and ideological charges. Even the most heartfelt or best intentions did not always work out for the good when put into practice by mere humans with physical and psychological frailties. As we struggle over the meaning of the "revolution" and ask ourselves who, in fact, *won*, it helps to untangle the threads and reject the conflation of radically different impulses into a singular revolution.

Part 5

THE VIETNAM WAR

The war in Vietnam was America's longest and most agonizing war. More than anything else, it was the wedge that divided the nation in two during the turbulent years of the sixties.

In many ways, the growing U.S. involvement in Vietnam illustrates the logic of the Cold War doctrine of containment. In the years following World War II, despite U.S. wartime promises to end colonialism in Southeast Asia, President Truman chose to support French colonial power in Indochina rather than the nationalist independence movement there led by Vietnamese insurgent and, significantly, *communist*, Ho Chi Minh. Truman believed it was crucial to secure European support for the United States in its growing conflict with the Soviet Union, and this was an attempt to mollify France. But the implications of this action would be enormous. When Ho Chi Minh and his followers defeated the French colonial power in 1954, the United States stepped into the breach, creating a divided Vietnam and setting up a puppet government friendly to the United States in South Vietnam.

As the Cold War escalated, President John F. Kennedy promised the world in his inaugural address that Americans were prepared to "pay any price" and "bear any burden" to contain the threat of communism. In the logic of this Cold War world view, Vietnam (like Korea and even the Bay of Pigs invasion of Cuba) was a hot battle in the Cold War. Relying on the belief that the struggles in Vietnam might prove the "domino" that began the fall of Southeast Asia to communism, John Kennedy sent increasing numbers of military "advisors" to Vietnam, launched programs of counterinsurgency, and greatly increased programs of financial and military aid to South Vietnam.

America's growing involvement in Vietnam may also be seen as a byproduct of the "politics of affluence" discussed in Part 2. In creating a divided Vietnam, the United States launched an experiment in nation building. Could the United States, through its great resources, technological expertise, and example of democracy, construct a democratic, free-market state that would serve as a bulwark against the spread of communism in the region?

The war had begun as a war for Vietnamese independence from the French. It continued as a civil war between the Vietnamese people, but also as a proxy war in the larger Cold War struggle between the United States and the Soviet Union. Under John Kennedy, American troop presence grew from 900 to 15,000; under Lyndon Johnson, from 15,000 to 555,000.

The war had a devastating effect on the people of Vietnam. Perhaps one-third of the South Vietnamese population became refugees, uprooted from their ancestral homes, surviving as beggars, criminals, and prostitutes in an alien urban culture. The use of napalm and defoliants, and the dropping of more than seven million tons of bombs on Indochina—three times the total tonnage of explosives dumped on all the enemy nations during World War II—demolished Vietnam's agricultural base and crippled its economy. As one American major declared after a particularly brutal battle, "We had to destroy the village in order to save it."

The war also created profound conflict within the United States. A significant portion of the American people came to distrust their government. More and more Americans—and not just the young—came to believe that the war had no purpose, that it was without morality, justification, even self-interest. As more and more young men came home in body bags and "the light at the end of the tunnel" seemed no closer, large numbers of Americans concluded, with CBS news anchor Walter Cronkite, that the war was "mired in stalemate."

Not everyone, of course, came to oppose the war. Bumper stickers proclaimed, "America, love it or leave it." The American public's division over the war in Vietnam coalesced with all the other divisions in American society: over civil rights and Black Power, over feminism, over what seemed the cultural revolution of youth. With tanks in the streets of Chicago at the 1968 Democratic National Convention, it seemed that the nation would be torn apart. And even within the antiwar movement, there was no unity. The small minority of the antiwar movement that proclaimed solidarity with the Vietnamese National Liberation Front (NLF) had little in common with most of the 61 percent of Americans who, by 1971, saw U.S. involvement in Vietnam as a "mistake."

In the following readings, we try to capture some of the range of Americans' understandings of the Vietnam War, both then and now. In an excerpt from *We Were Soldiers Once . . . and Young*, readers are taken back to 1965, a moment when patriotic innocence seemed possible, and when Americans faced—for the first time—the realities of an escalating war. An SDS antiwar leaflet from the same year shows the early antiwar protestors' strength of commitment, as well as the larger concerns that led them to protest the war. Historian William Chafe's article on Allard Lowenstein and the Dump Johnson Movement highlights the efforts of some Americans to bring about change through peaceful electoral means in an increasingly polarized nation. John Kerry's 1971 testimony before Congress on behalf of the Vietnam Veterans Against the War takes us back to the experience of American servicemen in Vietnam, and offers a window into the horror of the war for the Vietnamese people. And William Jefferson Clinton's letter to the director of the ROTC in 1969 shows how at least one young student chose to find a way out of fighting in Vietnam.

The American public has not come fully to terms with the legacy of the Vietnam War. Neither have its historians. The section ends with two very controversial pieces from recent books on the Vietnam War. Robert McNamara, secretary of defense under Kennedy and Johnson and a key architect of the nation's Vietnam policy, argues that the war was wrong and explains why. Journalist Michael Lind, in contrast, argues that although the war was a failure, it was both right and necessary.

The questions that arise from this section are not easy ones. What should be America's role in the world? How should the United States define its own self-interest? What are the proper limits of U.S. intervention? Does U.S. policy in Vietnam show a fatal flaw in the idea that America has the moral right to impose its own values and beliefs on other nations? If that is the lesson of Vietnam, how would the logic of that lesson shape our foreign policy?

Other critical questions remain. Why did the United States lose the Vietnam War? Was there ever a way that U.S. involvement could have led to a democratic government in Vietnam? How can we understand the atrocities committed against the Vietnamese and reported by John Kerry in his congressional testimony? Was American involvement in Vietnam a mistake, or was it a failure?

We Were Soldiers Once . . . and Young

Lt. Gen. Harold G. Moore
and Joseph L. Galloway

The Vietnam Memorial, a wall of polished black granite bearing the name of each and every American who fell in Vietnam, graphically illustrates the toll of the war in loss and heartbreak. The names are listed in the order that the men died, and the wall begins low, with just a handful of names from the years before 1960. It rises to tower above the people who stand reading the names before tapering down again with the names of those who died toward the end of the war.

It was on November 14, 1965, in Vietnam's Ia Drang Valley, that American servicemen began dying in large numbers. In the following excerpt from We Were Soldiers Once . . . and Young, *the commander of the 1st Battalion, 7th Cavalry and the only journalist with the battalion tell the story of the first major battle of America's Vietnam War. Writing from hindsight, they attempt to show us a moment in time, a "watershed year when one era was ending in America and another was beginning."*

PROLOGUE

In thy faint slumbers I by thee have watch'd
And heard thee murmur tales of iron wars . . .
—Shakespeare, *Henry IV, Part One,* Act II, Scene 3

This story is about time and memories. The time was 1965, a different kind of year, a watershed year when one era was ending in America and another was beginning. We felt it then, in the many ways our lives changed so suddenly, so dramatically, and looking back on it from a quarter-century gone we are left in no doubt. It was the year America decided to directly intervene in the Byzantine affairs of obscure and distant Vietnam. It was the year we went to war. In the broad, traditional sense, that "we" who went to war was all of us, all Americans, though in truth at that time the larger majority had little knowledge of, less interest in, and no great concern with what was beginning so far away.

So this story is about the smaller, more tightly focused "we" of that sentence: the first American combat troops, who boarded World War II–era troopships, sailed to that little-known place, and fought the first major battle of a conflict that would drag on for ten long years and come as near to destroying America as it did to destroying Vietnam.

The Ia Drang campaign was to the Vietnam War what the terrible Spanish Civil War of the 1930s was to World War II: a dress rehearsal; the place where new tactics, techniques, and weapons were tested, perfected, and validated. In the Ia Drang, both sides claimed victory and both sides drew lessons, some of them dangerously deceptive, which echoed and resonated throughout the decade of bloody fighting and bitter sacrifice that was to come.

This is about what we did, what we saw, what we suffered in a thirty-four-day campaign in the Ia Drang Valley of the Central Highlands of South Vietnam in November 1965, when we were young and confident and patriotic and our countrymen knew little and cared less about our sacrifices.

Another war story, you say? Not exactly, for on the more important levels this is a love story, told in our own words and by our own actions. We were the children of the 1950s and we went where we were sent because we loved our country. We were draftees, most of us, but we were proud of the opportunity to serve that country just as our fathers had served in World War II and our older brothers in Korea. We were members of an elite, experimental combat division trained in the new art of airmobile warfare at the behest of President John F. Kennedy.

Just before we slipped out to Vietnam the Army handed us the colors of the historic 1st Cavalry Division and we all proudly sewed on the big yellow-and-black shoulder patches with the horsehead silhouette. We went to war because our country asked us to go, because our new President, Lyndon B. Johnson, ordered us to go, but more importantly because we saw it as our duty to go. That is one kind of love.

Another and far more transcendent love came to us unbidden on the battlefields, as it does on every battlefield in every war man has ever fought. We discovered in that depressing, hellish place, where death was our constant companion, that we loved each other. We killed for each other, we died for each other, and we wept for each other. And in time we came to love each other as brothers. In battle our world shrank to the man on our left and the man on our right and the enemy all around. We held each other's lives in our hands and we learned to share our fears, our hopes, our dreams as readily as we shared what little else good came our way.

We were the children of the 1950s and John F. Kennedy's young stalwarts of the early 1960s. He told the world that Americans would "pay any price, bear any burden, meet any hardship" in the defense of freedom. We were the down payment on that costly contract, but the man who signed it was not there when we fulfilled his promise. John F. Kennedy waited for us on a hill in Arlington National Cemetery, and in time we came by the thousands to fill those slopes with our white marble markers and to ask on the murmur of the wind if that was truly the future he had envisioned for us.

Among us were old veterans, grizzled sergeants who had fought in Europe and the Pacific in World War II and had survived the frozen hell of Korea, and now were about to add another star to their Combat Infantryman's Badge. There were regular-army enlistees, young men from American's small towns whose fathers told them they would learn discipline and become real men in the Army. There were other young men who chose the Army over an equal term in prison. Alternative sentencing, the judges call it now. But the majority were draftees, nineteen- and twenty-year-old boys summoned from all across America by their local Selective Service Boards to do their two years in green. The PFCs soldiered for $99.37 a month; the sergeants first class for $343.50 a month.

Leading us were the sons of West Point and the young ROTC lieutenants from Rutgers and The Citadel and, yes, even Yale University, who had heard Kennedy's call and answered it. There were also the young enlisted men and NCOs who passed through Officer Candidate School and emerged newly minted officers and gentlemen. All laughed nervously when confronted with the cold statistics that measured a second lieutenant's combat life expectancy in minutes and seconds, not hours. Our second lieutenants were paid $241.20 per month.

The class of 1965 came out of the old America, a nation that disappeared forever in the smoke that billowed off the jungle battlegrounds where we fought and bled. The country that sent us off to war was not there to welcome us home. It no longer existed. We answered the call of one President who was now dead; we followed the orders of another who would be hounded from office, and haunted, by the war he mismanaged so badly.

Many of our countrymen came to hate the war we fought. Those who hated it the most—the professionally sensitive—were not, in the end, sensitive enough to differentiate between the war and the soldiers who had been ordered to fight it. They hated us as well, and we went to ground in the cross fire, as we had learned in the jungles.

In time our battles were forgotten, our sacrifices were discounted, and both our sanity and our suitability for life in polite American society were publicly questioned. Our young-old faces, chiseled and gaunt from the fever and the heat and the sleepless nights, now stare back at us, lost and damned strangers, frozen in yellowing snapshots packed away in cardboard boxes with our medals and ribbons.

We rebuilt our lives, found jobs or professions, married, raised families, and waited patiently for America to come to its senses. As the years passed we searched each other out and found that the half-remembered pride of service was shared by those who had shared everything else with us. With them, and only with them, could we talk about what had really happened over there—what we had seen, what we had done, what we had survived.

We knew what Vietnam had been like, and how we looked and acted and talked and smelled. No one in America did. Hollywood got it wrong every damned time, whetting twisted political knives on the bones of our dead brothers.

So once, just this once: This is how it all began, what it was really like, what it meant to us, and what we meant to each other. It was no movie. When it was over the dead did not get up and dust themselves off and walk away. The wounded did not wash away the red and go on with life, unhurt. Those who were, miraculously, unscratched were by no means untouched. Not one of us left Vietnam the same young man he was when he arrived.

This story, then, is our testament, and our tribute to 234 young Americans who died beside us during four days in Landing Zone X-Ray and Landing Zone Albany in the Valley of Death, 1965. That is more Americans than were killed in any regiment, North or South, at the Battle of Gettysburg, and far more than were killed in combat in the entire Persian Gulf War. Seventy more of our comrades died in the Ia Drang in desperate skirmishes before and after the big battles at X-Ray and Albany. All the names, 305 of them including one Air Force pilot, are engraved on the third panel to the right of the apex, Panel 3-East, of the Vietnam Veterans Memorial in Washington, D.C., and on our hearts. This is also the story of the suffering of families whose lives were forever shattered by the death of a father, a son, a husband, a brother in that Valley.

While those who have never known war may fail to see the logic, this story also stands as tribute to the hundreds of young men of the 320th, 33rd, and 66th Regiments of the People's Army of Vietnam who died by our hand in that place. They, too, fought and died bravely. They were a worthy enemy. We who killed them pray that their bones were recovered from that wild, desolate place where we left them, and taken home for decent and honorable burial.

This is our story and theirs. For we were soldiers once, and young.

HEAT OF BATTLE

You cannot choose your battlefield,
God does that for you;
But you can plant a standard
Where a standard never flew.
—Stephen Crane, "The Colors"

The small bloody hole in the ground that was Captain Bob Edwards's Charlie Company command post was crowded with men. Sergeant Herman R. Hostuttler, twenty-five, from Terra Alta, West Virginia, lay crumpled in the red dirt, dead from an AK-47 round through his throat. Specialist 4 Ernest E. Paolone of Chicago, the radio operator, crouched low, bleeding from a shrapnel wound in his left forearm. Sergeant James P. Castleberry, the artillery forward observer, and his radio operator, PFC Ervin L. Brown, Jr., hunkered down beside Paolone. Captain Edwards had a bullet hole in his left shoulder and armpit, and was slumped in a contorted sitting position, unable to move and losing blood. He was holding his radio handset to his ear with his one good arm. A North Vietnamese machine gunner atop a huge termite hill no more than thirty feet away had them all in his sights.

"We lay there watching bullets kick dirt off the small parapet around the edge of the hole," Edwards recalls. "I didn't know how badly I had been hurt, only that I couldn't stand up, couldn't do very much. The two platoon leaders I had radio contact with, Lieutenant William W. Franklin on my right and Lieutenant James L. Lane on Franklin's right, continued to report receiving fire, but had not been penetrated. I knew that my other two platoons were in bad shape and the enemy had penetrated to within hand-grenade range of my command post."

The furious assault by more than five hundred North Vietnamese regulars had slammed directly into two of Captain Edwards's platoons, a thin line of fifty Cavalry troopers who were all that stood between the enemy and my battalion command post, situated in a clump of trees in Landing Zone X-Ray, Ia Drang Valley, in the Central Highlands of South Vietnam, early on November 15, 1965.

America had drifted slowly but inexorably into war in this far-off place. Until now the dying, on our side at least, had been by ones and twos during the "adviser era" just ended, then by fours and fives as the U.S. Marines took the field earlier this year. Now the dying had begun in earnest, in wholesale lots, here in this eerie forested valley beneath the 2,401-foot-high crest of the Chu Pong massif, which wandered ten miles back into Cambodia. The newly arrived 1st Cavalry Division (Airmobile) had already interfered with and changed North Vietnamese brigadier general Chu Huy Man's audacious plans to seize the Central Highlands. Now his goal was to draw the Americans into battle—to learn how they fought and teach his men how to kill them.

One understrength battalion had the temerity to land by helicopter right in the heart of General Man's base camp, a historic sanctuary so far from any road that neither the French nor the South Vietnamese army had ever risked penetrating it in the preceding twenty years. My battalion, the 450-man 1st Battalion, 7th Cavalry of the U.S. Army, had come looking for trouble in the Ia Drang; we had found all we wanted and more. Two regiments of regulars of the People's Army of Vietnam (PAVN)—more than two thousand men— were resting and regrouping in their sanctuary near here and preparing to resume combat operations, when we dropped in on them the day before. General Man's commanders reacted with speed and fury, and now we were fighting for our lives.

One of Captain Edwards's men, Specialist 4 Arthur Viera, remembers every second of Charlie Company's agony that morning. "The gunfire was very loud. We were getting overrun on the right side. The lieutenant [Neil A. Kroger, twenty-four, a native of Oak Park, Illinois] came up in the open in all this. I thought that was pretty good. He yelled at me. I got up to hear him. He hollered at me to help cover the left sector."

Viera adds, "I ran over to him and by the time I got there he was dead. He had lasted a half-hour. I knelt beside him, took off his dog tags, and put them in my shirt pocket. I went back to firing my M-79 grenade launcher and got shot in my right elbow. The M-79 went flying and I was knocked down and fell back over the lieutenant. I had my .45 and fired it with my left hand. Then I got hit in the neck and the bullet went right through. Now I couldn't talk or make a sound.

"I got up and tried to take charge, and was shot a third time. That one blew up my right leg and put me down. It went in my leg above the ankle, traveled up, came back out, then went into my groin and ended up in my back, close to my spine. Just then two stick grenades blew up right over me and tore up both my legs. I reached down with my left hand and touched grenade fragments on my left leg and it felt like I had touched a red-hot poker. My hand just sizzled."

When Bob Edwards was hit he radioed for his executive officer, Lieutenant John Arrington, a twenty-three-year-old South Carolinian who was over at the battalion command post rounding up supplies, to come forward and take command of Charlie Company. Edwards says, "Arrington made it to my command post and, after a few moments of talking to me while lying down at the edge of the foxhole, was also hit and wounded. He was worried that he had been hurt pretty bad and told me to be sure and tell his wife that he loved her. I thought: 'Doesn't he know I'm badly wounded, too?' He was hit in the arm and the bullet passed into his chest and grazed a lung. He was in pain, suffering silently. He also caught some shrapnel from an M-79 that the North Vietnamese had apparently captured and were firing into the trees above us."

Now the North Vietnamese were closing in on Lieutenant John Lance (Jack) Geoghegan's 2nd Platoon. They were already intermingled with the few survivors of Lieutenant Kroger's 1st Platoon and were maneuvering toward Bob Edwards's foxhole. Clinton S. Poley, twenty-three, six feet three inches tall, and the son of an Ackley, Iowa, dirt farmer, was assistant gunner on one of Lieutenant Geoghegan's M-60 machine guns. The gunner was Specialist 4 James C. Comer, a native of Seagrove, North Carolina.

Poley says, "When I got up something hit me real hard on the back of my neck, knocked my head forward and my helmet fell off in the foxhole. I thought a guy had snuck up behind me and hit me with the butt of a weapon, it was such a blow. Wasn't anybody there; it was a bullet from the side or rear. I put my bandage on it and the helmet helped hold it on. I got up and looked again and there were four of them with carbines, off to our right front. I told Comer to aim more to the right. After that I heard a scream and I thought it was Lieutenant Geoghegan."

It wasn't. By now, Lieutenant Geoghegan was already dead. His platoon sergeant, Robert Jemison, Jr., saw him go down trying to help a wounded man. "Willie Godboldt was twenty yards to my right. He was wounded, started hollering: 'Somebody help me!' I yelled: 'I'll go get him!' Lieutenant Geoghegan yelled back: 'No, I will.' He moved out of his position in the foxhole to help Godboldt and was shot." Just five days past his twenty-fourth birthday, John Lance Geoghegan of Pelham, New York, the only child of proud and doting parents, husband of Barbara and father of six-month-old Camille, lay dead, shot through the head and back, in the tall grass and red dirt of the Ia Drang Valley. PFC Willie F. Godboldt of Jacksonville, Florida, also twenty-four years old, died before help ever reached him.

Sergeant Jemison, who helped fight off five Chinese divisions at Chipyong-ni in the Korean War, now took a single bullet through his stomach but kept on fighting. Twenty minutes later the order came down for every platoon to throw a colored smoke grenade to mark friendly positions for the artillery and air strikes. Jemison got up to throw one and was hit again, this time knocked down by a bullet that struck him in the left shoulder. He got up, more slowly now, and went back to firing his M-16. Jemison fought on until he was hit a third time: "It was an automatic weapon. It hit me in my right arm and tore my weapon all to pieces. All that was left was the plastic stock. Another bullet cut off the metal clamp on my chin strip and knocked off my helmet. It hit so hard I thought my neck was broke. I was thrown to the ground. I got up and there was nothing left. No weapon, no grenades, no nothing."

James Comer and Clinton Poley, thirty feet to Jemison's left, had been firing their M-60 machine gun for almost an hour, an eternity. "A stick-handled potato-masher grenade landed in front of the hole. Comer hollered, 'Get down!' and kicked it away a little bit with his foot. It went off. By then we were close to being out of ammo and the gun had jammed. In that cloud of smoke and dust we started to our left, trying to find other 2nd Platoon positions. That's when I got hit in the chest and I hit the ground pretty hard."

Poley adds, "I got up and then got shot in my hip, and went down again. Comer and I lost contact with each other in the long grass. We'd already lost our ammo bearer [PFC Charles H. Collier from Mount Pleasant, Texas], who had been killed the day before. He was only eighteen and had been in Vietnam just a few days. I managed to run about twenty yards at a time for three times and finally came to part of the mortar platoon. A sergeant had two guys help me across a clearing to the battalion command post by the large anthill. The battalion doctor, a captain, gave me first aid."

Meantime, Specialist Viera was witness to scenes of horror: "The enemy was all over, at least a couple of hundred of them walking around for three or four minutes; it seemed like three or four hours. They were shooting and machine-gunning our wounded and laughing and giggling. I knew they'd kill me if they saw I was alive. When they got near, I played dead. I kept my eyes open and stared at a small tree. I knew that dead men had their eyes open."

Viera continues, "Then one of the North Vietnamese came up, looked at me, then kicked me, and I flopped over. I guess he thought I was dead. There was blood running out of my mouth, my arm, my legs. He took my watch and my .45 pistol and walked on. I watched them strip off all our weapons; then they left, back where they came from. I remember the artillery, the bombs, the napalm everywhere, real close around me. It shook the ground underneath me. But it was coming in on the North Vietnamese soldiers, too."

All this, and much more, took place between 6:50 A.M. and 7:40 A.M. on November 15, 1965. The agonies of Charlie Company occurred over 140 yards of the line. But men were fighting and dying on three sides of our thinly held American perimeter. In the center, I held the lives of all these men in my hands. The badly wounded Captain Bob Edwards was now on the radio, asking for reinforcements. The only reserve I had was the reconnaissance platoon, twenty-two men. Was the attack on Charlie Company the main enemy threat? Delta Company and the combined mortar position were also under attack now. Reluctantly, I told Captain Edwards that his company would have to fight on alone for the time being.

The din of battle was unbelievable. Rifles and machine guns and mortars and grenades rattled, banged, and boomed. Two batteries of

105mm howitzers, twelve big guns located on another landing zone five miles distant, were firing nonstop, their shells exploding no more than fifty yards outside the ring of shallow foxholes.

Beside me in the battalion command post, the Air Force forward air controller, Lieutenant Charlie W. Hastings, twenty-six, from La Mesa, New Mexico, radioed a special code word, "Broken Arrow," meaning "American unit in danger of being overrun," and within a short period of time every available fighter-bomber in South Vietnam was stacked overhead at thousand-foot intervals from seven thousand feet to thirty-five thousand feet, waiting its turn to deliver bombs and napalm to the battlefield.

Among my sergeants there were three-war men—men who parachuted into Normandy on D day and had survived the war in Korea— and those old veterans were shocked by the savagery and hellish noise of this battle. Choking clouds of smoke and dust obscured the killing ground. We were dry-mouthed and our bowels churned with fear, and still the enemy came on in waves.

March on Washington: The War Must Be Stopped (1965)

Students for a Democratic Society

On April 17, 1965, thousands of people came together in Washington, D.C., for the first national protest against the war in Vietnam. Few Americans questioned their government's actions in Vietnam at this point; for most, the war was a peripheral issue. There were very few American military personnel in Vietnam before 1965. But questions about the war had begun to surface, especially on the nation's college and university campuses. This first national protest was organized by Students for a Democratic Society, still a small and virtually unknown group. SDS members had come to believe that the war was immoral, a threat to the cause of democracy both at home and abroad, and they meant to shake the nation from what they saw as a dangerous complacency. In a stirring speech, Paul Potter, president of SDS, linked the war in Vietnam to failures of democracy within American society. American intervention in Vietnam, he argued that day, did not represent the will of the American people but instead the interests of an interlocking set of elites—military, financial, technocratic. "We must name the system," he declared.

The following document is an SDS leaflet from November 1965, calling for a second protest, a March on Washington. Some historians have argued that the sort of logic set forth in this leaflet represents a critical flaw in this strand of the American antiwar movement: some leaders drew a false equivalency—largely based on ignorance of Vietnam and its history—between social problems in the United States and the civil war in Vietnam, between civil rights protesters in America and the Vietnamese National Liberation Front. How might such an understanding of America's involvement in Vietnam shape the course of antiwar protest? Why might the authors of this leaflet have seen the relationship between domestic social problems and foreign policy this way?

Students for a Democratic Society, leaflet.

260

In the name of freedom, America is mutilating Vietnam. In the name of peace, America turns that fertile country into a wasteland. And in the name of democracy, America is burying its own dreams and suffocating its own potential.

Americans who can understand why the Negroes of Watts can rebel should understand too why Vietnamese can rebel. And those who know the American South and the grinding poverty of our northern cities should understand that our real problems lie not in Vietnam but at home—that the fight we seek is not with Communism but with the social desperation that makes good men violent, both here and abroad.

THE WAR MUST BE STOPPED

Our aim in Vietnam is the same as our aim in the United States: that oligarchic rule and privileged power be replaced by popular democracy where the people make the decisions which affect their lives and share in the abundance and opportunity that modern technology makes possible. This is the only solution for Vietnam in which Americans can find honor and take pride. Perhaps the war has already so embittered and devastated the Vietnamese that that ideal will require years of rebuilding. But the war cannot achieve it, nor can American military presence, nor our support of repressive unrepresentative governments.

The war must be stopped. There must be an immediate cease fire and demobilization in South Vietnam. There must be a withdrawal of American troops. Political amnesty must be guaranteed. All agreements must be ratified by the partisans of the "other side"—the National Liberation Front and North Vietnam.

We must not deceive ourselves: a negotiated agreement cannot guarantee democracy. Only the Vietnamese have the right of nationhood to make their government democratic or not, free or not, neutral or not. It is not America's role to deny them the chance to be what they will make of themselves. That chance grows more remote with every American bomb that explodes in a Vietnamese village.

But our hopes extend not only to Vietnam. Our chance is the first in a generation to organize the powerless and the voiceless at home to confront America with its racial injustice, its apathy, and its poverty, and with that same vision we dream for Vietnam: a vision of a society in which all can control their own destinies.

We are convinced that the only way to stop this and future wars is to organize a domestic social movement which challenges the very legitimacy of our foreign policy; this movement must also fight to end racism, to end the paternalism of our welfare system, to guarantee decent incomes for all, and to supplant the authoritarian control of our universities with a community of scholars.

This movement showed its potential when 25,000 people—students, the poverty-stricken, ministers, faculty, unionists, and others— marched on Washington last April. This movement must now show its force. SDS urges everyone who believes that our warmaking must be ended and our democracy-building must begin, to join in a March on Washington on November 27, at 11 A.M. in front of the White House.

"Dump Johnson"

William H. Chafe

For those young antiwar protesters who wished to retain "political viability within the system," Allard Lowenstein provided a powerful role model. A bundle of political energy and charismatic charm, Lowenstein through the late 1940s, 1950s, and 1960s had seemed like a youthful knight in shining armor, leading various student crusades for reforming the political process, and redeeming America's promise to the ideals of equal opportunity, peace, and justice.

Lowenstein's politics represented a perfect amalgam of anticommunism and social reform. As one of the first presidents of the National Student Association (NSA) in 1950–51, the young, New York City–raised graduate of the University of North Carolina had pioneered both a tough anticommunist position for NSA on foreign policy and a commitment to racial equality and social progress at home. His exposé of the evils of apartheid in South Africa in 1962 helped highlight the genius and moral passion of Nelson Mandela's fight for black majority rule in that country. Then, Lowenstein became the primary white leader stirring northern white students to go South to Mississippi and join the civil rights struggle. Now, in 1967, Lowenstein assumed the most daunting mantle of all—leading an insurgency from the left within the Democratic Party to end the war in Vietnam, all the while working within the system. The following selection describes Lowenstein's tactical and strategic brilliance in creating the move to "dump" Lyndon Johnson as the Democratic Party's standard bearer in 1968. But in the process, the article also raises the larger question of whether it is possible to walk the thin line between rebellion against a policy of a political regime, and operating within the ground rules of that same regime.

Stunning in its tactics and bold in its assumptions about the vulnerability of those in power, the campaign to "Dump Lyndon Johnson" as

Excerpted from William H. Chafe, *Never Stop Running: Allard K. Lowenstein and the Struggle to Save American Liberalism,* copyrighted in 1993 by Harper Collins. Reprinted by permission.

the presidential nominee of the Democratic Party in 1968 was the effort of a few reformers, propelled by conscience, to marshal enough political power to achieve, in essence, a peaceful coup d'état. Led by the young reformer Allard Lowenstein, this insurgent movement pledged to accomplish radical ends through reformist means. Rarely, if ever, had political activists reposed more faith in the capacity of a democratic process to turn its leaders and policies upside down. Between 1966 and 1968, in effect, Lowenstein and his allies sought to transform American politics. The degree to which that effort was a success testified dramatically to the genius and political passion of Allard Lowenstein, and represented the apex of his political influence. The effort also ultimately defined the borderline between seeking change within the political system, and deciding that the system itself had to change.

In the aftermath of the student "teach-ins" and the onset of the draft resistance campaign, Lowenstein sought a viable plan to sustain and nourish a political alternative to radical confrontation with the government. Earlier meetings between Lowenstein and administration officials had left little hope that change could come from within the administration. In response, Lowenstein and his allies from various liberal organizations set upon a course of action based on their conclusion that Lyndon Johnson himself was the Achilles' heel of the Democratic Party and that with enough support, they might mobilize opposition to the president's renomination.

By May 1967, Lowenstein started broaching the nucleus of his emerging strategy to friends. "It is now clear what must be done," Lowenstein told two student associates at a meeting in Cambridge. "Dump Johnson. We can do it. No one wants him out there and all that we have to do is have someone say it. Like, 'The emperor has no clothes.' There's a movement within the party that is dying for leadership." Later in the summer—after returning from a trip to Africa—Lowenstein talked about this idea with other student allies.

In both cases, the first response was astonishment. "I've never had any questions about [Al's] political judgment in the past," student leader Barney Frank—later congressman—told one friend, "[but] I think he's crazy. The idea of upsetting a sitting president with the power of Lyndon Johnson . . . crazy." Others asked what kind of mushrooms Al had been eating in Africa. But Lowenstein persisted. The idea might sound brazen and bizarre when first set forth, he agreed; but his friends should think about the logical sequence. The public was changing its opinion on the war and had no enthusiasm for LBJ; all people needed was an outlet for their grievances. Momentum would develop, Johnson would plummet further in popularity, suddenly a candidate would emerge who "will get on the bandwagon that we've built," and voila! Johnson would fall. The idea suddenly sounded plausible, especially to those who were captured by the conviction and energy of the person presenting it.

Not surprisingly, Lowenstein used as his departure point the place from which he had first launched his political alternative to radical protest—the NSA. Why not mobilize these students as the vanguard for carrying the "dump Johnson" movement forward into the Democratic Party and the primary states. Thus when the NSA met for its annual Congress in August 1967, two headlines emerged: the student delegates had decided to sever their ties with CIA-supported international organizations; and they determined to organize an "alternative candidates task force" that would pave the way for unseating Lyndon Johnson. "This congress," Lowenstein told the delegates at College Park, Maryland, "can be a launching pad for a decision to make 1968 the year when students help change a society almost everyone agrees is headed for destruction."

Ironically, the attractiveness of Lowenstein's "dump Johnson" strategy was heightened by the dissension and disarray among radicals who met later that summer at the National Conference for New Politics (NCNP) convention. More than 3,000 delegates gathered in Chicago, representing a variety of antiwar, Black Power, and community action groups. Most appeared committed to a total overhaul of American society, rejecting the feasibility of working for change through existing institutions. Almost immediately, however, their deliberations were taken over by fractious infighting. A black caucus demanded unconditional acceptance of a thirteen point ultimatum requiring 50 percent black representation on all committees (later expanded to require 50 percent voting power throughout the convention), support for all wars of national liberation, condemnation of Zionist imperialism, and creation of "white civilizing committees" to extirpate "the savage and beastlike character that runs rampant through America." In what seemed to many a paroxysm of guilt, the overwhelmingly white delegates accepted the black caucus's demands. But then the convention devoted most of its energies to discussing how to create a revolution and barely mentioned the 1968 election or presidential politics. Thus the "new politics," especially as conveyed by the mass media, seemed to boil down to two essentials: a willingness to embrace inflammatory rhetoric as long as the source of the rhetoric was black; and an insistence that "politics," at least as conventionally defined, was beneath radical contempt—a tool of the establishment that should be abandoned as irrelevant.

From the point of view of Lowenstein and his allies, the NCNP's activities simply confirmed the legitimacy of their own effort, while removing one source of possible competition for the loyalties of those who still wanted to make a political fight against the president. "The third party had died with the New Politics," one student leader noted. "The chance of denying the army the manpower to fight [through draft resistance] . . . was equally impossible." The counterculture's assertion that revolution would come "when you could fuck in the streets" was a disaster. "So Allard's stuff—even as implausible as it sounded—still made more sense than [anything else around]." Suddenly, Lowenstein's contention that mainstream college students could provide the organizational infrastructure for unseating the president became not only credible but, for many antiwar activists, the only ball game in town.

At just this critical juncture, other political voices began to provide reinforcement. Writing in the *New Yorker* under the pseudonym Bailey Laird, Richard Goodwin, a speech writer for Robert Kennedy and a former aide to John Kennedy, cleverly dissected the conventional wisdom that an incumbent president could not be unseated. "The rules [of politics]," Goodwin wrote, "are only a summary of what's happened before. The trick is in trying to see what's going to happen next." According to the "rules," John Kennedy could never have been elected because "he was too young and a Catholic." But Kennedy chose to ignore the rules and create his own new reality. So, too, with the 1968 election, Goodwin reasoned. "People just don't like [Johnson]," he pointed out. "You can go around the country and you just don't meet anyone who's enthusiastic about [him]. . . . People tend to vote against someone rather than for someone, and I think they could really turn on the President." Thus, Goodwin concluded, "this nomination is really up for grabs. . . . People are looking for a fresh face . . . a man who really stands for something. . . . I think someone like that would find help . . . in the most unexpected places."

Allard Lowenstein could hardly have asked for a more ringing endorsement of both his own political assessment and his plan of action. He had maneuvered much of the student leadership of the country into a position of supporting his mainstream political approach to the war. Now he had escalated that campaign to an explicit assault on the president himself. The challenge he faced was to use his student base as a foundation from which to build buttresses of support to other segments of the party. Goodwin had written that "once in a while you have to take a big chance. Knowing when that time has come is what separates the great ones from the others. [But] I tell you, the big prize is hanging right up there ready to be grabbed." Lowenstein had decided that *this* was the time to turn fantasy into reality and reach for the prize.

He coordinated a remarkable team effort. Forces in the field were deployed far beyond what anyone could imagine, based on the number of people involved, and the results were literally stunning. One group, working from their postage-stamp office at Union Theological Seminary, made contact with campuses where Al might speak, and lined up potential canvassers for primary campaigns. Harold Ickes (later in the Clinton administration) dropped out of law school to spend up to twenty hours a day as "dispatch central," his New York studio apartment serving as the headquarters for scheduling "dump Johnson" activities. "I would literally work as the sun moved," he recalled, "from the East Coast to the West Coast. Al would call in and give me names of people I should follow up with, whom I should call, introduce myself to, etc. There was just this bewildering array of people that I kept in touch with." Pivotal to the whole operation, of course, were Lowenstein himself and his coworker Curtis Gans, who resigned from his ADA job to devote all his time to the "dump Johnson" project he had helped to create. Gans in Washington and Lowenstein in New York would target key constituencies to visit, orchestrate their travel schedules, pool their political contacts and resources, then hit the road in a political assault pattern that might well have made old time politicians feel outclassed.

The scenario became routine. Collecting lists of names and phone numbers of all the "friendlies" they could identify from sources like ADA, Women Strike for Peace, and antiwar advertisements, Gans and Lowenstein would schedule a series of meetings in a local area. Lowenstein was teaching constitutional law at City College every Tuesday and Thursday, so he made East Coast trips after class on Tuesday and on Wednesday, then headed west from Thursday night through Monday. "I never missed a class," he boasted. Gans's role was to "advance" the joint mission, meeting with local politicos, scouting the territory for potential allies as well as minefields, and setting up speaking locations and private meetings for Lowenstein. A few days later, Lowenstein would parachute in for his part of the tandem operation, while Gans moved on to prepare the next landing site. Lowenstein would meet privately with important political figures, give a public address about the "dump Johnson" campaign in a community setting, then sometimes speak to a university group. Always the message was the same: this campaign was a mainstream effort of concerned Democrats; its purpose was to save the country and the party, not destroy them; the nation was full of people convinced that Johnson's Vietnam policy was disastrous, and working together, these people could make a difference and turn the country in a new direction. As reassuring as it was bold, the Lowenstein message hammered home the theme that concerted political action—within the party—was the highest form of Democratic loyalty, and the only way to save the country.

Almost magically, the pieces started to fall into place. Right after the NSA meeting in August 1967, Lowenstein flew to California, where he enlisted the support of Gerald Hill of the California Democratic Council, along with a $1,000 donation from the council to help defray his travel expenses. Shortly thereafter, $5,000 was collected from an East Coast antiwar source. The actor Robert Vaughn helped establish a group called Dissenting Democrats for antiwar activists who were outside the Democratic Party structure. By early September, the "dump Johnson" forces took the first giant step toward credibility *within* the party structure when Donald Peterson, the Democratic Party chairman of the tenth congressional district in Wisconsin, signed on, soon to be joined by Alpha Smaby, a widely respected legislator from Hubert Humphrey's home state of Minnesota. Newspaper stories proliferated as the campaign took on a life of its own. "Al seemed to be at every airport, every college campus, every state," Harold Ickes said. "It was just amazing where you would get calls from."

By the end of October, the "dump Johnson" movement had achieved a momentum that even hardened politicians could no longer ignore. The state party chairman in Michigan—a critical Democratic stronghold—embraced the campaign, as did the "young Democrat" organizations in Iowa, Michigan, and Wisconsin. Affiliate organizations multiplied, from the Coalition for a Democratic Alternative (CDA) to the Conference of Concerned Democrats ("concerned demagogues," Ickes called them) and Concerned Democrats of America. In a devastating blow to traditional Democrats, the liberal *New Republic* endorsed the campaign in a front-page editorial—"We don't know whether Lyndon Johnson can be denied. . . . We do know the attempt must be made"—and public opinion polls showed a growing groundswell of support for an alternative to Johnson, accompanied by a near free-fall decline in Johnson's public standing. It was as if everything Lowenstein had predicted in August were a carefully drawn blueprint for what was happening in October and November.

All that was missing was a candidate. From the beginning, Lowenstein had argued—undoubtedly with greater self-assurance than he felt—that once his coalition of forces had proved the depth and breadth of political alienation in the land, a candidate would "jump on the bandwagon." Furthermore, he insisted that such a demonstration had to come from "responsible, broadly based" groups within the party who could not be dismissed as marginal—thus providing another persuasive argument for excluding the "crazies." "These [potential candidates] cannot be expected to undertake so gruelling a contest [as an assault on the president]," he wrote, "unless they can be shown that it will not be an act of political hari-kari." But now that demonstration had been made and it was time to deliver on the final promise, without which the entire "dump Johnson" edifice might crumble.

Throughout the campaign, it had been clear that Lowenstein's ideal candidate was Robert Kennedy. The two had initially been wary of each other when Kennedy ran for the U.S. Senate from New York in 1964, but rapidly they became closer, especially after Kennedy enlisted Lowenstein's aid in drafting his antiapartheid speech at the University of Capetown in South Africa in February 1966. "He and Bobby [developed] a tremendous affection for each other," columnist Jack Newfield commented. When Lowenstein found himself on the same plane Kennedy was taking to California in the spring of 1967, therefore, he took the opportunity to brief Kennedy on his plans. Student-manned organizations would drive Johnson from the presidential race during the primaries, he told the senator, and the nomination would then be wide open. Although he did not ask Kennedy to become a candidate at that point, he nevertheless hoped to plant a seed that would grow. Kennedy responded with interest but contented himself primarily with speculating about other potential candidates, especially General James Gavin, a prominent military hero who had turned against the war. Lowenstein viewed Kennedy's response overall as "very friendly."

In their next meeting, the issue was broached more directly. At Hickory Hill, Kennedy's house in McLean, Virginia, after the ADA's board meeting in September 1967, Lowenstein and Jack Newfield engaged in a three-hour debate with Arthur Schlesinger, Jr., and James Loeb on the merits of Kennedy entering the race. "Argue it out," Kennedy told them, and while Schlesinger and Loeb defended the tactic of supporting a peace plank, Lowenstein and Newfield—with Lowenstein doing most of the talking—insisted that Johnson was going to fall and that Kennedy had a moral and political responsibility to step in. "Al was eloquent," Newfield said; he pulled out all the stops. At different points, Kennedy made remarks suggesting his fundamental agreement with Lowenstein. "When was the last time millions of people rallied behind a plank?" Kennedy asked Schlesinger. He also agreed that Johnson was vulnerable, "I think Al may be right," he said. "I think Johnson might quit the night before the convention opens. I think he is a coward." But Kennedy also told Lowenstein and Newfield that he saw no politically convincing argument for jumping in. Mayor Richard Daley of Chicago and other politicos were giving him no encouragement. Furthermore, any action Kennedy took would be seen as "splitting the party" out of personal spite toward LBJ. As Newfield later wrote, Kennedy's gut instincts were all for going in. But he could not bring himself to make the leap. "You understand, of course, that there are those of us who think the honor and direction of the country are at stake," Lowenstein told Kennedy as he left. "We're going to do it without you, and that's too bad, because you could have become president of the United States." It was a poignant moment, two politicians in quest of redemptive meaning in their public lives exchanging bittersweet comments on the larger struggle of conscience that engulfed them both.

In the meantime, Lowenstein took Kennedy's advice and approached a series of other potential candidates. General Gavin was interested but, in Lowenstein's view, completely naive, and more important he indicated that he would run as a Republican if he ran at all. George McGovern also responded positively to the idea and was seen by some as the best overall candidate because he understood the need for far-reaching reform in the political system. But McGovern was deeply concerned about the impact a presidential candidacy would have on his chances for reelection to the Senate from conservative South Dakota. When Lowenstein went to Sioux Falls, he discovered a mood substantially different from that of the rest of the country. "The picture of [South Dakota] unravelling" under the impact of the war just was not present, Lowenstein concluded. For McGovern to run for both president and the Senate, therefore, would create a problem of "two vocabularies, two emotional tones"—a prospect that seemed to confirm McGovern's doubts.

That left the one name that was on everyone's list, Eugene McCarthy. The senior senator from Minnesota, McCarthy had once been a close ally of Lyndon Johnson. His eloquent nomination speech for Adlai Stevenson at the 1960 Democratic convention was widely viewed as a last-ditch effort to block the Kennedy juggernaut and buy time for Johnson. In 1964, moreover, LBJ had publicly toyed with the idea of McCarthy as his vice-presidential choice (going to Humphrey only at the last minute). On the other hand, McCarthy had become a powerful voice against the war. His daughter Mary served as a persuasive intermediary for the "dump Johnson" forces, having been deeply impressed by Lowenstein's NSA speech in August. From talking to Mary, it seemed clear to Lowenstein that McCarthy was more ready to make a positive decision than anyone else.

Pressed especially by Gans, Lowenstein finally agreed to initiate a formal approach to the Minnesota senator. A man of deep Catholic morality but appropriately moderate demeanor, McCarthy in many ways was the ideal torchbearer. He would scare no one with his gray hair, his gray suit, and his dignified appeal for people to "speak out if you agree . . . there is no justification for continuing this war." But he could also inspire audiences with the simplicity of his moral commitment. "There comes a time," he said repeatedly, "when an honorable man simply has to raise the flag." Now, when Lowenstein and Gans went to him, McCarthy appeared ready to raise his—and to carry the banner for the "dump Johnson" movement.

On a three-day trip through the Northeast to test the political winds, the response was overwhelmingly positive. At a hastily massed rally in Cambridge, hand-lettered signs proclaimed, "The war is obscene, we want Eugene." In response, McCarthy told the crowds, "Vietnam is part of a much larger question, which is, is America going to police the planet?" the crowd went wild. Political supporters of the "dump Johnson" effort began to believe in it. "A month back," observed Gerald Hill, "I would have said our effort was an attempt to modify Johnson's policies by giving him a scare. Now it is becoming a real attempt to beat him." Having already scheduled a national Conference of Concerned Democrats in Chicago for December on the presumption a candidate would have emerged by then, Lowenstein and Gans were now confident that they had their man. "There are some things that are just so wrong that you have to take a stand," McCarthy said as he left Boston, "no matter what." Eleven months after the student body presidents' letter to LBJ, six months after first articulating the idea of "dumping Johnson" to student allies, and four months after the NSA convention at College Park, the final piece of Lowenstein's "impossible" plan had fallen into place. A candidate had emerged "to jump on the bandwagon."

No matter what political observers or historians think about Allard Lowenstein's style and effectiveness, his success in putting together a mainstream Democratic effort to defeat a sitting president was one of the most remarkable political achievements of contemporary American history. With unerring singleness of purpose, Lowenstein identified his objective, created a brilliant strategy, and mobilized an elite battalion of supporters to achieve his goal.

At the root of Lowenstein's success was his passionate preoccupation with showing that protest could triumph within the system. Countless thousands of other opponents of the war believed that the political process was so contaminated by militaristic values and materialism that only a struggle to change the soul of America and destroy capitalism could bring about the kind of change that was necessary. But whatever sympathy Lowenstein occasionally showed for the genuine alienation and idealism of these antiwar critics, he refused to play in their ball game and, in the way he defined their tactics, made sure they would not be accepted in his. Lowenstein denounced the "hate philosophy" he identified with the New Left and dismissed the inflammatory rhetoric that first decried the "system" and then tried to trash it. "Al [not only] didn't have much use for [the hard left]," Greg Craig noted, "[he had] some contempt for [them]."

To isolate and defeat the left, however, Lowenstein had to show that the politics of the center could work in addressing grievances identified by the left and shared by liberals. Thus, he had to reach out to the mainstream and simultaneously move it leftward, cultivating a heightened consciousness among "moderates" about the dimension of the problems that existed. It was like an upward spiral: you appealed to people's traditional values as the basis for mobilizing them, then kept them activated and working inside the system, initially as a way to prevent the left from triumphing, but ultimately as the only means of defeating the warhawks on the right. In everything Lowenstein did, one student ally noted, "there was an ongoing assumption that he defined the limits of the [permissible] left, wherever he was. Beyond that [there'd] be dragons." Thus, Lowenstein made his program the definition of acceptable dissent, galvanizing support precisely because the effort was to make democracy work, not destroy it. As one student supporter said, "Al [gave] me a way to do what I believed, and honor where I came from at the same time. . . . There was no way I was going to go against the system altogether, because I knew what it had done for my family. And here was an opportunity to take the tools of the system and make it work for what I believed in. I always believed that was what he wanted to do."

At every stage, Lowenstein devised ways of proceeding that reinforced such instincts. Al emphasized what united people behind a common cause and how their collective commitment could be turned to practical effect. "Al's greatest contribution," the journalist David Halberstam said, "was in making people feel they were not alone. He once told me, 'You know, the students think they're the only ones who are angry, and the middle-class women in the suburbs think they're the only ones who don't like the war' . . . and what Al did was [make] those people feel they were not alone. He was the ultimate moralist-activist . . . and he could touch in you and evoke in you those things that you believed in when you were very young."

There were some who believed Lowenstein took too much credit for the "dump Johnson" movement. "If the author supplies the idea and the architect the blueprint," Curtis Gans said, "he was neither the author nor the architect" of the campaign. Clearly, countless individuals were involved, some—like Gans—more important than others. Still, Lowenstein was the source, the inspiration, and the genius that made it all happen. "Al had the ability of taking very complex issues," Harold Ickes said, "and redefining them so that people who were not that sophisticated . . . really understood them in a very profound way." He could translate the most byzantine political strategy into terms that others could immediately identify with. Others provided the mechanical skill, an associate pointed out, but Lowenstein had the creativity to make the impossible seem doable.

"He was articulate as hell . . . he knew a bunch of reporters, [and] he was eminently quotable," the associate observed, thus becoming the critical pivot around which the movement turned.

Because of his talents, Lowenstein may have been the only person who could have achieved the triumph of 1967. Acknowledged as a member of mainstream, anticommunist America, he could articulate his position without automatically incurring dismissal as a "crazy." Yet, as a perennial student leader and reformer, he could reach out to the angry young and get their attention. Combined with an extraordinary political intelligence, these qualifications placed him in the unique position of being able to chart, direct, and then put into place a plan to show that the American democratic system would work, and that people who cared could make a difference.

What had begun as "a classic Don Quixote maneuver that no one believed in except himself" was now on the verge of victory. The fall of 1967, *Newsweek* observed, had been "one of the most histrionic autumns America has ever known . . . a season of blustery rhetoric and even stormier deeds." Into that autumn, Allard Lowenstein had brought a vision of change. "He said that . . . we're going to organize the students of this country and go in and do the work that the political hacks normally do," the Amherst student body president said, "[and he said] the students of this country are gong to bring it back to sanity . . . and the most marvelous thing . . . is that he really predicted [what was going to happen]. And then he said . . . 'It will be the biggest news story of 1968.'"

With astonishing insight, Allard Lowenstein had prophesied—then helped bring to reality—a program of political protest that promised to redeem the faith of Americans in peaceful change through democratic processes. In the parlance of the day, he had delivered a "heavy" message and done so with style, brilliance, and panache. What was not yet clear was whether 1968 would bring the fulfillment of the promise he had made.

Vietnam Veterans against the War (1971)

John Kerry

By the early 1970s the American people's initial support of the government policy in Vietnam had become a yearning for an end to what seemed an interminable and unwinnable war. Americans from all walks of life now openly questioned and protested against the war. The antiwar movement had come to include groups such as Business Executives Move for a Vietnam Peace, the Federation of American Scientists, and Another Mother for Peace.

Vietnam Veterans against the War was one of the most influential and controversial antiwar organizations. Created by six Vietnam Veterans in 1967, it had thousands of members by the end of the decade. In April 1971, more than one thousand VVAW members—many in wheelchairs or on crutches—joined a 200,000 strong antiwar protest in Washington, D.C. "Bring our brothers home," they chanted. On April 23, thousands of veterans gathered at the U.S. Capitol, took the medals they'd been given by their nation—including Purple Hearts and Silver Stars—and threw them away.

Inside the Capitol building that day, one of their own, John Kerry, testified before the Senate Foreign Relations Committee. Kerry, a graduate of Yale University, had joined the navy and served as an officer on a gunboat in the Mekong Delta. He had received a Silver Star, Bronze Star, and three Purple Hearts. What he told the Senate committee was devastating. "How do you ask a man to be the last man to die for a mistake?" he demanded.

John Kerry was elected to the U.S. Senate (D., MA) in 1984 and has served since that date.

I would like to talk on behalf of all those veterans and say that several months ago in Detroit we had an investigation at which over 150 honorably discharged, and many very highly decorated, veterans testified

From "Vietnam Veterans against the War" statement by John Kerry to the Senate Committee on Foreign Relations, April 23, 1971.

to war crimes committed in Southeast Asia. These were not isolated incidents but crimes committed on a day-to-day basis with the full awareness of officers at all levels of command.

It is impossible to describe to you exactly what did happen in Detroit—the emotions in the room and the feelings of the men who were reliving their experiences in Vietnam. They relived the absolute horror of what this country, in a sense, made them do.

They told stories that at times they had personally raped, cut off ears, cut off heads, taped wires from portable telephones to human genitals and turned up the power, cut off limbs, blown up bodies, randomly shot at civilians, razed villages in fashion reminiscent of Genghis Khan, shot cattle and dogs for fun, poisoned food stocks, and generally ravaged the countryside of South Vietnam in addition to the normal ravage of war and the normal and very particular ravaging which is done by the applied bombing power of this country.

We call this investigation the Winter Soldier Investigation. The term Winter Soldier is a play on words of Thomas Paine's in 1776 when he spoke of the Sunshine Patriots and summer time soldiers who deserted at Valley Forge because the going was rough.

We who have come here to Washington have come here because we feel we have to be winter soldiers now. We could come back to this country, we could be quiet, we could hold our silence, we could not tell what went on in Vietnam, but we feel because of what threatens this country, not the reds, but the crimes which we are committing that threaten it, that we have to speak out. . . .

In our opinion and from our experience, there is nothing in South Vietnam which could happen that realistically threatens the United States of America. And to attempt to justify the loss of one American life in Vietnam, Cambodia or Laos by linking such loss to the preservation of freedom, which those misfits supposedly abuse, is to us the height of criminal hypocrisy, and it is that kind of hypocrisy which we feel has torn this country apart.

We found that not only was it a civil war, an effort by a people who had for years been seeking their liberation from any colonial influence whatsoever, but also we found that the Vietnamese whom we had enthusiastically molded after our own image were hard put to take up the fight against the threat we were supposedly saving them from.

We found most people didn't even know the difference between communism and democracy. They only wanted to work in rice paddies without helicopters strafing them and bombs with napalm burning their villages and tearing their country apart. They wanted everything to do with the war, particularly with this foreign presence of the United States of America, to leave them alone in peace, and they practiced the art of survival by siding with whichever military force was present at a particular time, be it Viet Cong, North Vietnamese or American.

We found also that all too often American men were dying in those rice paddies for want of support from their allies. We saw first hand how monies from American taxes were used for a corrupt dictatorial regime. We saw that many people in this country had a one-sided idea of who was kept free by our flag, and blacks provided the highest percentage of casualties. We saw Vietnam ravaged equally by American bombs and search and destroy missions, as well as by Viet Cong terrorism and yet we listened while this country tried to blame all of the havoc on the Viet Cong.

We rationalized destroying villages in order to save them. We saw America lose her sense of morality as she accepted very coolly a My Lai and refused to give up the image of American soldiers who hand out chocolate bars and chewing gum.

We learned the meaning of free fire zones, shooting anything that moves, and we watched while America placed a cheapness on the lives of Orientals.

We watched the United States falsification of body counts, in fact the glorification of body counts. We listened while month after month we were told the back of the enemy was about to break. We fought using weapons against "oriental human beings." We fought using weapons against those people which I do not believe this country would dream of using were we fighting in the European theater. We watched while men charged up hills because a general said that hill has to be taken, and after losing one platoon or two platoons they marched away to leave the hill for reoccupation by the North Vietnamese. We watched pride allow the most unimportant battles to be blown into extravaganzas, because we couldn't lose, and we couldn't retreat, and because it didn't matter how many American bodies were lost to prove that point, and so there were Hamburger Hills and Khe Sanhs and Hill 81s and Fire Base 6s, and so many others.

Now we are told that the men who fought there must watch quietly while American lives are lost so that we can exercise the incredible arrogance of Vietnamizing the Vietnamese.

Each day to facilitate the process by which the United States washes her hands of Vietnam someone has to give up his life so that the United States doesn't have to admit something that the entire world already knows, so that we can't say that we have made a mistake. Someone has to die so that President Nixon won't be, and these are his words, "the first President to lose a war."

We are asking Americans to think about that because how do you ask a man to be the last man to die in Vietnam? How do you ask a man to be the last man to die for a mistake? . . . We are here in Washington also to say that the problem of this war is not just a question of war and diplomacy. It is part and parcel of everything that we are trying as human beings to communicate to people in this country—the question of racism which is rampant in the military, and so many other questions such as the use of weapons; the hypocrisy in our taking umbrage at the Geneva Conventions and using that as justification for a continuation of this war when we are more guilty than any other body of violations of those Geneva Conventions: in the use of free fire zones, harassment interdiction fire, search and destroy missions, the bombings, the torture of prisoners, the killing of prisoners, all accepted policy by many units in South Vietnam. That is what we are trying to say. It is part and parcel of everything.

An American Indian friend of mine who lives in the Indian Nation of Alcatraz put it to me very succinctly. He told me how as a boy on an Indian reservation he had watched television and he used to cheer the cowboys when they came in and shot the Indians, and then suddenly one day he stopped in Vietnam and he said "my God, I am doing to these people the very same thing that was done to my people," and he stopped. And that is what we are trying to say, that we think this thing has to end.

We are here to ask, and we are here to ask vehemently, where are the leaders of our country. Where is the leadership? We're here to ask where are McNamara, Rostow, Bundy, Gilpatrick, and so many others. Where are they now that we, the men they sent off to war, have returned. These are commanders who have deserted their troops. And there is no more serious crime in the laws of war. The Army says they never leave their wounded. The marines say they never leave even their dead. These men have left all the casualties and retreated behind a pious shield of public rectitude. They've left the real stuff of their reputations bleaching behind them in the sun in this country. . . .

We wish that a merciful God could wipe away our own memories of that service as easily as this administration has wiped away their memories of us. But all that they have done and all that they can do by this denial is to make more clear than ever our own determination to undertake one last mission—to search out and destroy the last vestige of this barbaric war, to pacify our own hearts, to conquer the hate and the fear that have driven this country these last ten years and more. And more. And so when thirty years from now our brothers go down the street without a leg, without an arm, or a face, and small boys ask why, we will be able to say "Vietnam" and not mean a desert, not a filthy obscene memory, but mean instead the place where America finally turned and where soldiers like us helped it in the turning.

Letter to the Draftboard (1969)

William Jefferson Clinton

In many respects, the 1992 presidential campaign represented a referendum on how Americans felt about the 1960s, and even more important, on which perception of the 1960s would prevail—the one that saw it as an era of reform and optimism, or one which perceived it as a time of polarization and bitterness. Nothing better highlighted the relevance of the 1960s to the 1992 presidential race than the disclosure that Bill Clinton had consciously sought to evade the draft, and the possibility of serving in Vietnam.

On February 12, 1992—in the midst of the New Hampshire primary campaign—Clinton released a letter he had sent in December 1969 to the head of the Reserve Officers Training Corps (ROTC) at the University of Arkansas. In that letter (reprinted here in its entirety) Clinton described the anguish, ambivalence, and outrage he felt about the possibility of serving in Vietnam. Already a Rhodes Scholar at Oxford University in England, he had returned to the United States in the summer of 1969; while at home, he struck a bargain, agreeing to join the ROTC unit at the University of Arkansas after his return from England. This action won him a deferment from the draft and reduced the likelihood that he might have to go to Vietnam. Once back in England, however, Clinton decided upon reflection that this course of action was not consistent with his moral revulsion against the war; hence, he chose to renege on the commitment—although only after his deferment had gone through.

The Clinton letter can be read in either of two ways—as the clever footwork of a schemer willing to do anything in order to escape fighting; or as the principled and tortured confession of someone so deeply troubled by the issue of how to serve his conscience and country that he fell into a state of moral and intellectual paralysis. There is also a third option: that Clinton's letter reflects both motivations simultaneously.

Whatever the case, the key to Clinton's behavior seems contained in his overriding objective, stated in the letter, "to maintain my political viability within the system." While others either served in the military or engaged in outright resistance, Clinton chose a middle course. Readers of the letter today, thirty years

Excerpted from *The New York Times*. February 13, 1992.

after the war, might well ponder just what it tells us about the realities facing students in the late 1960s.

As context, is it useful to know that of the 26.8 million American men who came of draft age during the Vietnam War, 16 million—legally—did not serve in the military. Another 2 percent evaded the draft illegally. Of the 26.8 million men of draft age, 2.7 million (or roughly 10 percent) served in Vietnam, approximately half of them in combat or close support for combat troups. Graduates of elite colleges—such as George W. Bush—were unlikely to see military service in Vietnam; Harvard's twelve-hundred member graduating class of 1970 sent two men to Vietnam. One exception was Clinton's vice president, Al Gore, who graduated from Harvard in 1969 and enlisted in the army. He spent approximately six months of his twenty-two-month military service in Vietnam as a military journalist.

I am sorry to be so long in writing. I know I promised to let you hear from me at least once a month, and from now on you will, but I have had to have some time to think about this first letter. Almost daily since my return to England I have thought about writing, about what I want to and ought to say.

First, I want to thank you, not just for saving me from the draft, but for being so kind and decent to me last summer, when I was as low as I have ever been. One thing which made the bond we struck in good faith somewhat palatable to me was my high regard for you personally. In retrospect, it seems that the admiration might not have been mutual had you known a little more about me, about my political beliefs and activities. At least you might have thought me more fit for the draft than for R.O.T.C.

Let me try to explain. As you know, I worked for two years in a very minor position on the Senate Foreign Relations Committee. I did it for the experience and the salary but also for the opportunity, however small, of working every day against a war I opposed and despised with a depth of feeling I had reserved solely for racism in America before Vietnam. I did not take the matter lightly but studied it carefully, and there was a time when not many people had more information about Vietnam at hand than I did.

I have written and spoken and marched against the war. One of the national organizers of the Vietnam Moratorium is a close friend of mine. After I left Arkansas last summer, I went to Washington to work in the national headquarters of the Moratorium, then to England to organize the Americans here for demonstrations Oct. 15 and Nov. 16.

Interlocked with the war is the draft issue, which I did not begin to consider separately until early 1968. For a law seminar at Georgetown I wrote a paper on the legal arguments for and against allowing, within the Selective Service System, the classification of selective conscientious objection, for those opposed to participation in a particular war, not simply to "participation in war in any form."

From my work I came to believe that the draft system itself is illegitimate. No government really rooted in limited, parliamentary democracy should have the power to make its citizens fight and kill and die in a war they may oppose, a war which even possibly may be wrong, a war which, in any case, does not involve immediately the peace and freedom of the nation.

The draft was justified in World War II because the life of the people collectively was at stake. Individuals had to fight, if the nation was to survive, for the lives of their countrymen and their way of life. Vietnam is no such case. Nor was Korea an example, where, in my opinion, certain military action was justified but the draft was not, for the reasons stated above.

Because of my opposition to the draft and the war, I am in great sympathy with those who are not willing to fight, kill, and maybe die for their country (i.e., the particular policy of a particular government) right or wrong. Two of my friends at Oxford are conscientious objectors. I wrote a letter of recommendation for one of them to his Mississippi draft board, a letter which I am more proud of than anything else I wrote at Oxford last year. One of my roommates is a draft resister who is possibly under indictment and may never be able to go home again. He is one of the bravest, best men I know. His country needs men like him more than they know. That he is considered a criminal is an obscenity.

The decision not to be a resister and the related subsequent decisions were the most difficult of my life. I decided to accept the draft in spite of my beliefs for one reason: to maintain my political viability within the system. For years I have worked to prepare myself for a political life characterized by both practical political ability and concern for rapid social progress. It is a life I still feel compelled to try to lead. I do not think our system of government is by definition corrupt, however dangerous and inadequate it has been in recent years. (The society may be corrupt, but that is not the same thing, and if that is true we are all finished anyway.)

When the draft came, despite political convictions, I was having a hard time facing the prospect of fighting a war I had been fighting against, and that is why I contacted you. R.O.T.C. was the one way left in which I could possibly, but not positively, avoid both Vietnam and resistance. Going on with my education, even coming back to England, played no part in my decision to join R.O.T.C. I am back here, and would have been at Arkansas Law School because there is nothing else I can do. In fact, I would like to have been able to take a year out perhaps to teach in a small college or work on some community action project and in the process to decide whether to attend law school or graduate school and how to begin putting what I have learned to use.

But the particulars of my personal life are not nearly as important to me as the principles involved. After I signed the R.O.T.C. letter of intent I began to wonder whether the compromise I had made with myself was not more objectionable than the draft would have been, because I had no interest in the R.O.T.C. program in itself and all I seemed to have done was to protect myself from physical harm. Also, I began to think I had deceived you, not by lies—there were none—but by failing to tell you all the things I'm writing now. I doubt that I had the mental coherence to articulate them then.

At that time, after we had made our agreement and you had sent my 1-D deferment to my draft board, the anguish and loss of my self-regard and self-confidence really set in. I hardly slept for weeks and kept going by eating compulsively and reading until exhaustion brought sleep. Finally, on Sept. 12 I stayed up all night writing a letter to the chairman of my draft board, saying basically what is in the preceding paragraph, thanking him for trying to help in a case where he really couldn't, and stating that I couldn't do the R.O.T.C. after all and would he please draft me as soon as possible.

I never mailed the letter, but I did carry it on me every day until I got on the plane to return to England. I didn't mail the letter because I didn't see, in the end, how my going in the army and maybe going to Vietnam would achieve anything except a feeling that I had punished myself and gotten what I deserved. So I came back to England to try to make something of this second year of my Rhodes scholarship.

And that is where I am now, writing to you because you have been good to me and have a right to know what I think and feel. I am writing too in the hope that my telling this one story will help you to understand more clearly how so many fine people have come to find themselves still loving their country but loathing the military, to which you and other good men have devoted years, lifetimes, of the best service you could give. To many of us, it is no longer clear what is service and what is disservice, or if it is clear, the conclusion is likely to be illegal.

Forgive the length of this letter. There was much to say. There is still a lot to be said, but it can wait. Please say hello to Col. Jones for me.

Merry Christmas.

Sincerely,

Bill Clinton

In Retrospect

Robert McNamara

Robert McNamara, secretary of defense from 1961 through 1968, was one of the key architects of America's war in Vietnam. Though he at first supported escalation of America's involvement in Vietnam, growing doubts about the war led him to resign in 1968. In 1995, twenty years after the end of the Vietnam War, McNamara published In Retrospect: The Tragedy and Lessons of Vietnam. *"We of the Kennedy and Johnson administrations who participated in the decisions on Vietnam acted according to what we thought were the principles and traditions of this nation. We made our decisions in light of those values," he wrote. "Yet we were wrong, terribly wrong." McNamara's book was controversial: some pointed to his role in the war and called his self-criticism "too little, too late"; others saw his analysis as a betrayal of those who fought and died in a far-off land. Such controversy shows how raw the wounds of Vietnam may still be. But questions of responsibility aside, McNamara's larger interpretation is very much in line with the interpretations of many historians of the war. In the following excerpt from his book, he lays out what he sees as the major causes for America's "disaster" in Vietnam. Compare McNamara's analysis here with the radically different one that follows, drawn from Michael Lind's* Vietnam: The Necessary War.

By the time the United States finally left South Vietnam in 1973, we had lost over 58,000 men and women; our economy had been damaged by years of heavy and improperly financed war spending; and the political unity of our society had been shattered, not to be restored for decades.

Were such high costs justified?

Dean Rusk, Walt Rostow, Lee Kwan Yew, and many other geopoliticians across the globe to this day answer yes. They conclude that without U.S. intervention in Vietnam, Communist hegemony—both Soviet and Chinese—would have spread farther through South and East Asia to include control of Indonesia, Thailand, and possibly India. Some would go further and say that the USSR would have been led to take greater risks to extend its influence elsewhere in the world, particularly in the Middle East, where it might well have sought control of the oil-producing nations. They might be correct, but I seriously question such judgments.

When the archives of the former Soviet Union, China, and Vietnam are opened to scholars, we will know more about those countries' intentions, but even without such knowledge we know that the danger of Communist aggression during the four decades of the Cold War was real and substantial. Although during the 1950s, 1960s, 1970s, and 1980s the West often misperceived, and therefore exaggerated, the power of the East and its ability to project that power, to have failed to defend ourselves against the threat would have been foolhardy and irresponsible.

That said, today I question whether either Soviet or Chinese behavior and influence in the 1970s and 1980s would have been materially different had the United States not entered the war in Indochina or had we withdrawn from Vietnam in the early or mid-1960s. By then it should have become apparent that the two conditions underlying President Kennedy's decision to send military advisers to South Vietnam were not being met and, indeed, could not be met: political stability did not exist and was unlikely ever to be achieved; and the South Vietnamese, even with our training assistance and logistical support, were incapable of defending themselves.

Given these facts—and they are facts—I believe we could and should have withdrawn from South Vietnam either in late 1963 amid the turmoil following Diem's assassination or in late 1964 or early 1965 in the face of increasing political and military weakness in South Vietnam. And, as the table opposite suggests, there were at least three other occasions when withdrawal could have been justified.

I do not believe that U.S. withdrawal at any of these junctures, if properly explained to the American people and to the world, would have led West Europeans to question our support for NATO and, through it, our guarantee of their security. Nor do I believe that Japan would have viewed our security treaties as any less credible. On the contrary, it is possible we would have improved our credibility by withdrawing from Vietnam and saving our strength for more defensible stands elsewhere.

Date of Withdrawal	U.S. Force Levels in South Vietnam	US Killed in Action	Basis for Withdrawal
November 1963	16,300 advisers[a]	78	Collapse of Diem regime and lack of political stability
Late 1964 or early 1965	23,300 advisers	225	Clear indication of South Vietnam's inability to defend itself, even with U.S. training and logistical support
July 1965	81,400 troops	509	Further evidence of the above
December 1965	184,300 troops	1,594	Evidence that U.S. military tactics and training were inappropriate for the guerrilla war being waged
December 1967	485,600 troops	15,979	CIA reports indicating bombing in the North would not force North Vietnam to desist in the face of our inability to turn back enemy forces in South Vietnam
January 1973	543,400 troops (April 1969)	58,191[b]	Signing of Paris Accords, marking an end of U.S. military involvement

[a]This and all subsequent figures in the table have been supplied by the U.S. Army Center of Military History, Washington, D.C.

[b]As of December 31, 1968, the number of U.S. killed-in-action in Vietnam totaled 30,568.

It is sometimes said that the post–Cold War world will be so different from the world of the past that the lessons of Vietnam will be inapplicable or of no relevance to the twenty-first century. I disagree. That said, if we are to learn from our experience in Vietnam, we must first pinpoint our failures. There were eleven major causes for our disaster in Vietnam:

1. We misjudged then—as we have since—the geopolitical intentions of our adversaries (in this case, North Vietnam and the Vietcong, supported by China and the Soviet Union), and we exaggerated the dangers to the United States of their actions.
2. We viewed the people and leaders of South Vietnam in terms of our own experience. We saw in them a thirst for—

and a determination to fight for—freedom and democracy. We totally misjudged the political forces within the country.

3. We underestimated the power of nationalism to motivate a people (in this case, the North Vietnamese and Vietcong) to fight and die for their beliefs and values—and we continue to do so today in many parts of the world.

4. Our misjudgments of friend and foe alike reflected our profound ignorance of the history, culture, and politics of the people in the area, and the personalities and habits of their leaders. We might have made similar misjudgments regarding the Soviets during our frequent confrontations—over Berlin, Cuba, the Middle East, for example—had we not had the advice of Tommy Thompson, Chip Bohlen, and George Kennan. These senior diplomats had spent decades studying the Soviet Union, its people and its leaders, why they behaved as they did, and how they would react to our actions. Their advice proved invaluable in shaping our judgments and decision. No Southeast Asian counterparts existed for senior officials to consult when making decisions on Vietnam.

5. We failed then—as we have since—to recognize the limitations of modern, high-technology military equipment, forces, and doctrine in confronting unconventional, highly motivated people's movements. We failed as well to adapt our military tactics to the task of winning the hearts and minds of people from a totally different culture.

6. We failed to draw Congress and the American people into a full and frank discussion and debate of the pros and cons of a large-scale U.S. military involvement in Southeast Asia before we initiated the action.

7. After the action got under way and unanticipated events forced us off our planned course, we failed to retain popular support in part because we did not explain fully what was happening and why we were doing what we did. We had not prepared the public to understand the complex events we faced and how to react constructively to the need for changes in course as the nation confronted uncharted seas and an alien environment. A nation's deepest strength lies not in its military prowess but, rather, in the unity of its people. We failed to maintain it.

8. We did not recognize that neither our people nor our leaders are omniscient. Where our own security is not directly at stake, our judgment of what is in another people's or country's best interest should be put to the test of open discussion in international forums. We do not have the God-given right to shape every nation in our own image or as we choose.

9. We did not hold to the principle that U.S. military action—other than in response to direct threats to our own security—should be carried out only in conjunction with multinational forces supported fully (and not merely cosmetically) by the international community.

10. We failed to recognize that in international affairs, as in other aspects of life, there may be problems for which there are no immediate solutions. For one whose life has been dedicated to the belief and practice of problem solving, this is particularly hard to admit. But, at times, we may have to live with an imperfect, untidy world.

11. Underlying many of these errors lay our failure to organize the top echelons of the executive branch to deal effectively with the extraordinarily complex range of political and military issues, involving the great risks and costs—including, above all else, loss of life—associated with the application of military force under substantial constraints over a long period of time. Such organizational weakness would have been costly had this been the only task confronting the president and his advisers. It, of course, was not. It coexisted with the wide array of other domestic and international problems confronting us. We thus failed to analyze and debate our actions in Southeast Asia—our objectives, the risks and costs of alternative ways of dealing with them, and the necessity of changing course when failure was clear—with the intensity and thoroughness that characterized the debates of the Executive Committee during the Cuban Missile Crisis.

These were our major failures, in their essence. Though set forth separately, they are all in some way linked: failure in one area contributed to or compounded failure in another. Each became a turn in a terrible knot.

The Genuine Lessons of the Vietnam War

Michael Lind

In his "reinterpretation" of the Vietnam War, Michael Lind rejects what he sees as the dominant interpretations of the war—left, liberal, and conservative— and returns to the Cold War vision of the men who committed America to the course that proved so disastrous. In the context of the Cold War, he argues, the Vietnam War was not a "tragic error" or an "inexplicable mistake." It was failure, but it was a just and necessary war.

Lind, who has written both for the left-progressive Nation *and for the right- conservative* National Review, *is difficult to pigeonhole ideologically, but his book has been highly controversial among historians of the Vietnam War. It is useful to contrast the "lessons" Lind draws from America's experience in Viet- nam with those outlined by McNamara in the previous selection. What are the implications of Lind's "lessons" for American foreign policy in the post–Cold War world?*

In the mid-1960s, the sound and ultimately successful Cold War grand strategy of global military containment of the communist bloc required Presidents Kennedy and Johnson to escalate the U.S. in- volvement in Vietnam rather than withdraw without a major effort. Any president in office at the time probably would have done so. On February 17, 1965, former president Dwight Eisenhower told Presi- dent Johnson that "the U.S. has put its prestige onto the proposition of keeping SE Asia free. . . . We cannot let the Indo-Chinese penin- sula go. [Eisenhower] hoped it would not be necessary to use the six to eight divisions mentioned, but if it should be necessary then so be it." Similarly, any president in the 1960s probably would have led the United States to war if North Korea had invaded South Korea a second time, or if China had invaded Taiwan. In the circumstances of the Cold War, a president who abandoned any of the three fronts in Asia to the communist bloc without a major struggle would have been guilty of dereliction of his duties as commander-in-chief and leader of the worldwide American alliance system. To argue otherwise is ahistorical. If the United States today, a decade after the demise of the Soviet Union, is prepared to go to war on behalf of South Korea and possibly Taiwan as well, then it makes no sense to argue that it was irrational for the United States to defend its Indochinese protectorate at the height of the Third World War.

Once the Vietnam War is viewed in the context of the Cold War, it looks less like a tragic error than like a battle that could hardly be avoided. The Cold War was fought as a siege in Europe and as a series of duels elsewhere in the world—chiefly, in Korea and Indochina. Both the siege and the duels were necessary. Power in world politics is perceived power, and perceived power is a vector that results from perceived military capability and perceived political will. The U.S. forces stationed in West Germany and Japan demonstrated the capability of the United States to defend its most important allies. U.S. efforts on behalf of minor allies in peripheral regions such as South Korea and South Vietnam and Laos proved that the United States possessed the will to be a reliable ally. Had the United States repeatedly refused to take part in proxy-war duels with the Soviet Union, and with China during its anti-American phase, it seems likely that there would have been a dramatic pro-Soviet realignment in world politics, no matter how many missiles rusted in their silos in the American West and no matter how many U.S. troops remained stationed in West Germany.

Most of the major duels between the American bloc and the communist bloc took place in countries that were peripheral (so that proxy wars between the superpowers would be unlikely to escalate into all-out global war) and symbolic (because they were divided between communist and noncommunist states). Along with China, which was divided between the communist mainland and Nationalist Taiwan, and partitioned Korea, Vietnam was one of a handful of front-line countries. The argument that the United States should have "chosen its battles" more carefully and avoided peripheral regions in which its allies were at a disadvantage posits a false alternative. It would have been foolish for Moscow or Beijing to risk general war by attacking major U.S. allies, or to sponsor military challenges to the U.S. alliance system in places where the United States and its allies had a clear military and political advantage. The United States, then, was fated to forfeit the Cold War, or to fight in difficult conditions in battlefields that its enemies chose.

While the need to preserve a surplus of American credibility required the United States to escalate its involvement in Indochina by going to war, the need to preserve a surplus of American public support for the Cold War in its entirety required the U.S. government to avoid escalating the war in Indochina too much. Presidents Johnson and Nixon defended America's Cold War credibility, at the cost of eroding America's Cold War consensus. The high costs of the Vietnam War between 1965 and 1968 destroyed U.S. public support for an open-ended commitment to the defense of the noncommunist states of Indochina, while the additional costs of the prolonged withdrawal between 1968 and 1973 endangered public support for the Cold War on any front.

In the United States, the domestic result of the Vietnam War was a neoisolationist consensus in the 1970s. Disaffected moderate supporters of the Cold War teamed up with the permanent antiinterventionist made up of mostly northern progressive isolationists and Marx-influenced leftists. The neoisolationism of the U.S. Congress and the Carter administration in its first years permitted and encouraged the Soviet Union, with the assistance of its Vietnamese and Cuban auxiliaries, to engage in empire-building in the Third World without fear of American reprisal. The perception of rising Soviet power and American retreat inspired European appeasement of Moscow in the mid-seventies and also inspired bandwagoning with Moscow on the part of Third World states in the UN General Assembly. Only the Second Cold War of 1979–89, orchestrated in the face of significant leftist and neutralist opposition by Ronald Reagan, Margaret Thatcher, Helmut Kohl, François Mitterrand, and other western democratic leaders, reversed the pro-Soviet trend in world politics and drove the Soviet Union into bankruptcy by raising the costs of its bid for world military primacy. Far from having no affect in world politics, the U.S. defeat in Indochina inaugurated a period in which the relative power, influence, and ambition of the Soviet empire peaked. . . .

THE VERDICT ON VIETNAM

In the House of Commons on April 4, 1940, Winston Churchill described the British retreat from Dunkirk: "We must be careful not to assign to this deliverance the attributes of a victory." Indochina was the Dunkirk of the American effort in the Cold War. The Vietnam War will never be understood as anything other than a horrible debacle. At the same time, it cannot be understood except as a failed campaign in a successful world war against imperial tyrannies that slaughtered and starved more of their own subjects than any regimes in history.

For the past generation, the Vietnam War has been considered not only a disastrous defeat (which it was), but an easily avoidable mistake (which it was not, any more than was the Korean War) and a uniquely horrible conflict (more Americans were killed in three months in the trenches in World War I than in a decade in Vietnam). The anti–Vietnam War orthodoxy is so exaggerated, and so implausible, that it is certain to change as younger historians uninfluenced by the partisan battles of the Vietnam era write a more accurate and dispassionate history.

In the long run, the greatest danger is that the Vietnam War will be treated by mainstream historians as an inexplicable mistake. It is only a slight exaggeration to say that academic historians are paid to explain why what happened had to happen more or less as it did happen. Historians tend to applaud success and to condemn failure without considering that a successful policy may have been a mistake and that a failed policy might have been worth attempting. . . .

How will the Vietnam War be considered a generation or two from now? It seems likely that historians free from the biases of Marxist leftism, liberal isolationism, and minimal realism will consider the Korean and Vietnam Wars to have been comparable Cold War proxy battles between the United States and the Soviet Union and China. It will be taken for granted that the United States was able to bring about a stalemate in the Korean War in large part because the enemy was vulnerable to American conventional forces backed by nuclear threats. The United States won a Pyrrhic victory in Indochina and withdrew because the U.S. military's misguided conventional-war approach to combating what, in the early years, was predominantly an insurgency piled up American casualties too quickly and destroyed

American public support, first for the U.S. commitment to Indochina and then, temporarily, for the Cold War in general. Disinterested historians of the twenty-first century will also take it for granted that similar coalitions of progressive isolationists, Marxist radicals, and pacifists opposed U.S. intervention in World War I, World War II, and the major and minor conflicts of the Cold War, the Gulf War, and no doubt wars yet to come. The continuities in the ethnic and regional influences on isolationists and interventionists in the American population will be understood just as well.

Here, then, is a provisional verdict. The Vietnam War was a just, constitutional and necessary proxy war in the Third World War that was waged by methods that were often counterproductive and sometimes arguably immoral. The war had to be fought in order to preserve the military and diplomatic credibility of the United States in the Cold War, but when its costs grew excessive the war had to be forfeited in order to preserve the political consensus within the United States in favor of the Cold War.

The Vietnam War was neither a mistake nor a betrayal nor a crime. It was a military defeat.

Part 6

YEARS OF POLARIZATION

During the late 1960s American society was more profoundly divided than at any time since the Civil War. As the peaceful petitions of the nonviolent Civil Rights movement were replaced by Black Power slogans, white support for blacks plummeted. The emergence of feminism created profound divisions over traditional family roles and definitions of masculinity and femininity. The student movement began as a request for moderate changes, but with the growing crisis over Vietnam it began to challenge to the very structure of the university. As the protests over Vietnam grew, many cities and university campuses became domestic battlefields, with police barricades confronting student demonstrators.

The seeds of division lay in what many saw as the quiescent years of the 1950s. As a generation of youth came of age, raised in at least relative security and optimism, they—like their presidents—believed in great possibilities. Some measured American principles against its reality and found the nation wanting. They would be the core of what, by 1968, seemed a whole generation of activists. What's important to remember, however, is that all the youth inspired to activism in the 1960s were not on the left; conservative youth also measured the nation against its principles—though different ones—and set out to change the world.

The Civil Rights movement was crucial to the development of political activism on America's campuses. As white students and black students joined together in civil rights protests, they came face to face with the duplicity and brutality of law enforcement officials in the South. When, as frequently happened, the federal government failed to provide corrective assistance, demonstrators began to suspect that even those authorities they thought they would trust were part of the problem. What had begun as a specific protest against southern racism gradually developed into a more critical challenge to established authority generally.

When Mario Savio and others came back to campus from summer civil rights demonstrations in Mississippi in 1964, they carried their newfound criticism to university life itself. After officials at the University of California at Berkeley attempted to control distribution of political materials on a campus plaza, the Berkeley free speech movement began. Significantly, the issues were not specific, but involved protest against the "university machine" itself as a manifestation of corporate control of America. Students protested the depersonalization of the multiversity with its computerized systems, its huge classrooms, and its insensitivity to issues of human community.

By 1967 and 1968, the spirit of Berkeley had spread across the country, fueled by the fires of antiwar demonstrations. Universities were denounced for being instruments of the military-industrial complex. Students demanded the cancellation of university contracts to conduct research on weapons development. Army and Navy ROTC courses came under attack for providing a bond between the university and U.S. policy in Vietnam. When weapons manufacturers came to campus to recruit, students protested their presence, insisting that the university had no right to support the war effort—even indirectly—by making its facilities available to those who profited from the war.

Culture and politics became intermixed as long hair, marijuana, more casual attitudes toward sex, and rejection of middle-class values became associated with the antiwar movement. When students took over university buildings to protest the war, they boasted of their communal lifestyle, their hostility to monogamy, and their freedom to carve out a different lifestyle than that of their parents or elders. The so-called generation gap involved not only political disagreement, but also fundamental personal conflicts over how one would dress, what kind of language one would use, and whom one would sleep with. By the end of the 1960s the moderate reformism of the Students for a Democratic Society in 1962 had given way to the militant and violent rhetoric of the Weathermen. In the meantime, reaction against youthful protest and the counterculture had spread. Commentators developed a new phrase—"Middle America"—to describe those who rejected totally the assault on middle-class values by young people of the left. And Spiro Agnew, Richard Nixon's vice president, made a cottage industry out of denouncing antiwar protestors as "ideological eunuchs" who were encouraged in their rabble-rousing "by an effete corps of impudent snobs who characterize themselves as intellectuals."

The following selections, both documents from the time and historians' analyses, highlight some of the tensions of the time. While Americans were profoundly divided, the divisions were complicated, and rarely simply two-sided. The 1960 "Sharon Statement" by the young conservatives of Young Americans for Freedom (YAF) contrasts with the 1962 Port Huron Statement by the young leftists in Students for a Democratic Society (SDS). SDS's Port Huron Statement, in turn, offers a vivid contrast to the Weatherman SDS statement of the late 1960s, illustrating how a radical faction of the SDS moved from a vision of social transformation through participatory democracy to an ideology that justified violent revolution.

There were also divisions between the political activists of the New Left and the burgeoning counterculture. Historian Terry H. Anderson describes the rise and fall of the sixties counterculture, taking seriously its claims to a politics of its own. And, in a 1969 article for *Harper's* magazine, Peter Schrag vividly describes the counterrevolt against counterculture and New Left alike in his portrait of "the forgotten American." Finally, historian Kim McQuaid describes the culminating event of this era of division: Watergate.

How did America become so polarized? Why did the earlier, more moderate protests of the 1960s meet with little success? Did the intransigence of those in power necessitate the shift toward a more radical position? Was the counterculture really a challenge to the values and ways of life of mainstream America, or was it nothing more than a lifestyle, built around its own forms of consumption? Were the New Left political activists right to be suspicious of the counterculture? Which approach was more effective in yielding social change? Is the "forgotten American" described by Peter Schrag still a force in American politics today? Was the polarization chronicled in the following readings unavoidable?

The Port Huron Statement (1962)

Students for a Democratic Society

To young Americans in the early 1960s, everything seemed possible. A youthful, activist president had come into office promising that "we can do better." Black students throughout the South had demonstrated through sit-ins and kneel-ins that people willing to act on their convictions could help to turn society around. Inspired by these examples and given hope by the new leadership in Washington, young white reformers came together to draw up a manifesto for social change. Those who formed Students for a Democratic Society (SDS) were deeply critical of the complacency and indifference of their society. They hoped to marshall the resources of technology, the university, corporations, and government to eliminate poverty and racism. Hence, their agenda of reform. What remains most impressive from the Port Huron Statement, however, is its moderation, its faith that change can take place within the system, its conviction that social democracy could be achieved quickly and effectively, without revolution. The Port Huron Statement speaks eloquently to the idealism of a generation of student activists. Just as eloquently, it testifies to their innocence.

INTRODUCTION: AGENDA FOR A GENERATION

We are people of this generation, bred in at least modest comfort, housed now in universities, looking uncomfortably to the world we inherit.

When we were kids the United States was the wealthiest and strongest country in the world; the only one with the atom bomb, the least scarred by modern war, an initiator of the United Nations that we thought would distribute Western influence throughout the world. Freedom and equality for each individual, government of, by, and for

Excerpted from Tom Hayden et al., Port Huron Statement, mimeographed (n.p., Students for a Democratic Society, 1962).

the people—these American values we found good, principles by which we could live as men. Many of us began maturing in complacency.

As we grew, however, our comfort was penetrated by events too troubling to dismiss. First, the permeating and victimizing fact of human degradation, symbolized by the Southern struggle against racial bigotry, compelled most of us from silence to activism. Second, the enclosing fact of the Cold War, symbolized by the presence of the Bomb, brought awareness that we ourselves, and our friends, and millions of abstract "others" we knew more directly because of our common peril, might die at any time. We might deliberately ignore, or avoid, or fail to feel all other human problems, but not these two, for these were too immediate and crushing in their impact, too challenging in the demand that we as individuals take the responsibility for encounter and resolution.

While these and other problems either directly oppressed us or rankled our consciences and became our own subjective concerns, we began to see complicated and disturbing paradoxes in our surrounding America. The declaration "all men are created equal . . ." rang hollow before the facts of Negro life in the South and the big cities of the North. The proclaimed peaceful intentions of the United States contradicted its economic and military investments in the Cold War status quo. . . .

Our work is guided by the sense that we may be the last generation in the experiment with living. But we are a minority—the vast majority of our people regard the temporary equilibriums of our society and world as eternally-functional parts. In this is perhaps the outstanding paradox: we ourselves are imbued with urgency, yet the message of our society is that there is no viable alternative to the present. Beneath the reassuring tones of the politicians, beneath the common opinion that America will "muddle through," beneath the stagnation of those who have closed their minds to the future, is the pervading feeling that there simply are no alternatives, that our times have witnessed the exhaustion not only of Utopias, but of any new departures as well. . . .

Some would have us believe that Americans feel contentment amidst prosperity—but might it not better be called a glaze above deeply-felt anxieties about their role in the new world? And if these anxieties produce a developed indifference to human affairs, do they not as well produce a yearning to believe there *is* an alternative to the present, that something *can* be done to change circumstances in the school, the workplaces, the bureaucracies, the government? It is to this latter yearning, at once the spark and engine of change, that we direct our present appeal. The search for truly democratic alternatives to the present, and a commitment to social experimentation with them, is a worthy and fulfilling human enterprise, one which moves us and, we hope, others today. On such a basis do we offer this document of our convictions and analysis: as an effort in understanding and changing the conditions of humanity in the late twentieth century, an effort rooted in the ancient, still unfulfilled conception of man attaining determining influence over his circumstances of life. . . .

THE STUDENTS

If student movements for change are still rareties on the campus scene, what is commonplace there? The real campus, the familiar campus, is a place of private people, engaged in their notorious "inner emigration." It is a place of commitment to business-as-usual, getting ahead, playing it cool. It is a place of mass affirmation of the Twist, but mass reluctance toward the controversial public stance. Rules are accepted as "inevitable," bureaucracy as "just circumstances," irrelevance as "scholarship," selflessness as "martyrdom," politics as "just another way to make people, and an unprofitable one, too." . . .

Tragically, the university could serve as a significant source of social criticism and an initiator of new modes and molders of attitudes. But the actual intellectual effect of the college experience is hardly distinguishable from that of any other communications channel—say, a television set—passing on the stock truths of the day. Students leave college somewhat more "tolerant" than when they arrived, but basically unchallenged in their values and political orientations. With administrators ordering the institution, and faculty the curriculum, the student learns by his isolation to accept elite rule within the university, which prepares him to accept later forms of minority control. The real function of the educational system—as opposed to its more rhetorical function of "searching for truth"—is to impart the key information and styles that will help the student get by, modestly but comfortably, in the big society beyond.

THE SOCIETY BEYOND

Look beyond the campus, to America itself. That student life is more intellectual, and perhaps more comfortable, does not obscure the fact that the fundamental qualities of life on the campus reflect the habits of society at large. The fraternity president is seen at the junior manager levels; the sorority queen has gone to Grosse Pointe; the serious poet burns for a place, any place, to work; the once-serious and never-serious poets work at the advertising agencies. The desperation of people threatened by forces about which they know little and of which they can say less; the cheerful emptiness of people "giving up" all hope of changing things; the faceless ones polled by Gallup who listed "international affairs" fourteenth on their list of "problems" but who also expected thermonuclear war in the next few years; in these and other forms, Americans are in withdrawal from public life, from any collective effort at directing their own affairs. . . .

The very isolation of the individual—from power and community and ability to aspire—means the rise of a democracy without publics. With the great mass of people structurally remote and psychologically hesitant with respect to democratic institutions, those institutions themselves attenuate and become, in the fashion of the vicious circle, progressively less accessible to those few who aspire to serious participation in social affairs. The vital democratic connection between community and leadership, between the mass and the several elites, has been so wrenched and perverted that disastrous policies go unchallenged time and again.

POLITICS WITHOUT PUBLICS

The American political system is not the democratic model of which its glorifiers speak. In actuality it frustrates democracy by confusing the individual citizen, paralyzing policy discussion, and consolidating the irresponsible power of military and business interests. . . .

A most alarming fact is that few, if any, politicians are calling for changes in these conditions. Only a handful even are calling on the President to "live up to" platform pledges; no one is demanding structural changes, such as the shuttling of Southern Democrats out of the Democratic Party. Rather than protesting the state of politics, most politicians are reinforcing and aggravating that state. . . .

THE ECONOMY

We live amidst a national celebration of economic prosperity while poverty and deprivation remain an unbreakable way of life for millions in the "affluent society," including many of our own generation. We hear glib references to the "welfare state," "free enterprise," and "shareholder's democracy" while military defense is the main item of "public" spending and obvious oligopoly and other forms of minority rule defy real individual initiative or popular control. Work, too, is often unfulfilling and victimizing, accepted as a channel to status or plenty, if not a way to pay the bills, rarely as a means of understanding and controlling self and events. In work and leisure the individual is regulated as part of the system, a consuming unit, bombarded by hard-sell, soft-sell, lies and semitrue appeals to his basest drives. He is always told that he is a "free" man because of "free enterprise." . . .

The Military-Industrial Complex

The most spectacular and important creation of the authoritarian and oligopolistic structure of economic decision-making in America is the institution called "the military-industrial complex" by former President Eisenhower—the powerful congruence of interest and structure among military and business elites which affects so much of our development and destiny. Not only is ours the first generation to live with the possibility of world-wide cataclysm—it is the first to experience the actual social preparation for cataclysm, the general militarization of American society. . . .

Since our childhood these two trends—the rise of the military and the installation of a defense-based economy—have grown fantastically. The Department of Defense, ironically the world's largest single organization, is worth $160 billion, owns 32 million acres of America and employs half the 7.5 million persons directly dependent on the military for subsistence, has an $11 billion payroll which is larger than the net annual income of all American corporations. Defense spending in the Eisenhower era totaled $350 billions and President Kennedy entered office pledged to go even beyond the present defense allocation of 60 cents from every public dollar spent. Except for a war-induced boom immediately after "our side" bombed Hiroshima, American economic prosperity has coincided with a growing dependence on military outlay—from 1911 to 1959 America's Gross

National Product of $5.25 trillion included $700 billion in goods and services purchased for the defense effort, about one-seventh of the accumulated GNP. . . .

TOWARD AMERICAN DEMOCRACY

Every effort to end the Cold War and expand the process of world industrialization is an effort hostile to people and institutions whose interests lie in perpetuation of the East-West military threat and the postponement of change in the "have not" nations of the world. Every such effort, too, is bound to establish greater democracy in America. The major goals of a domestic effort would be:

1. America must abolish its political party stalemate. . . .
2. Mechanisms of voluntary association must be created through which political information can be imparted and political participation encouraged. . . .
3. Institutions and practices which stifle dissent should be abolished, and the promotion of peaceful dissent should be actively promoted.
4. Corporations must be made publicly responsible. . . .
5. The allocation of resources must be based on social needs. A truly "public sector" must be established, and its nature debated and planned. . . .
6. America should concentrate on its genuine social priorities: abolish squalor, terminate neglect, and establish an environment for people to live in with dignity and creativeness. . . .

The Sharon Statement (1960)

Young Americans for Freedom

When we talk about the 1960s as an era of radicalism, as a time when young people rejected the status quo and attempted to transform American life and politics, we are almost always talking about the Left and groups such as Students for a Democratic Society. But in the 1960s, the sense of possibility that motivated young people to seek fundamental changes in American society was by no means restricted to the Left. Beginning at the dawn of the decade, conservative youth also rejected the domestic policies of what was called the "liberal consensus," a dominant political understanding that combined relatively modest government-sponsored social programs with a faith in capitalism and economic individualism. Unlike their peers in the New Left, however, conservative youth did not reject the two-party political system, but instead attempted to capture the Republican Party and move it dramatically to the right.

Young Americans for Freedom was the most important organization for conservative youth in the 1960s. The organization was founded in September 1960, at the Sharon, Connecticut, family estate of conservative columnist and National Review *editor William F. Buckley. Like the authors of the Port Huron Statement, which was written two years later, the ninety young men and women who gathered for the Sharon Conference believed that the United States was at a critical turning point in its history. Their "Sharon Statement" was a statement of principles for a time of "moral and political crises." It affirmed what the authors called "eternal truths" derived from the individual's right to use his "God-given free will," central to which was an unrestricted free market economy. The Sharon Statement also offered a justification for States' Rights and called for victory over—not coexistence with—communism.*

In the mid-1960s, the YAF had roughly the same membership as the historically much-better-known SDS, and wielded greater political power. YAF played a critical role in securing the 1964 Republican presidential nomination for the "true conservative" Goldwater over more moderate Republican candidates such as Nelson Rockefeller. Though Goldwater was defeated, YAF saw victory in its ability to shift the party to the right. At the same time, it had to contend

with new supporters drawn not by what it defined as "traditional" conserva-
tive principles but by a States' Rights platform that defined racial segregation
and discrimination as local issues beyond the purview of the federal govern-
ment. In the latter half of the decade, YAF splintered and lost visibility, but it
served as a training ground for leaders who claimed political power in the
1980s.

In this time of moral and political crises, it is the responsibility of the youth of America to affirm certain eternal truths.

We, as young conservatives, believe:

That foremost among the transcendent values is the individual's use of his God-given free will, whence derives his right to be free from the restrictions of arbitrary force;

That liberty is indivisible, and that political freedom cannot long exist without economic freedom;

That the purpose of government is to protect those freedoms through the preservation of internal order, the provision of national defense, and the administration of justice;

That when government ventures beyond these rightful functions, it accumulates power, which tends to diminish order and liberty;

That the Constitution of the United States is the best arrangement yet devised for empowering government to fulfill its proper role, while restraining it from the concentration and abuse of power;

That the genius of the Constitution—the division of powers—is summed up in the clause that reserves primacy to the several states, or to the people, in those spheres not specifically delegated to the Federal government;

That the market economy, allocating resources by the free play of supply and demand, is the single economic system compatible with the requirements of personal freedom and constitutional government, and that it is at the same time the most productive supplier of human needs;

That when government interferes with the work of the market economy, it tends to reduce the moral and physical strength of the nation; that when it takes from one man to bestow on another, it diminishes the incentive of the first, the integrity of the second, and the moral autonomy of both;

That we will be free only so long as the national sovereignty of the United States is secure; that history shows periods of freedom are rare, and can exist only when free citizens concertedly defend their rights against all enemies;

That the forces of international Communism are, at present, the greatest single threat to these liberties;

That the United States should stress victory over, rather than coexistence with, this menace; and

That American foreign policy must be judged by this criterion: does it serve the just interests of the United States?

Counterculture

Terry H. Anderson

In the middle years of the decade of "The Sixties," it seemed that the Movement had two distinct branches. There were the politicos, serious young men and women who had worked for civil rights and against the war in Vietnam. And then there were the hippies: long-haired boys and braless girls; sex, drugs, and rock 'n' roll. In fact, many of the men and women who devoted themselves to creating a counterculture were also people of great commitment and serious-ness. As Terry Anderson argues below, they meant to overthrow the dominant Cold War culture, just as the New Left meant to challenge the political es-tablishment. Many in the counterculture believed that mindblowing experi-ences with sex or drugs or music were much more likely to alter the world view of America's young people than were all the earnest speeches and political exhortations in which the avowedly political strand of "the Movement" placed so much trust. As counterculture hero John Sinclair explained, "So you listen to the band . . . you just go crazy and have a good time. . . . Rather than go up there and make some speech about our moral commitment in Viet-nam, you just make 'em so freaky they'd never want to go in the army in the first place. . . ."

By the late 1960s, America's youth culture had come to look very much like the counterculture, and the obvious distinction between the political and cul-tural radicals had faded. In this excerpt from his book, The Movement and the Sixties, *historian Terry Anderson analyzes the rise—and fall—of the American counterculture and the polarization of American society. As you read this piece, consider the following: Did the spread of counterculture style into the general youth culture transform it from a true "counter" culture to lit-tle more than a "lifestyle"? Were the hippies and freaks who believed culture was a more powerful tool than politics right? Do you think this counterculture contained the seeds of its own destruction? Was "Middle America" right to fear this movement?*

Living your lifestyle, doing your own thing, was a significant theme of the movement as it blended with the counterculture during the second wave, the four or five years after Chicago. Some became involved in politics, working for causes that attacked the establishment and transferred power to the people: *empowerment.* Others felt politics died with Martin Luther King and Bobby Kennedy and they became consumed with personal pursuits that freed them from their past: *liberation.* All the while, most experienced an individual transformation that made them "Sixties People," different from the cold war generation. "Remember," Tuli Kupferberg told the emerging new culture: "The *first* revolution (but not of course the last) is in yr own head. Dump out *their* irrational goals, desires, morality."

The counterculture must be defined broadly. The movement developed as a counter to the political establishment: the counterculture was a counter to the dominant cold war culture. After the rip tide the press reported, somewhat ironically, that there were 200,000 "full time hippies" and another 300,000 who shared the practices and beliefs, that some 20,000 were dropping out each year, and that "the number is accelerating geometrically." By the end of the decade hippies had established thousands of communes, hip communities in almost every major city, and they were hitch-hiking around the country and throughout the world—from Marrakech to Kabul to Kathmandu. By the early years of the next decade perhaps 3 million people felt part of the counterculture, yet they always were a minority within another minority—the movement. While it must be remembered that within the sixties generation were more conservative kids who were eager apprentices for the system, it was the hippies who confronted and disturbed the establishment, regardless of their numbers. "No one knows for sure just how large this massive generational upheaval really was," wrote a researcher. "We can only be sure that it took place on a scale unprecedented in our history."

During the second wave the counterculture became a phenomenon that affected many young Americans, and as baby boomers flooded campuses the division between activists and hippies faded like tie-dye. The underground was surfacing, gently infiltrating the movement. What started with blue jeans and work shifts during Freedom Summer had become bell bottoms and peasant dresses by Woodstock. Hip was a sign of the times, a symbol that the sixties generation had shifted from surfing and bundling on the beach to protesting and smoking dope, from "Love me do" to "Why don't we do it in the road." After the March on the Pentagon, participant Keith Lampe wrote, "Just two weeks ago we were talking about 'hippies' of 'the psychedelic movement' on the one hand, and 'straight peace activists' or 'resisters' as something quite distinct. Now the two are tightly communal aspects of the same thing—and who can hang a name on it? It's like wind, or water. Superbly leaderless. The bull horns at the Pentagon were passed around almost as freely as the joints and sandwiches and water jugs."

Many commentators have discussed the origins of the counterculture. Most have mentioned that throughout American history there have been those who do not fit into the mainstream, misfits. In earlier times they might have been roamers, drifters, mountain men, or utopians at communities such as Oneida, New Harmony, or various Shaker or Hutterite settlements. As America urbanized they clustered in cities—bohemians after the First World War, student radicals during the Depression, beatniks during the cold war. Since future hippies were being raised during the postwar era, some were influenced by contemporary intellectuals and poets. Paul Goodman discussed *Growing Up Absurd*, William Whyte challenged students to "*fight* The Organization," and beat poets ridiculed society and urged readers to get "On the Road." "We gotta go and never stop going till we get there," said one of Jack Kerouac's characters, and in *Desolation Angels* the author spoke of "a 'rucksack revolution' with all over America 'millions of Dharma bums' going up to the hills to meditate and ignore society." Some writers emphasized that the counterculture was a response to technology, that during the atomic age America had become a "civilization sunk in an unshakeable commitment to genocide, gambling madly with the universal extermination of our species." Others viewed the growth of hippiedom as a result of a massive sixties generation that came of age. More kids meant more dissension from social norms. Throw in the Beatles, and presto: The Summer of Love. . . .

Why did such a small part of the sixties generation during the Summer of Love—less than 100,000 kids—bloom into a garden of millions of flower people during the second wave? The behavior of the establishment stimulated the growth of the anti-establishment. The cool generation of mid-decade became the alienated generation during and after the rip tide.

It began as baby boomers entered "duck and cover" elementary schools, matriculated into crewcut high schools, and graduated into college, "the best years of your life," promised their parents. Instead,

"Welcome to lines, bureaucracy and crowds," the *Daily Californian* editorialized as students were herded from advisers to classrooms down the maze toward matriculation. Welcome to rules and regulations. True, the situation at some universities improved, but for most students campus life resembled an article published by Jerry Farber and reprinted endlessly in undergrounds, "The Student as Nigger." Professors would not stand up for students, or to deans and politicians, because they were "short on balls." Instead, teachers terrorized students. "The grade is a hell of a weapon." A student smiles and shuffles for the professor, learning the most important rule of college: "Tell the man what he wants to hear or he'll fail your ass out of the course." Change was slow at many universities. . . . Students felt powerless, and many dropped out in their own way. For 120 student government positions at the University of Minnesota not even a hundred ran for election in a university with 45,000 enrolled. Others moved off campus and established undergrounds without censors, or as hip writers for the Austin *Rag* proclaimed: "I'm not a student here, so you can go to hell." Buttons appeared:

I AM A HUMAN BEING

DO NOT FOLD, SPINDLE OR MUTILATE

There were other sayings that appeared on buttons, bumper stickers, and T-shirts that gave clues to the counterculture:

MAKE LOVE NOT WAR

The older generation was fighting a war, one that many younger citizens felt was illegal, inhumane, and immoral. For draft-age youth, the war forced a response. A young man could either go along with the establishment and join the military, fight the machine by protesting and resisting the draft, or drop out. The first two had not stopped the war, and after Nixon's election it was clear that the conflict would continue for years. What to do? Country Joe McDonald answered, "You take drugs, you turn up the music very loud, you dance around, you build yourself a fantasy world where everything's beautiful."

Most kids blamed the war on the older generation. "What's happening," wrote an activist, "is that a whole generation is starting to say to its parents, 'You can no longer get us to kill & be killed for your uptight archaic beliefs.'" Many returning soldiers agreed. Unlike fathers coming home after World War II, Vietnam veterans rarely talked of heroism, duty, honor. Instead, the "endless war" became an endless barrage of horror stories and disillusionment. "I just lost respect for everything after Vietnam," Lieut. Al Wilder commented. "Everything I learned as a kid turned out to be a damn lie." . . .

Other kids were distressed by a nation that continued to discriminate against some of its own citizens. One son asked his parents: " 'What would you do if a Negro moved in next door?' and they'd say, 'Nothing! We don't mind.' And I'd say, 'What would you do if I wanted to marry a Negro?' and that was completely different. 'No. You can't marry a Negro. No, no. You can't do that.' And I couldn't understand why, because I'd been raised to believe Negroes were just like anyone else. Two and two just never made four." . . .

Thus, the behavior of the culture boosted the counterculture. Without racism, war, and campus paternalism, the population of hippiedom would have been proportionately about the same size as that of the beats in the postwar society. There would have been more hippies, of course, because of the enormous number of baby boomers, but the counterculture would have been relatively small, confined to the usual bohemian enclaves of the East and West coasts and a few college towns. . . .

"The hippies have passed beyond American society," wrote an underground journalist. "They're not really living in the same society. It's not so much that they're living on the leftovers, on the waste of American society, as that they just don't give a damn."

They did give a damn about their own culture, however, and they began to build one that expressed values that they felt were positive, healthy—building a peaceful, gentle society that discriminated against no one and that practiced love. "All you need is love," they sang. "Love is other, love is being and letting be, love is gentle, love is giving and love is dropping out, love is turning on, love is a trip, a flower, a smile, a bell." Other values were honesty, tolerance, personal freedom, and fun. Hugh Romney of the Hog Farm stated a hippie truism: "Do anything you want as long as nobody gets hurt."

IF IT FEELS GOOD, DO IT

A theme of cold war culture (and a later era) was "just say no." The creed was the Protestant Ethic: work. The motif of the sixties was "just say yes," and the canon was the Pleasure Ethic: fun. Live for the moment. Have a Happy Day.

Freaks said yes to many things that their parents had told them to reject—especially drugs and sex. . . .

Various surveys reported that at the beginning of the sixties only 4 percent of youth aged 18 to 25 had tried marijuana, and that twelve years later that figure was almost 50 percent; 60 percent for college students; and much higher at some universities: 70 percent at the University of Kansas, and almost 90 percent at Boston University College of Law. Underground papers conducted their own unscientific surveys, and while unreliable, it appears that of those who responded usually 80 or 90 percent smoked marijuana, half to two-thirds had experimented with LSD, and perhaps 10 percent had tried heroin. . . .

Making love and smoking dope was behavior usually conducted behind closed doors; dress was for the public, and it was a symbol. Hair represented rebellion from the crew-cut cold war era, and identity with the new generation. "Almost cut my hair," sang Crosby, Stills, and Nash, but instead they let their "freak flag fly," because, as Nash later stated, "if they had long hair you knew how they thought, that they were into good music, a reasonable life, that they probably hated the government." Hair, and dress, sequestered them from mom and pop, declared independence. Hip men threw out sport coats and ties, and hip women abandoned cosmetics and undergarments and for the first time in memory revealed the soft contours of unbound bodies. "Long hair, beads, no bras and freaky clothes represent a break from Prison Amerika," declared Jerry Rubin. . . .

Counterculture social thought generally had two parallel themes that often appeared in the lives of many hippies. Some revolted and searched for personal liberation, and the freedom that they practiced often was unstructured, libertarian, even anarchistic. Through experimentation, they often grew into what they felt was a more independent and holistic person. Others rebelled, tasted freedom, and rushed to a more authoritarian form of counterculture. These freaks often joined others in spiritual retreats or ashrams, where leaders developed a more structured, disciplined day, and where members practiced religious beliefs aimed at personal growth or inner development. Both of these avenues aimed to balance self-realization and fulfillment with community, and the eventual results depended on each individual.

All the while, hippies developed their alternative society—some dropping out by going to the country while a larger number remained in the city and became involved in cultural activism. Both built various types of hip enclaves that they called communes, cooperatives, collectives, or experimental communities, all difficult to define because freaks interchanged these names and because those living arrangements always were evolving. While there probably were over 2000 rural and at least 5000 urban communes by the end of the decade, no one knows the number because most communards wanted to be left alone and usually would not reply to surveys. . . .

Activists such as Tom Hayden called them escapists—dropping out meant copping out—but these builders of the dawn were not listening. Aware that they were politically powerless, they no longer cared about changing the establishment. "Like it's so obvious that civilization is doomed," a communard said, "and we don't want to go with it. . . . We're retribalizing . . . it's the beginning of a whole new age." The new age would be different, said [Marty] Jezer, for they were building communities, "learning self-sufficiency and rediscovering old technologies that are not destructive to themselves and the land. . . . And we are doing this, as much as possible, outside the existing structures, saying, as we progress, a fond farewell to the system, to Harvard, Selective Service, General Motors, Bank of America, IBM, A&P, BBD&O, IRS, CBS, DDT, USA and Vietnam." . . .

Woodstock . . . was destined to become the most famous event of the era, to live on in mythology. "It was like balling the first time," wrote a participant after the festival; "historians will have to reckon with it" for "these young revolutionaries are on their way . . . to slough away the life-style that isn't theirs . . . and find one that is."

Woodstock began as a commercial enterprise. The four producers offered Max Yasgur $50,000 to use his thousand-acre farm near Bethel, New York. They hoped that 50,000 people would come to "The Woodstock Music and Art Fair: An Aquarian Exposition," and pay $18 for three days to hear over two dozen bands, including Jimi Hendrix, Janis Joplin, Joan Baez, Arlo Guthrie, Canned Heat, The Who, the Grateful Dead, Jefferson Airplane, Creedence Clearwater Revival, Country Joe and the Fish, Ten Years After, and Crosby, Stills, Nash and Young.

Yet Woodstock became much, much more. Before the first band began to play, a pilgrimage of young people streamed toward Yasgur's farm in unprecedented numbers, clogging the roads for miles, creating the most massive traffic jam in New York history. The kids rarely honked, and instead took out their guitars and tambourines and played songs, shared foods and drinks, and passed joints in perhaps the most patient jam of the decade. Vehicles slowly passed by: Volkswagens with riders hanging outside, a microbus with freaks on the roof smoking a gigantic water pipe, psychedelic motorcycles, a van painted like a tiger, another like a speckled trout. The generation streamed onto the farm, to alfalfa fields and pastures, pitched tents and tepees. Eventually 400,000 were camping, and as far as any one could see there were young people "walking, lying down, drinking, eating, reading, singing. Kids were sleeping, making love, wading in the marshes, trying to milk the local cows and trying to cook the local corn."

"We were exhilarated," one participant recalled. "We felt as though we were in liberated territory." They were, and since their numbers overwhelmed local authorities, the young quickly established their own culture with their own rules, rituals, costumes, and standards of behavior. An observer noted that the cops were like "isolated strangers in a foreign country," and they made little attempt to enforce drug or nudity laws as the counterculture blossomed. "We used to think of ourselves as little clumps of weirdos," said Janis Joplin. "But now we're a whole new minority group."

The gathering of the tribe, however, also was ripe for disaster. Overcrowding created nightmares. Sanitation facilities were inadequate and some waited an hour to relieve themselves. Toilets overflowed. The hungry crowd consumed half a million hamburgers and hot dogs on the first day and food ran out, as did almost all drinkable water. Dope was sold and given away openly, and many consumed too much. Medical supplies became dangerously low. All the while the traffic jam meant that musicians, medicine, doctors, and food had to be flown in by helicopter at tremendous expense. Officials grew concerned, and thinking there would be a riot, the governor considered sending in the national guard. Then, the rains came, and came, and people huddled and slept in meadows that turned to mud.

Before the music began the first evening, a voice boomed out of the speakers: "We're going to need each other to help each other work this out, because we're taxing the systems that we've set up. We're going to be bringing the food in. But the one major thing that you have to remember tonight is that the man next to you is your brother." For many participants, the growing sense of community turned this rock festival into an unforgettable countercultural experience. "Everyone needed other people's help, and everyone was ready to share what he had as many ways as it could be split up. Everyone could feel the good vibrations.". . .

In a vague way, most leaving the rainy festival felt warm, and they sang along with Joni Mitchell,

> We are stardust
> We are golden
> And we've got to get ourselves
> Back to the garden

If freaks could stay in the garden, cultivating their culture, many thought that it could happen—a cultural revolution. "Woodstock is the great example of how it is going to be in the future," Tim Leary wrote to John Sinclair. "We have the numbers. The loving and the peaceful are the majority. The violent and the authoritarian are the minority. We are winning. And soon." Hippie culture was having an impact on the idea of revolution, for cultural activists began talking about the development of a Youth Nation committed to nonviolence concerned about one another, an idea popularized by Abbie Hoffman in his *Woodstock Nation*. Steve Haines of the *Berkeley Tribe* advocated more festivals, using the receipts to buy land and supplies to build large regional communes for one to two thousand freaks, and Sinclair talked about various tribes of black militants and white cultural activists signing treaties as the first step in developing a Sun Dance Nation. During the Indian summer after Woodstock it appeared to many that some sort of cultural upheaval finally was under way that would bring about a New America. . . .

Just four months after already famous Woodstock, hip Californians were eager to have "Woodstock West." "We're all headed the same way," Andy Gordon wrote, "drawn by the power of the Woodstock myth. Gotta make it to that historic get-together. Altamont! The magic hits me—it's like Shangri-La. Xanadu."

But nirvana did not appear for most participants, and some described a reality closer to Hades. The audience was enormous, about 300,000, and most were good-natured, sitting on the surrounding hills, far from the stage. People got high, and there were very few arrests. The problems appeared closer to the stage, where about fifty became violent. Shari Horowitz reported: "Scanning the audience, I

could see the chaos mounting—drunken brawls and bad acid trips.
. . . I felt a sense of loss. My people hadn't the strength to transcend
rudeness and get it all together." Numerous bands played in the af-
ternoon, and the scene became more chaotic. In perhaps the most
short-sighted move in the history of rock concerts, the Stones gave
$500 worth of beer to the Hell's Angels with orders to guard the
stage. When the crowd moved closer to the music, when some
drugged kids began to dance wildly, the motorcycle thugs beat them,
busting pool cues over heads, causing so much commotion that
bands stopped the music and asked for peace. "Please people," said
Grace Slick of Jefferson Airplane, "please stop hurting each other." At
dusk, the Stones finally appeared, and while Mick Jagger sang "Street
Fighting Man," the Angels grabbed a young black, Meredith Hunter.
Reports conflicted; he did or did not have a gun at the love-in. Never
mind, the black-leather gang stabbed him repeatedly and kicked in
his face. Horrified and stunned, the crowd did nothing. Hunter died
in a pool of blood.

Altamount disgusted many, especially those in the counterculture.
"Pearl Harbor to the Woodstock Nation" wrote one participant, and
Gordon noted just how far down the psychedelic path the counterculture had stumbled in almost three years since the Human Be-in:
"scabrous, syphilitic Hell's Angels, and a few luscious random teenie-
chiclets, with a hippier-than-thou look. And not a smile in a carload."
After the music began, "I saw they were no longer joining hands
and dancing together in spontaneous joy, as at the first gathering
of the tribes." Commercialization had massacred the tribes, for at Altamount the magic between the hip community and musicians had
evaporated. The people no longer were the show; they simply were
the audience, and that agonized many. The younger generation was
acting like the older one. A cultural activist wrote that the concert
"exploded the myth of innocence," and many other underground
writers felt that Altamount signaled "The Failure of the Counter Culture." Robert Somma lamented that it was the "last gasp from a dying
decade. . . . It made you want to go home. It made you want to
puke."

Three weeks later the decade chronologically ended and during
the next year, *Business Week* claimed, "Middle America has come to
view festivals as harbingers of dope, debauchery, and destruction."
State and county officials drafted regulations aimed at preventing
rock festivals, and conservatives turned up their attack on the coun-

terculture. "You can be the irresponsible creature you are, the drones living off the work of others," the editor of *Christian Economics* told hippies, "only because most people are not like you." Conservative Tom Anderson was more livid: "Dear spoiled, deluded, arrogant, brainwashed brats and know-it-alls: I am sick of you," and he gave some advice: "Learn to speak Russian. And Chinese." Oddly enough, the Russians agreed and became strange bedfellows with conservative Americans. One Soviet historian referred to hippies as bourgeois bloodsuckers living off society, and adding that "no one with any common sense can believe that the hippies and Yippies are capable of effecting any changes in American society." . . .

The middle continued to collapse. The generation gap expanded, perhaps to the largest size since the 1920s. When two researchers asked a mother if she would like to comment on her hippie son who lived in Kabul, Afghanistan, she responded: "I have nothing to say about him. He's gone. Far away. Dead." An opinion poll asked citizens to list the most harmful groups in the nation, and the result: Communists, prostitutes, and hippies. . . .

Regardless of the reaction, hippies did not fade away during the second wave. Repression might make them move on to more friendly communities, but it did not bring them back into the mainstream. Just the opposite. . . . Instead, hippiedom expanded exponentially. Freaks did their own thing. Detroit's *South End* put it like this: "We are a generation that is sucking in life in gulps while others are trying to swallow. We are making the American cultural revolution." . . . "Flower Power," wrote an observer, "is as revolutionary as Black Power, and after it America will never be the same again."

Nor would many young Americans. They were changing, some hoping, and some singing along with John Lennon. If they could make "Imagine" a reality, then, as the Moody Blues told the new generation, they were "On the Threshold of a Dream."

What was dream? What was reality in the counterculture? Did they get back to the garden? Some times. Some places. Other times and other places they did not. As mundane as it sounds, hippies were simply people who possessed all the human frailties as those in the Establishment. . . .

How can the counterculture be evaluated? Reliable surveys and statistics on this amorphous blob do not exist, so it is difficult to judge. Subsequently, most assessments have been personal and emotional.

Many of the older generation loathed the children for rejecting traditional values, and many kids loathed the parents for holding on to what they considered archaic beliefs. To some, the sight of a longhair or one death from an overdose was too much and they condemned the entire culture experiment. To others, just seeing a policeman or another death in Vietnam was too much and they condemned the entire Establishment. The result was the largest generational gap in memory—the "war at home," one observer labeled it, who suggested that the nation's greatest internal conflict was "not between the rich and the poor, or the black and the white, or even the young and the old, but the people with long hair and the people with short hair."

To the longhairs, the question of whether the counterculture was a failure or success missed the point. Hippies were not taking a college course, trying to pass an exam, earn a grade, get ahead. The counterculture looked at it a different way. "How good were communes?" Compared with what, they asked, the best or the worst families in America? The fact that they experimented with their lifestyle was success enough for most of them, for they no longer were normal. They were different, had dropped out of the rat race, challenged their past. They had considered their existence on planet Earth, and in some ways, many had changed their lives. "If, through participation in the communal experience, individuals feel more alive and fulfilled (greater awareness of self and others, etc.), such a commune must be deemed a success," wrote Richard Fairfield. To hippies, then, the political revolution shifted to an individual revolution, and some felt proud that they had taken the chance, such as the communards at Twin Oaks who published a booklet declaring *The Revolution Is Over: We Won!*

Those people probably had won—for themselves—while others were not so sure. From his commune in Vermont, Marty Jezer described the pros and cons of the counterculture:

> At its best the amorphous and vaguely defined movement we call the counter-culture is working, and that there exists now, in cities and on farms everywhere in the country, a visible alternative community that is creating new ways of living out of a tired, frightened, and dying land. (There is another, darker side to the counter-culture symbolized by Altamount and Manson; rock-star millionaires; the dehumanizing attitudes longhaired men still have for women; the heavy consumer-

trip so many people are on, buying bellbottoms and beads, records, tape machines, flashy new cars with peace stickers on the bumpers to make it all seem all right; the continued high price of dope and the availability of speed, smack, and other bummers; the ambitious and competitive ego-tripping, disguised in groovy garb and mystical language, but still a mirrored reflection of the dominant values of the old way; and more: all the baggage, possessions, psychic junk and garbage we carry with us from the past.) But despite the glorification of a lifestyle that so often manifests style at the expense of life, there are people moving ahead, experimenting with and leading lives that a few years ago they'd never had dreamed possible.

The counterculture eventually changed the sixties by altering cold war culture, but it also had a more immediate impact on the movement during the second wave. Jerry Rubin mused that "grass destroyed the left" and created a youth culture, and in a sense dope clouded the political focus. "The New Left no longer exists," SDS founder Richard Flacks said at the end of the decade. "The ideals of the New Left have now merged into whole new cultural situations in enclaves like Isla Vista, the youth communities outside the system, which may or may not have coherent politics." Little seemed coherent as the movement splintered into numerous factions, as earlier organizations and initial leaders continued to fade. Some older activists grew frustrated, dropped out, and began building their own society. As former SDS president Carl Oglesby recalled: "There were a lot of good, righteous people showing up in places like Vermont and New Hampshire in those days. Lots of parties, great reefer, good acid. Lovely friends . . . I remember it with great fondness. It was almost the best part of the struggle. The best part of the struggle was the surrender."

Some surrendered. Some did not, for many baby boomers were coming of age during the second wave and the counterculture idea of continual experimentation created different possibilities and activities. Cultural rebellion and political activism continued to merge and flourish. . . .

A community was emerging, "the people" cooperating for a common goal that usually concerned their empowerment or liberation in a New America. While some activists remained concerned with national affairs, others shifted their involvement toward themselves, their people, their neighborhoods. A new motto appeared for the movement: Think Global, Act Local. "Back in the city, it was like you were a Weatherman type or a plastic hippie or you didn't do anything but talk revolution," said a freak who left Brooklyn for Eugene. "Here . . . all these alternatives have come into being. They may be small, they may not be all that new, but there is some progress you can put your finger on. Beginnings rather than endings."

You Don't Need a Weatherman to Know Which Way the Wind Blows (1969)

Submitted by Karin Ashley, Bill Ayers, Bernardine Dohrn, John Jacobs, Jeff Jones, Gerry Long, Howie Machtinger, Jim Mellen, Terry Robbins, Mark Rudd, and Steve Tappis

Just seven years after the Port Huron Statement, SDS met again in national convention. In the intervening years the war in Vietnam had expanded dramatically, the integrationist petitions of the early Civil Rights movement had turned into demands for Black Power and a movement for student autonomy had generated massive protests on university campuses. For at least some, the primary lesson of the sixties had been the impossibility of securing change peacefully. Teach-ins at universities had not changed the government's Vietnam policy; campaigns on behalf of antiwar candidates seemed an exercise in futility; for those who were most bitter and radicalized, revolution seemed the only answer. With young people as an advance party, these activists demanded that SDS support a worldwide revolution against capitalism and imperialism. The following selection from the Weatherman Manifesto—"You don't need a weatherman to know which way the wind blows"—appears, in retrospect, a hopelessly doctrinaire plea. Just one year later three of those who endorsed it blew themselves to pieces making bombs in Greenwich Village. Yet the statement also reflects just how corrosive the 1960s had been in destroying the idealism of seven years earlier.

Excerpted from Karin Ashley et al. "You Don't Need a Weatherman to Know Which Way the Wind Blows," mimeographed statement, 1969.

INTERNATIONAL REVOLUTION

> *The contradiction between the revolutionary peoples of Asia Africa and Latin America and the imperialists headed by the United States is the principal contradiction in the contemporary world. The development of this contradiction is promoting the struggle of the people of the whole world against US imperialism and its lackeys.*
>
> Lin Piao
> *Long Live the Victory of People's War!*

People ask, what is the nature of the revolution that we talk about? Who will it be made by, and for, and what are its goals and strategy?

The overriding consideration in answering these questions is that the main struggle going on in the world today is between US imperialism and the national liberation struggles against it. . . .

So the very first question people in this country must ask in considering the question of revolution is where they stand in relation to the United States as an oppressor nation, and where they stand in relation to the masses of people throughout the world whom US imperialism is oppressing. . . .

It is in this context that we must examine the revolutionary struggles in the United States. We are within the heartland of a world-wide monster, a country so rich from its world-wide plunder that even the crumbs doled out to the enslaved masses within its borders provide for material existence very much above the conditions of the masses of people of the world. The US empire, as world-wide system, channels wealth, based upon the labor and resources of the rest of the world, into the United States. The relative affluence existing in the United States is directly dependent upon the labor and natural resources of the Vietnamese, the Angolans, the Bolivians and the rest of the peoples of the Third World. All of the United Airlines Astrojets, all of the Holiday Inns, all of Hertz's automobiles, your television set, car and wardrobe already belong, to a large degree, to the people of the rest of the world. . . .

The goal is the destruction of US imperialism and the achievement of a classless world: world communism. Winning state power in the US will occur as a result of the military forces of the US overextending themselves around the world and being defeated piecemeal; struggle within the US will be a vital part of this process, but when the revolution triumphs in the US it will have been made by the people of the whole world. For socialism to be defined in national terms within so extreme and historical an oppressor nation as this is only imperialist national chauvinism on the part of the "movement."

In this context, why an emphasis on youth? Why should young people be willing to fight on the side of Third World peoples? . . .

As imperialism struggles to hold together this decaying, social fabric, it inevitably resorts to brute force and authoritarian ideology. People, especially young people, more and more find themselves in the iron grip of authoritarian institutions. Reaction against the pigs or teachers in the schools, welfare pigs or the army is generalizable and extends beyond the particular repressive institution to the society and the State as a whole. The legitimacy of the State is called into question for the first time in at least 20 years, and the anti-authoritarianism which characterizes the youth rebellion turns into rejection of the State, a refusal to be socialized into American society. Kids used to try to beat the system from inside the army or from inside the schools; now they desert from the army and burn down the schools.

The crisis in imperialism has brought about a breakdown in bourgeois social forms, culture and ideology. The family falls apart, kids leave home, women begin to break out of traditional "female" and "mother" roles. There develops a "generation gap" and a "youth problem." Our heroes are no longer struggling businessmen, and we also begin to reject the ideal career of the professional and look to Mao, Che, the Panthers, the Third World, for our models, for motion. We reject the elitist, technocratic bullshit that tells us only experts can rule, and look instead to leadership from the people's war of the Vietnamese. Chuck Berry, Elvis, the Temptations brought us closer to the "people's culture" of Black America. The racist response to the civil rights movement revealed the depth of racism in America, as well as the impossibility of real change through American institutions. And the war against Vietnam is not "the heroic war against the Nazis"; it's the big lie, with napalm, burning through everything we had heard this country stood for. Kids begin to ask questions: Where is the Free World? And who do the pigs protect at home?

THE RYM AND THE PIGS

A major focus in our neighborhood and citywide work is the pigs, because they tie together the various struggles around the state as the enemy, and thus point to the need for a movement oriented toward power to defeat it.

The pigs are the capitalist state, and as such define the limits of all political struggles; to the extent that a revolutionary struggle shows signs of success, they come in and mark the point it can't go beyond. . . . Our job is not to avoid the issue of the pigs as "diverting" from anti-imperialist struggle, but to emphasize that they are our real enemy if we fight that struggle to win.

The most important task for us toward making the revolution, and the work our collectives should engage in, is the creation of a mass revolutionary movement, without which a clandestine revolutionary party will be impossible. A revolutionary mass movement is different from the traditional revisionist mass base of "sympathizers." Rather it is akin to the Red Guard in China, based on the full participation and involvement of masses of people in the practice of making revolution; a movement with a full willingness to participate in the violent and illegal struggle. It is a movement diametrically opposed to the elitist idea that only leaders are smart enough or interested enough to accept full revolutionary conclusions. It is a movement built on the basis of faith in the masses of people.

The task of collectives is to create this kind of movement. (The party is not a substitute for it, and in fact is totally dependent on it.) This will be done at this stage principally among youth, through implementing the Revolutionary Youth Movement strategy discussed in this paper. It is practice at this, and not political "teachings" in the abstract, which will determine the relevance of the political collectives which are formed.

The strategy of the RYM for developing an active mass base, tying the city-wide fights to community and city-wide anti-pig movement, and for building a party eventually out of this motion, fits with the world strategy for winning the revolution, builds a movement oriented toward the power, and will become one division of the International Liberation Army, while its battlefields are added to the many Vietnams which will dismember and dispose of US imperialism. Long Live the Victory of People's War!

The Forgotten American (1969)

Peter Schrag

Inevitably, the social protests of the 1960s provoked a counter-response. By the end of the decade a group, dubbed "middle Americans" by the media, had rallied to the defense of the flag, traditional authority, and good manners. One definition of "middle Americans" was primarily economic. Earning between $5,000 and $15,000 a year, they made up 55 percent of the population. The majority were blue-collar workers, lower-echelon bureaucrats, schoolteachers, and white-collar employees. As they saw the federal government pour money into impoverished areas, they developed a sense of neglect and resentment, believing that they were being ignored while vocal protestors received all the attention. Just as important, however, was a sense of crisis in cultural values, a belief that the rules were being changed in midstream. As Newsweek's *Karl Fleming observed, middle Americans felt "threatened by a terrifying array of enemies: hippies, Black Panthers, drugs, the sexually liberated, those who questioned the sanctity of marriage and the morality of work." Antiwar protests galvanized these middle Americans into action. From their perspective, it was blasphemy to wear the American flag on the seat of one's pants, burn one's draft card, or shout obscenities at authorities. In the following article, published in 1969, Peter Schrag describes the resentments and values of this group, illuminating just how profound the polarization of the 1960s was, and perceptively explaining why so many would turn from the party of the New Deal to increasingly conservative candidates.*

There is hardly a language to describe him, or even a set of social statistics. Just names: racist-bigot-redneck-ethnic-Irish-Italian-Pole Hunkie-Yahoo. The lower middle class. A blank. The man under whose hat lies the great American desert. Who watches the tube, plays the horses, and keeps the niggers out of his union and his neighborhood. Who might vote for Wallace (but didn't). Who cheers when the cops beat up on demonstrators. Who is free, white, and twenty-one, has a job, a home, a family, and is up to his eyeballs in credit. In the guise of the working class—or the American yeoman or John Smith—he was once the hero of the civics books, the man that Andrew Jackson called "the bone and sinew of the country." Now he is "the forgotten man," perhaps the most alienated person in America.

Nothing quite fits, except perhaps omission and semi-invisibility. America is supposed to be divided between affluence and poverty, between slums and suburbs. John Kenneth Galbraith begins the foreword to *The Affluent Society* with the phrase, "Since I sailed for Switzerland in the early summer of 1955 to begin work on this book. . . ." But *between* slums and suburbs, between Scarsdale and Harlem, between Wellesley and Roxbury, between Shaker Heights and Hough, there are some eighty million people (depending on how you count them) who didn't sail for Switzerland in the summer of 1955, or at any other time, and who never expect to go. Between slums and suburbs: South Boston and South San Francisco, Bell and Parma, Astoria and Bay Ridge, Newark, Cicero, Downey, Daly City, Charlestown, Flatbush. Union halls, American Legion posts, neighborhood bars, and bowling leagues, the Ukrainian Club and the Holy Name. Main Street. To try to describe all this is like trying to describe America itself. If you look for it, you find it everywhere: the rows of frame houses overlooking the belching steel mills in Bethlehem, Pennsylvania; two-family brick houses in Canarsie (where the most common slogan, even in the middle of a political campaign, is "curb your dog"); the Fords and Chevies with a decal American flag on the rear window (usually a cut-out from the *Reader's Digest,* and displayed in counter-protest against peaceniks and "those bastards who carry Vietcong flags in demonstrations"); the bunting on the porch rail with the inscription, "Welcome Home, Pete." The gold star in the window. . . .

He does all the right things, obeys the law, goes to church and insists—usually—that his kids get a better education than he had. But the right things don't seem to be paying off. While he is making more than he ever made—perhaps more than he'd ever dreamed—he's still struggling while a lot of others—"them" (on welfare, in demonstrations, in the ghettos) are getting most of the attention. "I'm working my ass off," a guy tells you on a stoop in South Boston. "My kids don't have a place to swim, my parks are full of glass, and I'm supposed to bleed for a bunch of people on relief." In New York a man who drives a Post Office trailer truck at night (4:00 P.M. to midnight) and a cab during the day (7:00 A.M. to 2:00 P.M.), and who hustles radios for his Post Office buddies on the side, is ready, as he says, to "knock somebody's ass." "The colored guys work when they feel like it. Sometimes they show up and sometimes they don't. One guy tore up all the time cards. I'd like to see a white guy do that and get away with it."

WHAT COUNTS

Nobody knows how many people in America moonlight (half of the eighteen million families in the $5000 to $10,000 bracket have two or more wage earners) or how many have to hustle on the side. "I don't think anybody has a single job anymore," said Nicholas Kisburg, the research director for a Teamsters Union Council in New York. "All the cops are moonlighting, and the teachers; and there's a million guys who are hustling, guys with phony social security numbers who are hiding part of what they make so they don't get kicked out of a housing project, or guys who work as guards at sports events and get free meals that they don't want to pay taxes on. Every one of them is cheating. They are underground people—*Untermenschen.* . . . We really have no systematic data on any of this. We have no ideas of the attitudes of the white worker. (We've been too busy studying the black worker.) And yet he's the source of most of the reaction in this country."

The reaction is directed at almost every visible target: at integration and welfare, taxes and sex education, at the rich and the poor, the foundations and students, at the "smart people in the suburbs." In New York State the legislature cuts the welfare budget; in Los Angeles, the voters reelect Yorty after a whispered racial campaign against the Negro favorite. In Minneapolis a police detective named Charles Stenvig, promising "to take the handcuffs off the police," wins by a margin stunning even to his supporters: in Massachusetts the voters mail tea bags to their representatives in protest against new taxes, and in state after state legislatures are passing bills to punish student demonstrators. ("We keep talking about permissiveness in training kids," said a Los Angeles labor official, "but we forget that these are our kids.")

And yet all these things are side manifestations of a malaise that lacks a language. Whatever law and order means, for example, to a man who feels his wife is unsafe on the street after dark or in the park at any time, or whose kids get shaken down in the school yard, it also means something like normality—the demand that everybody play it by the book, that cultural and social standards be somehow restored to their civics-book simplicity, that things shouldn't be as they are but as they were supposed to be. If there is a revolution in this country— a revolt in manners, standards of dress and obscenity, and, more importantly, in our official sense of what America is—there is also a counter-revolt. Sometimes it is inarticulate, and sometimes (perhaps most of the time) people are either too confused or apathetic—or simply too polite and too decent—to declare themselves. In Astoria, Queens, a white working-class district of New York, people who make $7000 or $8000 a year (sometimes in two jobs) call themselves affluent, even though the Bureau of Labor Statistics regards an income of less than $9500 in New York inadequate to a moderate standard of living. And in a similar neighborhood in Brooklyn a truck driver who earns $151 a week tells you he's doing well, living in a two-story frame house separated by a narrow driveway from similar houses, thousands of them in block after block. This year, for the first time, he will go on a cruise—he and his wife and two other couples—two weeks in the Caribbean. He went to work after World War II ($57 a week) and he has lived in the same house for twenty years, accumulating two television sets, wall-to-wall carpeting in a small living room, and a basement that he recently remodeled into a recreation room with the help of two moonlighting firemen. "We get fairly good salaries, and this is a good neighborhood, one of the few good ones left. We have no smoked Irishmen around."

Stability is what counts, stability in job and home and neighborhood, stability in the church and in friends. At night you watch television and sometimes on a weekend you go to a nice place—maybe a downtown hotel—for dinner with another couple. (Or maybe your sister, or maybe bowling, or maybe, if you're defeated, a night at the track.) The wife has the necessary appliances, often still being paid off and the money you save goes for your daughter's orthodontist, and later for her wedding. The smoked Irishmen—the colored (no one says black; few even say Negro)—represent change and instability, kids who cause trouble in school, who get treatment that your kids never got, that you never got. ("Those fucking kids," they tell you in South Boston, "raising hell, and not one of 'em paying his own way. Their fucking mothers are all on welfare.") The black kids mean a change in the rules, a double standard in grades and discipline, and—vaguely—a challenge to all you believed right. Law and order is the stability and predictability of established ways. Law and order is equal treatment—in school, in jobs, in the courts—even if you're cheating a little yourself. The Forgotten Man is Jackson's man. He is the vestigial American democrat of 1840: "They all know that their success depends upon their own industry and economy and that they must not expect to become suddenly rich by the fruits of their toil." He is also Franklin Roosevelt's man—the man whose vote (or whose father's vote) sustained the New Deal. . . .

AT THE BOTTOM OF THE WELL

American culture? Wealth is visible, and so, now, is poverty. Both have become intimidating clichés. But the rest? A vast, complex, and disregarded world that was once—in belief, and in fact—the American middle: Greyhound and Trailways bus terminals in little cities at midnight, each of them with its neon lights and its cardboard hamburgers; acres of tar-paper beach bungalows in places like Revere and Rockaway; the hair curlers in the supermarket on Saturday, and the little girls in the communion dresses the next morning; pinball machines and the *Daily News,* the *Reader's Digest* and Ed Sullivan; houses with tiny front lawns (or even large ones) adorned with statues of the Virgin or of Sambo welcomin' de folks home; Clint Eastwood or Julie Andrews at the Palace; the trotting tracks and the dog tracks—Aurora Downs, Connaught Park, Roosevelt, Yonkers, Rockingham, and forty others—where gray men come not for sport and beauty, but to read numbers, to study and dope. (If you win you have figured something, have in a small way controlled your world, have surmounted your impotence. If you lose, bad luck, shit. "I'll break his goddamned head.") Baseball is not the national pastime; racing is. For every man who goes to a major-league baseball game there are four who go to the track and probably four more who go to the candy store or the barbershop to make their bets. (Total track attendance in 1965: 62 million plus another 10 million who went to the dogs.)

There are places, and styles, and attitudes. If there are neighborhoods of aspiration, suburban enclaves for the mobile young execu-

tive and the aspiring worker, there are also places of limited expectation and dead-end districts where mobility is finished. But even there
you can often find, however vestigial, a sense of place, the roots of old
ethnic loyalties, and a passionate, if often futile, battle against intrusion and change. "Everybody around here," you are told, "pays his
own way." In this world the problems are not the ABM or air pollution (have they heard of Biafra?) or the international population crisis; the problem is to get your street cleaned, your garbage collected,
to get your husband home from Vietnam alive; to negotiate installment payments and to keep the schools orderly. Ask anyone in Scarsdale or Winnetka about the schools and they'll tell you about new
programs, or about how many are getting into Harvard, or about the
teachers; ask in Oakland or the North Side of Chicago, and they'll
tell you that they have (or haven't) had trouble. Somewhere in his
gut the man in those communities knows that mobility and choice
in this society are limited. He cannot imagine any major change for
the better; but he can imagine change for the worse. And yet for a
decade he is the one who has been asked to carry the burden of social reform, to integrate his schools and his neighborhood, has been
asked by comfortable people to pay the social debts due to the poor
and the black. In Boston, in San Francisco, in Chicago (not to mention Newark or Oakland) he has been telling the reformers to go to
hell. The Jewish schoolteachers of New York and the Irish parents of
Dorchester have asked the same question: "What the hell did Lindsay
(or the Beacon Hill Establishment) ever do for us?"

The ambiguities and changes in American life that occupy discussions in university seminars and policy debates in Washington, and
that form the backbone of contemporary popular sociology, become
increasingly the conditions of trauma and frustration in the middle.
Although the New Frontier and Great Society contained some programs for those not already on the rolls of social pathology—federal
aid for higher education, for example—the public priorities and the
rhetoric contained little. The emphasis, properly, was on the poor, on
the inner cities (e.g., Negroes) and the unemployed. But in Chicago
a widow with three children who earns $7000 a year can't get them
college loans because she makes too much; the money is reserved for
people on relief. New schools are built in the ghetto but not in the
white working-class neighborhoods where they are just as dilapidated.
In Newark the head of a white vigilante group (now a city council-
man) runs, among other things, on a platform opposing pro-Negro

discrimination. "When pools are being built in the Central Ward—don't they think white kids have got frustration? The white can't get a job; we have to hire Negroes first." The middle class, said Congressman Roman Pucinski of Illinois, who represents a lot of it, "is in revolt. Everyone has been generous in supporting anti-poverty. Now the middle-class American is disqualified from most of the programs."

"SOMEBODY HAS TO SAY NO . . ."

The frustrated middle. The liberal wisdom about welfare, ghettos, student revolt, and Vietnam has only a marginal place, if any, for the values and life of the workingman. It flies in the face of most of what he was taught to cherish and respect: hard work, order, authority, self-reliance. He fought, either alone or through labor organizations, to establish the precincts he now considers his own. Union seniority, the civil-service bureaucracy, and the petty professionalism established by the merit system in the public schools become sinecures of particular ethnic groups or of those who have learned to negotiate and master the system. A man who worked all his life to accumulate the points and grades and paraphernalia to become an assistant school principal (no matter how silly the requirements) is not likely to relinquish his position with equanimity. Nor is a dock worker whose only estate is his longshoreman's card. The job, the points, the credits become property:

> Some men leave their sons money [wrote a union member to the *New York Times*], some large investments, some business connections, and some a profession. I have only one worthwhile thing to give: my trade. I hope to follow a centuries-old tradition and sponsor my sons for an apprenticeship. For this simple father's wish it is said that I discriminate against Negroes. Don't all of us discriminate? Which of us . . . will not choose a son over all others?

Suddenly the rules are changing—all the rules. If you protect your job for your own you may be called a bigot. At the same time it's perfectly acceptable to shout black power and to endorse it. What does it take to be a good American? *Give the black man a position because he is black, not because he necessarily works harder or does the job better.* What does it take to be a good American? Dress nicely, hold a job, be clean-cut, don't judge a man by the color of his skin or the country of his origin. What about the demands of Negroes, the long hair of the students, the dirty movies, the people who burn drafts cards and American flags? Do you have to go out in the street with picket signs, do you have to burn the place down to get what you want? What does it take to be a good American? *This is a sick society, a racist society, we are fighting an immoral war.* ("I'm against the Vietnam war, too," says the truck driver in Brooklyn. "I see a good kid come home with half an arm and a leg in a brace up to here, and what's it all for? I was glad to see *my kid* flunk the Army physical. Still, somebody has to say no to these demonstrators and enforce the law.") What does it take to be a good American?

The conditions of trauma and frustration in the middle. What does it take to be a good American? Suddenly there are demands for Italian power and Polish power and Ukrainian power. In Cleveland the Poles demand a seat on the school board, and get it, and in Pittsburgh, John Pankuch, the seventy-three-year-old president of the National Slovak Society, demands "action, plenty of it to make up for lost time." Black power is supposed to be nothing but emulation of the ways in which other ethnic groups made it. But have they made it? In Reardon's Bar on East Eighth Street in South Boston, where the workmen come for their fish-chowder lunch and for their rye and ginger, they still identify themselves as Galway men and Kilkenny men; in the newsstand in Astoria you can buy *Il Progresso, El Tiempo,* the *Staats-Zeitung,* the *Irish World,* plus papers in Greek, Hungarian, and Polish. At the parish of Our Lady of Mount Carmel the priests hear confession in English, Italian, and Spanish and, nearby, the biggest attraction is not the stickball game, but the *bocce* court. Some of the poorest people in America are white, native, and have lived all of their lives in the same place as their fathers and grandfathers. The problems that were presumably solved in some distant past, in that prehistoric era before the textbooks were written—problems of assimilation, of upward mobility—now turn out to be very much unsolved. The melting pot and all: millions made it, millions moved to the affluent suburbs; several million—no one knows how many—did not. The median income in Irish South Boston is $5100 a year but the community-action workers have a hard time convincing the local citizens that any white man who is not stupid or irresponsible can be poor. Pride still keeps them from applying for income supplements or Medicaid, but it does not keep them from resenting those who do. In Pittsburgh, where the members of Polish-American organizations earn an estimated $5000 to $6000 (and some fall below the poverty line), the Poverty Programs are nonetheless directed primarily to Negroes, and almost everywhere the thing called urban backlash associates itself in some fashion with ethnic groups whose members have themselves only a precarious hold on the security of affluence. Almost everywhere in the old cities, tribal neighborhoods and their styles are under assault by masscult. The Italian grocery gives way to the supermarket, the ma-and-pa store and the walk-up are attacked by urban renewal. And almost everywhere, that assault tends to depersonalize and to alienate. It has always been this way, but with time the brave new world that replaces the old patterns becomes increasingly bureaucratized, distant, and hard to control.

Yet beyond the problems of ethnic identity, beyond the problems of Poles and Irishmen left behind, there are others more pervasive and more dangerous. For every Greek or Hungarian there are a dozen American-Americans who are past ethnic consciousness and who are as alienated, as confused, and as angry as the rest. The obvious manifestations are the same everywhere—race, taxes, welfare, students—but the threat seems invariably more cultural and psychological than economic or social. What upset the police at the Chicago convention most was not so much the politics of the demonstrators as their manners and their hair. (The barbershops in their neighborhoods don't advertise Beatle Cuts but the Flat Top and the Chicago Box.) The affront comes from middle-class people—and their children—who had been cast in the role of social exemplars (and from those cast as unfortunates worthy of public charity) who offend all the things on which working class identity is built: "hippies [said a San Francisco longshoreman] who fart around the streets and don't work"; welfare recipients who strike and march for better treatment; "all those [said a California labor official] who challenge the precepts that these people live on." If ethnic groups are beginning to organize to get theirs, so are others: police and firemen ("The cop is the new nigger"); schoolteachers; lower-middle-class housewives fighting sex education and bussing; small property owners who have no ethnic communion but a passionate interest in lower taxes, more policemen, and stiffer penalties for criminals. In San Francisco the Teamsters, who had never been known for such interests before, recently demonstrated in support of the police and law enforcement and, on another occasion, joined a group called Mothers Support Neighborhood Schools at a school-board meeting to oppose—with their presence and later, apparently, with their fists—a proposal to integrate the schools through bussing. . . .

WHEN HOPE BECOMES A THREAT

The imponderables are youth and tradition and change. The civics book and the institution it celebrates—however passé—still hold the world together. The revolt is in their name, not against them. And there is simple decency, the language and practice of the folksy cliché, the small town, the Boy Scout virtues, the neighborhood charity, the obligation to support the church, the rhetoric of open opportunity: "They can keep Wallace and they can keep Alabama. We didn't fight a dictator for four years so we could elect one over here." What happens when all that becomes Mickey Mouse? Is there an urban ethic to replace the values of the small town? Is there a coherent public philosophy, a consistent set of beliefs to replace family, home, and hard work? What happens when the hang-ups of upper-middle-class kids are in fashion and those of blue-collar kids are not? What happens when Doing Your Own Thing becomes not the slogan of the solitary deviant but the norm? Is it possible that as the institutions and beliefs of tradition are fashionably denigrated a blue-collar generation gap will open to the Right as well as to the Left? (There is statistical evidence, for example, that Wallace's greatest support within the unions came from people who are between twenty-one and twenty-nine, those, that is, who have the most tenuous association with the liberalism of labor.) Most are politically silent; although SDS has been trying to organize blue-collar high-school students, there are no Mario Savios or Mark Rudds—either of the Right or the Left—among them. At the same time the union leaders, some of them old hands from the Thirties, aren't sure that the kids are following them either. Who speaks for the son of the longshoreman or the Detroit auto worker? What happens if he doesn't get to college? What, indeed, happens when he does?

Vaguely but unmistakably the hopes that a youth-worshiping nation historically invested in its young become threats. We have never been unequivocal about the symbolic patricide of Americanization and upward mobility, but if at one time mobility meant rejection of older (or European) styles it was, at least, done in the name of America. Now the labels are blurred and the objectives indistinct. Just at the moment when a tradition-bound Italian father is persuaded that he should send his sons to college—that education is the only future—the college blows up. At the moment when a parsimonious taxpayer begins to shell out for what he considers an extravagant state university system the students go on strike. Marijuana, sexual liberation, dress styles, draft resistance, even the rhetoric of change become monsters and demons in a world that appears to turn old virtues upside down. The paranoia that fastened on Communism twenty years ago (and sometimes still does) is increasingly directed to vague conspiracies undermining the schools, the family, order and discipline. "They're feeding the kids this generation-gap business," says a Chicago housewife who grinds out a campaign against sex education on a duplicating machine in her living room. "The kids are told to make their own decisions. They're all mixed up by situation ethics and open-ended questions. They're alienating children from their own parents." They? The churches, the schools, even the YMCA and the Girl Scouts, are implicated. But a major share of the villainy is now also attributed to "the social science centers," to the apostles of sensitivity training, and to what one California lady, with some embarrassment, called "nude therapy." "People with sane minds are being altered by psychological methods." The current major campaign of the John Birch Society is not directed against Communists in government or the Supreme Court, but against sex education. . . .

CAN THE COMMON MAN COME BACK?

Beneath it all there is a more fundamental ambivalence, not only about the young, but about institutions—the schools, the churches, the Establishment—and about the future itself. In the major cities of the East (though perhaps not in the West) there is a sense that time is against you, that one is living "in one of the few decent neighborhoods left," that "if I can get $125 a week upstate (or downstate) I'll move." The institutions that were supposed to mediate social change and which, more than ever, are becoming priesthoods of information and conglomerates of social engineers, are increasingly suspect. To attack the Ford Foundation (as Wright Patman has done) is not only to fan the embers of historic populism against concentrations of wealth and power, but also to arouse those who feel that they are trapped by an alliance of upper-class Wasps and lower-class Negroes.

If the foundations have done anything for the blue-collar worker he doesn't seem to be aware of it. At the same time the distrust of professional educators that characterizes the black militants is becoming increasingly prevalent among the minority of lower-middle-class whites who are beginning to discover that the schools aren't working for them either. ("Are all those new programs just a cover-up for failure?") And if the Catholic Church is under attack from its liberal members (on birth control, for example) it is also alienating the traditionalists who liked their minor saints (even if they didn't actually exist) and were perfectly content with the Latin Mass. For the alienated Catholic liberal there are other places to go; for the lower-middle-class parishioner in Chicago or Boston there are none.

Perhaps, in some measure, it has always been this way. Perhaps none of this is new. And perhaps it is also true that the American lower middle has never had it so good. And yet surely there is a difference, and that is that the common man has lost his visibility and, somehow, his claim on public attention. There are old liberals and socialists—men like Michael Harrington—who believe that a new alliance can be forged for progressive social action:

> From Marx to Mills, the Left has regarded the middle class as a stratum of hypocritical vacillating rear-guarders. There was often sound reason for this contempt. But is it not possible that a new class is coming into being? It is not the old middle class of small property owners and entrepreneurs, nor the new middle class of managers. It is composed of scientists, technicians, teachers, and professionals in the public sector of the society. By education and work experience it is predisposed toward planning. It could be an ally of the poor and the organized workers—or their sophisticated enemy. In other words, an unprecedented social and political variable seems to be taking shape in America.
>
> The American worker, even when he waits on a table or holds open a door, is not servile; he does not carry himself like an inferior. The openness, frankness, and democratic manner which Tocqueville described in the last century persists to this very day. They have been a source of rudeness, contemptuous ignorance, violence—and of a creative self-confidence among great masses of people. It was in this latter spirit that the CIO was organized and the black freedom movement marched.

There are recent indications that the white lower middle class is coming back on the roster of public priorities. Pucinski tells you that liberals in Congress are privately discussing the pressure from the middle class. There are proposals now to increase personal income-tax exemptions from $600 to $1000 (or $1200) for each dependent, to protect all Americans with a national insurance system covering catastrophic medical expenses, and to put a floor under all incomes. Yet these things by themselves are insufficient. Nothing is sufficient without a national sense of restoration. What Pucinski means by the middle class has, in some measure, always been represented. A physician earning $75,000 a year is also a working man but he is hardly a victim of the welfare system. Nor, by and large, are the stockholders of the Standard Oil Company or U.S. Steel. The fact that American ideals have often been corrupted in the cause of self-aggrandizement does not make them any less important for the cause of social reform and justice. "As a movement with the conviction that there is more to people than greed and fear," Harrington said, "the Left must . . . also speak in the name of the historic idealism of the United States."

The issue, finally, is not *the program* but the vision, the angle of view. A huge constituency may be coming up for grabs, and there is considerable evidence that its political mobility is more sensitive than anyone can imagine, that all the sociological determinants are not as significant as the simple facts of concern and leadership. When Robert Kennedy was killed last year, thousands of working-class people who had expected to vote for him—if not hundreds of thousands—shifted their loyalties to Wallace. A man who can change from a progressive democrat into a bigot overnight deserves attention.

Watergate

Kim McQuaid

*The sixties, the era we remember for heroic struggles for civil rights and the po-
larization of the nation over the war in Vietnam, came to a kind of symbolic
end in 1974, with the resignation of President Richard Nixon over his betrayal of the trust of the American people. Through a bizarre series of events,
the Nixon administration found itself in a situation where, in order to cover
up high-level White House involvement in a burglary, it created a set of circumstances that brought down the entire administration. The ironies of the situation were endless. Nixon had such a commanding lead over his opponents
in the 1974 presidential election that no one could really challenge him, yet in
order to gain a still greater edge, Nixon's political associates authorized a
break-in at Democratic national headquarters in the Watergate Hotel. Even
with the evidence turned up by journalists and congressional hearings, Nixon
would probably have remained in office, yet the taping system he himself had
installed in order to document his role in the nation's history tripped him up.
Perhaps appropriately, the man who sought office in order to "bring us together again" accomplished his purpose by uniting most of the country in revulsion against his unconstitutional actions.*

In the following excerpts from his much longer discussion in The Anxious Years, *historian Kim McQuaid speculates on the significance of Watergate. Focusing on the tapes, the Senate Judiciary Committee hearings, and
finally Nixon's resignation (to avoid impeachment), McQuaid raises questions about what Americans expect of their president. Was Watergate, as he
argues, a "watershed in American innocence"? How does the effort to impeach President Nixon compare to the impeachment trial of President Clinton
(Part 7)?*

HISTORY AS KALEIDOSCOPE

It is easy to enunciate brittle profundities about Watergate. Americans who lived through over two years worth of break-ins, cover-ups, hearings, resignations, and on- and off-camera debates know that this political trial of a president and his closest associates mattered. We know it proved something about Richard Nixon, presidential power, government in general, and the laws upon which the nation is dependent. When it comes to being precise, however, eloquence often evaporates into knee-jerk phrases: "Nixon is a crook"; "No one is above the law"; "Nixon got railroaded"; "All politicians are only out for themselves"; and so forth.

This imprecision is hardly surprising. Watergate was a many-sided skirmish that roiled into a full-scale war. As combat proliferated, utterly ambitious people found their careers in danger and fought to protect them. Loyalties were strained or broken by fear; alliances were formed and reformed; associates were destroyed and replaced; and layers of rhetoric, lies, evasions, ad hominem abuse, guesstimation, press leaks, and instantaneous analysis obscured the landscape.

It was, to millions of concerned Americans, just one damned thing after another—surprises galore, a wildly burgeoning cast of characters, crisis rhetoric, and a review of basic principles about as easy to keep straight as a catalog of volcanoes on Mars or gaseous layers of Neptune. Watergate certainly wasn't the intellectualized government of political-science textbooks. It was a soap opera come to life, with a plot that was like the layers of an onion.

Watergate produced a result which Vietnam never had. The war made the United States look ineffective and divided, but Watergate made America look ridiculous in the eyes of its own people. The leaders often appeared to be buffoons, and the led hedged their political loyalties accordingly. The view that "government is the problem" grew. Washington looked as illegitimate and pathetic as it did misguided or criminal. The process—full of fits, starts, alarms, and diversions—took place in five major stages, which are summarized here and will be discussed in detail later.

An initial judicial and journalistic stage of the Watergate investigation lasted for eleven months, from June 1972 to May 1973. Then, during May, June, and July, the first stage of the political trial commenced before the Senate Watergate Committee. Once John Dean and Alexander Butterfield did so much to legitimize the Watergate investigation and to put the criminal spotlight on Richard Nixon himself, a second judicial and journalistic struggle took place from July to October 1973. At issue was whether the courts could gain custody of the Watergate tapes. After the first special prosecutor was fired for his legal troubles in October, and continuing on until April 1974, political, judicial, and journalistic opposition gradually, and sometimes hesitantly, converged on the White House. Finally, from April to August 1974, this process of convergence had gone far enough so that the second and last stage of the political trial of Watergate drove Nixon from the presidency.

By the end, almost nobody felt triumphant and almost everybody was emotionally drained. Watergate, in this important sense, marked a watershed in American innocence. It symbolized the end of three decades when Americans could assume, in bland arrogance, that they were a special, powerful, and uniquely favored nation existing outside of history. If there was one thing that everybody, from Richard Milhous Nixon himself to the most thorough Nixon-hater, agreed with after two-and-one-third years of repeatedly failed cover-up, it was this maxim from La Rochefoucauld: "Almost all our failings are more pardonable than the means we use to hide them." The adage captured the mood of unflattering self-awareness that characterized the period.

Watergate was a twenty-seven-month struggle during which . . . America's constitutional system of checks and balances was faced with its most divisive and overt challenges since the Depression decade of the 1930s. In the process of attempting to resolve the conflict about the proper scope of presidential, congressional, and judicial power in the United States, the judges, legislators, and executive branch officials—with assists from investigative journalists—were faced with the fact that presidential power had vastly increased during the Cold War which had characterized United States foreign policy since the end of the Second World War. Watergate had flowed from Vietnam and from the polarized domestic politics the failed American war in Indochina had induced.

It was now up to the Congress and the courts to determine how far to scale back executive privileges and the assumptions about national security that rationalized so many of those privileges. The process was daunting and threatening. Courts and Congress alike proceeded carefully and often hesitantly. Had Richard Nixon not made the incredible error of tape-recording his own conversations, and then of needlessly alienating many of his own congressional allies—as, for example, by claiming a right to impound funds—it is more than likely that he would have survived Watergate and that only a relatively small number of deniable intermediaries would have been punished for activities in which he was fully implicated. . . .

On April 29th, [1974,] Nixon went on prime-time TV to announce he was freely making available information about his knowledge and actions relating to the Watergate break-in and cover-up which would demonstrate that both were "just as I have described them to you from the very beginning." Framing the president as he spoke were several score bound volumes of transcript, or so it appeared. The volumes were stage props. Four-fifths of their pages were empty. The 1,200 pages remaining were heavily edited. Even with the White House's editing, however, the transcripts demonstrated no such "from the very beginning" honesty as Nixon claimed before an audience of over half the nation's adult population.

Honesty, however, was the last thing on the president's mind. Nixon was using his office as an "electronic pulpit" to make it appear that he was doing what he was not, in fact, doing—that is, providing evidence long desired by the courts and two special prosecutors and which had been demanded of him only two weeks earlier by a Congressional Judiciary Committee subpoena. All presidents engage in this sort of prevarication, but Nixon's lies were more brazen than most. For not quite ten months, the tapes had been a slowly tightening noose around his neck. So Nixon finally tried to slip the noose by "letting the people know" what was on the growing numbers of tapes the special prosecutor and Congress wanted to see, in hopes that his judicial and political opponents would then be forced to keep pressing for genuine evidence.

The strategy almost worked. Nixon gave one of his better Watergate performances, one good enough to elicit kudos from the *Washington Post* and the *New York Times*. He did this because he was initially able to make it appear as though he was finally obeying the law, and the appearance briefly cast Nixon's opponents as partisan villains. Here was the president giving everyone all anybody could ask for, so who was Congress to refuse it? Who was the special prosecutor to keep insisting on more? Congress now had all it needed to determine whether an impeachment trial was necessary.

Nixon's was a bold and unexpected stroke which only just failed. Had the House Judiciary Committee accepted the edited transcripts that Nixon advertised as genuine, Nixon could have eviscerated the political trial, continued to stymie criminal justice as it applied to himself, and kept his presidency alive. But the committee's staff, of course, knew that appearances were not realities. They knew that Nixon had released only sanitized versions of the tapes—including those which Sirica, grand jury members, the special prosecutor's lawyers, and the committee had seen entire—to avoid a clear refusal to obey a special congressional subpoena for many Watergate tapes which the Judiciary Committee had finally made on April 11th. Nixon submitted his *sanitized* transcripts the day before the deadline which the House Judiciary Committee had set for their receipt of the *unsanitized* evidence. . . .

They knew all of that. Still, they almost played Nixon's game. . . . On the evening of May 1st, the House Judiciary Committee's members were called upon to decide. Would they accept the transcripts Nixon had made public several days before as sufficient, or would they not? They wouldn't, but only just. By a vote of 20 to 18, the committee refused to allow Nixon to set the terms of his own investigation any longer. . . . They guessed what the public's reaction to Nixon's edited tapes might be, and they guessed right. Within two weeks after Nixon released his version of Watergate, his presidency was on the road toward dissolution.

Nixon's staff had deleted a lot from the transcripts—pithy instructions, for example, which the president gave John Mitchell on March 22, 1973, one day after his "cancer on the presidency" meeting with John Dean: "I want you all to stonewall it, let them plead the Fifth Amendment, cover up or anything else" to "save the plan." But the transcripts were peppered with "(expletives deleted)" and the expletives mattered. Off-color expressions, present and absent, shocked the majority of Americans who did not then believe that their presidents swore.

The idea seems quaint now, yet it existed then. The United States of 1974 was steeped in an era of American Greatness, weaned during decades when presidents loomed ever larger in the nation's political imagination. America had become the greatest country in the world, a land with missions to match its greatness. Majesty was accordingly expected of the men who led that nation and who symbolized it to hundreds of millions at home and abroad—and majesty meant moral grandeur and spotless behavior. "Give 'em Hell" Harry Truman had used salty language, but Richard Nixon and many another rising politician had pilloried such verbal pyrotechnics as unacceptable. Truman was common, and the day of the common president who used common language was over. Nixon and others cast their words and actions in heroic styles pioneered by successful presidents like Franklin Delano Roosevelt and John F. Kennedy. Heroic strategies paid off for presidents. It gave them a divinity which doth hedge kings and leaders of nations with thermonuclear arsenals. It allowed their power and repute to survive shocks which other leaders, like "fixer" Lyndon Johnson, did not survive.

But it also exacted a price. Richard Nixon paid that price after April 30th, 1974. Politicians who knew what presidential image making was all about guessed what was coming, as House Judiciary Committee member James Mann of South Carolina did when he talked with journalist Elizabeth Drew on the eve of the committee's crucial vote of May 1st. Mann referred, Drew wrote:

> as people have been doing all day, to the "(expletive deleted)"s. They all seem curious to know what those parentheses are hiding. "The more that people know about him, it seems, the more trouble he's in," he says. "It's not that they think he's guilty of an impeachable offense, necessarily, but that he's not the man they thought he was."

No, Nixon wasn't the man they thought he was, any more than Jack Kennedy had been, but Kennedy hadn't been exposed while still in office. And it cost Nixon heavily with those who had come to expect their president to be a democratic monarch. Nixon's image problem then was a major reason that the Judiciary Committee risked moving ahead—though only just—on May 1st. Enough members believed that Nixon's edited words would explode in his face. Congress fought to replace Nixon's evidentiary agenda with its own and, during the next several weeks, the truth of perceptions like Representative Mann's was borne out. Mann's constituents didn't like what they read or heard about the tapes, and they heard and read lots more than the White House reckoned they would.

The reading began when the *New York Times*, in a repeat of its Pentagon Papers revelations, serialized the White House's transcripts verbatim. On May 1st, CBS News broadcast a prime-time special in which reporters read segments of the tape transcripts. Three days later, NBC News used professional actors to do the same thing. Meanwhile, both the *Washington Post* and the *New York Times* rushed the transcripts into paperback, with commentaries to help readers make sense of seven hundred pages of text. Both books, available on news-stands by May 14th, quickly became best-sellers.

The more exposure Nixon's edited transcripts got, the less willing congressional Republicans and conservative Democrats were to defend their content. Republican House Minority Leader John Rhodes of Arizona and his Senate counterpart, Hugh Scott of Pennsylvania, somersaulted from complimenting the president for supplying bowdlerized evidence to damning what Nixon had made public. Rhodes branded the transcripts a "deplorable, shabby, disgusting, and immoral performance by all," and later added that he'd be willing to accept Nixon's resignation if Nixon chose to offer it. Such strategic withdrawals by Congress's Republican leadership sent strong messages to fence sitters on the House Judiciary Committee. . . . The more Republicans who were willing to go after Nixon, the better for the Democrats. The Judiciary Committee would become a Chinese army, and Nixon simply couldn't shoot them *all*. . . .

For six months, the House Judiciary Committee moved glacially. . . . Through all of this, Washington's power brokers watched public-opinion polls like hawks, especially after Nixon's tape transcripts gambit failed. . . . Never before had the grass roots wanted Nixon out so badly. "Expletive deleted"s and a lot else besides had undermined Nixon to a point that a political indictment and a political trial were now acceptable. . . .

Thirty-eight percent believed Nixon should be impeached at the beginning of May, while 49 percent did not and 13 percent had no opinion. By mid-May, 48 percent wanted Nixon tossed out, 37 percent didn't, and 15 percent weren't sure. At the end of May, 44 percent wanted Nixon removed, 41 percent didn't, and the remainder stayed bemused. Six percent more of the adult population wanted Nixon tried at the end of May than at its start. Six percent more also believed that Nixon was guilty of crimes unbecoming a president, 9 percent ceased their opposition to trying Nixon, and 8 percent ceased opposing his impeachment. The release of the tapes had backfired. Millions of Americans had believed the president when he'd stated repeatedly that he hadn't been involved in Watergate at *all*. Nixon might be a dupe, but they didn't think of him as a liar or crook. Even with excisions, however, the White House tapes showed that Nixon *had* been involved. Sloughing everything off on bad advisers like John Dean no longer worked: the question was no longer whether Nixon was involved, but how involved he was. . . .

[Finally, on July 24th, 1974,] it was the Supreme Court's turn to make political determinations. This it did by deciding by a vote of 8 to 0 (one justice excusing himself) that Nixon must obey the subpoenas obtained by the special prosecutor for more Watergate tapes. Both the judicial trial and the political trial of the Watergate case, the judges had decided, required the best evidence available. The justices made a political decision that removed most of the final executive privilege and national security barriers to the impeachment trial. The power circle ringing Richard Milhous Nixon had finally closed—a year after the existence of the White House tapes had first become known.

No one recognized this better than the men and women of the House Judiciary Committee. Once the Court ruled unanimously against a president who had appointed four of its members, including Chief Justice Warren Burger, Nixon had few political friends left. Within hours, southern Democrats and moderate Republicans on the committee met to determine strategies for the impeachment debates that began the same evening.

THE JUDICIARY COMMITTEE DECIDES

What followed focused the country's attention as nothing about Watergate had before. Not even the Senate Watergate Committee hearings of the summer of 1973 became an instantaneous folk event the way the week-long House Judiciary Committee debates and votes on five separate impeachment articles did. Via live television and radio, interested citizens were symbolically and actually admitted into the elite regions of their political order. In the process, it was easy—even natural—for tens of millions of people to think of themselves, too, as members of the political grand jury debating and deciding the issues before them.

Realities were otherwise, and very much went on behind the scenes, but Watergate was visible as it had never been before. The fundamental question the House Judiciary Committee had to decide was whether Richard Nixon still deserved to lead. The audience knew that, whether they had ever read the Constitution or not, or whether they knew much about the nuances of the many different aspects of the case. Everyone—audience and participants—was a part of history now. This vote mattered.

Rarely before had members of Congress played to such a large, diverse, and involved national audience. The experience was heady and intimidating. Fundamental issues of political power and privilege were very clearly at issue. The thirty-eight committee members at the center of the national stage worried, therefore. They would not have been human—or politically successful—if they had not. Sandwiched between an opening speech by Democrat Committee Chair Peter Rodino of New Jersey and a closing speech by ranking committee Republican Edward Hutchinson of Michigan, all the members—Democrat and Republican alternating—were given fifteen minutes to make an opening statement of their views on the overall case for or against Richard M. Nixon.

Nine and one-half hours of speechifying by thirty-eight people could have induced yawns or worse, but it didn't. For, in giving each member a quarter-hour before the cameras, the Judiciary Committee made itself known to a national audience for the first time. The committee became less of an abstract whole and much more a collection of individuals arguing different views in differing ways. Moreover, the opening statements were, in effect, a poll of a political grand jury, and the tens of millions in the television and radio audiences, listening to the general arguments for and against, could more easily understand and identify with the process of judgement.

The audience was also a jury, of course, one which would soon deliver electoral judgements on all of the assembled members of Congress. So all the committee's members did their best to couch their opening statements in fashions which would best make their case and best reflect upon their motives in arguing as they did. They sought to involve their electorates on their behalf. The president's opponents provided long sequences of details about his involvement in the cover-up. The president's defenders countered that the committee's Democratic majority was mostly engaged in a partisan vendetta using a "grab bag of allegations." . . .

The process was full of last-minute fits and starts. After the nine-and-one-half hours of nationally televised opening statements were completed on the evening of July 25th, Nixon's defenders on the House Judiciary Committee knew they didn't have the votes to stop the committee from voting out some impeachment charges. Representative Charles Sandman of New Jersey said as much near the start of the proceedings, but by their conclusion, the numbers were clear. The twenty-one Democratic members all intended to charge Nixon with something and six of the seventeen Republicans were off the reservation. Three were leaning strongly toward indictment, and another three (Cohen of Maine, Hogan of Maryland, and Railsback of Illinois) were definitely going to vote to indict.

At long last, the Democrats had the bipartisan alliance they had been trying to create for more than six months. The eleven Republicans who intended to vote against any and all charges hadn't convinced a single Democrat that Nixon had done nothing wrong, but the president's defenders did not lack for political energy. They intensified their efforts to make whatever charges were brought as innocuous and narrowly drawn as possible. As so often before, Nixon's defenders were arguing that the president should enjoy every conceivable benefit of a criminal justice system he had repeatedly flouted. With the last act in the Watergate drama about to be played, Nixon's congressional supporters kept on defending him.

They were not fools, these people. They mixed ideals with self-interest, just as their opponents did. Regarding interests, most feared that the Republican Party would be branded as the "party of Watergate" for as long as the Democrats could get away with it and that this political equation would cost the G.O.P. and themselves dearly.

Their ideals enabled them to rationalize and explain their concerns about their political interests and also to express some legitimate indignation. Hypocrisy and double standards were the charges the president's defenders hurled at his attackers, privately and publicly. Nixon was no saint and nobody was arguing that he was. But he hadn't done anything that every recent president before him hadn't also done, and most of these presidents had been Democrats. "Post-Watergate morality" was all very well, but all the Democrats were doing was obscuring their own domestic dirty tricks by blaming Nixon (and, through him, the Republicans) for everything, just as they had earlier done about sins committed in Vietnam.

These charges had substance, enough to make it clearer why Watergate took so long, and why a Democratic Congress was so very often hesitant to proceed quickly or expeditiously to resolve the case. Watergate had evolved out of the Vietnam War and the divisions and fears spawned by it. The politics of fear and discord that Nixon exploited was no peculiar creation of his. He was more its creation than its creator. So it appeared unfair to make Nixon what Democrat John Conyers of Michigan had called him at the start of the House Judiciary Committee's debates: "in a very real sense a casualty of the Vietnam war."

Nixon's defenders also opposed making Nixon a casualty because of his various domestic sins. Lyndon Johnson had been a thief and worse, but the Democratic congressional leaders who had known that hadn't mounted any sort of coup against him. Instead, they had stonewalled Republican efforts to trace millions of dollars in kickbacks and favoritism and misuse of government property and corruption of favored subordinates like Bobby Baker in the White House inner sanctum. Now these same people, joined by journalists and bureaucrats and uppity lawyers and judges, were out to get Nixon. They were mounting a coup because they were "marinated in hatred" for Nixon and all he stood for. So, thinking in this way, it was comparatively easy for some Republican members of Congress to keep fighting for Nixon. Watergate was, in this view, merely a skirmish in a much wider Cold War. If Nixon were denied office because he had mismanaged a skirmish, the nation might lose its war against foreign and domestic radicalism, and America could swiftly return to the bad old days of 1968.

Had Watergate not happened when and how it had, this hypocrisy and double-standard argument of the president's defenders might have had far more force. But popular fears about Vietnam, Black Power, and the New Left were passé in July 1974. Moreover, the White House had blundered far too many times in its efforts to squelch the case. The combination of these two factors removed just enough of the inhibitions within the House Judiciary Committee against charging Nixon with broadly defined political crimes. . . .

The resignation came first. On the morning of August 8th, people learned that Nixon had finally given up. In a televised address to the country at 9 P.M. that evening, Nixon gave his explanation of what had happened. "In all the decisions I have made in my political life," he began, "I have always tried to do what was best for the Nation." Regarding Watergate, Nixon had had a "duty to persevere" to "complete the term of office to which you elected me." But perseverance was no longer possible. Congressional support had eroded to such a point that there was no more point in fighting against what might be a "dangerously destabilizing precedent [impeachment] for the future," much as he "would have preferred to carry through to the finish." "I have never been a quitter . . . But, as President, I must put the interests of America first. America needs a full-time President and a full-time Congress" to deal with pressing national and international problems. Vice President Ford would be president as of noon on August 9th. Ford should be supported because a "process of healing" was "desperately needed in America." Nixon had made wrong judgements and some of these had hurt people, but all he had done had been done for America, not for himself. . . .

Nixon's more revealing statements came later. At 9:30 A.M. on August 9th, Nixon gathered his Cabinet and staff around him for the last time as president. Here, before what remained of his administration, Nixon came as close as he ever did to explaining himself as a human being during the entire twenty-six months of the Watergate struggle. It wasn't a neat performance; such public intimacies rarely are. Nixon mixed gallant gestures, self-justification, hope, and anger in about equal proportions. . . .

Nixon was leaving the presidency, but not disappearing from political life. A defeat was not an end. "It is only a beginning always." Only those who have "been in the deepest valley can . . . even know how magnificent it is to be on the highest mountain." Every one in government should remember this. They also needed to realize something else, Nixon added as he closed: "Always give your best, never get discouraged, never get petty; always remember, others may hate you; but those who hate you don't win unless you hate them, and then you destroy yourself."

There, finally, amidst tears and the more hard-eyed emotions, was the distilled personalized wisdom of the Watergate case. Nixon had hated well and excessively. That hate, in turn, had destroyed him. Minutes later, Richard Nixon and his family left the White House for a plane trip home to San Clemente, California, on a presidential aircraft named the Spirit of '76. In flight, shortly after noon on August 9th, 1974, Nixon's presidency ended.

Part 7

AN ERA OF TRANSFORMATION

The 1970s represented the end of an era. Throughout the thirty years after World War II American politics had functioned on the premise that nothing was impossible if America wished to achieve it. We would be guardians of freedom, send a man to the moon, conquer social injustice, eliminate poverty, develop impressive technology—in short, control the universe. That sense of confidence and of power had been a hallmark of all political factions in the country, even young radicals who thought that by their own endeavors they could change the world. In the 1970s, however, a new sense of limits struck home. The United States suffered its first loss in war. Richard Nixon became the first president forced to resign in disgrace, in large part because he himself had no sense of limits to his own presidential power. The oil-producing countries of OPEC quickly made Americans conscious of their dependence on the rest of the world during the 1973–74 oil boycott and the sporadic shortages thereafter. When Iranian revolutionaries held American diplomats hostage for more than a year, the sense of being subject to powers beyond one's control became a reality reinforced by every newscast. The American tendency toward hubris—the arrogant confidence that one can do anything—had come face to face with the realities of human frailty, mortality, and interdependency.

By the time that President Richard M. Nixon resigned in disgrace, Americans' basic faith in their political system had been shaken. The years of polarization and the Vietnam War had taken an enormous toll on the American public. And as more and more evidence of governmental wrongdoing surfaced—Nixon's secret bombing of Cambodia; Watergate—the nation felt betrayed. Jimmy Carter spoke directly to that sense of betrayal when in 1976 he told the American people that they deserved a government as good as they were, one based upon faith, honesty, integrity, dignity, and respect for traditional

American values. Gerald Ford, Nixon's vice president, had done a superb job of healing the immediate wounds left by Watergate, but Carter offered an almost religious salve designed to reverse the damage. Running on the platform of an outsider who would bring a fresh perspective to Washington, Carter—a southerner and our first "born again" president—seemed to represent the simplicity and decency that would restore the faith of Americans in their political process.

The problem was that Carter knew very little about getting along in Washington. Oftentimes insensitive toward Congress, he entered into a permanent deadlock. Although he accomplished some positive goals in foreign policy, particularly with the Camp David accords on the Middle East, he was never able to deliver on his pledge of turning the government around. While he diagnosed and articulated the crisis of confidence that existed in the American political process in the post-Nixon years, he was unable to mobilize support for constructive solutions to that crisis. The intractable problems of energy and Iran seemed to paralyze his administration.

The election of Ronald Reagan represented still another effort to recover what had been lost, this time by going back to a rhetoric and program that reminded the United States of its former sense of invincibility. Reagan—originally a Hollywood actor—could communicate what he saw as simple verities. America should be strong. Communism represented a false God and the Soviet Union an "evil empire." Free enterprise worked. And every individual should be responsible for him- or herself. With remarkable skill, the new president pushed through legislation to cut taxes—and social welfare benefits—while dramatically increasing military spending.

Reagan's success coincided with the rapid growth of the New Right, conservatives grounded not in free-market or libertarian philosophies but in the convictions of evangelical, often fundamentalist, Christianity. Whether galvanized by the Equal Rights Amendment, abortion, school busing, homosexuality, or prayer in the schools, such New Right groups added a different dimension to the American political scene. Though America appeared less divided than during the years of protests and police barricades, many observers sensed the consolidation of a deeper division in American society—one that came to be described as the "culture wars." On one side were the urban, more affluent, more educated, more sophisticated; on the other the former bedrock of the Democratic Party, now increasingly Republican: small town, less educated, less affluent, more religious. This shift would alter the balance of national politics, and also shape the national debate on social issues over the rest of the twentieth century and beyond. Such divisions would become very apparent in the impeachment trial of President Clinton in the final years of the twentieth century.

Clinton represented a new generation of American leadership. Born in 1946, he was the first postwar president from the generation of Vietnam, not World War II. Unlike presidents before or since, Clinton was married to a woman who was his professional peer, a figure of importance in her own right. He was a charismatic figure whose own excesses would compromise his presidency. Clinton, in many ways, promised the nation a return to an age of possibility. He presided over a period of relative peace and great prosperity and a revival of national confidence. But his ambitious legislative agenda was largely defeated by an aggressive Republican Congress, and the coalition of "New Democrats" that had voted him into office twice failed to maintain a Democratic presidency in the 2000 election. No clear winner emerged in the three-way race among Clinton's vice president, Al Gore; Republican son of a former president, George W. Bush; and Green Party candidate Ralph Nader. Gore had a majority in the popular vote, but the election turned on the electoral college count, with Florida's results too close to call. After weeks of uncertainty the Supreme Court, in a 5–4 and clearly partisan vote, ended the possibility of a Florida recount, thus giving Bush the presidency by a margin of one electoral college vote.

The last third of the twentieth century was not simply a reaction to the end of an era; it was also a time of transformation. Policies implemented in the 1960s—such as the major revision of immigration law—began to have major impacts on American society. Political parties were reconfigured. The end of the Cold War created a new set of challenges for foreign policy. The United States, as the only remaining superpower, faced a world in which national boundaries were ever less meaningful, as everything from the environment to the economy were increasingly subject to global forces and interrelations.

This section and the next examine these transformations and their legacies. Author Nicholas Lemann argues for the importance of the often-neglected decade of the seventies in American history. E. J. Dionne, Jr., analyzes the rise of the New Right. Ronald Reagan's 1985 State of the Union address illustrates the ideas and the optimism of "the Reagan Revolution." In an article from the late 1980s, Nobel

Prize–winning economist James Tobin explains "Reaganomics" and offers a sharp critique of their effects on the nation. A report from the U.S. Census Bureau demonstrates the increasing diversity of the nation's population, and reveals some of the great differences that exist among immigrant groups. Four speeches from members of Congress in the impeachment trial of President Clinton illustrate some of the divisions that exist within American society. Finally, law professor Alan Dershowitz critiques the role the Supreme Court played in deciding the result of the 2000 presidential election.

The questions that emerge from this section are ones that we are currently debating. What lasting implications do differing economic policies have for the United States? How will the rapidly increasing diversity of the American people affect the nation? Are the divisions represented by the "culture wars" to be the most important force in contemporary American politics? What role should religion play in America's public life, and in the political sphere?

How the Seventies Changed America

Nicholas Lemann

The only major historical account of "The Seventies" to appear before the year 2000 was titled It Seemed Like Nothing Happened. *And much of what did happen was bad: Watergate, recession, the oil crisis, the Iranian hostage situation, polyester leisure suits. The 1970s have passed into the historical imagination as a wasteland, a failure of a decade lost between the great dreams of the 1960s and the "Reagan revolution" of the 1980s. But in this article from* American Heritage, *respected journalist Nicholas Lemann argues that this "runt" of a decade was in fact far more significant than anyone dreamed.*

"That's it," Daniel Patrick Moynihan, then U.S. ambassador to India, wrote to a colleague on the White House staff in 1973 on the subject of some issue of the moment. "Nothing will happen. But then nothing much is going to happen in the 1970s anyway."

Moynihan is a politician famous for his predictions, and this one seemed for a long time to be dead-on. The seventies, even while they were in progress, looked like an unimportant decade, a period of cooling down from the white-hot sixties. You had to go back to the teens to find another decade so lacking in crisp, epigrammatic definition. It only made matters worse for the seventies that the succeeding decade started with a bang. In 1980 the country elected the most conservative President in its history, and it was immediately clear that a new era had dawned. (In general the eighties, unlike the seventies, had a perfect dramatic arc. They peaked in the summer of 1984, with the Los Angeles Olympics and the Republican National Convention in Dallas, and began to peter out with the Iran-contra scandal in 1986 and the stock market crash in 1987.) It is nearly impossible to engage in magazine-writerly games like discovering "the day the seventies

died" or "the spirit of the seventies"; and the style of the seventies—
wide ties, sideburns, synthetic fabrics, white shoes, disco—is so far interesting largely as something to make fun of.

But somehow the seventies seem to be creeping out of the loser-
decade category. Their claim to importance is in the realm of sweeping historical trends, rather than memorable events, though there
were some of those too. In the United States today a few basic propositions shape everything: The presidential electorate is conservative and
Republican. Geopolitics revolves around a commodity (oil) and a religion (Islam) more than around an ideology (Marxism-Leninism). The
national economy is no longer one in which practically every class, region, and industry is upwardly mobile. American culture is essentially
individualistic, rather than communitarian, which means that notions
like deferred gratification, sacrifice, and sustained national effort are a
very tough sell. Anyone seeking to understand the roots of this situation has to go back to the seventies.

The underestimation of the seventies' importance, especially during the early years of the decade, is easy to forgive because the character of the seventies was substantially shaped at first by spillover
from the sixties. Such sixties events as the killings of student protesters at Kent State and Orangeburg, the original Earth Day, the invasion of Cambodia, and a large portion of the war in Vietnam took
place in the seventies. Although sixties radicals (cultural and political) spent the early seventies loudly bemoaning the end of the revolution, what was in fact going on was the working of the phenomena
of the sixties into the mainstream of American life. Thus the first
Nixon administration, which was decried by liberals at the time for
being nightmarishly right-wing, was actually more liberal than the
Johnson administration in many ways—less hawkish in Vietnam,
more free-spending on social programs. The reason wasn't that
Richard Nixon was a liberal but that the country as a whole had continued to move steadily to the left throughout the late sixties and
early seventies; the political climate of institutions like the U.S. Congress and the boards of directors of big corporations was probably
more liberal in 1972 than in any year before or since, and the Democratic party nominated its most liberal presidential candidate ever.
Nixon had to go along with the tide.

In New Orleans, my hometown, the hippie movement peaked in
1972 or 1973. Long hair, crash pads, head shops, psychedelic posters,

underground newspapers, and other Summer of Love–inspired institutions had been unknown there during the real Summer of Love,
which was in 1967. It took even longer, until the middle or late seventies, for those aspects of hippie life that have endured to catch on
with the general public. All over the country the likelihood that an
average citizen would wear longish hair, smoke marijuana, and
openly live with a lover before marriage was probably greater in 1980
than it was in 1970. The sixties' preoccupation with self-discovery became a mass phenomenon only in the seventies, through home-brew
psychological therapies like est. In politics the impact of the black en-
franchisement that took place in the 1960s barely began to be felt
until the mid- to late 1970s. The tremendously influential feminist
and gay-liberation movements were, at the dawn of the 1970s, barely
under way in Manhattan, their headquarters, and certainly hadn't
begun their spread across the whole country. The sixties took a long
time for America to digest; the process went on throughout the seventies and even into the eighties.

The epochal event of the seventies as an era in its own right was the
Organization of Petroleum Exporting Countries' oil embargo, which
lasted for six months in the fall of 1973 and the spring of 1974. Everything that happened in the sixties was predicated on the assumption
of economic prosperity and growth; concerns like personal fulfillment and social justice tend to emerge in the middle class only at
times when people take it for granted that they'll be able to make a
living. For thirty years—ever since the effects of World War II on the
economy had begun to kick in—the average American's standard of
living had been rising, to a remarkable extent. As the economy grew,
indices like home ownership, automobile ownership, and access to
higher education got up to levels unknown anywhere else in the
world, and the United States could plausibly claim to have provided a
better life materially for its working class than any society ever had.
That ended with the OPEC embargo.

While it was going on, the embargo didn't fully register in the national consciousness. The country was absorbed by a different story,
the Watergate scandal, which was really another sixties spillover, the
final series of battles in the long war between the antiwar liberals and
the rough-playing anti-Communists. Richard Nixon, having engaged
in dirty tricks against leftish politicians for his whole career, didn't
stop doing so as President; he only found new targets, like Daniel
Ellsberg and Lawrence O'Brien. This time, however, he lost the Es-

tablishment, which was now far more kindly disposed to Nixon's enemies than it had been back in the 1950s. Therefore, the big-time press, the courts, and the Congress undertook the enthralling process of cranking up the deliberate, inexorable machinery of justice, and everybody was glued to the television for a year and a half. The embargo, on the other hand, was a non video-friendly economic story and hence difficult to get hooked on. It pertained to two subcultures that were completely mysterious to most Americans—the oil industry and the Arab world—and it seemed at first to be merely an episode in the ongoing hostilities between Israel and its neighbors. But in retrospect it changed everything, much more than Watergate did.

By causing the price of oil to double, the embargo enriched—and therefore increased the wealth, power, and confidence of—oil-producing areas like Texas, while helping speed the decline of the automobile-producing upper Midwest; the rise of OPEC and the rise of the Sunbelt as a center of population and political influence went together. The embargo ushered in a long period of inflation, the reaction to which dominated the economics and politics of the rest of the decade. It demonstrated that America could now be "pushed around" by countries most of us had always thought of as minor powers.

Most important of all, the embargo now appears to have been the pivotal moment at which the mass upward economic mobility of American society ended, perhaps forever. Average weekly earnings, adjusted for inflation, peaked in 1973. Productivity—that is, economic output per man-hour—abruptly stopped growing. The nearly universal assumption in the post–World War II United States was that children would do better than their parents. Upward mobility wasn't just a characteristic of the national culture; it was the defining characteristic. As it slowly began to sink in that everybody wasn't going to be moving forward together anymore, the country became more fragmented, more internally rivalrous, and less sure of its mythology.

Richard Nixon resigned as President in August 1974, and the country settled into what appeared to be a quiet, folksy drama of national recuperation. In the White House good old Gerald Ford was succeeded by rural, sincere Jimmy Carter, who was the only President elevated to the office by the voters during the 1970s and so was the decade's emblematic political figure. In hindsight, though, it's impossible to miss a gathering conservative stridency in the politics of the late seventies. In 1976 Ronald Reagan, the retired governor of California, challenged Ford for the Republican presidential nomination. Reagan lost the opening primaries and seemed to be about to drop out of the race when, apparently to the surprise even of his own staff, he won the North Carolina primary in late March.

It is quite clear what caused the Reagan campaign to catch on: He had begun to attack Ford from the right on foreign policy matters. The night before the primary he bought a half-hour of statewide television time to press his case. Reagan's main substantive criticism was of the policy of détente with the Soviet Union, but his two most crowd-pleasing points were his promise, if elected, to fire Henry Kissinger as Secretary of State and his lusty denunciation of the elaborately negotiated treaty to turn nominal control of the Panama Canal over to the Panamanians. Less than a year earlier Communist forces had finally captured the South Vietnamese capital city of Saigon, as the staff of the American Embassy escaped in a wild scramble into helicopters. The oil embargo had ended, but the price of gasoline had not retreated. The United States appeared to have descended from the pinnacle of power and respect it had occupied at the close of World War II to a small, hounded position, and Reagan had hit on a symbolic way of expressing rage over that change. Most journalistic and academic opinion at the time was fairly cheerful about the course of American foreign policy—we were finally out of Vietnam, and we were getting over our silly Cold War phobia about dealing with China and the Soviet Union—but in the general public obviously the rage Reagan expressed was widely shared.

A couple of years later a conservative political cause even more out of the blue than opposition to the Panama Canal Treaty appeared: the tax revolt. Howard Jarvis, a seventy-five-year-old retired businessman who had been attacking taxation in California pretty much continuously since 1962, got onto the state ballot in 1978 an initiative, Proposition 13, that would substantially cut property taxes. Despite bad press and the strong opposition of most politicians, it passed by a two to one margin.

Proposition 13 was to some extent another aftershock of the OPEC embargo. Inflation causes the value of hard assets to rise. The only substantial hard asset owned by most Americans is their home. As the prices of houses soared in the mid-seventies (causing people to dig deeper to buy housing, which sent the national savings rate plummeting and made real estate prices the great conversation starter in the social life of the middle class), so did property taxes, since they are based on the values of the houses. Hence, resentment over taxation became an issue in waiting.

The influence of Proposition 13 has been so great that it is now difficult to recall that taxes weren't a major concern in national politics before it. Conservative opposition to government focused on its activities, not on its revenue base, and this put conservatism at a disadvantage, because most government programs are popular. Even before Proposition 13, conservative economic writers like Jude Wanniski and Arthur Laffer were inventing supply-side economics, based on the idea that reducing taxes would bring prosperity. With Proposition 13 it was proved—as it has been proved over and over since—that tax cutting was one of the rare voguish policy ideas that turn out to be huge political winners. In switching from arguing against programs to arguing against taxes, conservatism had found another key element of its ascension to power.

The tax revolt wouldn't have worked if the middle class hadn't been receptive to the notion that it was oppressed. This was remarkable in itself, since it had been assumed for decades that the American middle class was, in a world-historical sense, almost uniquely lucky. The emergence of a self-pitying strain in the middle class was in a sense yet another sixties spillover. At the dawn of the sixties, the idea that *anybody* in the United States was oppressed might have seemed absurd. Then blacks, who really were oppressed, were able to make the country see the truth about their situation. But that opened Pandora's box. The eloquent language of group rights that the civil rights movement had invented proved to be quite adaptable, and eventually it was used by college students, feminists, Native Americans, Chicanos, urban blue-collar "white ethnics," and, finally, suburban homeowners.

Meanwhile, the social programs started by Lyndon Johnson gave rise to another new, or long-quiescent, idea, which was that the government was wasting vast sums of money on harebrained schemes. In some ways the Great Society accomplished its goal of binding the country together, by making the federal government a nationwide provider of such favors as medical care and access to higher education; but in others it contributed to the seventies trend of each group's looking to government to provide it with benefits and being unconcerned with the general good. Especially after the economy turned sour, the middle class began to define its interests in terms of a rollback of government programs aimed at helping other groups.

As the country was becoming more fragmented, so was its essential social unit, the family. In 1965 only 14.9 percent of the population was single; by 1979 the figure had risen to 20 percent. The divorce rate went from 2.5 per thousand in 1965 to 5.3 per thousand in 1979. The percentage of births that were out of wedlock was 5.3 in 1960 and 16.3 in 1978. The likelihood that married women with young children would work doubled between the mid-sixties and the late seventies. These changes took place for a variety of reasons—feminism, improved birth control, the legalization of abortion, the spread across the country of the sixties youth culture's rejection of traditional mores—but what they added up to was that the nuclear family, consisting of a working husband and a nonworking wife, both in their first marriage, and their children, ceased to be so dominant a type of American household during the seventies. Also, people became more likely to organize themselves into communities based on their family status, so that the unmarried often lived in singles apartment complexes and retirees in senior citizens' developments. The overall effect was one of much greater personal freedom, which meant, as it always does, less social cohesion. Tom Wolfe's moniker for the seventies, the Me Decade, caught on because it was provably true that the country had placed relatively more emphasis on individual happiness and relatively less on loyalty to family and nation.

Like a symphony, the seventies finally built up in a crescendo that pulled together all its main themes. This occurred during the second half of 1979. First OPEC engineered the "second oil shock," in which by holding down production, it got the price for its crude oil (and the price of gasoline at American service stations) to rise by more than 50 percent during the first six months of that year. With the onset of the summer vacation season, the automotive equivalent of the Depression's bank runs began. Everybody considered the possibility of not being able to get gas, panicked, and went off to fill the tank; the result was hours-long lines at gas stations all over the country.

It was a small inconvenience compared with what people in the Communist world and Latin America live through all the time, but the psychological effect was enormous. The summer of 1979 was the only time I can remember when, at the level of ordinary life as opposed to public affairs, things seemed to be out of control. Inflation was well above 10 percent and rising, and suddenly what seemed like a quarter of every day was spent on getting gasoline or thinking about getting gasoline—a task that previously had been completely routine, as it is again now. Black markets sprang up; rumors flew about well-connected people who had secret sources. One day that summer, after an hour's desperate and fruitless search, I ran out of gas on the Central Expressway in Dallas. I left my car sitting primly in the right lane and walked away in the hundred-degree heat; the people driving by looked at me without surprise, no doubt thinking, "Poor bastard, it could have happened to me just as easily."

In July President Carter scheduled a speech on the gas lines, then abruptly canceled it and repaired to Camp David to think deeply for ten days, which seemed like a pale substitute for somehow setting things aright. Aides, cabinet secretaries, intellectuals, religious leaders, tycoons, and other leading citizens were summoned to Carter's aerie to discuss with him what was wrong with the country's soul. On July 15 he made a television address to the nation, which has been enshrined in memory as the "malaise speech," although it didn't use that word. (Carter did, however, talk about "a crisis of confidence . . . that strikes at the very heart and soul and spirit of our national will.")

To reread the speech today is to be struck by its spectacular political ineptitude. Didn't Carter realize that Presidents are not supposed to express doubts publicly or to lecture the American people about their shortcomings? Why couldn't he have just temporarily imposed gas rationing, which would have ended the lines overnight, instead of outlining a vague and immediately forgotten six-point program to promote energy conservation?

His describing the country's loss of confidence did not cause the country to gain confidence, needless to say. And it didn't help matters that upon his return to Washington he demanded letters of resignation from all members of his cabinet and accepted five of them. Carter seemed to be anything but an FDR-like reassuring, ebullient presence; he communicated a sense of wild flailing about as he tried (unsuccessfully) to get the situation under control.

I remember being enormously impressed by Carter's speech at the time because it was a painfully honest and much thought-over attempt to grapple with the main problem of the decade. The American economy had ceased being an expanding pie, and by unfortunate coincidence this had happened just when an ethic of individual freedom as the highest good was spreading throughout the society, which meant people would respond to the changing economic conditions by looking out for themselves. Like most other members of the word-manipulating class whose leading figures had advised Carter at Camp David, I thought there *was* a malaise. What I didn't realize, and Carter obviously didn't either, was that there was a smarter way to play the situation politically. A President could maintain there was nothing wrong with America at all—that it hadn't become less powerful in the world, hadn't reached some kind of hard economic limit, and wasn't in crisis—and, instead of trying to reverse the powerful tide of individualism, ride along with it. At the same time, he could act more forcefully than Carter, especially against inflation, so that he didn't seem weak and ineffectual. All this is exactly what Carter's successor, Ronald Reagan, did.

Actually, Carter himself set in motion the process by which inflation was conquered a few months later, when he gave the chairmanship of the Federal Reserve Board to Paul Volcker, a man willing to put the economy into a severe recession to bring back price stability. But in November fate delivered the coup de grâce to Carter in the form of the taking hostage of the staff of the American Embassy in Teheran, as a protest against the United States' harboring of Iran's former shah.

As with the malaise speech, what is most difficult to convey today about the hostage crisis is why Carter made what now looks like a huge, obvious error: playing up the crisis so much that it became a national obsession for more than a year. The fundamental problem with hostage taking is that the one sure remedy—refusing to negotiate and thus allowing the hostages to be killed—is politically unacceptable in the democratic media society we live in, at least when the hostages are middle-class sympathetic figures, as they were in Iran.

There isn't any good solution to this problem, but Carter's two successors in the White House demonstrated that it is possible at least to negotiate for the release of hostages in a low-profile way that will cause the press to lose interest and prevent the course of the hostage negotiations from completely defining the Presidency. During the last year of the Carter administration, by contrast, the hostage story absolutely dominated the television news (recall that the ABC show *Nightline* began as a half-hour five-times-a-week update on the hostage situation), and several of the hostages and their families became temporary celebrities. In Carter's defense, even among the many voices criticizing him for appearing weak and vacillating, there was none that I remember willing to say, "Just cut off negotiations and walk away." It was a situation that everyone regarded as terrible but in which there was a strong national consensus supporting the course Carter had chosen.

So ended the seventies. There was still enough of the sixties spillover phenomenon going on so that Carter, who is now regarded (with some affection) as having been too much the good-hearted liberal to maintain a hold on the presidential electorate, could be challenged for renomination by Ted Kennedy on the grounds that he was too conservative. Inflation was raging on; the consumer price index rose by 14.4 percent between May 1979 and May 1980. We were being humiliated by fanatically bitter, premodern Muslims whom we had expected to regard us with gratitude because we had helped ease out their dictator even though he was reliably pro–United States. The Soviet empire appeared (probably for the last time ever) to be on the march, having invaded Afghanistan to Carter's evident surprise and disillusionment. We had lost our most recent war. We couldn't pull together as a people. The puissant, unified, prospering America of the late 1940s seemed to be just a fading memory.

I was a reporter for the *Washington Post* during the 1980 presidential campaign, and even on the *Post*'s national desk, that legendary nerve center of politics, the idea that the campaign might end with Reagan's being elected President seemed fantastic, right up to the weekend before the election. At first Kennedy looked like a real threat to Carter; remember that up to that point no Kennedy had ever lost a campaign. While the Carter people were disposing of Kennedy, they were rooting for Reagan to win the Republican nomination because he would be such an easy mark.

He was too old, too unserious, and, most of all, too conservative. Look what had happened to Barry Goldwater (a sitting officeholder, at least) only sixteen years earlier, and Reagan was so divisive that a moderate from his own party, John Anderson, was running for president as a third-party candidate. It was not at all clear how much the related issues of inflation and national helplessness were dominating the public's mind. Kennedy, Carter, and Anderson were all, in their own way, selling national healing, that great post-sixties obsession; Reagan, and only Reagan, was selling pure strength.

In a sense Reagan's election represents the country's rejection of the idea of a sixties-style solution to the great problems of the seventies—economic stagnation, social fragmentation, and the need for a new world order revolving around relations between the oil-producing Arab world and the West. The idea of a scaled-back America—husbanding its resources, living more modestly, renouncing its restless mobility, withdrawing from full engagement with the politics of every spot on the globe, focusing on issues of internal comity—evidently didn't appeal. Reagan, and the country, had in effect found a satisfying pose to strike in response to the problems of the seventies, but that's different from finding a solution.

Today some of the issues that dominated the seventies have faded away. Reagan and Volcker did beat inflation. The "crisis of confidence" now seems a long-ago memory. But it is striking how early we still seem to be in the process of working out the implications of the oil embargo. We have just fought and won a war against the twin evils of Middle East despotism and interruptions in the oil supply, which began to trouble us in the seventies. We still have not really even begun to figure out how to deal with the cessation of across-the-board income gains, and as a result our domestic politics are still dominated by squabbling over the proper distribution of government's benefits and burdens. During the seventies themselves the new issues that were arising seemed nowhere near as important as those sixties legacies, minority rights and Vietnam and Watergate. But the runt of decades has wound up casting a much longer shadow than anyone imagined.

The Religious Right and the New Republican Party

E. J. Dionne, Jr.

As the young conservatives who wrote the Sharon Statement (Part 6) discov-
ered when they worked for Goldwater's election in 1964 and found many sup-
porters motivated by anti-integration States' Rights doctrines rather than by
belief in the free market, American conservatism is not a single, coherent move-
ment. The tensions within conservatism—and, by extension, within the Re-
publican Party—have played a major role in shaping American politics in the
last half of the twentieth century and beyond. In this excerpt from his best-
selling book, Why Americans Hate Politics, *E. J. Dionne explores some of*
these tensions and their implications, focusing on the rise to power of the Reli-
gious Right in the 1970s and 1980s.

Dionne's analysis was published near the end of the era of Reagan and
Bush, Sr. How did the New Right continue to influence American politics dur-
ing the Clinton and Bush, Jr., administrations? Is the troubled relationship
Dionne describes between "Old" and "New" Right resolved, or does it still play
a role in the nation's political life?

In 1965, a young Baptist minister explained why he felt it inappropriate for fundamentalists such as himself to become involved in politics.
"We have few ties to this earth," the minister explained. "Believing in
the Bible as I do, I would find it impossible to stop preaching the pure
saving Gospel of Jesus Christ and begin doing anything else, including
fighting communism or participating in civil rights reforms," he said.
"Preachers are not called upon to be politicians but to be soul winners.
Nowhere are we commissioned to reform the externals." The minister
who spoke these words was the pastor of the Thomas Road Baptist
Church in Lynchburg, Virginia, the Reverend Jerry Falwell.

Falwell's statement is remarkable only in light of his subsequent history. At the time he spoke, his words were well within the fundamentalist and evangelical mainstream. Until the 1970s, a polite disrespect for politics characterized much of the fundamentalist and evangelical movement. If Christ's Kingdom was not of "this world," then His followers had no political obligations beyond a relatively narrow definition of what they should "render unto Caeser." Baptists, whether fundamentalist such as Falwell or not, had long been the most ardent advocates of separating church and state, even on the touchiest issues such as prayer in public schools and abortion. The Baptists' dissenting, popular tradition and their mistrust of state religion had deep roots. In colonial America, the Established churches had been the churches of the upper classes. Baptists, with their deep belief in individual conscience and their disdain for hierarchy, knew instinctively that if a religion was established by the state, it would not be theirs.

But there were other reasons for the fundamentalists' mistrust of politics.

Fundamentalism was plunged into crisis by its two great public crusades of the teens and twenties, the wars against evolution and alcohol. Ironically, both wars initially appeared successful. Prohibition was enacted into law, passed with the support of the culturally "advanced" as well as the culturally "backward." . . . Prohibition, of course, proved to be a disaster and was forever after invoked by all who insisted that government efforts to regulate personal morality were doomed.

The Scopes "monkey trial" actually ended in the conviction of John T. Scopes for teaching evolution, another fundamentalist victory. But few victories better deserved to be called Pyrrhic. The fundamentalists' claims about evolution were held up for scorn throughout the nation. . . . And so the fundamentalists went underground, disdaining a presence in public life that had done their movement so much harm. . . .

Yet in 1980, the entire nation was discussing the fundamentalists and the evangelicals—vaguely aware that the two groups overlapped but were not quite the same. A religious movement that the broader society had dismissed as hopelessly unsophisticated proved exceptionally adept at using the tools of modern politics: television, precinct organization, direct mail. The religiously hip and liberal had drawn much notice in the 1960s. But by the 1970s, the declining churches were the liberal churches, which had rejected the "fundamentals" of Christianity, as the fundamentalists saw it. The churches on the rise were the most *conservative*—those preaching the most old-fashioned Gospel, those demanding adherence to the strictest moral codes. . . .

Still, the growth of conservative churches was one thing; the rise of a *politicized* Christian right was something else again. The apparent power of the Religious Right caused alarm around the nation. Books with titles such as *God's Bullies* and *Holy Terror* warned that tolerance and individual freedom were in jeopardy.

Some of the Religious Rights' leaders did indeed sound alarming. . . . "We have enough votes to run the country," said the Reverend Pat Robertson. "And when the people say, 'We've had enough,' we are going to take over."

If Americans outside the fundamentalist and evangelical communities were worried by what was going on, they were also baffled. After all, most of what had happened in the 1960s and 1970s moved the country in a *liberal* direction. In this "greening of America," sexual attitudes were freer, drugs were more widely used, abortion was legal, women were marching toward equality. If America was indeed as dangerously secularized as the leaders of the Religious Right proclaimed, how could their movement sneak up on the country and become so powerful? . . .

In light of the growth experienced by the evangelical and fundamentalist movements through the 1970s, a political reassertion by conservative Protestantism was inevitable. But the insurgency need never have been as loud, as widespread, or as right wing as it proved to be. The sparks that inflamed the Religious Right came from the judiciary—specifically, the Supreme Court's decisions on issues such as school prayer, abortion, pornography, and government aid to religious schools. *The paradox of the Religious Right is that it became an important factor in American politics primarily because of liberal victories.* . . .

Jerry Falwell himself wrote in his autobiography that he began changing his mind about the involvement of preachers in politics on January 23, 1973, the day the Supreme Court issued the *Roe v. Wade* decision that struck down the nation's abortion laws. If advocates of the Social Gospel had spoken of "social sin," Falwell began to speak of "national sin." A new Prohibitionist movement was about to be born. . . .

If Jerry Falwell began moving toward political action in 1973 because of the *Roe* decision on abortion, an influential group of conservatives were ready to encourage him. Falwell arrived on the scene at precisely the point when conservative political operatives were searching for new political constituencies and new ways to move them. . . .

Class resentment clearly played a key role in New Right politics and its founders. They were eager to identify with George Wallace and his followers among both the working class and the unvarnished new rich. Among the key figures was Richard Viguerie, a onetime direct-mail fund-raiser for Young Americans for Freedom who was hired by George Wallace to handle his mail solicitations. "Compared to a William Buckley . . . ," wrote Paul Gottfried and Thomas Fleming, two conservative historians, "Viguerie resembles a car salesman attending, uninvited, a formal dinner." Among Viguerie's direct-mail clients and allies was Paul Weyrich, a former congressional staffer who helped found two new conservative institutions in the early 1970s. The Committee for the Survival of a Free Congress was the forerunner to the dozens of conservative political action committees that would proliferate in the 1970s. . . . Weyrich's other creation was the Heritage Foundation, which he set up with Ed Feulner, another Capitol Hill veteran. Heritage was to be a militant think tank that would feed ideas directly to the conservative movement and to its allies in Congress. . . . Heritage wanted political victory *now!* Weyrich saw little point in the niceties of academic debate, since he took the warfare analogy to heart. "It may not be with bullets," he was once quoted by Viguerie as saying, "and it may not be with rockets and missiles, but it is a war nevertheless. It is a war of ideology, it's a war of ideas, and it's a war about our way of life. And it has to be fought with the same intensity, I think, and dedication as you would fight a shooting war."

Clearly, the stylistic differences between *National Review* and the New Right were profound, and they betrayed a fundamental difference in emphasis between the two schools of conservatism. For *National Review* conservatives, the centerpiece of postwar conservatism had been anticommunism. Despite *National Review*'s traditionalism, it was still more comfortable with libertarian antigovernment themes than with the New Right's "populism." Following their hero George Wallace, the New Rightists were much more prepared than the older conservatives to use government for their own ends. Kevin Phillips

noted that the New Right, while sharing with the Old Right a sympathy for a strong military and a suspicion of government, believed
that the primary political questions were "domestic social issues."
What he really had in mind were domestic social *resentments.* He listed
these as "public anger over busing, welfare spending, environmental
extremism, soft criminology, media bias and power, warped education, twisted textbooks, racial quotas, various guidelines and an
ever-expanding bureaucracy." It is no accident that Phillips's list
seemed to define the difference between Barry Goldwater and
George Wallace.

. . . "The New Right is looking for issues that people care about,"
Weyrich said. "Social issues, at least for the present, fit the bill." The
Moral Majority was born out of a series of meetings among Falwell,
Viguerie, Howard Phillips, another early New Right leader, and oth-
ers. Falwell credits Weyrich with coming up with the name, though
Howard Phillips appears to have used it first. "Jerry, there is in
America a moral majority that agrees about the basic issues," Weyrich
told Falwell in 1979. "But they aren't organized. They don't have a
platform. The media ignore them. Somebody's got to get that moral
majority together."

For the New Right, religious issues offered an opportunity to expand the movement's social-issue repertoire. Abortion had emerged
first during the Nixon campaign in 1972. After the 1973 Supreme
Court decision, all the pressure on the issue moved right, since the
Roe v. Wade decision gave liberals what they thought was the decisive
victory; now it was the conservatives who had to organize against the
status quo.

The Falwell movement also allowed the New Right to speak more
effectively on a host of other issues. Where George Wallace's attacks
on the educational establishment could not help but smack of
racism, the Religious Right's approach emphasized not race but
values—the right of parents to influence the content of their children's education, the right of schoolchildren to recite prayers. The
Moral Majority was also a natural complement to the antifeminist
movement. Support for Phyllis Schlafly's campaign against the Equal
Rights Amendment was especially strong among women with conservative religious commitments. With Schlafly concentrating her efforts
in states where the ERA was up for ratification, the Moral Majority
helped give her sympathizers elsewhere an alternative organizational
voice.

The Moral Majority gave bite to the political approach that F. Clifton White had proposed to Barry Goldwater when he made his "Choice" documentary on declining American values. White's film spoke to a generalized unease that many Americans felt about the country's moral direction. But in 1964, those Americans were unorganized, and the evangelicals and fundamentalists had still not achieved their political breakthrough. Falwell's activities gave Weyrich and his allies a chance to turn vague discontent into a real lever of political power. And with the growth of the evangelical and fundamentalist churches, such a movement had more political potential than ever.

It is a sign of the distance between the Old and New Right that in 1980, Ronald Reagan was not the first choice of many of the conservatives who gathered around Viguerie and Weyrich. For them, Reagan was a throwback to the Goldwater campaign, a champion of the Buckleyite past rather than the populist future. . . .

The populism of the Religious Right made the conservatives affiliated with *National Review* uncomfortable. Russell Kirk, for one, detested the very idea of a "populist conservatism," calling populism "the ignorant democratic conservatism of the masses." But the *National Review* conservatives could put their doubts aside because they understood the political potential of the Religious Right and its electoral sympathizers. Here, at last, was the mass constituency that traditionalist conservatism had lacked. In the 1950s, traditionalism seemed to be a hopelessly antiquated creed, an antidemocratic doctrine supported by a handful of marginal conservative intellectuals. It turned out that traditionalism had a genuine base among those who looked to the Bible rather than Edmund Burke for authority. . . .

For conservative evangelicals and fundamentalists, the elections of 1976 and 1980 created a sense of triumph. The first had allowed evangelicals to rejoin the political mainstream. The second confirmed their power. . . . Yet in retrospect, it is clear that the Religious Right was never as powerful as it claimed to be, or as its liberal critics feared. . . .

For example, the notion that the Moral Majority had "elected" Ronald Reagan is almost certainly wrong. The evidence suggests strongly that Reagan would have won with or without the Moral Majority. According to the *New York Times*/CBS News poll surveying over 12,000 voters after they had cast their ballots in 1980, "born-again white Protestants" accounted for 17 percent of the electorate. Reagan carried this group over Carter 61 percent to 34 percent. *Even if Carter had defeated Reagan by the same 61 to 34 percent among born-again white Protestants, Reagan would still have won.* And this analysis makes every effort to *exaggerate* rather than underestimate the Moral Majority's influence. For example, it assumes that *all* born-again white Protestants were influenced by the Moral Majority, which was certainly not the case, since polls showed that substantial numbers of born-again white Protestants actually disagreed with the Moral Majority on many issues. . . .

What happened in 1980, then, was not a Republican breakthrough but a ratification of earlier trends toward the Republicans that had been interrupted by Jimmy Carter in 1976. White evangelicals and fundamentalists had begun backing Republicans long before anyone outside of Lynchburg, Virginia, had heard of Jerry Falwell. These shifts did not occur because a group of preachers told their followers to abandon the party of Roosevelt. Nor did Republican politicians win the evangelical vote on the basis of conservative religious themes alone. Most of the evangelical conservatives were white Southerners who *began voting against the Democrats because of civil rights.* Many of them did so when not a campaign word was spoken about faith or morals. Even in his 1964 landslide victory, Lyndon Johnson could not manage a majority in the nation's most heavily Baptist counties. Johnson's share of the Baptist vote was 13 percentage points *lower* than his share in the nation as a whole. . . .

What is important about the Religious Right, then, is not that it created new political facts, but that it reinforced trends that had begun long ago because of the reaction of conservative Southern whites to civil rights. In the process, the Religious Right transformed both the Republican Party and the conservative movement. At least as late as 1976, it was possible for a candidate with moderate—which is to say nonconservative—views on social issues to win the Republican nomination. By 1980, that had become virtually impossible. . . .

Nonetheless, for all the much-touted strength of the Religious Right, the movement's successes during the 1980s were actually quite modest. Reagan proved himself to be very much a man of the Old Right, just as some of the New Right leaders had feared. Although Reagan could speak as movingly about traditional values as he spoke about everything else, his priorities were elsewhere: in cuts in domestic programs, in reductions in marginal tax rates, and in large increases in military spending to counter the Soviet threat. In the meantime, abortions continued, women kept flooding the work-place—and not a word of prayer was recited in the schools to petition the Almighty to turn these trends around.

Reagan himself, moreover, seemed to embody the broader society's ambivalence in the battle between modernity and traditionalism; he seemed very much the sort of person who could pray for Prohibition and vote for Gin. He was the nation's first divorced president. He rarely attended church. He had been formed by Hollywood and demonstrated enormous personal tolerance for "alternative" lifestyles. As one Republican put it, young voters who liked Reagan but were liberal on the social issues always sensed that Reagan was winking at them when he tossed a rhetorical bone to the Religious Right. How serious could a man of his experience and background really be about Jerry Falwell's agenda?

Indeed, the 1980s could hardly be seen as a time when the nation embraced the old Protestant virtues of thrift, self-denial, and self-discipline. The Republican Party abandoned dour, if "responsible," fiscal policies for deficit spending. The dominant ethos of the age seemed to be acquisitive, materialistic, self-indulgent. The clichés of the 1980s were Madonna's "Material Girl," insider trading, MTV, MBAs, BMWs, yuppies. The traditionalists who streamed to evangelical churches could no more identify with these symbols than they could with the Rolling Stones, LSD, or the yippies of the 1960s. . . .

For the more ardent religious conservatives, many of whom repaired to Pat Robertson's candidacy in 1988, the Reagan years had meant little progress at all. . . . They sought much firmer commitments from conservatives to social and religious traditionalism. To the extent that they pressed their demands too forcefully, they threatened the Republican coalition and conservatism's delicate philosophical balance. For the rise of the Religious Right had strengthened the hand of the traditionalist wing of conservatism—the wing that had always seen values as more important than markets, religious faith as more important than economic growth, tradition more important than progress. As a result, the old conservative war between traditionalists and libertarians that Frank Meyer and *National Review* conservatives had tried to settle was raging with greater ferocity than ever. For the libertarians, who profoundly disagreed with the traditionalists on many issues, had also made real gains under Reagan. Many conservatives sensed danger ahead.

"The Second American Revolution" (1985)

Ronald W. Reagan

Whether political observers are hostile or friendly to Ronald Reagan, nearly every political commentator agrees that Reagan possessed extraordinary skill in articulating his point of view and rallying support for it. Although Reagan retained a level of popular backing usually reserved for "consensus" politicians of a moderate persuasion, he presented, and argued effectively for, a singularly partisan definition of America's purpose and goals. Reagan had clear ideas, many of them in deep conflict with the direction of American government and policies since the New Deal. He wished to dismantle the "welfare state," cut taxes severely, restore a laissez-faire economy, and simultaneously construct a huge new military machine. In fact, Reagan did seek a new American revolution, one that would alter dramatically the shape and substance of American politics. Here in his State of the Union Address in 1985, the dimensions of that revolution are outlined, suggesting the degree to which Reagan sought publicly to build support for his strong ideas.

Mr. Speaker, Mr. President, distinguished members of the Congress, honored guests and fellow citizens. I come before you to report on the state of our union. And I am pleased to report that, after four years of united effort, the American people have brought forth a nation renewed—stronger, freer and more secure than before.

Four years ago, we began to change—forever, I hope—our assumptions about government and its place in our lives. Out of that change has come great and robust growth—in our confidence, our economy and our role in the world. . . .

Four years ago, we said we would invigorate our economy by giving people greater freedom and incentives to take risks, and letting them keep more of what they earned.

We did what we promised, and a great industrial giant is reborn. Tonight we can take pride in 25 straight months of economic growth, the strongest in 34 years: a three-year inflation average of 3.9 percent the lowest in 17 years; and 7.3 million new jobs in two years, with more of our citizens working than ever before. . . .

We have begun well. But it's only a beginning. We are not here to congratulate ourselves on what we have done, but to challenge ourselves to finish what has not yet been done.

We are here to speak for millions in our inner cities who long for real jobs, safe neighborhoods and schools that truly teach. We are here to speak for the American farmer, the entrepreneur and every worker in industries fighting to modernize and compete. And, yes, we are here to stand, and proudly so, for all who struggle to break free from totalitarianism; for all who know in their hearts that freedom is the one true path to peace and human happiness. . . .

We honor the giants of our history not by going back, but forward to the dreams their vision foresaw. My fellow citizens, this nation is poised for greatness. The time has come to proceed toward a great new challenge—a Second American Revolution of hope and opportunity; a revolution carrying us to new heights of progress by pushing back frontiers of knowledge and space; a revolution of spirit that taps the soul of America, enabling us to summon greater strength than we have ever known; and, a revolution that carries beyond our shores the golden promise of human freedom in a world at peace.

Let us begin by challenging conventional wisdom: There are no constraints on the human mind, no walls around the human spirit, no barriers to our progress except those we ourselves erect. Already, pushing down tax rates has freed our economy to vault forward to record growth.

In Europe, they call it "the American Miracle." Day by day, we are shattering accepted notions of what is possible. . . .

We stand on the threshold of a great ability to produce more, do more, be more. Our economy is not getting older and weaker, it's getting younger and stronger; it doesn't need rest and supervision, it needs new challenge, greater freedom. And that word—freedom—is the key to the Second American Revolution we mean to bring about.

Let us move together with an historic reform of tax simplification for fairness and growth. Last year, I asked then-Treasury Secretary Regan to develop a plan to simplify the tax code, so all taxpayers would be treated more fairly, and personal tax rates could come further down.

We have cut tax rates by almost 25 percent, yet the tax system remains unfair and limits our potential for growth. Exclusions and exemptions cause similar incomes to be taxed at different levels. Low-income families face steep tax barriers that make hard lives even harder. The Treasury Department has produced an excellent reform plan whose principles will guide the final proposal we will ask you to enact.

One thing that tax reform will not be is a tax increase in disguise. We will not jeopardize the mortgage interest deduction families need. We will reduce personal tax rates as low as possible by removing many tax preferences. We will propose a top rate of no more than 35 percent, and possibly lower. And we will propose reducing corporate rates while maintaining incentives for capital formation. . . .

Tax simplification will be a giant step toward unleashing the tremendous pent-up power of our economy. But a Second American Revolution must carry the promise of opportunity for all. It is time to liberate the spirit of enterprise in the most distressed areas of our country.

This government will meet its responsibility to help those in need. But policies that increase dependency, break up families and destroy self-respect are not progressive, they are reactionary. Despite our strides in civil rights, blacks, Hispanics and all minorities will not have full and equal power until they have full economic powers. . . .

Let us resolve that we will stop spreading dependency and start spreading opportunity; that we will stop spreading bondage and start spreading freedom.

There are some who say that growth initiatives must await final action on deficit reductions. The best way to reduce deficits is through economic growth. More business will be started, more investments made, more jobs created and more people will be on payrolls paying taxes. The best way to reduce government spending is to reduce the need for spending by increasing prosperity. . . .

To move steadily toward a balanced budget we must also lighten government's claim on our total economy. We will not do this by raising taxes. We must make sure that our economy grows faster than growth in spending by the federal government. In our fiscal year 1986 budget, overall government program spending will be frozen at the current level; it must not be one dime higher than fiscal year 1985. And three points are key:

First, the social safety net for the elderly, needy, disabled and unemployed will be left intact. Growth of our major health care pro-grams, Medicare and Medicaid, will be slowed, but protections for the elderly and needy will be preserved.

Second, we must not relax our efforts to restore military strength just as we near our goal of a fully equipped, trained and ready profes-sional corps. National security is government's first responsibility, so, in past years, defense spending took about half the federal budget. Today it takes less than a third.

We have already reduced our planned defense expenditures by nearly $100 billion over the past four years, and reduced projected spending again this year. You know, we only have a military industrial complex until a time of danger. Then it becomes the arsenal of democracy. Spending for defense is investing in things that are price-less: peace and freedom.

Third, we must reduce or eliminate costly government subsidies. For example, deregulation of the airline industry has led to cheaper airfares, but on Amtrak taxpayers pay about $35 per passenger every time an Amtrak train leaves the station. It's time we ended this huge federal subsidy.

Our farm program costs have quadrupled in recent years. Yet I know from visiting farmers, many in great financial distress, that we need an orderly transition to a market-oriented farm economy. We can help farmers best, not by expanding federal payments, but by making fundamental reforms, keeping interest rates heading down and knocking down foreign trade barriers to American farm exports. . . .

In the long run, we must protect the taxpayers from government. And I ask again that you pass, as 32 states have now called for, an amendment mandating the federal government spend no more than it takes in. And I ask for the authority used responsibly by 43 gover-nors to veto individual items in appropriations bills. . . .

Nearly 50 years of government living beyond its means has brought us to a time of reckoning. Ours is but a moment in history. But one moment of courage, idealism and bipartisan unity can change Ameri-can history forever. . . .

Every dollar the federal government does not take from us, every decision it does not make for us, will make our economy stronger, our lives more abundant, our future more free. . . .

There is another great heritage to speak of this evening. Of all the changes that have swept America the past four years, none brings greater promise than our rediscovery of the value of faith, freedom, family, work and neighborhood.

We see signs of renewal in increased attendance in places of worship; renewed optimism and faith in our future; love of country rediscovered by our young who are leading the way. We have rediscovered that work is good in and of itself; that it ennobles us to create and contribute no matter how seemingly humble our jobs. We have seen a powerful new current from an old and honorable tradition— American generosity. . . .

I thank the Congress for passing equal access legislation giving religious groups the same right to use classrooms after school that other groups enjoy. But no citizen need tremble, nor the world shudder, if a child stands in a classroom and breathes a prayer. We ask you again—give children back a right they had for a century-and-a-half or more in this country.

The question of abortion grips our nation. Abortion is either the taking of human life, or it isn't; and if it is—and medical technology is increasingly showing it is—it must be stopped. . . .

Of all the changes in the past 20 years, none has more threatened our sense of national well-being than the explosion of violent crime. One does not have to have been attacked to be a victim. The woman who must run to her car after shopping at night is a victim; the couple draping their door with locks and chains are victims; as is the tired, decent cleaning woman who can't ride a subway home without being afraid.

We do not seek to violate rights of defendants, but shouldn't we feel more compassion for victims of crime than for those who commit crime? For the first time in 20 years, the crime index has fallen two years in a row; we've convicted over 7,400 drug offenders, and put them, as well as leaders of organized crime, behind bars in record numbers.

But we must do more. I urge the House to follow the Senate and enact proposals permitting use of all reliable evidence that police officers acquire in good faith. These proposals would also reform the *habeas corpus* laws and allow, in keeping with the will of the overwhelming majority of Americans, the use of the death penalty where necessary.

There can be no economic revival in ghettos when the most violent among us are allowed to roam free. It is time we restored domestic tranquility. And we mean to do just that. . . .

Tonight I have spoken of great plans and great dreams. They are dreams we can make come true. Two hundred years of American history should have taught us that nothing is impossible. . . . Anything is possible in America if we have the faith, the will and the heart.

History is asking us, once again, to be a force for good in the world. Let us begin—in unity, with justice and love.

Thank you and God bless you.

Reaganomics in Retrospect

James Tobin

James Tobin, winner of the 1981 Nobel Prize in economics and a former member of President Kennedy's Council of Economic Advisors, published this analysis of "Reaganomics" in 1988, close to the end of the Reagan administration. Reagan, he argues, was most interested in an ideologically driven agenda centered on reducing the size of government and of government spending on civilian programs, and his economic policies were crafted in service to those goals. Here, Tobin explains and critiques the key economic principles underlying Reagan's economic policy. For readers, this article presents a clear explanation of these economic principles and their application, along with a contemporary liberal critique of Reaganomics. Do you think Tobin's prediction, that the Reagan era would not really bring about a "counterrevolution" that turned the American government away from liberalism, has proved true? What is the legacy of Reagan if, as Tobin argues below, "an antigovernment president leaves few monuments"?

Rarely in a democracy does a new government take office determined to change course radically and endowed with the electoral mandate that enables it to do so. Franklin Roosevelt in 1933 and Lyndon Johnson in 1965 were the only United States presidents in my lifetime who had and used this opportunity, until Ronald Reagan was inaugurated in 1981. Most administrations veer only moderately from the established compromise consensus they inherit. Their minor course adjustments reflect the difference from their predecessors and opponents in the balance of interests in the coalition that elected them. Leaders like FDR, LBJ, and Reagan—and across the sea, Margaret Thatcher—manage to shift boldly the whole path of

From James Tobin, "Reaganomics in Retrospect," in B. B. Kymlicka and Jean V. Matthews, eds., *The Reagan Revolution?* (Dorsey Press, 1988). Reprinted by permission of the James Tobin estate.

policy. After them, the centrist consensus from which successors will deviate is forever different.

Ronald Reagan came to Washington with a strong and distinctive social and economic ideology. Roosevelt and Johnson, both pragmatists, were definitely not ideologues. They responded decisively and imaginatively to the situations they confronted; the New Deal and the Great Society were not preordained by any long-held doctrinal beliefs of their builders. Liberalism, in its twentieth century meaning, is a loose set of attitudes and values rather than a coherent ideology. But there is a ready-made right-wing ideology, and Reagan came to Washington in 1981 with a programmatic agenda conceived in its image.

THE ECONOMIC IDEOLOGY OF THE REAGAN ADMINISTRATION

What was the economic ideology President Reagan brought to Washington? Basically, it was the ancient theme of nineteenth century liberalism—celebrating the miracle of Adam Smith's Invisible Hand, the virtues of free markets, free enterprise, and laissez faire. It has long been espoused by the Right in the United States. After World War II, conservative intellectuals, business leaders, and politicians rallied to this flag even when it was outside the general consensus. Barry Goldwater was their hero in 1964, but Johnson clobbered him. Ronald Reagan became a public figure and a potential political leader by his talent for communicating the ideology on radio, television, and in person under the sponsorship of General Electric.

The Invisible Hand

Free-market ideology is an extravagant version of the central paradigm of economic theory. The modern theory of general competitive equilibrium and its theorem that such an equilibrium is, in some sense, a situation of optimal social welfare make rigorous the intuitive conjectures of Adam Smith and subsequent classical and neoclassical economists. Economists know the restrictive conditions of these proofs; they can list the standard caveats and qualifications. They are lost in the arena of politics and public opinion, and they are increasingly glossed over by economists. At the same time, and for the same reasons that conservative ideology was gaining public favor, its counterpart in economic theory was being taken more and more uncritically throughout the economics profession.

Every ideological movement has its own version of history. As Reagan tells it, the U.S. economy was a shambles when he came to its rescue in 1981. He lay[s] all the blame on federal economic policies under previous administrations since World War II: chronic deficits, over-taxation, large and growing government, loose monetary policy, macroeconomic fine tuning, intrusive regulation, bureaucratic waste, misguided welfare handouts, and so on. In this story, there is no credit for the remarkable performance of the economy in the 1950s and 1960s, and there is no acknowledgment of the roles of OPEC, the Iranian revolution, and other external shocks in the 1970s.

Government as Leviathan

In renascent conservative doctrine, government "is the problem, not the solution." In the 1970s, this message found receptive ears in a populace disillusioned by Vietnam, Watergate, and the economic disappointments of the decade. Government regulations and taxes, according to candidate and President Reagan, shackle the energies and initiatives of the citizens. Government, especially central government, has become a Leviathan, devouring the resources of the nation. Government has expanded far beyond its proper functions of national defense, internal order, protection of property rights, and enforcement of contracts. Government has no business redistributing income and wealth beyond minimal safety nets for the truly poor and disadvantaged. Even these needs should be met primarily by private charity supplemented by local governments.

The highest priority for the Reagan administration has been from the beginning to reduce the size of the federal government and budget relative to the economy. This implied severe cuts in federal civilian spending; Reagan was also committed to a sharp increase in military expenditures. The nondefense budget had been growing faster than the GNP. This growth was almost entirely in social security benefits: for old age and disability, medicare, and health insurance for the aged, introduced by Lyndon Johnson in 1966. These are universal entitlements, not needs-tested, and the growth of spending for them had been closely matched by earmarked payroll taxes. Social security growth reflected a combination of demographic trends, economic developments, fiscal miscalculations, and political generosities—

notably by the Nixon and Ford administrations and their Democratically controlled Congresses. The experts in the Reagan team knew these facts, but the president preferred to ignore them and talk about the excessive size of the budget as a whole.

The Strategy of Cutting Taxes First

The idea that the federal budget must stop growing faster than the GNP was not new; both Presidents Ford and Carter were committed to this objective. Reagan, however, was ready to slaughter cows that previous administrations and Congresses regarded as politically sacred. He was also ready to follow a strategy that his predecessors eschewed as unsound. That was to cut taxes first, accept the resulting deficits, and use the abhorrence of deficit spending among politicians, financiers, and the general public, as a bludgeon to force Congress to cut civilian spending. Cutting the budget—both civilian spending and taxes—was and is the prime goal.

Only a conservative Republican president could have adopted this strategy without provoking an outraged response from the financial community and negative reactions in financial markets. Such responses forced Jimmy Carter to modify several of his proposed budgets. For example, when his budget for fiscal 1979 was proposed in January 1978, it showed a deficit of $60 billion. The outcry forced Carter to submit a revised budget with a much lower expected deficit and to abandon some expenditure initiatives and scale down some tax cuts. While Reagan and his spokesmen routinely have given lip service to the old conservative orthodoxy of budget balance, it has always been a distinctly subordinate objective. The president has often explained the strategy of lowering taxes first by saying that the way for parents to keep kids from overspending is to cut their allowances.

The strategy did not work quite the way President Reagan had hoped. Although Congress acquiesced in drastic cuts for civilian spending, other than for social security entitlements, these cuts were insufficient to bring the federal deficit under control. The president succeeded in making it politically impossible for any major restoration of federal tax revenues. His landslide victory in 1984 over Walter Mondale, who courageously but recklessly told the electorate that taxes would have to rise, closed that road to fiscal sanity for the foreseeable future. The president eventually lost to Congressional opponents about half of his ambitious buildup of defense spending. Even so, the "unacceptably large" deficits continued. The Gramm-Rudman law of 1985 acknowledged the impasse. Its purpose was to force the president and Congress to agree on how to eliminate the deficit over the five fiscal years 1987–91 or else face mindlessly automatic cuts in both defense and civilian spending—cuts that neither side would like.

Supply-Side Economics and the Budget

Supply-side economics gave Reagan another argument for reducing taxes faster than he could hope to lower expenditures. This argument is not wholly consistent with the strategy just discussed, but ideology and political economics do not have to be consistent. The argument was that cutting tax rates would actually raise tax revenues—a claim that made famous the economist who made it famous. Arthur Laffer drew his curve on a cocktail napkin for the instruction of Congressman Jack Kemp. The curve dramatized the incontrovertible truth that beyond some point a rise in tax rates will discourage taxable activities so much that revenues actually decline. Laffer and Kemp jumped to the unsupported conclusion that U.S. rates were already there. This assertion was naturally an instant sensation in conservative political and business circles, lending apparent scientific authority to something they very much wanted to believe. Ronald Reagan believed it, and he still does. Raising taxes, he continues to say, will devastate the economy. Economic growth propelled by tax cuts, he continues to say, will balance the budget. Members of his administration who thought otherwise and had the courage to speak up—like Martin Feldstein, who never bought the Laffer line, and David Stockman, who once agreed but learned better—are now in private life.

Supply-side fiscal economics as espoused by Laffer, Kemp, and Reagan is reminiscent of extravagant claims advanced by some Keynesian enthusiasts that tax cuts would pay for themselves in revenues generated by the expansion of economic activity. The expansion they had in mind was demand-side. The scenario was that in an economy with excess unemployment and redundant industrial capacity, the spending of tax cuts would prime the pump. Sober Keynesians believed that tax cuts—or additional government expenditure—would stimulate activity in a slack economy—but not by enough to avoid an increase in the deficit.

The label *supply side,* which had a great deal to do with the attention the doctrine rapidly received, was coined satirically by Herbert Stein to distinguish what he called supply-side fiscalism from the old Keynesian demand-side brand. There are several differences in logic. From a demand-side viewpoint, additional government spending is at least as expansionary as private spending—mostly on consumption, induced by tax reductions. The supply-siders, however, contend that both cutting tax rates and *reducing* public spending are stimulating. The supply-side recipe is supposed to work by giving private individuals greater after-tax incentives to work, save, invest, innovate, and take risks—not to consume. These responses are supposed to augment productivity and raise the economy's capacity to produce from a given employed labor force, while demand-side fiscal stimuli are intended to raise the economy's production from given capacity by employing more of the available labor force. Laffer's theory, if valid, should work even if unemployment were at and remained at its full employment minimum, while a Keynesian fiscal prescription is intended only as therapy for recession or as a tonic for an uncompleted recovery.

These differences did not prevent the supply-side protagonists from claiming the 1964 Kennedy-Johnson tax cut as a precedent, even though its motivation and success were demand-side and even though there is no credible evidence that it alone led to a net reduction of the deficit. Also, logic has not prevented them from staking claim to the 1983–85 U.S. recovery, even though that fits a standard Keynesian scenario.

There is a less flamboyant, less novel, and more professional supply-side economics—namely good, straight microeconomics. Economists of all shades of opinion recognize that taxes and transfers have incentive and disincentive effects. This has been recognized in policy, too—for example, the Investment Tax Credit introduced in the Kennedy administration and the sliding scales relating welfare benefits and food stamps to recipients' own resources introduced under Johnson and Nixon. Martin Feldstein joined the Reagan administration after leading, for a decade, important research on the effects of taxation of capital income on investment and saving. The Reagan ideologues had the directions of effects right; the trouble was, as Charles Schultze observed, that they multiplied reasonable empirical magnitudes tenfold.

Monetarism

Monetarism was another ingredient in the triumphant conservative ideology of 1981. Strict control of money supply growth was accepted as necessary and sufficient for disinflation; the Federal Reserve should stick to noninflationary "M" targets and hit them. Supply-siders were somewhat uncomfortable; they feared that the Fed would not accommodate the expansion that their policies would generate. The administration feebly tried to argue that monetary stringency would take care of prices while supply-side stimuli raised output. Inflation is, after all, "too much money chasing too few goods," and their policies would shrink the money and multiply the goods! . . .

MACROECONOMIC MANAGEMENT 1981–85

In 1981, Congress adopted the president's economic and budgetary programs to an amazing degree. The Democrats retained nominal control in the House and a near majority in the Senate. But, bull-dozed by their disastrous defeat in the presidential election, they submitted with docility and me-too-ism. Tax cuts amounting to about 3 percent of the GNP were passed—to be phased in over three years. Simultaneously, a buildup of defense spending, designed to rise from 5.5 percent to 8 percent of the GNP, began. (As the administration points out, defense would still be 2–3 percent lower relative to the GNP than in the 1950s and 1960s.) Civilian budget cuts were passed in almost equal magnitude to defense increases. Entitlements were still growing, however. The administration made some noises about taking them on, but it drew back when the flak made clear that social security was one ancient monument that the opposition could and would defend.

The official 1981 forecasts of the economy and the budget were rosy. In part, they were phony, as Stockman admitted in his un-guarded interview with an *Atlantic* writer—for which the president took him to the proverbial woodshed; Stockman reiterated his claim in great detail in a later book. In part, the forecasts reflected unjusti-fied optimism about the economy shared by most private forecasters at the time.

In October 1979, Paul Volcker instituted a strict monetarist regi-men designed to rid the economy of the high inflation accompany-ing the second oil shock. A recession began in the spring of 1980—contributing to the defeat of Jimmy Carter—but there was a slight recovery at the end of the year. Anyone who understood Volcker's policy should have known that this was a temporary blip. Recession resumed with a vengeance only months after the inauguration—too late to be taken into account in the budget and economic prospectuses of the new administration.

Later in 1981, people began to recognize realities: Deficits of a new magnitude were in prospect. Moreover, they were not just cyclical; they were structural, that is, they would continue even when the economy was operating, and generating government revenues, at normal rates of unemployment and capacity utilization. One big reason was the growth of interest payments on federal debt. High interest rates were, in part, the consequence of the unprecedented fiscal stimulus superimposed on the Fed's monetary policy. High interest payments, in turn, enlarge the deficit—altogether a vicious spiral. . . .

The United States drifted into a bizarre and extreme mix of tight monetary and easy fiscal policies with several unpleasant consequences: The federal debt grew faster than the GNP as far as the eye could see, because interest on the debt alone increased the debt faster than the sustainable growth rate of the economy, while expenditures other than debt interest exceeded revenues even when the recovery was complete. High interest rates induced a net capital inflow and appreciated the dollar enough to yield an equivalent current account deficit. As a result, the recovery was unbalanced; manufacturing industries and agriculture suffered formidable international competitive disadvantage while services and other nontrade sectors flourished. Pressures for protection of jobs and markets in the disadvantaged sectors threatened the political consensus that had long supported a liberal U.S. commercial policy.

Let no one underestimate the drastic extent of the change in fiscal policy in 1981. While the federal government seldom ran surpluses in the last forty years, before 1981 its deficits were modest, virtually always less than 2 percent of the GNP—compared to the 4–5 percent deficits of the Reagan years. Before 1981, cyclical recoveries brought deficits down close to zero, and the structural high-employment budget was often in surplus. Now we have *structural* deficits of 3–4 percent of the GNP. Before 1981, the debt/GNP ratio had declined from more than 100 percent at the end of World War II to 25 percent in the 1970s. Five years of Reaganomics raised it to almost 40 percent. That figure is not a catastrophe, but the prospect that it will rise and accelerate endlessly portended future disaster. . . .

Greater Poverty and Inequality

During the Reagan years, poverty and inequality have increased in the United States. The president's promise that supply-side incentives would create a "rising tide" that "lifts all boats" has not been fulfilled. Even in 1985, after three years of recovery, 14 percent of all United States citizens were living in households below the official absolute poverty line—the same rate as in 1981, up from 11.4 in 1978 and 12.1 back in 1969. Inequality has increased in the 1980s—reversing modest trends in the other direction since 1960. In the two previous decades, families in the lowest quintile consistently received 5.2 to 5.5 percent of aggregate family money income; together, the lowest two quintiles received 16.8 to 17.6 percent; and the top quintile received between 40.9 and 41.6 percent. In 1984, the share of the lowest fifth was less than 5 percent, the share of the lowest two fifths was below 16 percent, and the share of the highest fifth was 43 percent. These figures are for pretax cash incomes. Tax changes in 1981 added to the absolute and relative gains of the higher income groups. The 1986 tax reform of personal income taxes will do the same, although it will also remove households in poverty from the tax rolls.

Cynics, like me, are bound to notice that the emphasis of supply-side tax reduction and reform has been to cut top-bracket income tax rates. . . .

THE LEGACY OF REAGANOMICS

The Crippled Public Sector

Ronald Reagan will bequeath a crippled federal government to his successor. He tried to squeeze ambitious growth for defense spending into a budget he was simultaneously depriving of tax revenues. Legislators of both parties, most of whom knew better, deserve a share of the blame for their supine surrender to the president's program.

President Johnson lost the place in history his domestic social policies could have earned him by the tragic error of embroiling the United States in the Vietnam war. His by-product error in fiscal policy, his insistence on "guns *and* butter," and his delay in asking for taxes to pay for the war all fatefully destroyed the economic stability achieved prior to 1966. The lesson of the Vietnam war may be saving President Reagan and the country from pushing his obsessions with communist threats in Central America to the point of U.S. military intervention. Yet, he is also likely to be seen in history as repeating the "guns and butter" mistake.

President Reagan is right that the country can afford the arms buildup he has asked for. Whether it is needed and whether it is good national policy are questions where an economist has no special expertise. Assuming the buildup is needed, it should neither be the victim of budget deficit control nor should its burden be placed narrowly on other government programs and their beneficiaries. A rich country can afford the defense it needs, and it can also afford the Library of Congress, public broadcasting, good statistics, environmental protection, and humane treatment of the poor and disadvantaged. Reagan's "butter" is different from Johnson's; it consists in the tax reductions he is determined to protect—largely to the benefit of the wealthier citizens of the country. The policy has had the adverse macroeconomic consequences discussed above—notably including the trade deficit. The policy has also brought federal budget making to the political impasse that ended in the colossal irrationality of Gramm-Rudman.

Income taxes have long been the major source of federal revenue. They yielded revenues equal to 11.3 percent of the GNP in 1959, 13.3 percent of the GNP in 1969, and 11.6 percent of the GNP in 1979. They will yield only 10.7 percent of the GNP in 1989. It is true that payroll tax revenues have risen from 2.4 percent of the GNP in 1959 to an estimated 6.8 percent for 1989. They are, however, earmarked for social insurance benefits—mostly for Old Age and Survivors Insurance. Social security stands on its own feet; it will run surpluses over the next twenty years—building a trust fund that will be needed later in the next century. The accounts are now officially off budget once more. Regular on-budget governmental activities depend on income taxes—or on deficits. In 1979, defense and debt interest took 6.4 percent of the GNP, and income tax revenues amounting to 4.1 percent were available for other activities. In 1989, defense and interest will take 8.7 percent of the GNP—leaving income taxes of only 2.0 percent for other activities.

The social costs and dangers of the resulting austerities in the civilian budget are already evident. Here are some examples:

- The federal government is abandoning revenue-sharing— federal support of state and local government expenditures

on infrastructure investments, education, and social programs. Those governments have responded partly by curtail-
ing those expenditures, as the administration intended, and
partly by raising their own taxes—generally more regressive
than the federal income tax.

- Secretary of State Shultz is right in complaining that Congress does not provide enough funds for foreign aid, for effective diplomatic representation around the world, and for
meeting U.S. obligations to international organizations. He
should address his complaint to the White House, too.

- President Reagan promised action on acid rain to Canadian
Prime Minister Mulroney, but the funds are missing from the
president's budget. President and Mrs. Reagan made headlines when they solemnly proclaimed an all-out war on drug
abuse, but his next budget cut the funds. American airports
and skies are increasingly congested, but there are no funds
for expanding facilities, air control personnel, and safety enforcement. National highways deteriorate, but gasoline taxes
supposedly earmarked for their maintenance and improvement remain unspent to hold down the deficit. The federal
government relies on tax-deductible private donations for
more and more purposes: for example, advancing the cause
of democracy throughout the world, and enabling the White
House and State Department to receive foreign dignitaries in
facilities worthy of a great and rich republic. Cutbacks in federal statistical programs hamper academic researchers, businesses, and others who rely upon them. Our national parks
deteriorate. Federal support of education and science is
shortchanged. Federal service is underpaid relative to the private sector, and at the same time reviled by its chief as a para-
sitic, power-hungry bureaucracy. (As I told an undergraduate
class recently, Paul Volcker, the most important economic official in the world, is paid less than Green Business School
graduates hired to guess what Volcker will do next week.)

There never was any reason to believe the Reagan thesis that the
trouble with the U.S. economy was that the public sector was too big,
either in its real economic activities or in its welfare-state transfers.
On both counts, the United States had smaller public sectors relative
to the size of the economy than any advanced capitalist democracy

except Japan and Australia. The administration's view that only the formation of physical capital by private business provides for the future of the nation is a vulgar error that has sacrificed public investment in human capital (education, health, natural resources, and the public infrastructure) to the construction of shopping malls and luxury casino hotels.

The current conservative fad is privatization. The administration's budget makers have hit upon sales of federal assets as a cute technical way to appear to comply with Gramm-Rudman. No business accountant would regard asset sales as deficit-reducing for current revenue. But privatization is welcomed by free-market ideologues anyway. Although some privatization may be desirable and cost-effective, current proposals reflect budget cosmetics and doctrinaire principle rather than case-by-case examinations of long-run costs and benefits.

Certainly some federal programs cut or eliminated over the past six years deserved Stockman's ax, and that is also true of some parts of the president's proposed budget for fiscal 1988. These expenditures would not have been vulnerable under the business-as-usual budget politics of previous administrations and Congresses. Yet, other cows that deserved slaying under free market principles have remained sacred. The most expensive example is federal agricultural policy; this administration has spent record amounts for farm price supports and related subsidies. Another example, of interest to Canadians, is our maritime policy. In both these cases, costly budgetary subventions are accompanied by regulations restricting competition.

As for deregulation, the major initiatives in energy, air and surface transportation, and finance were begun under President Carter. They have been continued and extended. The Reagan administration's own initiatives have concentrated less on dismantling anticompetitive regulations than on relaxing the regulations designed for environmental and social purposes. As Canadians know, it has been hard to get the president excited about acid rain. As blacks know, the administration is against affirmative action.

The administration deserves credit for defending liberal trade policies against the pressures of protectionism—all too tempting to Democratic politicians. But it was the administration's macroeconomic policies that, by appreciating the dollar, made American producers uncompetitive in world trade and invited protectionist demands from desperate industries and displaced workers. Moreover, the administration's rhetoric has been more liberal than its actions. Like his predecessors, the president has arranged import quotas and special duties for particularly hard-hit industries.

Missing Agenda

Two major economic problems have not been on the Reagan agenda at all. The first problem is macroeconomic; it has to do with unemployment and inflation. The greatest basic obstacle to full prosperity is the fear of policymakers at the central bank and throughout the government, and of the influential public, that a return to the low unemployment rates we reached in the prosperities of the 1970s would set off another inflationary spiral. This fear may be obsolete and unjustified, but it is a reality. If it is justified, then the inflation-safe unemployment rate is too high at 6 percent or more, and we should actively seek structural reforms that would lower it. These reforms could include pro-competitive labor market policies, changes in trade union legislation, incentives for employers and workers to adopt profit-sharing or revenue-sharing contracts, and the use of wage-price guideposts with tax-based inducements for compliance. This is not the occasion to discuss specific proposals; yet, this administration has no concern about this crucial matter.

The second problem conspicuously missing from the Reagan agenda is the pathology of urban ghettos inhabited by blacks and other minorities. These neighborhoods, the people who live in them, and the cities where they are located have been "losing ground," to use the title of [Charles] Murray's [1984] book. The war on poverty and the Great Society did not prevent or arrest the vicious downward spirals in these areas and populations. Subsequent neglect and a decline in the real public resources channeled to them also hurt. The only current administration response is to cut welfare spending further in the belief that this will cut both welfare dependency and poverty. Meanwhile, the lower Bronx and Harlem, Roxbury in Boston, Woodlawn and the West Side of Chicago—and similar areas of many other small and large cities—are a disgraceful and dangerous contrast to the affluent styles of life displayed in the centers of the same cities and flaunted on national television. President Reagan is fond of likening America to "a shining city on a hill." There is a Hill district here in my own New Haven, and it does not shine.

At the outset, I placed Ronald Reagan in the select class of government leaders who substantially and durably shift the course of policy and the center of political debate. Yet, I have some doubts about the permanence of the rightward Reagan counterrevolution. Prior to the Iran-contra scandals, opinion polls showed Ronald Reagan's high approval rating to be without precedent for a president in his sixth year; he still is remarkably popular as a person—even among citizens critical of his role in the adventures recently revealed. On few specific issues, however, have polls shown majorities favoring Reagan's side. In the nature of the case, an antigovernment president leaves few public monuments. This president will leave none comparable to Roosevelt's social security or Johnson's civil rights and health insurance.

The awful truth is that Reaganomics was a fraud from the beginning. The moral of its failures and of its legacies is that a nation pays a heavy price when it entrusts its government and economy to simplistic ideologues—however smooth their performances on television.

We, the American Foreign Born (1993)

United States Census Bureau

"America is a nation of immigrants." It's a truism, and a fairly accurate one. But who those immigrants are—where they come from and why; how big a proportion of the U.S. population they represent; where they settle and what they do—all has changed dramatically over the course of U.S. history. In the late twentieth century, Ellis Island and the Statue of Liberty have been replaced by LAX (the Los Angeles airport) or by the U.S.–Mexico border as immigrants' first glimpse of their new land.

And despite the patriotic rhetoric describing America as a nation of immigrants—whether the metaphor employed is melting pot, stew pot, or salad bowl—immigration has been a difficult issue in American life since well before the Civil War. A strong anti-immigration party emerged in the 1850s, following a dramatic rise in the number of Irish immigrants during Ireland's great potato famine. In 1882, Congress passed the Chinese Exclusion Act in response to pressure from native-born workers who wanted to prevent competition for jobs from low-paid Chinese laborers. In the 1920s, Congress enacted a series of Immigration Acts meant to stem the flow of immigrants—the "barbarian horde," in the words of one congressman—and to establish quotas based on "national origins" that favored immigrants from northern and western Europe over those from eastern and southern Europe.

Though the 1924 Immigration Act was modified somewhat through the years (in 1943 the United States opened its borders to 105 Chinese immigrants per year), it was the 1965 Immigration and Nationality Act that fundamentally changed American immigration policy—and the face of America. In keeping with other legislation aimed at ending racial discrimination, the act replaced the national quotas with hemispheric "ceilings," emphasized family reunification, and gave professionals and skilled workers high priority. In the years following 1965, immigration from Latin America and Asia grew dra-

We, the American Foreign Born, from "We, the Americans" Report Series, WE-7, Bureau of the Census, 1993.

matically. And so did the number of immigrants to the United States and the proportion of immigrants in the U.S. population.

The following document is a report by the U.S. Census Bureau: We, the American Foreign Born. *It offers a very informative statistical portrait of America's foreign-born population as of 1990. (The trends documented here have continued; the proportion of foreign-born in 1999 had risen to 9.5 percent, and Asia and Latin America continue to provide the largest number of immigrants.) How has the nation's immigrant population changed? What differences exist among immigrants from different nations and/or regions? What accounts for such differences? Be sure to read this document as a primary source, as well as a source of statistical information. Why might the Census Bureau, a government agency, use language that emphasizes the American-ness of the foreign born?*

INTRODUCTION

Most of us are descended from people who were born and reared in the United States. Almost 20 million of us, however, must go back to Mexico, the Philippines, Canada, Cuba, Germany, and many other countries to learn about previous generations. We, who were born in another country of foreign parents and now live in the United States, are America's foreign born. . . .

Where do we, the foreign born, come from? Where do we live in the United States? What kind of work do we do? What education do we have? How much do we earn? We are a mosaic of social and cultural characteristics.

The following pages provide a portrait of We, the American foreign born.

In 1990, We the American Foreign Born Reached Our Greatest Number in the History of the United States

In 1990, the foreign-born population was 19.8 million or 7.9 percent of the total population. This was the largest number of foreign-born persons in U.S. history and the highest proportion of foreign born in the past 40 years.

In 1980, the foreign-born population numbered 14.1 million or 6.2 percent of the total population; 1970 figures were 9.6 million or 4.7 percent and 1960 figures were 9.7 million or 5.4 percent.

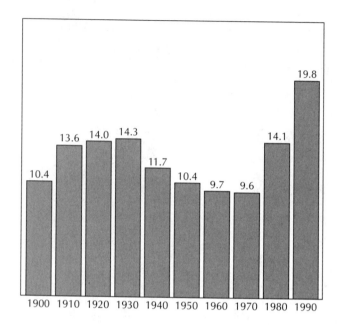

Figure 1. Foreign-Born Population: 1900 to 1990 (Millions)

Around the turn of the century, however, the proportions of foreign born were higher than in 1990. For example, in 1900, the foreign-born population was 13.6 percent of the population or 10.4 million; and in 1910, the proportion of foreign born was 14.8 percent or about 13.6 million.

Today, Most of Us Come from Asia or Latin America

Immigration records, started in 1820, show that until 1970 most of the foreign born came to America from Europe. Of the total of nearly 42 million people who immigrated between 1820 and 1960, 34 million were European. In the 30 years since then, only 2.7 of the 15 million immigrants who came to the United States were European.

The proportion of the total foreign born from European countries declined from 85 percent in 1900 to 22 percent in 1990.

The proportion of the total foreign born from Latin America and

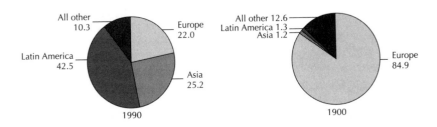

Figure 2. Percent Foreign Born by Region of Birth: 1900 and 1990

Asia increased from less than 1.5 percent each in 1900 to 43 percent and 25 percent, respectively, in 1990.

We Come from Many Countries, including Mexico, the Philippines, Canada, and Cuba

Ten countries contributed at least 500,000 people each to the foreign-born population living in the United States in 1990.

Poor economic conditions in Mexico combined with its proximity to the southern border and demand for unskilled labor in the United States resulted in a very large increase in the number of Mexican foreign born since 1970. More than 1 in 5 of the country's foreign born were born in Mexico, which was the largest foreign-born group in 1990.

Several foreign-born groups lost population between 1980 and 1990. Of the 40 groups with more than 100,000 foreign-born persons in 1990, 14 declined in size. With the exception of Canadians, all of these groups were European. Italians, followed by Scottish, Hungarians, Germans, and Greeks had the largest declines.

One of Every Four of Us Came to America Between 1985 and 1990

The largest wave of immigrants occurred between 1985 and 1990. During this period, 1 of every 4 foreign born arrived in the United States. Nearly 44 percent of the total foreign-born population arrived between 1980 and 1990.

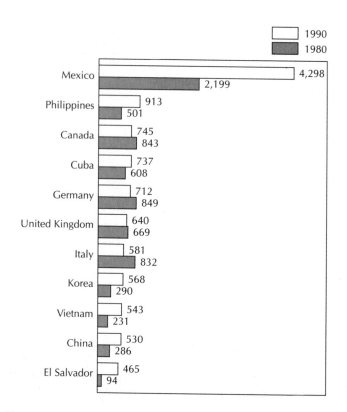

Figure 3. Largest Foreign-Born Groups by Country of Birth: 1980 and 1990 (Thousands)

Between 1980 and 1990, 3 of every 4 Salvadoran immigrants arrived along with more than half of the immigrants from Korea, Vietnam, and China, and nearly half of the Mexican and Filipino immigrants.

More than 70 percent of Canadian, German, and Italian immigrants arrived prior to 1970. Cubans arrived in large numbers during the 1950s and 1960s.

We Settle Near Our Ports of Entry

American immigrants tend to settle near their port of entry. More than two-thirds of those who came from Italy, for example, live in the northeastern part of the country, where they landed. Similarly, more than half of the foreign born who immigrated from China and Japan have remained in the West, and most immigrants from Mexico live in the States that border Mexico.

Throughout this century, both California and New York have had the largest share of immigrant population. As the source of immigration changed from mostly European to mostly Latin American and Asian, California and New York traded places in rank. In 1950, nearly 25 percent of immigrants lived in New York, while only 14 percent lived in California. In 1990, nearly one-third of the immigrants lived in California, while New York's share of immigrants decreased to 14 percent. Nearly half of all the foreign born in America live in California or New York. Eight of every 10 immigrants live in just 10 States. Florida, Texas, New Jersey, and Illinois each have between 5 and 8 percent of the foreign-born population.

In recent decades, most immigrants have settled in big cities and their suburbs. In 10 cities throughout America, foreign born account for half or more of the city's population. In Hialeah city, Florida, 7 out of every 10 people are foreign born.

We Are Older Than the Native-Born Population

Compared with the native-born population, a greater proportion of both male and female foreign born were between the ages of 20 and 64. One of every four foreign-born males was between the ages of 25 and 34. In 1990, about 13 percent of the foreign-born population was 65 years old and over, compared with about 12 percent of the native population. . . .

Among foreign-born groups, Mexicans, Salvadorans, and Vietnamese had the youngest populations with median ages of about 30. . . .

We Represent a Larger Share of Some Racial and Ethnic Population Groups

Among the foreign born, about 23 percent were Asian and Pacific Islander, 7 percent were Black, and nearly 40 percent were Hispanic. Among all Americans, 3 percent were Asian and Pacific Islander, 12 percent were Black, and 9 percent were Hispanic in 1990.

Our racial and ethnic composition has shifted during the past 20 years. In 1970, the foreign-born population was 90 percent White.

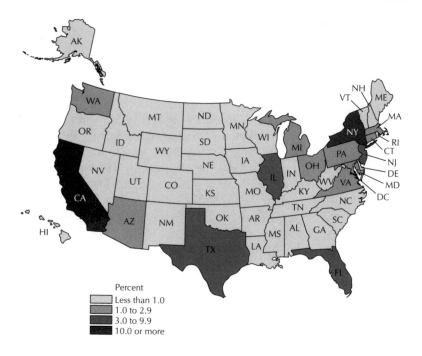

Figure 4. Percent of Total Foreign Born by State: 1990

The share of Whites among the foreign-born population decreased to about 50 percent in 1990.

The share of Hispanics among the foreign-born population increased from 15 percent in 1970 to 40 percent in 1990.

We Have About the Same Proportion of College Graduates but a Smaller Proportion of High School Graduates than the Native-Born Population

About 26 percent of the foreign-born population 25 years old and over had less than a 9th grade education compared with 9 percent of native-born Americans. About 59 percent of the foreign born had at least a high school diploma compared with about 77 percent of their native-born counterparts. About 20 percent of both groups have bachelor's degrees or higher.

About 6 percent of both the native and foreign-born populations

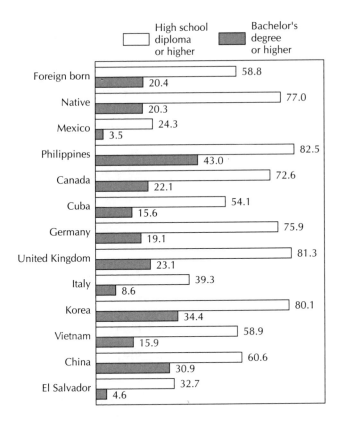

Figure 5. Educational Attainment for Selected Countries of Birth: 1990 (Percent of persons 25 years old and over)

have an associate's degree, and 13 percent and 12 percent, respectively, have a bachelor's degree. A larger share of foreign born (9 percent) than native Americans (7 percent) have graduate degrees.

About 43 percent of the foreign born from the Philippines had a college degree or higher compared to only 4 percent from Mexico.

Many of Us Speak a Language Other Than English in Our Homes

About 80 percent of the newcomers speak a language other than English at home compared with about 8 percent of the native-born population.

Over 95 percent of Mexicans, Cubans, or Salvadorans spoke Spanish at home. More than 9 of 10 foreign born from the Philippines, Korea, Vietnam, or China spoke an Asian language, and 79 percent of those from Italy and 58 percent of those from Germany spoke a language other than English.

More than half of those who spoke Spanish or an Asian and Pacific Islander language at home did not speak English "very well." In fact, 43 percent of the Mexican and nearly half of the Salvadoran foreign born were "linguistically isolated." . . .

Our Occupations Differ Depending on Our Country of Birth

The proportion of employed foreign-born workers 16 years old and over in managerial and professional occupations ranged from 6 percent for immigrants from Mexico to more than 40 percent for immigrants from the United Kingdom.

More than one-third of Canadian, German, United Kingdom, and Chinese foreign born worked as managers. One of every five Italians were engaged as craft and repair workers. . . .

Our Incomes Vary Depending on Our Country of Birth

Median family income varied widely by country of birth. In 1989, median income of the nearly 6 million families headed by a foreign-born person was $31,785 compared with $35,225 for all American families. However, median income for families with a householder born in the Philippines was $47,794. Medians among householders born in Mexico and El Salvador were the lowest at $21,585 and $21,818, respectively.

About 55 percent of the foreign-born population were living in households with incomes over $25,000, 24 percent had incomes over $50,000, and 5 percent had incomes over $100,000. . . .

More of Us Fall Below the Poverty Level Than the Total Population

Children of the foreign born were about twice as likely to be living in poverty than all children. Among both foreign born and the remainder of the population, children were more likely to be living in poverty than adults.

About one-third of the population 65 years old and over born in Cuba, Germany, or the United Kingdom were living below the poverty

level. Twenty-five percent of the Canadian elderly and 56 percent of
the Italian elderly were living in poverty.

Slightly smaller proportions of households maintained by a foreign-
born female with no husband present were living in poverty than
households maintained by a native-born counterpart.

The Clinton Impeachment Inquiry and Trial (1998–1999)

*Representatives Juanita Millender-McDonald (D., CA),
James Talent (R., MO), Gary Ackerman (D., NY),
and Bob Schaffer (R., CO)*

*On February 12, 1999, the U.S. Senate acquitted the 42nd president of the
United States, William Jefferson Clinton, on two articles of impeachment. The
charges, one of perjury and the other of obstruction of justice, stemmed from allegations that President Clinton had lied under oath about his sexual relationship with a White House intern, Monica Lewinsky, during a January
1998 deposition in a sexual harassment case brought against him by an
Arkansas woman, Paula Jones.*

*Clinton, at first, denied all charges. On national television, he told the
American public that he never had "sexual relations" with "that woman, Ms.
Lewinsky." Independent prosecutor Kenneth Starr, however, turned up material evidence—a stained blue dress belonging to Ms. Lewinsky—that proved
Clinton's denial was based on a very selective definition of "sexual relations,"
at best. On September 9, 1998, Starr submitted to Congress a 445-page report,
along with thirty-six boxes of evidence in the Clinton case. The Starr report
presented Clinton's sexual relationship with Lewinsky in such graphic detail
that mainstream Internet sites (on which the report was quickly posted) pref-
aced it with a warning that the explicit sexual material was not appropriate
for all readers.*

*The House of Representatives voted to begin an investigation, preparatory
to bringing charges of impeachment. The U.S. Constitution set forth procedure: the House must bring charges, in the form of articles of impeachment,
upon which the Senate must then vote. In the House, debate was bitter and
partisan. The widening gulf between congressional Republicans and Democrats seemed a graphic illustration of the nation's "culture wars," as Republicans portrayed Clinton's actions as moral failures. The president found few
defenders, but many House Democrats did not believe the charges, even if true,*

From the *Congressional Record*, 144 Cong Rec E 2333; 145 Cong Rec E 12; 145
Cong Rec E 35; 144 Cong Rec H 10509.

rose to the constitutionally required level for impeachment of "treason, bribery, or other high crimes and misdemeanors." Instead of impeachment, they proposed a motion of censure.

Others were concerned about the erosion of privacy signaled by the trial and the publication of the Starr report. Were not many senators, asked Sen. John Kerry (D., MA), "deeply disturbed by an independent counsel grilling a sitting President of the United States about his personal sex life, based on information from illegal phone recordings[?]" Reporters and pundits reminded the public of previous presidential liaisons and peccadilloes, most conspicuously those of John Kennedy and Franklin Roosevelt, which were kept from the public eye by a different understanding of the boundaries between president and public, media and public figures. Some—most notably the Reverend Jesse Jackson—saw the impeachment proceedings as simply one more cynical political ploy by a Republican Congress that had been willing to shut down the federal government for weeks in the winter of 1996 to forestall even the moderately liberal agenda of this Democratic president.

In the end the Senate, acting in a more restrained and bipartisan fashion than the House, rejected the charges. "This has been a long, tortured trial," one senator concluded. "There are no winners." The trial highlighted major divisions in American society, rifts not easily healed by the Senate's vote to acquit.

Following are excerpts from speeches made on the floor of Congress, two by Democrats and two by Republicans.

HON. JUANITA MILLENDER-MCDONALD (D., CA)

Thursday, November 12, 1998

Mr. Speaker, I come before you to ask a very important question:

Why did we bring this resolution to this floor?

I do not condone the President's behavior, but what I find truly abhorrent is the behavior of my Republican colleagues who have launched a partisan attack against the President.

Certainly I believe that the President's conduct should be investigated and that the Congress has a constitutional responsibility to hold hearings looking into the allegations made by the Independent Counsel. But these hearings cannot be entered into lightly. It is a grave and serious matter that faces us. What we decide here today will have ramifications for generations to come. How we conduct ourselves will serve as a precedent for those who follow.

We owe it to the American people to rise to the level of the challenge before us and to move forward with this investigation in a solemn and judicious fashion—not in the destructive partisan manner that we have seen so far.

The investigation of the President has gone on far too long and must be brought to a swift conclusion—through a focused, limited and fair investigation—for the sake of the nation and in the interest of returning the attention of Congress back to the business of families and their children.

The people of California's 37th Congressional District elected me to fight for better education, to fight for safer streets, to fight for the protection of Social Security. Instead I have had to spend the crucial last weeks of this Congress wading through more than 4,000 pages of what amounts to little more than pornography. By bogging down real legislative business with salacious details of sex and scandal, my Republican colleagues have done nothing to make a real difference in the lives of America's working families.

I call on my colleagues on the other side of the aisle today to change their do-nothing ways and finally make a real difference in Americans' lives by walking the high road on into the history books. Thus far this session, Republicans have turned their backs on our children, they have tried to rob money from our seniors and they have chipped away at a woman's right to choose. I urge my Republican colleagues to, at long last, do right by the American people and vote for a just investigative process—the limited, focused, fair proposal presented by my Democratic colleagues.

HON. JAMES M. TALENT (R., MO)

Wednesday, January 6, 1999

Mr. Speaker, it is not my preference or custom to speak on matters relating to the misconduct of others who hold public office. I have never done so before during my time in Congress. I hope never to have to do so again.

But the Constitution confides in Members of this House the obligation to decide whether high officers have acted in a manner that requires their impeachment. Where an official has a legal or moral obligation to judge misconduct and when that obligation cannot honorably be avoided, it is necessary to stand without flinching for what is clearly right.

Those failing to do so become inevitably part of the wrong against which they failed to act. The issue before the House is not whether Bill Clinton has acted with integrity. We all know the answer to that question. The issue is whether we have the integrity to do our duty under the Constitution and laws.

Public men and women commit private wrongs, just like everyone else. And just like everyone else, they are usually called to account for those wrongs in the fullness of time. If they act honorably when called to account, and accept responsibility for what they have done, they can emerge with a measure of their integrity intact. If they act less than honorably and refuse to own up to their actions, they may, and often are judged by the voters.

Their fellow officers in government have no warrant to judge them formally if they at least conform to the minimum standards of law and morality in how they react. But the minimum standards are just that: the minimum that we have the right to expect and insist upon. No one can fall below those standards with impunity. No officer of government can actively subvert the law, abuse the powers of his office and flout the standards of decency without facing the consequences that any other person in a position of trust would have to face.

That is the gravamen of the charges against President Clinton. The genesis of this matter was the President's liaison with Monica Lewinsky. But that affair, however sordid, was a private wrong. The Articles of Impeachment deal exclusively with what the President did to avoid the consequences when that private wrong reached the eyes and ears of the public. When the President was called to account before the people, he lied to the people; when he was called to account before a civil deposition, he lied under oath; and then, to cover up those initial lies, he tampered with witnesses, abused the trust of other officers of government, perjured himself before a federal grand jury, and abused the powers of the Presidency to avert investigations into his wrong doing.

From the record before the House, it is impossible to conclude anything other than that the President is guilty of these wrongs. He is therefore, in my judgment unfit to hold any position of trust, much less the Presidency. . . .

Some suggest that the misconduct in question does not meet the Constitutional standard for impeachment. But I believe the President's actions not only qualify as high crimes and misdemeanors; they present a classic example of what the term signifies, fully within the intentions of the Framers and the precedents of history.

The term *high crimes or misdemeanors* means a deliberate pattern of misconduct so grave as to disqualify the person committing it from holding a position of trust and responsibility. The President's misconduct qualifies as such an offense according to the commonly accepted understandings of civic responsibility, never before questioned until this controversy arose. No one would have argued a year ago that a President could perjure himself, obstruct justice, and tamper with witnesses without facing impeachment, and no one would argue that a business, labor, educational, or civic leader should stay in a position of trust having committed such misconduct. Congress has impeached and removed high officers for less than the President has done. Are we to lower the standards of our society because the President cannot live up to them? . . .

Mr. Speaker, this whole affair, distasteful as it is, presents an opportunity for the House to make a clear statement. There is such a thing as right and wrong. No society, and certainly not a constitutional republic like America, can endure without acknowledging that fact; and if we believe in right and wrong, we must give life to that belief by trusting that the right thing will be the best thing for our country. I urge each member of the House to do his duty today in the faith that only in that way can America emerge stronger.

HON. GARY L. ACKERMAN (D., NY)

Wednesday, January 6, 1999

Mr. Speaker, I rise tonight to strongly oppose the impeachment of the President of the United States. My President. The People's President.

Today we embarrass the memory of our country's Founders as we torture the intent of the genius of their system of balancing the awesome powers of Government. Once our votes are cast on this despicable issue, no longer will we be able to look upon ourselves and our House as honorable; or even as men and women who are here to serve as a check on the power of the Executive. Instead, we will have become a House that sits in moral judgment over another man, meting out punishment for personal deeds which we deem unacceptable. The Majority party, however, has decided that this course is predetermined, because we must uphold "the rule of law." Otherwise, our country will descend into chaos.

Yes, Mr. Speaker, no one is above the law—and there is no question that the law must be followed. But we also serve a greater document: and that is the Constitution of the United States. And it is the words within that great document that we must follow in this case as we decide whether the disgraceful behavior by the President merits his impeachment.

Mr. Speaker, under your leadership and that of your party, we stand here—small men with petty careers, and partisan of purpose, to diminish our great Republic. Devoid of a sense of proportion and overburdened with an excess of hubris, you claim conscience as your exclusive domain, and deny us the right to offer the People's Will—a motion of censure. I can only surmise the answer to that is because the Republican leadership is being driven by a core of short-sighted, bitter, and small-minded people who would do away with the highminded principles espoused and framed for time immemorial by the Founders of this Nation. And they would do this for the sole reason that they do not agree with the President's actions. However, the President's behavior does not put him in the category of those who would commit treason, except perhaps in the minds of those conspiracy theorists who are consuming the Majority party.

Let me be clear that what we do here today is an oligarchical act that attempts to recreate a presidency that would serve at the Majority's whim, rather than at the will of the people. Mr. Speaker, please believe me that the gravity of this action will not go unnoticed by the public that we purport to serve.

To be sure, the President has shamed himself greatly.

To be clear, it is we who are about to become the shame of the Nation.

HON. BOB SCHAFFER (R., CO)

Mr. Speaker, as Congress approaches the conclusion of what history will surely judge among the most solemn weeks in the history of Congress, I rise to address my colleagues tonight in this special order and in this great Chamber. For it was on this very floor that we all swore allegiance by the same oath, to the same Constitution, to one mighty Nation before the one true God.

In the hallways and passages beyond, this Congress has found itself consumed by the events leading up to a regrettable decision. Speculation of impending elections, national budgets, the economy, and the fate of legislation have all been proffered and examined through the prism of the President's uncertain fate.

Today, my remarks are not about politics. They concern things having nothing to do with party, power, or influence. Today I would like to send a strong message to my daughters, Jennifer, Emily, and Sara. They do not care about politics, they do not care about it any way. And at their young ages, they should not have to.

In fact, I am troubled as a father that they are now asking as many questions as they do about our President, broaching subjects that young girls should not have to consider, and about which no father in America should ever have to endure. But I want them to care very much about what I am about to say. . . .

My daughters, this controversy matters. It matters a lot. And it affects you and it will affect everyone in America.

America faces a moral crisis today, and as of this very moment, no one knows what the outcome will be. Americans are confused and divided about moral issues as they have rarely been before, and our moral confusion affects almost every aspect of our life, even if one does not care about politics. Even the word *moral* is confusing to people, and *values* is a word used endlessly by politicians, its meaning lost among the other slogans and buzzwords of the day.

Moral means it is about right and wrong. *Moral* means it is about good and bad. I try to teach my children about right and wrong every day, and their mother does too. It is the most important thing we teach. I want them to grow up with a clear sense of right and wrong. I do not want them to suffer from the same confusion that many others are suffering right at this moment.

Many people say that I have no right to tell anyone what is right and what is wrong, even though I am a father. Given the many rimes I have tried to teach my children right from wrong, they might find that to be pretty strange. But many people do not even believe that there is right and wrong anymore.

Jenny, Emily, and Sara, in time, you will come to your own conclusions about all this, but in the meantime you will hear us talk about right and wrong more than you would like. Again, because it is the most important thing we can give you, and because it is a sign that we care about what kind of people you grow up to be. It is a sign that we love you very, very much.

One thing we teach you is that it is wrong to lie. When we ask you a question, we expect you to tell the truth, no matter how much it hurts. Even if it means that you might get in big trouble, we know that telling the truth is habit forming.

People who get in the habit of lying just seem to have a hard time telling the truth about anything. Some people are such habitual liars that they never break out of the habit, and when you do not tell the truth, people no longer believe you. They will not trust you, and people you respect will not want to have anything to do with you.

My wife and I try to teach our children many other things, in addition to telling the truth, that are very important. Kindness to those who are suffering, or who are in need is another thing that we want our children to learn.

Taking advantage of a person who is weaker than you is wrong. Failing to extend kindness to a person in need is in the same category. Loyalty to your family and friends is right. Betrayal of those you love is wrong. . . .

I do not want to live in a country where people are afraid to make judgments or who could not even make them if they wanted to. I do not want to live in a country where people are indifferent to the truth, where lies are told and accepted as easily as the truth is. I do not want to live in a country where people are so morally confused that they have to ask why it all matters. I do not want to live in a country where wrongdoing, lies, deceit and betrayal are dismissed with the comment that "everyone else does it."

My daughters, I want you to know that, by God, everyone else does not do it. Everyone else does not do it. I do not care what the polls say. I do not care what sophisticated people living in New York or Washington, D.C., think. I do not care if the people who belong to exclusive clubs have something to say about it.

To each of my daughters, I do not care if you are the last person on this planet. I want you to be a person of honesty and integrity who knows right from wrong and who is not afraid to say so. I want you to think that honoring the promises you make to other people are promises that must not be broken. I want you to think that the promises you make to God are promises that matter even more.

Most of all, I want you to know that these are the things that matter most. And that is my message today from your father who loves you very, very much.

Supreme Injustice

Alan M. Dershowitz

Having survived the political partisanship of the Clinton impeachment trial, the nation was swept into controversy once again by the presidential election of 2000. For thirty-six days following the November 7 vote, the election remained undecided. Democratic candidate Al Gore clearly had won the popular vote. However, with Florida's results uncertain and contested, neither he nor Republican candidate George W. Bush had the necessary 270 electoral college votes to claim the presidency. In the end, the outcome of the election was determined by a 5–4 decision of the U.S. Supreme Court.

In this excerpt from his book, Supreme Injustice, *Harvard law professor Alan Dershowitz analyzes the process by which George W. Bush became what some commentators called the "president-select." Dershowitz is strongly critical of the actions of the Supreme Court, arguing elsewhere in his book that* "Bush v. Gore *showed [the Supreme Court justices] to be little differen[t] from ordinary politicians. Their votes reflected not any enduring constitutional values rooted in the precedents of the ages, but rather the partisan quest for immediate political victory."*

Many Americans believed that these contested origins would always shadow Bush's presidency. The terrorist attacks of September 11, 2001, however, pushed the divisive election struggle well into the background. Why, then, is the struggle over the 2000 election significant?

Shortly before 8 P.M. [on November 7, 2000,] the major television networks projected, based on exit polls, that Al Gore had won Florida. Within a few hours, they retracted this projection and declared the state too close to call. At approximately 2:15 A.M. on November 8, the networks declared that George W. Bush had won Florida by approximately fifty thousand votes and hence had won the presidency, despite

Gore's lead in the national popular vote. Gore called Bush to concede, but less than an hour later, Gore learned that the actual count had shrunk Bush's lead to the point where, under Florida law, an automatic machine recount was required. He again called Bush, this time to retract his private concession. At 4:15 A.M., the networks withdrew their projection that Bush had been elected. From this point on, confusion reigned, and the world turned its attention to Florida and to several key counties in particular. Within days, virtually every American had learned new terms such as "butterfly ballot," "chad," and "Votomatic." We were introduced to new characters in the unfolding drama, such as Florida secretary of state Katherine Harris and Florida attorney general Bob Butterworth. Images of weary vote counters holding perforated ballots up to the light flashed around the world.

The thirty-six days between November 7, when Americans voted, and December 13, when Al Gore finally conceded the presidency to George W. Bush, were among the most confusing, exhilarating, nerve-wracking, educational, divisive, uplifting, and depressing in our political history as a nation. We were exposed to what many called a high-stakes civics lesson on a subject about which most Americans had strong feelings but little prior knowledge. It was a wild ride for the candidates, their supporters, and a fascinated world that hadn't seen anything quite like this struggle for an Electoral College victory, which would determine the leadership of the free world based on several hundred disputed ballots in counties few people had ever heard of prior to November 7.

Shortly after the polls closed, several things became apparent: Gore appeared to have won the national popular vote by a razor-slim margin, but whichever candidate secured Florida's twenty-five electoral votes would win in the Electoral College and become president. More Floridians probably *intended* to vote for Gore than for Bush, but if the machine count was an accurate reflection of votes properly cast, more had *actually* voted for Bush. Gore was going to challenge the machine vote unless the automatic machine recount put him over the top, and Bush was going to resist any such challenge. This was going to be a fight to the finish, with neither candidate likely to concede until all hope was lost.

Both campaigns sent teams of lawyers, political operatives, and media mavens to Florida to conduct the anticipated litigation as the post–Election Day drama played itself out on several fronts: the legal, the political, the public relations, and the personal.

[Between November 7 and December 13, the Supreme Court rendered five crucial decisions.]

1. It agreed to review one aspect of the initial decision of the Florida Supreme Court, which had ordered the manual recount to continue and which extended the deadline for certifying the election by twelve days.
2. It vacated that decision and sent the case back to the Florida Supreme Court for clarification regarding the grounds of its decision.
3. It stayed the Florida Supreme Court's second decision, which had mandated a statewide recount of all undervotes and had ordered certain votes not counted by the machines but identified in the hand count to be included in the final certification.
4. It agreed to review that decision on its merits.
5. It reversed that decision and permanently stopped all hand counting of undervotes, thereby ending the election in favor of George W. Bush.

[This final] majority ruling in *Bush v. Gore* marked a number of significant firsts. Never before in American history has a presidential election been decided by the Supreme Court. Never before in American history have so many law professors, historians, political scientists, Supreme Court litigators, journalists who cover the high court, and other experts—at all points along the political spectrum—been in agreement that the majority decision of the Court was not only "bad constitutional law" but "lawless," "illegitimate," "unprincipled," "partisan," "fraudulent," "disingenuous," and motivated by improper considerations. In addition to the remarkable expert consensus regarding this case, there is also widespread popular outrage at what the high court did. Though the level of this outrage tends to mirror party affiliation, it is safe to say that the degree of confusion over what actually happened is not limited to one party. There are millions of Americans who do not strongly identify with the Democratic Party—indeed, even some who voted for George W. Bush—but who cannot understand how five justices could determine the outcome of a presidential election. Moreover, the furor within the Supreme Court itself—among some justices and law clerks—is unprecedented in the annals of this usually harmonious institution.

In light of these factors, many Americans who believed that the Court was an institution that could be trusted to remain above partisan politics are now experiencing a genuine loss of confidence in the impartiality of the judicial branch of our government. This widespread loss of confidence, reaching to the pinnacle of our judiciary, should be the concern of all Americans, because the Supreme Court has played such a critical role in the history of our nation. Without its moral authority, we would be a less tolerant, less vibrant, and less free democracy. The high court, throughout its long and distinguished history, has helped us—not always perfectly or swiftly—through crises of institutional racism, religious intolerance, McCarthyism, systematic malapportionment, presidents who deemed themselves above the law, and governors who defied the Constitution. The Court stepped in when the other branches of government were unwilling or unable to enforce the constitutional rights of unpopular minorities. The justices were always at their greatest when they could act unanimously and on principles that could be easily justified and widely accepted. When they act in an unprincipled and partisan manner—as they did in *Bush v. Gore*—they risk losing respect and frittering away the moral capital accumulated by their predecessors over generations. That is what Justice Stephen Breyer was referring to when he wrote in his dissent in *Bush v. Gore*:

> [I]n this highly politicized matter, the appearance of a split decision runs the risk of undermining the public's confidence in the Court itself. That confidence is a public treasure. It has been built slowly over many years. . . . It is a vitally necessary ingredient of any successful effort to protect basic liberty and, indeed, the rule of law itself. . . . [We] risk a self-inflicted wound—a wound that may harm not just the Court, but the Nation.

That is why all Americans must care about this case and must derive the appropriate lessons from it. The Supreme Court's moral capital will certainly again be needed in our future, and so it is a tragedy that it has been dissipated for short-term partisan gain in a case in which the Supreme Court had no proper role.

The Constitution, after all, places the power to elect our president in every institution of government but the judiciary. The people vote for electors. The electors vote for the president. If this process produces no clear winner, then the Constitution (and the laws enacted pursuant to it) assigns varying roles to the Senate, the House of Representatives, the state legislatures, and even the governors. No role, however, is explicitly given to the Supreme Court. James Madison, in recording his own views of the constitutional debate as to how the president should be elected, dismissed selection by the appointed judiciary as "out of the question."

Indeed, the justices themselves seemed to initially recognize the absence of a judicial role when they unanimously remanded *Bush v. Gore* back to the Florida Supreme Court for that court to explain whether it had improperly changed the election law as enacted by the Florida legislature. The high court suggested that if the state supreme court had changed duly enacted state legislation, then it may have violated Article II of the Constitution, which vests in state legislators the authority to select the manner by which electors should be chosen. It seems ironic that the U.S. Supreme Court would take upon itself a judicial function nowhere specified in the Constitution—effectively ending a presidential election—while seeming to deny to the Florida Supreme Court its traditional role in interpreting and reconciling conflicting statutes.

Some of the Court's defenders have argued that since, in their view, the Florida Supreme Court engaged in partisan judicial activism in support of Gore, it was permissible for the nation's highest court to "correct" the lower court and undo the harm it had done. Indeed, I am reliably informed that several of the majority justices were outraged at what they believed was crass partisanship by the Florida justices. I have been told that one of the dissenting U.S. Supreme Court justices characterized the mind-set of some of the majority justices as follows: "If the Florida Supreme Court is going to act like a bunch of Democratic political hacks, well, by God, we will act like a bunch of Republican political hacks." Even if it is true that some Florida justices acted in a partisan manner, that would not justify a retaliatory partisan decision by U.S. Supreme Court justices. Two partisan wrongs do not make a judicial right. Moreover, under the U.S. Constitution, a state court has the right to be wrong on matters of state law, and the Supreme Court has no power to correct it unless its mistake is a matter of federal constitutional or statutory law. Even then, the Supreme Court does not traditionally correct every error a state court makes. Citing death penalty cases, Justice Ruth Bader Ginsburg, in her dissenting opinion in *Bush v. Gore*, reminded her colleagues that "[n]ot uncommonly, we let stand state-court interpretations of *federal* law with which we might disagree." During oral argument, she put it even more directly to Bush's lawyer:

> "I do not know of any case where we have impugned a state supreme court the way you are doing in this case," Ginsburg scolded Olson. Florida's seven justices "may have been wrong; we might have interpreted it differently, but we are not the arbiters—they are."

The very justices who typically allow state prisoners to be executed even if their conviction was based on a mistaken reading of federal constitutional law jumped into this case on the ground that the Florida Supreme Court's decision violated the equal-protection clause of the U.S. Constitution in a manner never before suggested by any court. Even some scholars who supported Bush—Robert Bork, Harvey Mansfield, Michael McConnell, and Richard Epstein, among others—have found this conclusion unconvincing, troublesome, and wrongheaded.

It also seemed baffling to many that these five justices, whose records on the high court showed them to be the least sensitive to claims of equal protection, determined a presidential election on such doubtful equal-protection grounds.

These and many other questions have led many Americans to wonder whether the black-robed justices are really any less politically partisan than elected politicians. When Antonin Scalia—one of the architects of the majority decision—was still a law professor, he made an observation that aptly characterized the feelings of many scholars in regard to this decision:

> It is increasingly difficult to pretend to one's students that the decisions of the Supreme Court are tied together by threads of logic and analysis as opposed to what seems to be the fact that the decisions of each of the Justices on the Court are tied together by threads of social preference and predisposition.

In dissenting from the Supreme Court's decision ending the hand count, Justice John Paul Stevens, the court's senior associate justice, echoed Professor Scalia in strong words that will be long remembered and often quoted by those who follow the Court. He warned that the majority's position "can only lend credence to the most cynical appraisal of the work of judges throughout the land. It is," said Justice Stevens, "confidence in the men and women who administer the judicial system that is the true backbone of the rule of law. Time will one day heal the wound to that confidence that will be inflicted

by today's decision. One thing, however, is certain. Although we may
never know with complete certainty the identity of the winner of this
year's Presidential election, the identity of the loser is perfectly clear.
It is the Nation's confidence in the judge as an impartial guardian of
the rule of law."

Part 8

FACING THE NEW MILLENNIUM

In the aftermath of the September 11 terrorist attacks on the United States, commentators rushed to predict that everything about American life—from popular culture to foreign policy—had been changed forever. The attacks *were* unprecedented, and lives *were* forever changed—especially those of people who survived the attacks or who lost loved ones that day. But fairly quickly, for the vast majority of Americans, life returned to a semblance of normality.

The attacks, though, pointed to an irrefutable fact about the world at the beginning of the new millennium: its peoples and nations are increasingly interconnected. Political and national borders are compromised by global economies, by global communications, by the global environmental impact of national decisions, and by the proliferation of weapons of mass destruction. Despite unprecedented power, the United States is increasingly subject to global forces, and to the consequences of decisions made and actions taken in far off places.

In the last decades of the twentieth century, the United States led the world in the development of a "new economy," one driven by global capital, heavily reliant on new technologies, dynamic, flexible, and highly competitive. By the dawn of the twenty-first century, the economies of the world had become increasingly interdependent, with the economic fortunes of the United States tied directly to a growing number of nations. Europeans created a common market, moving to a single currency in January 2002, and the United States opened trade borders with Mexico and Canada in the 1994 North American Free Trade Agreements (NAFTA).

Throughout the 1990s, the American economy showed unparalleled sustained growth. The stock market climbed steadily and rapidly;

419

"dot-com" companies founded by twenty-something entrepreneurs made instant millionaires in a generation of computer-savvy youth. Unfounded assumptions about never-ending economic growth and rising prosperity were tempered by the recession that began in 2000 and that was exacerbated by the events of 9/11/01. But there were downsides to the new economy well before the recession. During the 1990s, the benefits of economic growth were not distributed equally: the top 1 percent of American households claimed more wealth than the lower 95 percent. Between 1980 and 1996, the real income of the top 5 percent grew 58 percent, while the income of the bottom 60 percent rose by just 4 percent. By 2000, the poverty rate had reached a low of 11.3 percent, close to the 1973 all-time low of 11.1 percent. But that 11.3 percent represented 31.1 million people, and it hid further inequities. More than 20 percent of African Americans and of Hispanics fell below the poverty line. While that figure represented an all-time low for both groups, it scarcely suggested economic quality.

In addition, because of the flow of global capital and the interdependency of markets in this new economy, the United States cannot stand fully insulated from events such as the longstanding economic recession in Japan or economic instability in Mexico, its neighbor to the south. Critics of NAFTA argue that "free trade" is hurting American workers, as cheap labor in Mexico drains jobs from the United States. Developing countries in Latin America, Africa, and South Asia increasingly compete for the same jobs as do the older industrialized countries—jobs that at an ever-increasing rate are leaving America and other "first world" countries—thus having a profound impact on their economic health and on the lives of their citizens. Nonetheless, the wealth of the United States and the vast majority of its citizens stands in stark contrast to the heartbreaking poverty of many of the world's peoples.

In the meantime, the structure of world geopolitics has undergone its own transformation. The terrorist attacks were evidence of the instability of the post–Cold War world, and of the threat of non-state actors in a world at least presumably stabilized by an alliance of nations. When, nearly three-quarters of a century after having come into existence, the Soviet Union suddenly disappeared in 1991, the United States became the only remaining superpower, the "winner" of the Cold War with the Soviet Union. It seemed a moment of triumph and possibility, but that confidence quickly faded as it became apparent that the end of the Cold War did not promise peace and stability. New international problems proliferated, with ethnic nationalism, indigenous civil wars, and religiously driven conflict souring hopes for a post–Cold War peace. Some even voiced nostalgia for the certainties of Cold War ideology. How was it possible to determine what was morally correct or politically advantageous when the choices in international affairs were so murky and muddled?

At home, meanwhile, Americans continued to struggle over the implications of its increasingly diverse population. An anti-immigrant backlash grew, beginning with California's Proposition 187, passed in 1994 by nearly 60 percent of those who voted. Proposition 187 sought to prevent illegal immigrants access to medical care, social services, and public education. Though it was declared unconstitutional in federal district court, struggles over immigration policy shifted to the U.S. Congress, where they proved highly divisive.

Issues of race continued to divide the American public, as well. Several states, including California and Texas, rejected affirmative action policies aimed primarily at African Americans and Latinos. As American culture shifted increasingly away from what had long been considered the white "mainstream," some celebrated the nation's growing diversity while others worried that the United States's "own" culture was being lost. As the percentage of Latinos moved to overtake the percentage of African Americans, and as both groups lagged economically while Asian American average family income became significantly higher than that of whites, issues of race, ethnicity, class, and culture remained highly charged and difficult topics for American people and policymakers alike.

The readings in this section build upon those in Part 7 that traced transformations in American society. Scholars from the Progressive Policy Institute, part of the Democratic Leadership Council, argue that the rise of the "new economy" is every bit as fundamental a transformation as the industrial revolution, and chart its impacts on the everyday lives of Americans. Stephan Thernstrom, in an article written for the conservative *National Review*, critiques the assumptions underlying the 2000 Census's definitions of race—and their policy implications. Historian J. R. McNeill offers a global perspective on environmental change and human action, looking ahead to an uncertain and increasingly volatile future. Diplomatic historian George Herring analyzes the impact of 9/11 in the context of post–Cold War foreign policy. And finally, novelist Don DeLillo captures the grief of the nation in the wake of September 11, 2001.

In the first decade of the new millennium, the challenges facing America seem as perilous and difficult to resolve as at any time during the last five decades of the twentieth century. As complex as the issues of post–World War II America were, they may well pale beside those of the post–Cold War world.

The New Economy Index and America's Metropolitan Areas

*Robert D. Atkinson, Randolph H. Court,
and Paul D. Gottleib
The Progressive Policy Institute*

One important piece of the reconfiguration of American politics has been the emergence of the "New Democrats," a coalition that claims to seek a "third way"—a "progressive alternative to the worn-out dogmas of traditional liberalism and conservatism." The key New Democratic group is the Democratic Leadership Council, which was closely allied with President Clinton. Critics argue that the New Democrats represent a move toward the center that shifts the balance of American politics rightward. The New Democrats and their supporters see themselves as breaking free of the constraints of liberal thought that was shaped in very different economic and social circumstances, in order to craft a progressive politics for the "information age" of the twenty-first century.

The Democratic Leadership Council's think tank, the Progressive Policy Institute, has crafted a series of policy papers on the "new economy." The following draws from two of those papers, The New Economy Index (*1998*) *and* The Metropolitan New Economy Index (*2001*). *While this document explains the "new economy" and some of its effects, it is also a policy statement and can be read both as scholarly analysis and as a primary document.*

INTRODUCTION

The U.S. economy is undergoing a fundamental transformation at the dawn of the new millennium. Some of the most obvious outward signs of change are in fact among the root causes of it: revolutionary tech-

From Robert D. Atkinson and Randolph H. Court, *The New Economy Index*, 1998, and Robert D. Atkinson and Paul Gottlieb, *The Metropolitan New Economy Index*, 2001. Reprinted with permission of the Progressive Policy Institute, www.ppionline.org.

nological advances, including powerful personal computers, high-speed telecommunications, and the Internet. The market environment facilitated by these and other developments in the last decade and a half has been variously labeled the "information economy," "network economy," "digital economy," "knowledge economy," and the "risk society." Together, the whole package is often simply referred to as the "New Economy."

The story of how businesses are changing in today's economy has been told and retold with such frequency in recent years that it has become something of a cliché: the new rules of the game require speed, flexibility, and innovation. New, rapidly growing companies are selling to global markets almost from their inception, and established companies are being forced to reinvent their operations to stay competitive in the new terrain. This is the part of the New Economy that was born in Steve Jobs's and Steve Wozniak's garage, at Bell Labs, Xerox PARC, and in the trunk of Michael Dell's car. It is Silicon Valley: Netscape, Yahoo!, and the next Big Thing. And of course it is Microsoft, with a market capitalization now second only to General Electric's.

But this New Economy is about more than high technology and the frenetic action at the cutting edge. Most firms, not just the ones actually producing technology, are organizing work around it. The New Economy is a metal casting firm in Pittsburgh that uses computer-aided manufacturing technology to cut costs, save energy, and reduce waste. It is a farmer in Nebraska who sows genetically altered seeds and drives a tractor with a global satellite positioning system. It is an insurance company in Iowa that uses software to flatten managerial hierarchies and give its workers broader responsibilities and autonomy. It is a textile firm in Georgia that uses the Internet to take orders from customers around the world.

It is also as much about new organizational models as it is about new technologies. The New Economy is the Miller brewery in Trenton, Ohio, which produces 50 percent more beer per worker than the company's next-most-productive facility, in part because a lean, 13-member crew has been trained to work in teams to handle the overnight shift with no oversight.[1]

---

1. Section 1 from *The New Economy Index*, PPI Policy Report, Robert D. Atkinson and Randolph H. Court.

THE TRANSFORMATION TO A NEW ECONOMY:
THE METROPOLITAN NEW ECONOMY INDEX

Was the New Economy a flash in the pan? Or, even worse, a myth spun by an overimaginative media? To paraphrase Mark Twain, reports of the New Economy's demise have been greatly exaggerated. The New Economy is here to stay. To be sure, the Nasdaq has fallen sharply, many dot-coms are going bust, and investment in information technology is down. When this news is conflated with the other negative economic indicators that surfaced in winter 2001, it is an easy but mistaken step to pronounce the death of the New Economy.

The fallacy of his leap rests on the belief that all the New Economy is about is the Internet and what investor Jim Clark and writer Michael Lewis dubbed the "next new thing." On the contrary, the New Economy embraces more fundamentally a profound transformation of all industries, the kind of transformation that happens perhaps twice in a century. The emergence of the New Economy is equivalent in scope and depth to the rise of the manufacturing economy in the 1890s and the emergence of the mass-production, corporate economy in the 1940s and '50s. As documented in PPI's New Economy Index the New Economy represents a complex array of forces including the reorganization of firms, more efficient and dynamic capital markets, more economic "churning" and entrepreneurial dynamism, globalization, economic competition and volatile labor markets.

But underlying and powering these changes is the information technology revolution, which, notwithstanding media reports of new "pure play" dot-com bankruptcies, is fundamentally healthy. The online market continues to grow at a robust pace, with more and more of its work done by traditional "bricks and mortar" companies diversifying into "clicks and mortar" operations. The Census Bureau reports that e-commerce retail sales grew seven times faster than all retail sales in the fourth quarter of 2000 and was 67 percent higher than in the fourth quarter of 1999. Moreover, between October 2000 and February 2001 Internet growth actually accelerated. Almost five million Internet domain names (e.g., dot-coms) and 17 million Internet hosts (Internet addresses) were added. Home broadband use increased 150 percent last year and is projected to continue growing rapidly. Worldwide Internet use is expected to more than triple by 2005 to more than 1.5 billion people.

But what about the slowdown in tech investments? Doesn't this mean that the tech revolution, and by extension, the New Economy has run its course? On the contrary, as a host of new technologies becomes ready for the market, IT investments will remain robust. These include voice recognition, expert systems, smart cards, e-books, cheap storage devices, new display devices and video software, intelligent transportation systems, "third generation" wireless communication devices, and robots.

In short, a New Economy has emerged: it is a global knowledge and idea-based economy where the keys to wealth and job creation are the extent to which ideas, innovation, and technology are embedded in all sectors of the economy—services, manufacturing, and agriculture.

THE NEW ECONOMY IN METROPOLITAN AREAS

The same forces that are driving the New Economy—new industries and jobs, globalization, competition and dynamism, and the information technology revolution—are also driving a new reordering of the economic geography of America, including its metropolitan regions.[2]

In the old economy most economic activity took place in large metropolitan areas. As the IT revolution gives companies and workers more locational freedom, a smaller share of employment is located in the largest metropolitan areas than was the case just 10 years ago. The share of employment located in the largest 61 metropolitan areas actually declined by 1.5 percent between 1988 and 1997, from 55.1 percent to 54.3 percent. In contrast, the share of jobs in mid-sized metros (between 250,000 and 1 million) increased by 4 percent, and the share in small metros (between 50,000 and 250,000) increased by 7 percent. But so far the deconcentrating forces of the New Economy are not all powerful—the share of jobs in rural counties not adjacent to metro areas declined by 11 percent.

These forces are also leading to a decentralization within metropolitan areas. The old economy metropolis was like an atom—most of a region's economic activity was concentrated densely at the center

---

2. Section 2 from *The Metropolitan New Economy Index*, PPI Policy Report, April 19, 2001, Robert D. Atkinson and Paul D. Gottlieb.

like a nucleus, with residents spread out in rings around the city, poorer ones close in, richer ones farther out. Nothing epitomized this better than the skyscrapers located in the downtown and the large factories adjacent to the downtown. Corporations erected skyscrapers that, as monuments, were intended to be as lasting as the companies themselves. Manufacturers in the core city were housed in sprawling factories that spewed out thousands of workers at the end of each shift.

But fundamental New Economy forces have acted like an atom smasher, breaking the nucleus up into hundreds of pieces and strewing it across the countryside. An office is more likely to be located in an anonymous building in a remote suburban office park, while the typical manufacturer is a small operation located in a metal "Butler" building located at the outer edges of a metro or in a small town.

In short, the common vision of the metropolitan area as a place with one economy, located among downtown skyscrapers and inner-ring factories, no longer describes the metropolis common to America at the beginning of the 21st century. By the early 1990s, 57 percent of office stock in America was located in the suburbs, up from 25 percent in 1970. Similarly, most high-tech jobs are in the suburbs as well.

And these trends are occurring not just in the newer metros of the West, but all over. Milwaukee's central city lost 14,000 jobs between 1979 and 1994, while inner-ring suburbs gained 4,800, and outer-ring suburbs gained a staggering 82,000. The District of Columbia's share of regional jobs fell from 33 percent in 1990 to only 25 percent in 1998, in part because office space in the high-tech outer-suburban Dulles Airport corridor increased from 20 million square feet in 1992 to 100 million in 1999. Atlanta's share of the metropolitan region's jobs declined from 40 percent in 1980 to 28 percent in 1990, with the northern, predominately white suburbs gaining all the share that the city lost—exacerbating the spatial mismatch for underemployed minorities, who are concentrated in the central and southern part of the city while jobs are increasing in the northern suburbs.

The bedroom suburb—little more than a home to workers commuting to the central city—is an anomaly, something to be experienced in reruns on Nickelodeon. Today, many people live and work in the suburbs and rarely visit the central city; others still commute to the core for work, but find any and all services needed for their daily lives available in the suburbs. These changes have proceeded to the

point where even the terms "cities" and "suburbs" have become artifacts of the old economy.

The centripetal forces sending businesses throughout all parts of
the metropolitan area mean that people can live farther from the
center and not face inordinately long commutes. In the old industrial
metropolis, when most jobs were downtown, few people wanted to
live 25 miles from the center city. With edge cities and office parks 20
miles from the center city, people now live 30, 40, and even 50 miles
from downtown and still have reasonable commutes. For example,
the growth of the high-tech I-270 corridor in the Washington, D.C.,
suburb of Montgomery County, Md., has meant that people who
work there are increasingly commuting from as far away as West
Virginia.

This kind of sprawl is not necessarily leading to lower population
densities within the current bounds of metro areas. On the contrary,
the fact that suburban areas are becoming urbanized accounts for
much of the concern over sprawl. Residents who moved to the suburbs to get away from it all—to experience the equivalent of Frank
Lloyd Wright's Broadacre City—are increasingly wondering what
happened to their semi-rural good life. For example, while population density in the city of Chicago fell from 16,000 persons per square
mile in 1950 to 12,000 in 1990, the density in already developed suburbs increased from 400 to 1,200 as infill and multifamily homes increased. Between 1980 and 1990, population density of the built-up
areas of the 40 largest metropolitan areas actually increased 14 percent, from 456 persons per square mile to 523. Thus, while many
urban core areas are getting less dense, inner and outer suburbs are
getting more dense.

But while inner and outer suburban densities may be increasing,
development on the far fringes of metropolitan areas, which often
leapfrogs existing metropolitan development by miles, has meant
that overall population densities are declining as many metro areas
encompass increasing amounts of land. For example, by the mid-
1990s the population of the Philadelphia metropolitan area was only
100,000 more today than it was in 1960, but it's spread out over a land
area 32 percent larger than in 1960, representing the development of
125,000 acres of open space. In Chicago, while the region's population grew only 4 percent, the residential land area expanded 50 percent. It is this low-density development at the fringes of metro areas
that is commonly referred to as sprawl.

But these patterns of dispersal differ by region. Places like Phoenix and Los Angeles are sprawling outward, but because they are gaining population, overall densities are going up. In contrast to this "dense sprawl," places like Rochester, N.Y., and other slow-growth metropolitan areas can be characterized as "thinning metropolises," where low-density exurbs continue to develop even as the population remains constant (or, as in the case of places like Buffalo, N.Y., even declines). In the New Economy, dispersed development is the dominant spatial form in virtually all areas.

But it's not just the spatial order of economic activity that the New Economy has transformed; it's also the industrial and occupational order. Because of superior productivity, in the last two decades manufacturing employment has declined as a share of total jobs and now accounts for only 14 percent of total employment. But in the 50 largest metro areas, its share is even less—only 11 percent of jobs.

With the relative decline in manufacturing employment, the economy has specialized in high-tech and business services (e.g., banking, consulting, insurance). Office jobs now account for over 40 percent of all jobs, while managerial, professional, and technical jobs account for almost 30 percent of employment. But these activities are even more concentrated in metro areas. While the 114 largest metro areas account for 67 percent of all jobs, they account for 81 percent of high-tech employment, and 91 percent of Internet domain names (e.g., dot-coms). Between 1988 and 1997, urban counties of large metropolitan areas (over 1 million in population) have seen advanced business services jobs increase by 21 percent, and high-tech by 24 percent, while their suburban areas have seen increases of 39 percent and 43 percent, respectively.

The inherent drivers of the New Economy—the rise of information and knowledge jobs, constant innovation and "churning," and competition, all coupled with a radical and deeply transformative information technology revolution—have enabled these changes. The New Economy gives both companies and workers more locational freedom. Whereas manufacturing and distribution facilities formerly needed to locate on water or rail lines, ubiquitous highway access now lets them locate almost anywhere. Likewise, many service facilities needed to locate downtown to facilitate face-to-face transactions, but now e-mail, faxes, and the Internet give them new freedom. As more and more Americans own cars and can afford single-family homes, they too can live in a much wider range of places. The result is that dispersed development of people and jobs—what critics call sprawl—is by its very nature a part of the New Economy.

This isn't to say that public policies should seek to exacerbate the centrifugal forces of the postindustrial New Economy. It is to say that policy makers need to understand and work with its systemic forces. It also is to say that, because the working economy now is not just the central city but the entire region, policy makers must view the region as a complex interconnected organism whose overall health is affected by the health of the parts. Because the metro area as a whole is the right unit for analysis, it's also the right unit for policy. Policy makers need to look at a host of issues, including transportation, education, training, and economic development, through a regional frame.

A Racialist's Census

Stephan Thernstrom

In the 2000 census, for the first time, Americans could identify themselves as belonging to more than one race. This change, while significant, was not the first time census racial categories had shifted: In the early part of the twentieth century, Americans were asked to select simply between "white" and "Negro and other races."

Much of the impetus for the 2000 census multiracial category came from the parents of multirace children. It is hard to chart the growth in the number of multiracial children in the United States, because the census did not gather that data. But fewer than half a million American children lived in "mixed-race" families in 1970. By 1990 almost two million (or about 4 percent of America's children) had parents drawn from different racial groups. Many of these parents did not want their children counted as belonging to only one race.

New understandings of "race" supported this change, as well. As Stephan Thernstrom notes below, the nineteenth-century notion that humans are divided into distinct biological races has been thoroughly discredited, and the single-race designations seemed uncomfortably reminiscent of the old Jim Crow "one-drop-of-blood" definition of race.

What seems a reasonable response to changing demographic realities and social understandings, however, became quite controversial. Census data is not gathered only to provide a portrait of the nation; it is meant as hard data for government policy and planning. Many who were concerned with questions of social justice and economic equality feared that the new census categories would undercount America's racial minorities and thus lessen their political power. Caught in a bind, the Clinton administration created a compromise.

In the following article from the conservative National Review, *historian and social commentator Stephan Thernstrom compares the attempts of civil rights organizations to maintain single-race categories to the Jim Crow laws of the early twentieth century. Thernstrom's argument is in part, a brief against*

*affirmative action. But he raises some difficult questions about the meanings
and uses of racial categories in the contemporary United States. How should
one's race be determined? Is identity a matter of blood? Of culture? Will racial
categories become more or less important in the future? Should we give up on
the notion of race altogether and substitute "ethnicity" instead? What are the
implications of Thernstrom's argument for government policies?*

"The United States is the only country in the world in which a white
woman can give birth to a black baby but a black woman cannot give
birth to a white baby." Not long ago, when the civil rights movement
was unquestionably on the side of the angels, liberals were fond of
pointing that out, with a mixture of dismay and smugness. How stupid! they said. You were deemed black if either of your parents was
black. Indeed, you were deemed black even if your only black ances-
tor was one great-grandparent—the infamous "drop" rule made it so.

That rule was essential to the either-or logic of the Jim Crow system, in which being only part-black was as inconceivable as being
part-pregnant. Nor was there room for people with other racial identities; those who were not white were thrown into the category of—
as the Census Bureau traditionally termed it—"Negroes and other
races." Under this system, if you recognized the remarkably mixed
ancestry of a Tiger Woods, what public school would you assign him
to? Where would you have him sit on the bus? Jim Crow is now dead,
but its legacy lives on in current racial-classification practices. Ironically, though, it is now those on the left, who are pleased to call themselves liberals, who insist that we all belong in rigid, mutually exclusive, color-coded compartments. Their views, alas, are reflected in the
decisions made recently about the Census of 2000, now in mailboxes
throughout the country.

In the past, the Census Bureau was not totally oblivious to the reality of the American marital melting pot. To the question about
"ancestry or ethnic origin" that appeared in both the 1980 and 1990
Censuses, it was allowable to give as many as three answers. You
could report your ancestry as German, Italian, and Irish, or as Polish,
Greek, and Swedish. But when it came to identifying yourself racially,
no such latitude was given. The "races" of the United States were assumed to be mutually exclusive categories, and you could name only
one.

This rigid rule came under growing criticism in the 1990s because of the spectacular surge in intermarriage between Americans of different "races." In some Asian groups—not so long ago categorized as "Orientals" and forbidden to marry non-Asians in some states—a majority of current marriages are to non-Asians, mostly whites. Fully half of all American Indians today are married to non-Indians. Even black/white intermarriages, once illegal in all southern states and taboo in all but the most cosmopolitan communities, are by now far from uncommon. More than one in eight African Americans who married in 1994 had white spouses, and that figure is doubtless higher by now. The rapid growth in the number of children born of racially mixed unions, and the resentment of their parents at being forced to put the child in just one racial box, forced the planners of the 2000 Census to recognize the new reality. It would now be possible, they announced, for racially mixed Americans to identify with more than one racial group when they fill out their forms.

In the infighting that led up to the decision, the battle to preserve the old, mutually exclusive conception of race was led, not by white dinosaurs, but by the major civil rights organizations. If a significant proportion of African Americans reported themselves as partly white, they worried, it could mean fewer affirmative action slots at colleges and universities, fewer jobs for black applicants, a smaller share of public contracts set aside for black-owned businesses, fewer safe black seats on city councils, in state legislatures, and in Congress. All of these programs take proportional representation as the goal, so a decline in the total numbers of a minority group means a reduced entitlement.

In a 1995 Vanderbilt Law Review article, an African American attorney pursued the implications of the new "civil rights" position on this issue to its appalling but logical conclusion. Since race was now being used to award societal benefits, and properly so, he argued, it was necessary to devise new legal tools to prevent "racial fraud." Whites would have a much better chance of getting into the school of their choice or of finding a desirable job if they claimed they were black. To prevent that, the author called for a stricter racial-classification system for all Americans, with "fines and immediate job or benefit termination" for those who "falsified their racial identity." What was needed was a new body of law that recognized the "permanent importance" of racial divisions.

Of course, many of our states had such laws before: these laws were essential to the Jim Crow system. For example, a 1924 Virginia statute required statewide racial registration and provided a year in jail as the penalty for making a "false" report of one's racial identity. Obviously, this was designed to discourage blacks from attempting to "pass" as white. One of the arguments advanced by the plaintiffs in *Plessy v. Ferguson* was that Homer Plessy was entitled to sit in the "white" railroad car because he was white, being only one-eighth black. But the Supreme Court was not impressed, declaring that it was up to the state of Louisiana to decide "the proportion of colored blood necessary to constitute a colored person." To be one-eighth black in Louisiana was to be black—that was that. It is breathtaking to find old ideas about "blood" now resuscitated in a respectable law review, and by an African American scholar. The fear now is that whites will try to "pass" as black. We have come a long, long way from the days of the *Brown* litigation, when Thurgood Marshall insisted that "classifications and distinctions based upon race or color have no moral or legal validity in our society."

Fortunately, the attempts of the civil rights organization to preserve "racial purity" were unsuccessful. The Census Bureau agreed to modify the instructions that accompanied the race question on the 2000 Census, and to indicate that it was possible to choose two or even more racial identities. Homer Plessy could say that he was both white and black, if he chose. Racially mixed Americans would be counted as they wished to be counted.

"Counted" in the simple sense that they may record their perceptions of their own racial identity. But what they report themselves to be, it has now become clear, will be of no practical import. The Office of Management and Budget has just issued guidelines governing how all federal agencies are to employ the racial and ethnic data gathered on the 2000 Census. Those guidelines reveal that the civil rights lobby lost the battle but won the war. When it comes to figuring out the racial composition of the population for purposes of "civil rights monitoring and enforcement" (i.e., to set quotas, goals, or targets in education, employment, and public contracting, and to determine whether racial minorities can claim that their right to political representation has been "diluted"), the complex identifications of racially mixed Americans will be ignored.

Though the Bureau will not tabulate data for every possible racial combination, it will keep track of a mind-boggling 63, so that we will have figures, for example, on the number of people who consider themselves part-white, part-black, and part-American Indian. But when the figures are to be used to determine whether civil rights laws have been violated, these distinctions will disappear. Citizens who say they are not only white but also a member of a "minority race" will be counted as belonging to the "minority race"—period. In other words, for these purposes, it is still the case that "a white woman can give birth to a black baby but a black woman cannot give birth to a white baby." If you have enough black or Asian "blood" to mention it on the census form at all, you will be put in the black or Asian column that the Equal Employment Opportunity Commission and similar agencies will be using to decide whether some company has "enough" employees of the right kind.

This decision means that civil rights groups need not fear that the number of their constituents will be reduced. Indeed, they will grow, if Americans of mixed race who reported themselves simply as white on past censuses now choose to mention that they have black ancestry as well. That mention will land them in the black column.

The most dramatic, indeed bizarre, effect will be on the enumeration of the American Indian population. A mere 2.1 million people checked the "American Indian, Eskimo, Aleut" box on the 1990 Census race question. That is the figure everyone uses for the Indian population in that year. But the separate question about "ancestry or ethnic origin" on the same Census, on which multiple choices were possible, yielded a staggering 8.7 million people who claimed to have some Indian ancestors. If all of the additional 6.6 million identify themselves as both Indian and something else on the 2000 Census race question, now that multiple race choices are possible, the Indian-population figures used for purposes of civil rights enforcement will suddenly quadruple. And most of these born-again Indians will be thoroughly assimilated Americans who have no contact or cultural connection to any Indian tribe today; but they will now count as if they had never left the reservation.

Some of us hoped that making it possible to give multiple answers to the race question would reveal a picture of such intricate complexity that it would call into question the very effort to divide us all into racial boxes. Sadly, our federal government today is attempting to prevent this fate, by retabulating the raw information in a manner that seems designed to ensure the "permanent importance"—as that Vanderbilt Law Review contributor put it—of race.

Deplorable though this is, it is too simple to say flatly that we should stop gathering any information at all about the racial and ethnic composition of the U.S. population. I have been strongly tempted to take the abolitionist position on this issue, and I respect Ward Connerly and others who do. I'm certainly disgusted to see that Americans who have been sent the Census short form—and they are five out of six of us—are asked to provide virtually no information except what racial box they belong in. Nevertheless, I have regretfully concluded that it is impractical and unwise to go to the extreme that many of my comrades in the anti-preference camp advocate.

Why? As early as the middle of the 19th century, the United States made its decennial census into something more than a simple head count of the population. The 1850 Census was the first to inquire into such matters as who had been born abroad and in what country, the occupations Americans were engaged in, and the school attendance of their children. Subsequent enumerations added questions about income and unemployment, housing, modes of travel to work, and dozens of other topics. All modern societies have felt compelled to compile such information, not least because businesses find such information extremely useful. The libertarian view that none of these matters is a proper concern of government is hopelessly utopian.

Even if all racial and ethnic questions were removed from the census, surely we would continue to hear complaints that blacks are far more likely than other Americans to live in poverty. Indeed, in the absence of authoritative data, the magnitude of such social problems would likely be even more exaggerated. Even with official statistics, a recent Gallup poll found that the American public thought that 32 percent of the population was black and 21 percent Hispanic (more than double the actual figures). Furthermore, it is only by gathering the facts that we are able to discern the close connection between black poverty, the remarkably high proportion of female-headed black families, and the huge racial gap in levels of literacy and numeracy. Surely we want to know if black third graders are far behind whites in reading and math competence, and the correlation between that difference and family structure or economic circumstances. It is at least possible that social-science knowledge will guide us toward solutions.

The problem, then, is not with the gathering of social and economic facts. The problem is what might be termed the "the privileging of race." The idea that mankind is divided into a very few, physically and cultural distinctive, racial groups is a thoroughly outmoded and discredited 19th-century notion. In setting out the officially recognized racial categories, the Office of Management and Budget cautions that "these classifications should not be interpreted as being scientific or anthropological in nature." That's for sure—but this admission only makes OMB's decision to use them more dubious. If these categories are not "scientific" or "anthropological," what are they? Why should the U.S. government distinguish some citizens from others on a basis that is not "scientific" or even "anthropological" (whatever that means) and use these distinctions in allocating public resources? "Race" is a bad idea whose time has come and gone. It does not belong in statistics that appear with the stamp of approval of the government of the United States.

Ethnicity (as distinct from crude, unidimensional race categories), however, is another matter. We cannot pretend that African Americans are not a distinctive group with an uniquely oppressive history they are still struggling to overcome, nor that Chinese Americans or Ukrainian Americans are like everyone else in every way. But we need not assume that Americans of Chinese origins are a separate "race," while classifying Ukrainians as "white." The census question on "ancestry or ethnic origin" is quite sufficient to identify subgroups of the population, and it will do the job nicely—with one important modification.

In the past, the Census Bureau has framed the instructions on the ancestry question in a manner that discourages the response "American." Despite that discouragement, 13 million people—5 percent of the population—said that their ancestry was "American" or "United States" on the 1990 Census, and another 27 million—11 percent of the population—said that they were unable or unwilling to specify any ancestry. If it were made clear that "American" is a perfectly acceptable response, those numbers might soar. And that would not be a bad thing at all.

Our Gigantic Experiment with Planet Earth

J. R. McNeill

In 1962, biologist Rachel Carson published the first of the articles that would become her bestselling book Silent Spring, *in the* New Yorker. *Carson's work redefined popular understandings of environmentalism, shifting focus from the preservation of unspoiled "wilderness" to an awareness of "the intricate web of life whose interwoven strands lead from microbes to man." America's environmental movement grew throughout the 1960s, drawing new members to existing groups such as the Sierra Club and lending support to a whole series of environmental protection initiatives, including the creation of the Environmental Protection Agency (EPA) in 1970.*

Increasingly in the latter part of the twentieth century, scientists and environmental activists attempted to draw Americans' attention to the global nature of environmental change and the global impact of our actions. Environmental policies have become key issues in recent elections, with Democratic candidates much more likely to support a range of environmental protections. The Clinton-Gore administration set aside large tracts of open land from development, adopted tough new standards for emissions and for air and water quality, and approached issues of environment and climate change as a global issue. George W. Bush began his administration, in contrast, by refusing to sign the Kyoto Protocols, a worldwide treaty aimed at reversing global warming by reducing the production of greenhouse gases, and by moving to open the Arctic National Wildlife Refuge to oil drilling.

In this excerpt from his influential book, Something New under the Sun, *historian J. R. McNeill argues that the environmental changes brought about by humankind are ultimately more significant than any other aspect of twentieth-century history. Even more than the other authors in this section, McNeill focuses on the global challenges of the twenty-first century. In a "total system of global society and environment," what role can a single nation—*

even one as powerful as the United States—play? Can the United States's wealth insulate it from ecological catastrophe?

Environmental change on earth is as old as the planet itself, about four billion years. Our genus, *Homo,* has altered earthly environments throughout our career, about four million years. But there has never been anything like the 20th century.

Asteroids and volcanoes, among other astronomical and geological forces, have probably produced more radical environmental changes than we have yet witnessed in our time. But humanity has not. This is the first time in human history that we have altered ecosystems with such intensity, on such scale and with such speed. It is one of the few times in the earth's history to see changes of this scope and pace. Albert Einstein famously refused to "believe that God plays dice with the world." But in the 20th century, humankind has begun to play dice with the planet, without knowing all the rules of the game.

The human race, without intending anything of the sort, has undertaken a gigantic uncontrolled experiment on the earth. In time, I think, this will appear as the most important aspect of 20th-century history, more so than World War II, the communist enterprise, the rise of mass literacy, the spread of democracy, or the growing emancipation of women. To see just how prodigal and peculiar this century was, it helps to adopt long perspectives of the deeper past.

In environmental history, the 20th century qualifies as a peculiar century because of the screeching acceleration of so many processes that bring ecological change. Most of these processes are not new; we have cut timber, mined ores, generated wastes, grown crops, and hunted animals for a long time. In modern times we have generally done more of these things than ever before, and since 1945, in most cases, far more. Although there are a few kinds of environmental change that are genuinely new in the 20th century, such as human-induced thinning of the ozone layer, for the most part the ecological peculiarity of the 20th century is a matter of scale and intensity.

Sometimes differences in quantity can become differences in quality. So it was with 20th-century environmental change. The scale and intensity of changes were so great that matters that for millennia were local concerns became global. One example is air pollution. Since people first harnessed fire half a million years ago, they have polluted air locally. Mediterranean lead smelting in Roman times even polluted air in the Arctic. But lately, air pollution has grown so comprehensive and large-scale that it affects the fundamentals of global atmospheric chemistry.

Beyond that, in natural systems as in human affairs, there are thresholds and so-called nonlinear effects. In the 1930s, Adolf Hitler's Germany acquired Austria, the Sudetenland, and the rest of Czechoslovakia without provoking much practical response. When in September 1939 Hitler tried to add Poland, he got a six-year war that ruined him, his movement, and (temporarily) Germany. Unknowingly—although he was aware of the risk—he crossed a threshold and provoked a nonlinear effect. Similarly, water temperature in the tropical Atlantic can grow warmer and warmer without generating any hurricanes. But once that water passes 26° Celsius, it begins to promote hurricanes; a threshold passed, a switch was thrown, simply by an incremental increase. The environmental history of the 20th century is different from that of time past not merely because ecological changes were greater and faster, but also because increased intensities threw some switches. For example, incremental increases in fishing effort brought total collapse in some oceanic fisheries. The cumulation of many increased intensities may throw some grand switches, producing very basic changes on the earth. No one knows, and no one will know until it starts to happen—if then. . . .

In 1930 the American physicist and Nobel Prize–winner Robert Millikan (1868–1953) said that there was no risk that humanity could do real harm to anything so gigantic as the earth. In the same year the American chemical engineer Thomas Midgley invented chlorofluorocarbons, the chemicals responsible for thinning the stratospheric ozone layer. Millikan, although certainly a man "of talents," did not understand what was brewing. What Machiavelli said of affairs of state is doubly true of affairs of global ecology and society. It is nearly impossible to see what is happening until it is inconveniently late to do much about it.

It is impossible to know whether humankind has entered a genuine ecological crisis. It is clear enough that our current ways are ecologically unsustainable, but we cannot know for how long we may yet sustain them, or what might happen if we do. In any case, human history since the dawn of agriculture is replete with unsustainable societies, some of which vanished but many of which changed their ways and survived. They changed not to sustainability but to some new and different kind of unsustainability. Perhaps we can, as it were, pile one unsustainable regime upon another indefinitely, making adjustments large and small but avoiding collapse, as China did during its "3,000 years of unsustainable development." Imperial China, for all its apparent conservatism, was . . . adopting new food crops, new technologies, shifting its trade relations with its neighbors, constantly adapting—and surviving several crises. However, unsustainable society on the global scale may be another matter entirely, and what China did for millennia the whole world perhaps cannot do for long. If so, then collapse looms, as prophets of the ecological apocalypse so often warn. Perhaps the transition from our current unsustainable regime to another would be horribly wrenching and a fate to be avoided—or at least delayed—at all costs, as beneficiaries of the status quo so regularly claim. We cannot know for sure, and by the time we do know, it will be far too late to do much about it.

The future, even the fairly near future, is not merely unknowable; it is inherently uncertain. Some scenarios are more likely than others, no doubt, but nothing is fixed. Indeed, the future is more volatile than ever before: a greater number of radically different possibilities exist because technology has grown so influential, because ideas spread so rapidly, and because reproductive behavior—usually a variable that changes at a glacial pace—is in rapid flux. Moreover, all these variables are probably more tightly interactive than at most times in the past, so the total system of global society and environment is more uncertain, more chaotic, than ever.

All that said, the probability is that sharp adjustments will be required to avoid straitened circumstances. Many of the ecological buffers—open land, unused water, unpolluted spaces—that helped societies weather difficult times in the past are now gone. The most difficult passages will probably (or better put, least improbably) involve shortage of clean fresh water, the myriad effects of warmer climate, and of reduced bio-diversity.

While one cannot say with any confidence what forms an ecological crunch might take, when it might happen, or how severe it might be, it is easier to predict who will have the worst of it. The poor and powerless cannot shield themselves from ecological problems today, nor will they be able to in the future. The wealthy and powerful in the past have normally had the wherewithal to insulate themselves from the effects of pollution, soil erosion, or fishery collapse. Only in a very severe crunch are they likely to face heavy costs. Of course, just who is rich and who is poor is subject to change: consider South Koreans, who in 1960 were on average poorer than Ghanaians, but by the 1990s were among the world's richer populations. This very fact inspires great efforts, individual and collective, to escape poverty and weakness, which efforts often aggravate ecological problems. South Koreans after 1960 paid dearly for their economic miracle, suffering from noxious urban air, toxic industrial effluent in the rivers, and many other disagreeable conditions. But now they are in a much better position than Ghanaians to weather serious ecological dislocations—because they are much richer.

If one accepts the notion that there is a significant chance that more serious ecological problems lie ahead, then, bearing Machiavelli in mind, it is prudent to address the prospect sooner rather than later. My interpretation of modern history suggests that the most sensible things to do are to hasten the arrival of a new, cleaner energy regime and to hasten the demographic transition toward lower mortality and fertility. The former implies concentrated scientific and engineering work, and probably interventions in the marketplace that encourage early retirement of existing energy infrastructures and faster diffusion of new ones. The latter implies furthering the formal education of girls and women in poor countries, because poor countries are where the demographic transition is incomplete, and because female education is the strongest determinant of fertility. There may be other desirable initiatives, such as converting the masses to some new creed of ecological restraint or coaxing rulers into considering time horizons longer than the next election or coup. These are more difficult and less practical, precisely because they are more fundamental.

From the Persian Gulf War to 9/11/2001: Confronting a New World Order

George C. Herring

When the Cold War came to an end, millions of Americans reached the conclusion, perhaps understandably, that foreign policy issues no longer would dominate American political discussion and decision making. For fifty years, the bipolar vision of the Cold War world had shaped American foreign policy. Now the situation was dramatically different. What criteria would the country use for determining its policies toward other nations? Would the United States maintain its military presence in Europe? Was a large military still necessary? In cases of civil strife, starvation, or ethnic rivalry, by what standards would the United States define its response? Was self-interest the key? But how was self-interest defined? Did morality matter? But who defined what was morally correct in disputes between warring ethnic factions?

There was only a decade between the end of the Cold War and the terrorist attacks that precipitated the war in Afghanistan. That decade, as George Herring demonstrates in his analysis of post–Cold War foreign policy, was far from peaceful, and the foreign policy issues facing the United States were far from easy. What is the logic behind American foreign policy since the terrorist attacks of September 11, 2001? Does it demonstrate continuity with previous approaches, or dramatic change? Herring points to unintended consequences from U.S. interventions and foreign policy decisions. What are the key unintended consequences that shape current foreign relations? What does the emergence of non-state actors mean for U.S. foreign policy? Was the world more stable at the height of the Cold War?

For a fleeting moment in the early 1990s, peace and world order seemed within reach. The end of the Cold War and the subsequent collapse of the Soviet Union removed the major cause of international tension for the past half century and eased, if they did not eliminate altogether, the dreadful threat of a nuclear holocaust. The emergence of democracies and market economies in the former Soviet satellites, Latin America, and even in South Africa offered the hope of a new age of freedom and prosperity. The victory in the 1991 Persian Gulf War of a powerful allied coalition, headed by the United States and working under the aegis of the United Nations, seemed to hail the triumph of Woodrow Wilson's dreams of collective security where peace would be maintained and aggression repelled by international collaboration. In the aftermath of the Gulf War, President George Bush proclaimed the birth of a new world order under American leadership. State Department official Frances Fukayama went farther, exulting in the "end of history," the absolute triumph of capitalism and democracy over fascism and communism and the promise of a just and peaceful world made up of stable and prosperous democracies in which geopolitics would be a thing of the past.

It did not take long for such prophecies to be exposed as at best wishful thinking, at worst, absolute folly. The Cold War had imposed a crude form of order on inherently unstable regions of the world, and its end unleashed powerful forces that had been held in check for years. Especially in Central Europe, the Middle East, and Central Asia, national loyalties gave way to explosive ethnic rivalries and secessionist movements. Most prominent were the brutal wars between Serbs, Croats, and Muslims in the former Yugoslavia and the conflict between Sunni and Shiite Muslims and Kurds in the Middle East, but the *New York Times* counted in early 1993 forty-eight such conflicts scattered across the globe. "Get ready for fifty new countries in the world in the next fifty years," a pessimistic New York Senator Daniel P. Moynihan admonished, most of them "born in bloodshed." Wilson's ideal of self-determination seemed to have returned with a vengeance, threatening to tear the world apart rather than bring it together.

Other commentators predicted even more gloomy scenarios. Some warned that the Cold War struggle between East and West would give way to a new conflict between North and South, between the haves and have-nots of the world, "the West and the rest." Runaway population growth in the developing countries portended a possibly disastrous drain on already scarce resources, enormous environmental crises that could afflict the entire globe, and the rampant spread of crime, disease, and war. Some commentators warned that international migration would be the greatest problem of the twenty-first century and foresaw an assault on the borders of developed countries through massive emigration. Others predicted that the anarchy already gripping Africa would spread across the globe, the chaos in less-developed countries eventually contaminating the developed ones. Although such predictions appeared unnecessarily pessimistic and even reflected a false nostalgia for the "order" of the Cold War, it seemed clear that the end of history was not in view. Conflict and disorder would characterize the post–Cold War era.

The position of the United States in the new world order was paradoxical. During the 1990s, America enjoyed a preponderance of power unprecedented in world history. Its economy was 40 percent larger than that of the second ranked nation, its defense spending six times that of the next six nations combined. Because of its wealth and security, it had unrivaled freedom of action. Ironically, however, it seemed less threatened by and had less to gain from the world and therefore was less disposed to act. The "central paradox of unipolarity," according to political scientist Stephen Walt, was that the United States "enjoys enormous influence but has little idea what to do with its power or even how much effort it should expend."[1] These peculiar conditions caused an always fickle American public to lose interest in the world. Both reflecting and shaping public opinion, the media drastically reduced its coverage of developments abroad, and Congress slashed the foreign affairs budget.

Not surprisingly, the United States responded uncertainly to the new world order. Its contours were fuzzy at best, and Americans lacked any sort of blueprint for dealing with it. The absence of an obvious threat to national security removed any compelling inducement to take the lead in solving world problems. Americans recognized that there could be no return to isolationism in a world shrunken by technology and bound by economic interdependence, but after forty years of international commitment and massive Cold War expenditures they yearned for normalcy and relief from the burdens of leadership. As in the aftermath of World Wars I and II, they preferred to focus on domestic problems, and support for foreign policy ventures waned. Bitter memories of the Vietnam debacle

---

1. Stephen Walt, "Two Cheers for Clinton," *Foreign Affairs* (March/April 2000), 64–65.

haunted the nation for a quarter century after the event, adding yet another restraint against global involvement.

The halting response of the Bush administration to the new order it had once hailed foreshadowed the difficulties of the post–Cold War era. If the administration looked to the future and reassessed America's global role, it did not reach any firm conclusions or confront in any fundamental way such urgent issues as world population growth and the environment. After its forceful leadership in the Persian Gulf War, it did little to address longer-range but still pressing problems in the Middle East. Its response to a mounting crisis in Bosnia in the Balkans suggested its hesitancy. Despite warnings from some quarters of a new holocaust and its own bold rhetoric, it did nothing to halt Serbia's "ethnic cleansing." "Where is it written that the United States is the military policeman of the world?" State Department spokesperson Margaret Tutwiler asked. "We don't have a dog in that fight," her boss, Secretary of State James Baker, curtly proclaimed. In his last days in office, President Bush authorized a humanitarian rescue mission in Somalia, sending troops to prevent rivalries among local warlords from causing mass starvation. But the administration appears never to have decided whether it was really committed to the new world order under American leadership that its rhetoric claimed, or, because of domestic constraints, it preferred retrenchment and retreat.

Even more than its predecessor, the administration of William Jefferson Clinton found adjustment to the new world order vexing and difficult. Clinton's aides had run their campaign on the slogan "It's the economy, stupid," and in many ways the new administration seemed more attuned to the new era, making clear its preeminent concern with domestic issues. Having spent his entire political career in state politics, the former governor of Arkansas was plainly less interested in, experienced with, and informed on foreign policy. At least at the outset, he appeared to hope that this team could hold the world at bay while he implemented an ambitious domestic agenda. His few campaign pronouncements on foreign policy seemed to promise more forthright U.S. leadership and a more active role in volatile areas such as Bosnia. Yet his foreign policy advisers came mainly out of the liberal Democratic mold—burned by Vietnam, nervous about unilateral interventions, and committed to working through the United Nations and persuading allies to share the burden of world leadership.

Clinton and his advisers quickly discovered the perils of the new world order. The administration was deeply committed to promoting domestic prosperity through the expansion of foreign trade. The president himself was an unabashed enthusiast for globalization, seeing trade as a primary means to promote free markets, democracy, and eventually peace and prosperity. "Since we don't have geopolitics any more," one Clinton adviser pronounced, "trade is the name of the game," and in embassies across the world diplomats turned their attention to economics. Clinton cashed in all his political chips to secure congressional passage in 1993 of the North American Free Trade Agreement (NAFTA). He also vigorously promoted the Asia-Pacific Economic Community as a modern economic NATO and the General Agreement on Tariffs and Trade (GATT). The Clinton administration eventually presided over the greatest expansion of foreign trade in U.S. history, helping to fuel the nation's most prolonged period of economic growth.

Promoting trade expansion raised all sorts of problems, however. Whatever its long-term benefits, it also brought huge short-term tradeoffs and costly job displacement. NAFTA contributed significantly to the prosperity of the 1990s, but it also eliminated more jobs in the nation's already moribund manufacturing sector. In the new world economy, promotion of trade often involved unprecedented and unwelcome intrusion into the internal politics of other nations, and globalization, which to many peoples meant Americanization, provoked a growing backlash abroad.

Committed to promoting human rights as well as expanding trade, the administration quickly discovered that the two might not always be compatible. Exports were increasingly important to domestic prosperity. In the most prominent cases, the administration therefore bowed to expediency without totally abandoning its principles. Two hundred thousand Americans were employed in the sale of some $9 billion worth of exports to China, for example, yet that country's abuses of human rights offended the sensibilities of pressure groups and some Washington officials. After much agonizing, the administration normalized trade relations with China, accepting more or less at face value that nation's promises to improve its human rights record.

Clinton also quickly discovered the painful truth that in foreign policy American presidents do not have to seek out trouble, it finds them. The administration was even less surefooted on the increasingly difficult questions posed by world order: peacekeeping and what came to be called humanitarian intervention to prevent human suffering in areas torn by ethnic conflict. In the campaign and in its early days in office, it sounded at least mildly interventionist. Clinton himself scored Bush's inaction on Bosnia and affirmed that "no national security issue is more urgent than securing democracy's triumph around the world." National security adviser Anthony Lake coined vague phrases such as "enlargement of democracy" and "pragmatic Wilsonianism" to describe an approach that hinted at greater activism. Before the end of its first year in office, however, the administration had beaten a hasty retreat. Unable to persuade its European allies to lift an arms embargo against Bosnia, it would go no further than sanction harmless NATO air strikes to defend embattled UN peacekeepers. It went along with expansion of the UN role in Somalia, but when eighteen American GIs were killed in bloody fighting in Mogadishu on October 3, 1993, it immediately scaled back the U.S. role and promised an alarmed Congress and public that Americans would be out of Somalia in six months. A week later, closer to home, and even more humiliating, a shipload of American soldiers and technicians dispatched to troubled Haiti as part of a larger effort to unseat a cruel military government turned back in the face of armed and jeering mobs on the docks at Port-au-Prince.

While rampant instability wracked the globe, the administration developed guidelines for intervention some critics denounced as "self-containment." The United States would only intervene in cases where international security was gravely threatened, a major disaster required urgent relief, or gross violation of human rights had occurred. Other nations would have to share the costs, but American troops would participate only under U.S. command. In response to proliferating UN commitments, the administration in May 1994 spelled out a total of seventeen even more restrictive guidelines for support of these peacekeeping operations. Making clear in the aftermath of Somalia its lack of enthusiasm for UN enterprises, it vowed that it would commit troops only in cases where vital U.S. interests were threatened. Congress would have to approve the mission, and funds would have to be available. Such missions must have a clearly stated objective, a reasonable assurance of success, and a strategy for completing the job. They must pose a major threat to international peace and security or gross violations of human rights. At the same time, Clinton urged the UN to scale back its own ambitions: "If the

American people are to say yes to UN peacekeeping, the United Nations must know when to say no." Parodying John F. Kennedy's inaugural address, critics claimed that in a troubled world Clinton's United States was willing to "pay only some prices, fight only some foes, and bear only some burdens in the defense of freedom." It was all but admitting to potential adversaries that when the going got tough, the United States would go home.

Not surprisingly in view of these guidelines, the United States and the rest of the world looked the other way in 1994 when ethnic rivalries in Rwanda in central Africa produced "the fastest, most efficient killing spree of the twentieth century."[2] While the world did nothing, the revenge-bent Hutu tribe murdered an estimated 800,000 rival Tutsis, some of them with machetes. It was a case where even a relatively small intervention might have made a difference, but the world chose to do nothing. Paralyzed by memories of Somalia and Haiti, the Clinton administration did not even discuss the possibility of intervention. As if to insulate themselves from guilt and responsibility, U.S. officials refused even to use what was called "the g-word," resorting instead to the euphemistic "acts of genocide" to describe what was happening. Their main concern was to get Americans out of Rwanda as quickly as possible.

The Clinton administration began to shift gears in the fall of 1994. After months of soul-searching, imposition of sanctions that hurt victims more than oppressors, and warnings that were ignored, it used the threat of a full-scale invasion of Haiti to remove a brutal military dictatorship and restore to power the erratic—but elected—president Jean-Bertrand Aristide. Clinton justified the move as necessary to "restore democracy" and, more pragmatically, to prevent a massive flight of Haitians to U.S. shores. To the shock of some observers, this time U.S. troops met a warm reception from Haitians, and after tense negotiations the military government agreed to leave. The intervention did not bring democracy to Haiti or lead to a new policy toward humanitarian interventions, but it probably spared some suffering in that troubled land and helped burnish a badly damaged Clinton image.

After years of hesitation, the United States in the summer of 1995 finally made its weight felt in the former Yugoslavia. The Serb mas-

---

2. Samantha Power, "Bystanders to Genocide: Why the United States Let the Rwanda Tragedy Happen," *The Atlantic Monthly* (September 2001), 84.

sacre of a Bosnian Muslim enclave in the village of Srebrenica, after three years of shelling with artillery, aroused anger throughout the world. In the United States a new coalition of liberal and neoconservative interventionists began to push the administration to do something. Humiliated by Somalia and Haiti, three years of inaction in the Balkans, and the blatant defiance of Serb leader Slobodan Milosevic, the president himself was moved to exclaim: "The United States cannot be a punching bag in the world anymore." In August 1995, with full U.S. backing, NATO began intensive bombing of Serb positions using the most modern technology and eventually taking out Milosevic's communications center. This decisive action forced the warring parties to the conference table in Dayton, Ohio, where U.S. diplomat Richard Holbrooke brokered "an imperfect peace to a very imperfect part of the world after an unusually cruel war."[3] Clinton followed by sending U.S. troops to participate in a Bosnian peace-keeping mission, to cover his political flanks limiting the commitment to twelve months (subsequently extended).

Clinton was reelected by a substantial margin in 1996, but foreign policy played an insignificant role in the campaign, and the election victory did not bring a firmer hand to the foreign policy wheel. In the absence of any clear threat and with the nation more prosperous than at any time in the twentieth century, there was little incentive for engagement. The result on the part of the American public was a form of "apathetic internationalism." A band of highly nationalist Republicans in Congress flaunted their hostility toward the outside world, boasting of not having passports. Republican House of Representatives leader Richard Armey of Texas even claimed that he did not need to go to Europe because he had already been there once. Network news focused increasingly on entertainment and trivia and further slashed its foreign coverage. After January 1998, moreover, Clinton was increasingly crippled when he first denied and then, faced with incontrovertible evidence, admitted, an affair with a young White House intern, Monica Lewinsky, prompting his foes in Congress to initiate impeachment proceedings.

While the administration was preoccupied with its own survival, the Balkans continued to seethe with violence. This time it was in Kosovo, the most volatile part of a most explosive region, with its own long

---

3. David Halberstam, *War in a Time of Peace: Bush, Clinton, and the Generals* (New York, 2001), 358.

and bitter history of ethnic hatreds. Populated predominantly by Kosovar Albanians who were also Muslims, Kosovo was viewed as sacred turf by Serbs. Left out of the Dayton discussions, it exploded in crisis shortly after. In 1997, the Kosovars began to form a Kosovo Liberation Army (KLA) to win their independence and launched guerrilla warfare against local Serbs. The Serbs struck back with a vengeance, burning villages and murdering those Kosovars they could get their hands on. At first, they moved slowly—"a village a day keeps NATO away"—was their sardonic slogan. Their intent was nevertheless unmistakable, and the results devastating. An especially bloody massacre at the village of Racak in late 1998 again provoked cries for international action.

Once more in early 1999, a reluctant administration was moved to do something. The Senate finally acquitted Clinton of impeachment charges in February 1999, freeing his hands. Still smarting from Vietnam and uneager to get entangled in a Balkans quagmire, the military stubbornly resisted calls for intervention. Within and outside the government, however, pressures grew. Some advocates of intervention compared the Serbs' ethnic cleansing to the Holocaust. The new Secretary of State, Madeline Albright, who had grown up in pre–World War II Czechoslovakia and viewed the United States as the "indispensable nation," fervently warned of another Munich and ridiculed the military's caution. Why do you insist on having all those modern forces if you are unwilling to use them, she once asked General Colin Powell. So important was her role that when war came it was known as "Madeline's War."

In March 1999, the administration finally went to war over Kosovo. If memories of World War II helped push the United States to do something, more recent and haunting memories of Vietnam dictated the way it fought. Clinton also hoped to repeat the Bosnian experience where a modest effort had forced Milosevic to the conference table. To assuage fears in Congress and among the European allies, the administration relied exclusively on airpower. In what turned out to be a huge miscalculation, the president even publicly vowed: "I do not intend to put ground troops into Kosovo to fight a war."

As is so often the case, the war turned out to be much more complicated than had been anticipated. The bombing was implemented gradually and the Serbs stubbornly withstood it, evoking memories of the Vietnam quagmire. As the war dragged on, Clinton and the NATO allies drastically escalated the bombing. It was a new kind of high-tech war, virtual war it seemed, fought by professional forces, waged from 50,000 feet, with no sacrifice required of the American people and little intrusion upon their lives. Using precision-guided weapons, U.S. aircraft attacked Serb airfields and ground forces and eventually Belgrade itself, causing troops to mutiny and political opposition to form. To increase the pressure, Clinton finally reneged on his promise not to use ground forces, warning that "all options are on the table." Milosevic conceded in June.

The war was fought clumsily—a "textbook case of how not to fight a war," in the words of two experts—and the results were less than satisfactory.[4] The always clever Milosesvic used the onset of war to drive the Albanians out of Kosovo, inflicting a great deal more human suffering and creating a million new refugees. A war fought to minimize Western military losses resulted in the death of an estimated 10,000 people, many of them civilians. As the war ended, the KLA seized the opportunity to drive the remaining Serbs out of Kosovo, ensuring further conflict. The war at least resolved the immediate problem without providing a long-term solution, and ultimately contributed to the removal of Milosevic.

The Clinton legacy in foreign policy was at best mixed. The administration took some measures in association with Russia to reduce the huge nuclear inventories left over from the Cold War, and opened a dialogue with North Korea to check its nuclear threat. It used American influence with some short-term success to try to settle long-standing disputes in Northern Ireland and the Middle East. It normalized relations with Vietnam, ending more than twenty-five years after the fall of Saigon the crippling and vindictive postwar sanctions imposed by loser on winner. It enlarged NATO to include some former Soviet satellites, rewrote the longstanding treaty with Japan, and sent warships in 1996 to defuse a dangerous crisis in the Taiwan Straits.

In the 1990s, as in the 1920s, the business of America was business, and in foreign policy as in domestic policy the administration's major claim to success was in the realm of economics. A timely bailout loan of $25 billion helped avert economic disaster in Mexico in 1995, and by keeping American markets open even at the cost of a huge short-term balance of payments deficit the administration helped contain

---

4. Ivo Daalder and Michael O'Hanlon, *Winning Ugly: NATO's War to Save Kosovo* (Washington, D.C., 2000).

the impact of the Asian economic meltdown of 1997. During the Clinton years, the United States concluded more than 300 trade agreements. While the United States prospered, however, there was little sign that globalization was producing the democratizing and stabilizing results its enthusiasts claimed. On the contrary, by the end of the century it had provoked a strong backlash from labor unions and some liberals at home and from leaders of the developing nations who on the one hand resented the competitive edge it gave the rich nations and on the other feared reformers from outside who sought to impose labor and environmental standards. Warfare in the streets of Seattle during the WTO meeting in November 1999 symbolized a clash that was likely to grow in the years ahead.

In the realm of international politics, as Garry Wills observed, Clinton was a "foreign policy minimalist, doing as little as possible as late as possible in place after place."[5] The administration responded perfunctorily to terrorist attacks on American interests in Saudi Arabia, New York City, and Africa, and on a U.S. Navy destroyer in Yemen, a sign of things to come unheeded. Clinton later felt compelled to apologize for U.S. inaction in Rwanda. He eventually employed U.S. power along with NATO to impose an uneasy peace on the Balkans, but the long-term prospects were still highly uncertain and the human cost of the delay was enormous. The administration never developed a doctrine for humanitarian intervention or a broader rationale for the use of American power in the new world order.

Without firm presidential leadership, the nation drifted. The mood in the aftermath of the Cold War was one of triumphalism and smug, insular complacency. In a 1998 poll, Americans did not even list foreign policy among the nation's major problems. On college campuses, the teaching of foreign languages declined drastically, and area studies gave way to modeling and game theory. Support for military spending, foreign aid, and the United Nations plummeted, and there was little backing for the use of ground troops abroad. Foreign policy played no more than a peripheral part in the 2000 campaign. Self-indulgent Americans reveled in their prosperity, a minority of the world's population recklessly consuming a huge proportion of the world's resources.

Not surprisingly, the new administration of George W. Bush took

---

5. Garry Wills, "The Clinton Principle," *New York Times Magazine* (January 19, 1997), 44.

its cues from this national mood. In the campaign and in his early statements, Bush went to some lengths to distance himself from the Wilsonian idealism he claimed had stamped Clinton's approach, and he expressed skepticism about humanitarian intervention and what he scornfully called nation-building. "We don't need to have the 82nd Airborne escorting kids to kindergarten" in the Balkans, future national security adviser Condoleeza Rice affirmed. The president and an experienced foreign policy team, headed by Secretary of State Colin Powell and Secretary of Defense Donald Rumsfeld, took an avowedly "realist" approach, stressing that they would focus on "what's in the best interests of the United States." Powell openly preached American exceptionalism. "Other systems do not work," he stated shortly after taking office. "We are going to show a vision to the world of the value system of America."

The new administration's early actions confirmed its unilateralist rhetoric. Bush and his advisers attached top priority to building the missile defense system that had been talked about in the Reagan years, a project that violated old treaties with the former Soviet Union and promised invulnerability to threats from abroad. They seemed to go out of their way in the first months to thumb their collective noses at international institutions and the rest of the world. Bush pointedly spurned the Middle East process Clinton had sought to nurture. Without any consultation, the administration withdrew from the 1997 Kyoto Protocol on global warming and suspended talks with North Korea aimed at stopping the development of long-range missiles. State Department spokesman Richard Haas labeled the new approach "'a la carte multilateralism.' We'll look at each agreement and make a decision, rather than come out with a broad-based approach." Others were not so sure. Critics at home denounced the administration's go-it-alone tendency as a new isolationism. "The Ugly American has a face again," a leading German periodical complained.

Terrorist attacks on New York City's World Trade Center and the Pentagon on the morning of September 11, 2001, causing massive destruction and the loss of more than 3,000 lives, wrought sudden and dramatic changes in U.S. attitudes and policies. For the first time since 1814, the United States itself had come under stunning, brutal attack, and in one fiery moment the complacency and sense of security that had marked the 1990s was swept aside in a surge of fear and anger. An already slowing economy was pushed into what economists finally admitted was a recession. Americans suddenly felt vulnerable. Patriotism was fashionable again. Speaking with a single voice for one of the few times since the 1964 Gulf of Tonkin Resolution, Congress granted the president sweeping authorization to use American military forces in a new war against international terrorism. In its shock and grief, a nation that since the Vietnam era had been chronically suspicious of government suddenly turned to government to avenge the appalling loss of life, repair the damage, heal an ailing economy, and provide security against future attacks. Just as Pearl Harbor had wiped away bitter recollections of America's participation in World War I, so also September 11, 2001, seemed to work a sea change in the mindset shaped by Vietnam and Watergate.

A government that had been unfocused and floundering suddenly found purpose, and in the immediate aftermath of the attacks, the Bush administration with universal popular support launched an all-out war against international terrorism. The terrorist attacks "hit the reset button" on foreign policy, Powell remarked, and those officials who had only recently shunned collaboration with other nations now under his leadership began cobbling together an unwieldy and fragile international coalition composed of old allies such as Britain and France, old enemies such as Russia, China, and even for a time Iran, and pariah states such as Pakistan to attack on a variety of fronts a new kind of foe and its sources of support. Responding slowly and deliberately, the administration also mobilized military forces to strike at the immediate source of the threat, terrorist mastermind Osama Bin Laden and the fundamentalist Islamic Taliban regime that sheltered him in Afghanistan. In the parlance of the old west, Bush promised to bring in "the evil one" dead or alive.

The first phase of the war confounded many experts. Because of geography and fierce tribal rivalries, Afghanistan was an extremely difficult place to fight, historically a graveyard of great power ambitions. Pessimists warned glumly of another quagmire, a "Vietnam with snow," one called it. The administration nevertheless conducted the war cautiously and with some skill. Applying on a much larger scale the new model of warfare first employed in the Balkans, the United States relied on airpower and Afghan proxies to eliminate the despised and surprisingly weak Taliban regime and Bin Laden's Al Qaeda fighters. Small numbers of U.S. Special Forces were dispatched to Afghanistan to work with rival tribes and direct bombs to their targets, and the United States unleashed a furious air attack on

suspected Taliban and Al Qaeda bases. In less than four months, the
Taliban was on the run and Al Qaeda had been crippled, although
Taliban leader Mullah Omar and Bin Laden remained at large. Only
one U.S. casualty was incurred from enemy fire.

The apparent success of the first phase of the war on terrorism
raised as many questions as it answered. Could victory in Afghanistan
be assured while the enemy leadership remained at large? Would the
bombing of Afghanistan cripple terrorism and increase worldwide
respect for U.S. credibility, as administration officials claimed, or intensify terrorism and replace the sympathy that welled up after September 11 with a more traditional fear and resentment? Could the
United States and its allies assist new Afghan leaders in rebuilding a
society devastated by more than two decades of brutal war? Where
would the next front be in a war Bush repeatedly described as global
and warned would last for years? Would the United States go after
Saddam Hussein's Iraq, as some Defense Department officials insistently urged, eliminating a menacing leader with weapons of mass destruction and finishing the job left undone by the president's father
more than ten years earlier? Or should it return to Somalia, the scene
of the 1993 debacle, whose continuing anarchy offered another possible haven for Bin Ladin–type terrorists? Or in association with its allies would an administration that now at least talked in internationalist terms mount a major effort to resolve the issues that helped
Islamic terrorism flourish, the still volatile dispute between Israel and
the Palestinians, the failure of leading Arab states such as Egypt and
Saudi Arabia to address the needs of their people and their willingness to tolerate militant Islamic groups inside their borders in order
to keep their own power intact? Each war causes as many problems as
it solves, and it was still far from clear what unintended consequences
would result from this war and whether they would be even more
threatening and intractable.

In a still larger sense, Americans inside and outside government
were sharply divided as to the role the nation should play in the
post–9/11/01 world. Some unabashedly spoke of a New American
Empire in which the United States would maintain a preponderance
of power and use that power as it saw fit without worrying about allies
or treaties to eliminate leaders or nations who threatened its "bene-
volent hegemony." Other more cautious internationalists advocated
continuing to work with allies in a pragmatic and less confrontational
manner to deal with international threats and resolve problems such

as the Israel–Palestine dispute that nurtured such threats. Still other self-styled "realists" proposed a less costly approach, abandoning the futile and expensive quest for preponderance, leaving to regional powers primary responsibility for dealing with threats in their areas with the United States serving as an offshore balancer. Looking beyond the dangers posed by terrorist organizations and so-called rogue states, liberals proposed an effort as coordinated and sustained as the war on terrorism to address urgent international problems such as runaway population growth, the environment, and growing disparities of wealth and thereby promote international order and peace.

Beneath all these issues lurked the question of how much American attitudes toward the world had really changed. While the smell of death still hung over Ground Zero in New York City, pundits claimed that September 11 had changed the United States forever, but as the war against terrorism went on this was less than clear. This war required no sacrifices of Americans. The administration did not even propose steps to reduce the dependence on foreign energy sources that restricted its leverage in the Middle East. Indeed, in the aftermath of September 11 purchases of gas-guzzling vehicles increased. Thus, it seemed entirely possible that if the war against terrorism appeared to be succeeding the United States might well revert to the selfish consumption and smug complacency that had characterized its outlook before the collapse of the World Trade Center.

The one thing that seemed certain was that the world would remain torn by conflict. The *New York Times* calculated in January 2002 that 59 of the world's 193 nations were involved in serious disputes ranging from separatist-ethnic violence to political discord and drug trafficking. A world already divided by conflict within and among states was rendered even more complex by the emergence of powerful non-state actors ranging from global financial markets to multinational corporations to Bin Laden's sinister worldwide network. The claims of its enthusiasts to the contrary notwithstanding, the onrushing process of globalization without the development of accompanying political and civic institutions to curb its abuses seemed as likely to produce conflict and disorder as peace and stability, thus creating an even more dangerous world. Because of its enormous power and the pervasiveness of its culture, America of necessity would remain central to this new world order, loved and hated, admired and feared. Americans have traditionally believed that what is good for them is good for the world, and hence many reacted with shock to the events of September 11, 2001. Other peoples do not agree. Because of its wealth and power they resent the United States for its own sake. They see its culture and its vast military power, put on full display in the war in Afghanistan, as possible threats to their way of life. The same people who on occasion may crave American support and protection may also hate the United States for its self-appointed role as world policeman and for imposing its culture. "America is the 800 pound gorilla that they must appease as they lie down with it uneasily each night," Ronald Steel has written. "Great powers may be admired or emulated, but they are rarely loved."[6] Whatever else it may have done, September 11 made clear—even though it was perpetrated by non-state actors—that history had not ended: geopolitics was alive and well. For Americans, like it or not, foreign policy was central to their survival. It was more urgent than ever to try to better understand the more complex and potentially more dangerous world in which they live and to develop a constructive role.

---

6. *New York Times,* October 15, 2000.

In the Ruins of the Future: Reflections on Terror and Loss in the Shadow of September (2001)

Don DeLillo

On the morning of September 11, 2001, terrorists hijacked two civilian airliners and crashed first one, then the other, into the twin towers of New York's World Trade Center. Another plane slammed into the Pentagon. A fourth exploded in a Pennsylvania field, brought down, seemingly, by brave passengers who refused to let it become another weapon of destruction.

In the days and weeks that followed, America grieved. These are novelist Don DeLillo's "reflections on terror and loss in the shadow of September."

1

In the past decade the surge of capital markets has dominated discourse and shaped global consciousness. Multinational corporations have come to seem more vital and influential than governments. The dramatic climb of the Dow and the speed of the Internet summoned us all to live permanently in the future, in the utopian glow of cyber-capital, because there is no memory there and this is where markets are uncontrolled and investment potential has no limit.

All this changed on September 11. Today, again, the world narrative belongs to terrorists. But the primary target of the men who attacked the Pentagon and the World Trade Center was not the global economy. It is America that drew their fury. It is the high gloss of our modernity. It is the thrust of our technology. It is our perceived godlessness. It is the blunt force of our foreign policy. It is the power of American culture to penetrate every wall, home, life, and mind.

Terror's response is a narrative that has been developing over years, only now becoming inescapable. It is *our* lives and minds that are occupied now. This catastrophic event changes the way we think and act, moment to moment, week to week, for unknown weeks and months to come, and steely years. Our world, parts of our world, have crumbled into theirs, which means we are living in a place of danger and rage.

The protesters in Genoa, Prague, Seattle, and other cities want to decelerate the global momentum that seemed to be driving unmindfully toward a landscape of consumer-robots and social instability, with the chance of self-determination probably diminishing for most people in most countries. Whatever acts of violence marked the protests, most of the men and women involved tend to be a moderating influence, trying to slow things down, even things out, hold off the white-hot future.

The terrorists of September 11 want to bring back the past.

2

Our tradition of free expression and our justice system's provisions for the rights of the accused can only seem an offense to men bent on suicidal terror.

We are rich, privileged, and strong, but they are willing to die. This is the edge they have, the fire of aggrieved belief. We live in a wide world, routinely filled with exchange of every sort, an open circuit of work, talk, family, and expressible feeling. The terrorist, planted in a Florida town, pushing his supermarket cart, nodding to his neighbor, lives in a far narrower format. This is his edge, his strength. Plots reduce the world. He builds a plot around his anger and our indifference. He lives a certain kind of apartness, hard and tight. This is not the self-watcher, the soft white dangling boy who shoots someone to keep from disappearing into himself. The terrorist shares a secret and a self. At a certain point the and his brothers may begin to feel less motivated by politics and personal hatred than by brotherhood itself. They share the codes and protocols of their mission here and something deeper as well, a vision of judgment and devastation.

Does the sight of a woman pushing a stroller soften the man to her humanity and vulnerability, and her child's as well, and all the people he is here to kill?

This is his edge, that he does not see her. Years here, waiting, taking flying lessons, making the routine gestures of community and home, the credit card, the bank account, the post-office box. All tactical, linked, layered. He knows who we are and what we mean in the world—an idea, a righteous fever in the brain. But there is no defenseless human at the end of his gaze.

The sense of disarticulation we hear in the term "Us and Them" has never been so striking, at either end.

We can tell ourselves that whatever we've done to inspire bitterness, distrust, and rancor, it was not so damnable as to bring this day down on our heads. But there is no logic in apocalypse. They have gone beyond the bounds of passionate payback. This is heaven and hell, a sense of armed martyrdom as the surpassing drama of human experience.

He pledges his submission to God and meditates on the blood to come.

3

The Bush Administration was feeling a nostalgia for the Cold War. This is over now. Many things are over. The narrative ends in the rubble, and it is left to us to create the counter-narrative.

There are a hundred thousand stories crisscrossing New York, Washington, and the world. Where we were, whom we know, what we've seen or heard. There are the doctors' appointments that saved lives, the cell phones that were used to report the hijackings. Stories generating others and people running north out of the rumbling smoke and ash. Men running in suits and ties, women who'd lost their shoes, cops running from the skydive of all that towering steel.

People running for their lives are part of the story that is left to us.

There are stories of heroism and encounters with dread. There are stories that carry around their edges the luminous ring of coincidence, fate, or premonition. They take us beyond the hard numbers of dead and missing and give us a glimpse of elevated being. For a hundred who are arbitrarily dead, we need to find one person saved by a flash of forewarning. There are configurations that chill and awe us both. Two women on two planes; best of friends who die together and apart. Tower 1 and Tower 2. What desolate epic tragedy might bear the weight of such juxtapostion? But we can also ask what symmetry, bleak and touching both, takes one friend, spares the other's grief?

The brother of one of the women worked in one of the towers. He managed to escape.

In Union Square Park, about two miles north of the attack site, the improvised memorials are another part of our response. The flags, flower beds, and votive candles, the lamppost hung with paper airplanes, the passages from the Koran and the Bible, the letters and poems, the cardboard John Wayne, the children's drawings of the Twin Towers, the hand-painted signs for Free Hugs, Free Back Rubs, the graffiti of love and peace on the tall equestrian statue.

There are many photographs of missing persons, some accompanied by hopeful lists of identifying features. (Man with panther tattoo, upper right arm.) There is the saxophonist, playing softly. There is the sculptured flag of rippling copper and aluminum, six feet long, with two young people still attending to the finer details of the piece.

Then there are the visitors to the park. The artifacts on display represent the confluence of a number of cultural tides, patriotic and multidevotional and retro hippie. The visitors move quietly in the floating aromas of candlewax, roses, and bus fumes. There are many people this mild evening, and in their voices, manner, clothing, and in the color of their skin they recapitulate the mix we see in the photocopied faces of the lost.

For the next fifty years, people who were not in the area when the attacks occurred will claim to have been there. In time, some of them will believe it. Others will claim to have lost friends or relatives, although they did not.

This is also the counter-narrative, a shadow history of false memories and imagined loss.

The Internet is a counter-narrative, shaped in part by rumor, fantasy and mystical reverberation.

The cell phones, the lost shoes, the handkerchiefs mashed in the faces of running men and women. The box cutters and credit cards. The paper that came streaming out of the towers and drifted across the river to Brooklyn back yards: status reports, résumés, insurance forms. Sheets of paper driven into concrete, according to witnesses. Paper slicing into truck tires, fixed there.

These are among the smaller objects and more marginal stories in the sifted ruins of the day. We need them, even the common tools of the terrorists, to set against the massive spectacle that continues to seem unmanageable, too powerful a thing to set into our frame of practiced response.

4

Ash was spattering the windows. Karen was half dressed, grabbing the kids and trying to put on some clothes and talking with her husband and scooping things to take out to the corridor, and they looked at her, twin girls, as if she had fourteen heads.

They stayed in the corridor for a while, thinking there might be secondary explosions. They waited, and began to feel safer, and went back to the apartment.

At the next impact, Marc knew in the sheerest second before the shock wave broadsided their building that it was a second plane, impossible, striking the second tower. Their building was two blocks away, and he'd thought the first crash was an accident.

They went back to the hallway, where others began to gather, fifteen or twenty people.

Karen ran back for a cell phone, a cordless phone, a charger, water, sweaters, snacks for the kids, and then made a quick dash to the bedroom for her wedding ring.

From the window she saw people running in the street, others locked shoulder to shoulder, immobilized, with debris coming down on them. People were trampled, struck by falling objects, and there was ash and paper everywhere, paper whipping through the air, no sign of light or sky.

Cell phones were down. They talked on the cordless, receiving information measured out in eyedrops. They were convinced that the situation outside was far more grave than it was here.

Smoke began to enter the corridor.

Then the first tower fell. She thought it was a bomb. When she talked to someone on the phone and found out what had happened, she felt a surreal relief. Bombs and missiles were not falling everywhere in the city. It was not all-out war, at least not yet.

Marc was in the apartment getting chairs for the older people, for the woman who'd had hip surgery. When he heard the first low drumming rumble, he stood in a strange dead calm and said, "Something is happening." It sounded exactly like what it was, a tall tower collapsing.

The windows were surfaced with ash now, blacked out completely, and he wondered what was out there. What remained to be seen and did he want to see it?

They all moved into the stairwell, behind a fire door, but smoke kept coming in. It was gritty ash, and they were eating it.

He ran back inside, grabbing towels off the racks and washcloths out of drawers and drenching them in the sink, and filling his bicycle water bottles, and grabbing the kids' underwear.

He thought the crush of buildings was the thing to fear most. This is what would kill them.

Karen was on the phone, talking to a friend in the district attorney's office, about half a mile to the north. She was pleading for help. She begged, pleaded, and hung up. For the next hour a detective kept calling with advice and encouragement.

Marc came back out to the corridor. I think we *might* die, he told himself, hedging his sense of what would happen next.

The detective told Karen to stay where they were.

When the second tower fell, my heart fell with it. I called Marc, who is my nephew, on his cordless. I couldn't stop thinking of the size of the towers and the meager distance between those buildings and his. He answered, we talked. I have no memory of the conversation except for his final remark, slightly urgent, concerning someone on the other line, who might be sending help.

Smoke was seeping out of the elevator shaft now. Karen was saying goodbye to her father in Oregon. Not hello-goodbye. But goodbye-I-think-we-are-going-to-die. She thought smoke would be the thing that did it.

People sat on chairs along the walls. They chatted about practical matters. They sang songs with the kids. The kids in the group were cooperative because the adults were damn scared.

There was an improvised rescue in progress. Karen's friend and a colleague made their way down from Centre Street, turning up with two policemen they'd enlisted en route. They had dust masks and a destination, and they searched every floor for others who might be stranded in the building.

They came out into a world of ash and near night. There was no one else to be seen now on the street. Gray ash covering the cars and pavement, ash falling in large flakes, paper still drifting down, discarded shoes, strollers, briefcases. The members of the group were masked and toweled, children in adults' arms, moving east and then north on Nassau Street, trying not to look around, only what's immediate, one step and then another, all closely focused, a pregnant woman, a newborn, a dog.

They were covered in ash when they reached shelter at Pace University, where there was food and water, and kind and able staff members, and a gas-leak scare, and more running people.

Workers began pouring water on the group. *Stay wet, stay wet.* This was the theme of the first half hour.

Later a line began to form along the food counter.

Someone said, "I don't want cheese on that."

Someone said, "I like it better not so cooked."

Not so incongruous really, just people alive and hungry, beginning to be themselves again.

5

Technology is our fate, our truth. It is what we mean when we call ourselves the only superpower on the planet. The materials and methods we devise make it possible for us to claim our future. We don't have to depend on God or the prophets or other astonishments. We are the astonishment. The miracle is what we ourselves produce, the system and networks that change the way we live and think.

But whatever great skeins of technology lie ahead, ever more complex, connective, precise, micro-fractional, the future has yielded, for now, to medieval expedience, to the old slow furies of cutthroat religion.

Kill the enemy and pluck out his heart.

If others in less scientifically advanced cultures were able to share, wanted to share, some of the blessings of our technology, without a threat to their faith or traditions, would they need to rely on a God in whose name they kill the innocent? Would they need to invent a God who rewards violence against the innocent with a promise of "infinite paradise," in the words of a handwritten letter found in the luggage of one of the hijackers?

For all those who may want what we've got, there are all those who do not. These are the men who have fashioned a morality of destruction. They want what they used to have before the waves of Western influence. They surely see themselves as the elect of God whether or not they follow the central precepts of Islam. It is the presumptive right of those who choose violence and death to speak directly to God. They will kill and then die. Or they will die first, in the cockpit, in clean shoes, according to instructions in the letter.

Six days after the attacks, the territory below Canal Street is hedged with barricades. There are few civilians in the street. Police at some checkpoints, troops in camouflage gear at others, wearing gas masks, and a pair of state troopers in conversation, and ten burly men striding east in hard hats, work pants, and NYPD jackets. A shop owner tries to talk a cop into letting him enter his place of business. He is a small elderly man with a Jewish accent, but there is no relief today. Garbage bags are everywhere in high broad stacks. The area is bedraggled and third-worldish, with an air of permanent emergency, everything surfaced in ash.

It is possible to pass through some checkpoints, detour around others. At Chambers Street I look south through the links of the National Rent-A-Fence barrier. There stands the smoky remnant of filigree that marks the last tall thing, the last sign in the mire of wreckage that there were towers here that dominated the skyline for over a quarter of a century.

Ten days later and a lot closer, I stand at another barrier with a group of people, looking directly into the strands of openwork facade. It is almost too close. It is almost Roman, I-beams for stonework, but not nearly so salvageable. Many here describe the scene to others on cell phones.

"Oh my god I'm standing here," says the man next to me.

The World Trade towers were not only an emblem of advanced technology but a justification, in a sense, for technology's irresistible will to realize in solid form whatever becomes theoretically allowable. Once defined, every limit must be reached. The tactful sheathing of the towers was intended to reduce the direct threat of such straight-edge enormity, a giantism that eased over the years into something a little more familiar and comfortable, even dependable in a way.

Now a small group of men have literally altered our skyline. We have fallen back in time and space. It is their technology that marks our moments, the small lethal devices, the remote-control detonators they fashion out of radios, or the larger technology they borrow from us, passenger jets that become manned missiles.

Maybe this is a grim subtext of their enterprise. They see something innately destructive in the nature of technology. It brings death to their customs and beliefs. Use it as what it is, a thing that kills.

6

Nearly eleven years ago, during the engagement in the Persian Gulf, people had trouble separating the war from coverage of the war. After the first euphoric days, coverage became limited. The rush of watching all that eerie green night vision footage, shot from fighter jets in combat, had been so intense that it became hard to honor the fact that the war was still going on, untelevised. A layer of consciousness had been stripped away. People shuffled around, muttering. They were lonely for their war.

The events of September 11 were covered unstintingly. There was no confusion of roles on TV. The raw event was one thing, the coverage another. The event dominated the medium. It was bright and totalizing, and some of us said it was unreal. When we say a thing is unreal, we mean it is too real, a phenomenon so unaccountable and yet so bound to the power of objective fact that we can't tilt it to the slant of our perceptions. First the planes struck the towers. After a time it became possible for us to absorb this, barely. But when the towers fell. When the rolling smoke began moving downward, floor to floor. This was so vast and terrible that it was outside imagining even as it happened. We could not catch up to it. But it was real, punishingly so, an expression of the physics of structural limits and a void in one's soul, and there was the huge antenna falling out of the sky, straight down, blunt end first, like an arrow moving backward in time.

The event itself has no purchase on the mercies of analogy or simile. We have to take the shock and horror as it is. But living language is not diminished. The writer wants to understand what this day has done to us. Is it too soon? We seem pressed for time, all of us. Time is scarcer now. There is a sense of compression, plans made hurriedly, time forced and distorted. But language is inseparable from the world that provokes it. The writer begins in the towers, trying to imagine the moment, desperately. Before politics, before history and religion, there is the primal terror. People falling from the towers hand in hand. This is part of the counter-narrative, hands and spirits joining, human beauty in the crush of meshed steel.

In its desertion of every basis for comparison, the event asserts its singularity. There is something empty in the sky. The writer tries to give memory, tenderness, and meaning to all that howling space.

7

We like to think America invented the future. We are comfortable with the future, intimate with it. But there are disturbances now, in large and small ways, a chain of reconsiderations. Where we live, how we travel, what we think about when we look at our children. For many people, the event has changed the grain of the most routine moment.

We may find that the ruin of the towers is implicit in other things. The new PalmPilot at fingertip's reach, the stretch limousine parked outside the hotel, the midtown skyscraper under construction, carrying the name of a major investment bank—all haunted in a way by what has happened, less assured in their authority, in the prerogatives they offer.

There is fear of other kinds of terrorism, the prospect that biological and chemical weapons will contaminate the air we breathe and the water we drink. There wasn't much concern about this after earlier terrorist acts. This time we are trying to name the future, not in our normally hopeful way but guided by dread.

What has already happened is sufficient to affect the air around us, psychologically. We are all breathing the fumes of lower Manhattan, where traces of the dead are everywhere, in the soft breeze off the river, on rooftops and windows, in our hair and on our clothes.

Think of a future in which the components of a microchip are the size of atoms. The devices that pace our lives will operate from the smart quantum spaces of pure information. Now think of people in countless thousands massing in anger and vowing revenge. Enlarged photos of martyrs and holy men dangle from balconies, and the largest images are those of a terrorist leader.

Two forces in the world, past and future. With the end of Communism, the ideas and principles of modern democracy were seen clearly to prevail, whatever the inequalities of the system itself. This is still the case. But now there is a global theocratic state, unboundaried and floating and so obsolete it must depend on suicidal fervor to gain its aims.

Ideas evolve and de-evolve, and history is turned on end.

8

On Friday of the first week a long series of vehicles moves slowly west on Canal Street. Dump trucks, flatbeds, sanitation sweepers. There are giant earthmovers making a tremendous revving sound. A scant number of pedestrians, some in dust masks, others just standing, watching, the indigenous people, clinging to walls and doorways, unaccustomed to traffic that doesn't bring buyers and sellers, goods and cash. The fire rescue car and state police cruiser, the staccato sirens of a line of police vans. Cops stand at the sawhorse barriers, trying to clear the way. Ambulances, cherry pickers, a fleet of Con Ed trucks, all this clamor moving south a few blocks ahead, into the cloud of sand and ash.

One month earlier I'd taken the same walk, early evening, among crowds of people, the panethnic swarm of shoppers, merchants, residents and passersby, with a few tourists as well, and the man at the curbstone doing acupoint massage, and the dreadlocked kid riding his bike on the sidewalk. This was the spirit of Canal Street, the old jostle and stir unchanged for many decades and bearing no sign of SoHo just above, with its restaurants and artists' lofts, or TriBeCa below, rich in architectural textures. Here were hardware bargains, car stereos, foam rubber and industrial plastics, the tattoo parlor and the pizza parlor.

Then I saw the woman on the prayer rug. I'd just turned the corner, heading south to meet some friends, and there she was, young and slender, in a silk headscarf. It was time for sunset prayer, and she was kneeling, upper body pitched toward the edge of the rug. She was partly concealed by a couple of vendors' carts, and no one seemed much to notice her. I think there was another woman seated on a folding chair near the curbstone. The figure on the rug faced east, which meant most immediately a storefront just a foot and a half from her tipped head but more distantly and pertinently toward Mecca, of course, the holiest city of Islam.

Some prayer rugs include a *mihrab* in their design, an arched element representing the prayer niche in a mosque that indicates the direction of Mecca. The only locational guide the young woman needed was the Manhattan grid.

I looked at her in prayer and it was clearer to me than ever, the daily sweeping taken-for-granted greatness of New York. The city will accommodate every language, ritual, belief, and opinion. In the rolls of the dead of September 11, all these vital differences were surrendered to the impact and flash. The bodies themselves are missing in large numbers. For the survivors, more grief. But the dead are their own nation and race and identity, young or old, devout or unbelieving—a union of souls. During the *hadj,* the annual pilgrimage to Mecca, the faithful must eliminate every sign of status, income, and nationality, the men wearing identical strips of seamless white cloth, the women with covered heads, all recalling in prayer their fellowship with the dead.

Allahu akbar. God is great.

Suggestions for Further Reading

On the origins and course of the Cold War consult W. I. Cohen, *America in the Age of Soviet Power, 1945–1991* (1993); and J. Gaddis, *The United States and the Origins of the Cold War* (1972), *The Long Peace* (1987), *Russia, the Soviet Union, and the United States* (2d ed., 1990), and *We Now Know: Rethinking Cold War History* (1997). For a more critical view, see T. J. McCormick, *America's Half Century: United States Foreign Policy in the Cold War* (1992). Other explanations include J. Gormly, *The Collapse of the Grand Alliance, 1945–1948* (1987); F. Harbutt, *The Iron Curtain: Churchill, America and the Origins of the Cold War* (1986); M. Hogan, *The Marshall Plan* (1987); W. LaFeber, *America, Russia, and the Cold War* (6th ed., 1991); V. Mastny, *Russia's Road to the Cold War* (1979); R. Pollard, *Economic Security and the Origins of the Cold War* (1985); H. Thomas, *Armed Truce: The Beginnings of the Cold War* (1987); and L. Wittner, *American Intervention in Greece, 1943–1949* (1982). Of particular interest are M. Leffler's prizewinning *A Preponderance of Power* (1992); R. Maddox's controversial *From War to Cold War: The Education of Harry S. Truman* (1988); T. Paterson's revisionist *Meeting the Communist Threat: Truman to Reagan* (1988), and *On Every Front: The Making and Unmaking of the Cold War* (1992). For a variety of interpretations of the Korean War see W. Stueck, *The Korean War: An International History* (1995); R. Appleman, *Disaster in Korea* (1992); R. Foot, *A Substitute for Victory* (1990); J. Halliday and B. Cumings, *Korea: The Unknown War* (1989); and C. A. MacDonald, *Korea* (1987). Also see S. G. Zhang, *Deterrence and Strategic Culture: Chinese–American Confrontations, 1949–1958* (1993). For the thinking of key American cold warriors, see W. Isaacson and E. Thomas, *The Wise Men* (1986); R. Messer, *The End of an Alliance (1982);* W. D. Miscamble, *George F. Kennan and the Making of American Foreign Policy* (1992); H. Schaffer,

Chester Bowles: New Dealer in the Cold War (1993); M. Schaller, *Douglas MacArthur* (1989); and S. Talbott, *The Master of the Game: Paul Nitze and the Nuclear Peace* (1988). Compare with H. W. Brands, *The Devil We Knew: Americans and the Cold War* (1993), and J. S. Walter, *Henry A. Wallace and American Foreign Policy* (1976). In G. F. Kennan, *At a Century's Ending: Reflections, 1982–1995* (1996), Kennan now argues that it was not so much the Soviet Union as the weapons race itself that needed to be contained. Excellent introductions to the meaning of McCarthyism are M. Barson, *Better Dead Than Red! A Nostalgic Look at the Golden Years of Russiophobia, Red-Baiting, and Other Commie Madness* (1992); and R. Fried, *Nightmare in Red* (1990). Fascinating full-scale accounts are J. Kovel, *Red Hunting in the Promised Land* (1994); D. Oshinsky, *A Conspiracy So Immense: The World of Joe McCarthy* (1983); and T. Reeves, *The Life and Times of Joe McCarthy* (1982). Evidence that spies were passing information from the U.S. to the U.S.S.R. appears in J. E. Haynes and H. Klehr, *Venona: Decoding Soviet Espionage in America* (1999). Clashing interpretations appear in D. Caute's biting *The Great Fear: The Anti-Communist Purge under Truman and Eisenhower* (1978); R. Griffith, *The Politics of Fear: Joseph R. McCarthy and the Senate* (rev. ed., 1987); E. Latham, *The Communist Controversy in Washington: From the New Deal to McCarthy* (1966); M. Rogin, *The Intellectuals and McCarthy: The Radical Specter* (1967); and A. Theoharis's revisionist *Seeds of Repression: Harry S. Truman and the Origins of McCarthyism* (1971). Also see H. Teres, *Renewing the Left: Politics, Imagination, and New York Intellectuals* (1996), and R. P. Newman, *Owen Lattimore and the Loss of China* (1992), as well as A. Bloom's enlightening *The New York Intellectuals: The Rise and Decline of the Anti-Stalinist Left* (1987); H. Brick, *Daniel Bell and the Decline of Intellectual Radicalism* (1986); W. Graebner, *The Age of Doubt: American Thought and Culture in the 1940s* (1991); R. Pells, *The Liberal Mind in a Conservative Age* (1985); M. McAuliffe, *Crisis on the Left: Cold War Politics and American Liberals* (1978); G. May, *Un-American Activities: The Trials of William Remington* (1994); L. May, ed., *Recasting America: Culture and Politics in the Age of Cold War* (1989); E. Schrecker, *No Ivory Tower: McCarthyism and the Universities* (1986); A. Theoharis and J. S. Cox, *The Boss: J. Edgar Hoover and the Great American Inquisition* (1988); and the provocative S. Whitfield, *The Culture of the Cold War* (1987).

The major developments in postwar American life are superbly described in J. Patterson, *Grand Expectations: Postwar America, 1945–1974*

(1996), and analyzed in S. Frazer and G. Gerstle, eds., *The Rise and Fall of the New Deal Order, 1930–1980* (1989), and A. Wolfe, ed., *America at Century's End* (1991). Key surveys of American social movements and politics are J. M. Blum, *Years of Discord* (1991); W. H. Chafe, *The Unfinished Journey: America since World War II* (4th ed., 1999); D. Chidester, *Patterns of Power: Religion and Politics in American Culture* (1988); J. Diggins, *The Proud Decades: America in War and Peace* (1988); D. Halberstam, *The Fifties* (1993); M. Jezer, *The Dark Ages* (1982); W. O'Neill, *American High: The Years of Confidence* (1988); and G. Reichard's analytical *Politics as Usual* (1988). On the Truman presidency, see A. Dunar, *The Truman Scandals and the Politics of Morality* (1984); A. Hamby, *Beyond the New Deal: Harry S. Truman and American Liberalism* (1973); M. Lacey, ed., *The Truman Presidency* (1989); D. McCullough's vivid *Truman* (1992); and W. Pemberton, *Harry S. Truman: Fair Dealer and Cold Warrior* (1989). For Eisenhower: P. Brendon, *Ike* (1986); R. Burk, *Dwight D. Eisenhower: Hero & Politician* (1986); C. Pach, Jr., and E. Richardson, *The Presidency of Dwight D. Eisenhower* (1991); and W. B. Pickett, *Dwight David Eisenhower and American Power* (1995). S. Dockrill, *Eisenhower's New-Look National Security Policy, 1953–61* (1996) is a valuable analysis. Also see J. Broadwater, *Adlai Stevenson and American Politics: The Odyssey of a Cold War Liberal* (1994); S. Gillon's perceptive *The ADA and American Liberalism*(1987); G. E. Elliot, *Senator Alan Bible and the Politics of the New West* (1994); N. C. Rae, *The Decline and Fall of the Liberal Republicans* (1989). Also see E. T. May, *Homeward Bound: American Families in the Cold War Era* (1988); B. Schulman, *From Cotton Belt to Sunbelt* (1991); and E. Taylor's challenging *Prime-Time Families: Television Culture in Postwar America* (1989). The Kennedy administration is best aproached in I. Bernstein's highly sympathetic *Promises Kept: John F. Kennedy's New Frontier* (1991); T. Brown, *JFK: History of an Image* (1988); D. Burner, *John F. Kennedy and a New Generation* (1988); J. Giglio, *The Presidency of John F. Kennedy* (1991); and T. Reeves's critical *A Question of Character: A Life of John F. Kennedy* (1991). The range of interpretations appears in K. Thompson, ed., *The Kennedy Presidency* (1985). For foreign policies, see M. Beschloss, *The Crisis Years* (1991). G. Posner, *Case Closed: Lee Harvey Oswald and the Assassination of JFK* (1993) is the most recent salvo fired in this continuing battle of theories. V. Bornet, *The Presidency of Lyndon B. Johnson* (1983); P. Conkin, *Big Daddy from the Pedernales: Lyndon Baines Johnson* (1986); R. Dallek's balanced *Lone Star Rising: Lyndon Johnson and His Times* (1990); R. Divine, ed., *The Johnson*

Years (1987); and D. Kearns's insightful *Lyndon Johnson and the American Dream* (1976) examine LBJ's life and presidency. Also see E. Berkowitz and K. McQuaid, *Creating the Welfare State* (1992); W. Leuchtenburg, *In the Shadow of FDR: From Harry Truman to Ronald Reagan* (1983); A. Matusow, *The Unraveling of America: A History of Liberalism in the 1960s* (1984); G. O'Brien, *Dream Time* (1988); and J. R. Williamson, *Federal Antitrust Policy during the Kennedy–Johnson Years* (1995). The growth of conservatism is analyzed in J. Andrew III, *The Other Side of the Sixties: Young Americans for Freedom and the Rise of Conservative Politics* (1997); M. C. Brennan, *Turning Right in the Sixties: The Conservative Capture of the GOP* (1995); D. T. Carter, *The Politics of Rage: George Wallace, the Origins of the New Conservatism, and the Transformation of American Politics* (1995); R. A. Goldberg, *Barry Goldwater* (1995); and R. Klatch, *Generation Divided: The New Left, the New Right, and the 1960s* (1999). Conflicting assessments of 1960s' liberalism appear in Charles Murray, *Losing Ground* (1984); J. Patterson, *America's Struggle against Poverty* (1981); L. Meade, *Beyond Entitlement* (1986); J. Schwarz, *America's Hidden Success* (1983); and D. Zarefsky, *President Johnson's War on Poverty: Rhetoric and History* (1986).

The literature on the African American freedom struggle continues to multiply rapidly, with insightful reminiscences and reflections as well as thoughtful monographs. An updated and comprehensive overview of the movement is H. Sitkoff, *The Struggle for Black Equality, 1954–1992* (rev. ed., 1993). Also see H. Hill and J. Jones, eds., *Race in America: The Struggle for Equality* (1993); R. King, *Civil Rights and the Idea of Freedom* (1992); R. Weisbrot, *Freedom Bound* (1991); and the photographic essay by D. Lyon, *Memories of the Southern Civil Rights Movement* (1992). On King, see T. Branch's dramatic *Parting the Waters, America in the King Years, 1954–63* (1988); J. Colaiaco, *Martin Luther King, Jr.: Apostle of Militant Nonviolence* (1993); D. Garrow, *Bearing the Cross* (1986); J. Ralph, Jr., *Northern Protest: Martin Luther King, Chicago, and the Civil Rights Movement* (1993); and the essays in P. Albert and R. Hoffman, eds., *We Shall Overcome: Martin Luther King, Jr., and the Black Freedom Struggle* (1990). Key monographs include E. Burner, *And Gently He Shall Lead Them: Robert Parris Moses and Civil Rights in Mississippi* (1994); R. Bush, *We Are Not What We Seem: Black Nationalism and Class Struggle in the American Century* (1999); C. Carson, *In Struggle: SNCC and the Black Awakening of the 1960s* (1981); W. H. Chafe, *Civilities and Civil Rights: Greensboro, North Carolina, and the Black Struggle for Freedom* (1980); D. Chappell, *Inside Agitators: White Southerners in the Civil Rights Movement* (1994); E. C. Clark, *The Schoolhouse Door: Segregation's Last Stand at the University of Alabama* (1993); J. Dittmer, *Local People: The Struggle for Civil Rights in Mississippi* (1994); Gerald Horne, *Fire This Time: The Watts Uprising and the 1960s* (1996); R. Norrell, *Reaping the Whirlwind: The Civil Rights Movement in Tuskegee* (1985); M. Stern, *Calculating Vision: Kennedy, Johnson, and Civil Rights* (1992); M. Tushnet, *Making Civil Rights Law: Thurgood Marshall and the Supreme Court, 1936–1961* (1994); T. Tyson, *Radio Free Dixie: Robert F. Williams and the Roots of Black Power* (1999); and W. L. Van Deburg's illuminating *New Day in Babylon: The Black Power Movement and American Culture* (1992). Major surveys include D. Goldfield, *Black, White, and Southern: Race Relations and Southern Culture* (1990), and S. Lawson, *Running for Freedom: Civil Rights and Black Politics in America since 1941* (1991). On the women of the freedom struggle, see M. King, *Freedom Song: A Personal Story of the 1960s Civil Rights Movement* (1987); K. Mills, *This Little Light of Mine: The Life of Fannie Lou Hamer* (1993); and G. Wade-Gayles, *Pushed Back to Strength: A Black Woman's Journey Home* (1993). Vital first-person accounts are R. Abernathy, *And The Walls Came Tumbling Down* (1989); E. Brown, *A Taste of Power: A Black Woman's Story* (1992); J. Forman, *The Making of Black Revolutionaries* (1972); D. Hilliard and L. Cole, *This Side of Glory: The Autobiography of David Hilliard and the Story of the Black Panther Party* (1993); and J. Lewis and M. D'Orso, *Walking with the Wind: A Memoir of the Movement* (1998). In addition to Malcom X, as told to Alex Haley, *The Autobiography of Malcolm X* (1965), see the essays on Spike Lee's feature film *Malcolm X* by N. Painter and G. Horne in the *American Historical Review* (April 1993). On the Chicano/a movement, see I. Garcia, *Chicanismo: The Forging of a Militant Ethos Among Mexican–Americans* (1997); M. V. Marin, *Social Protest in an Urban Bario: A Study of the Chicano Movement, 1966–1972* (1991); B. Marquez, *LULAC* (1993); and C. Muñoz, Jr., *Youth, Identity, Power: The Chicano Movement* (rev. ed., 2000). Native American movements are discussed in P. Smith and R. A. Warrior, *Like a Hurricane: The Indian Movement from Alcatraz to Wounded Knee* (1996).

The rebirth of feminism is analyzed in W. H. Chafe, *The Paradox of Change* (1991) and *Women and Equality* (1977); F. Davis, *Moving the Mountain: The Women's Movement in America since 1960* (rev. ed. 1999); R. Duplessis and A. Snitow, eds., *The Feminist Memoir Project: Voices from*

Women's Liberation (1998); A. Echols, *Daring to Be Bad: Radical Feminism in America, 1965–1975* (1989); S. Evans's controversial and important *Personal Politics: The Roots of Women's Liberation in the Civil Rights Movement and the New Left* (1978); R. Gatlin, *American Women since 1945* (1987); C. Harrison's carefully argued *On Account of Sex: The Politics of Women's Issues, 1945–1968* (1988); D. Horowitz, *Betty Friedan and the Making of the Feminine Mystique: The American Left, the Cold War, and Modern Feminism* (1998); E. Klein, *Gender Politics* (1984); S. Lynn, *Progressive Women in Conservative Times: Racial Justice, Peace, and Feminism, 1945 to the 1960s* (1992); and Ruth Rosen's impressive *The World Split Open: How the Modern Women's Movement Changed America* (2000). Useful works on abortion include L. Kaplan, *The Story of Jane: The Legendary Underground Feminist Abortion Service* (1995); K. Luker, *Abortion and the Politics of Motherhood* (1994); R. Petchesky, *Abortion and Women's Choice* (1984); and L. Reagan, *When Abortion Was a Crime: Women, Medicine, and the Law in the United States, 1867–1973* (1997). On *Roe v. Wade*, see D. Garrow, *Liberty and Sexuality: The Right to Privacy and the Making of Roe v. Wade* (1994). Analyses of the campaign for the Equal Rights Amendment include M. Berry, *Why the ERA Failed* (1986); J. Hoff-Wilson, *Rights of Passage: The Past and Future of the ERA* (1986); J. Mansbridge, *Why We Lost the ERA* (1986); and J. Sherron De Hart and D. Mathews, *The Equal Rights Amendment and the Politics of Cultural Conflict* (1988). Sexism and the color line is the subject of P. Cleage, *Deals with the Devil, and Other Reasons to Riot* (1993); P. Giddings, *When and Where I Enter: The Impact of Black Women on Race and Sex in America* (1984); and M. Wallace, *Black Macho and the Myth of the Superwoman* (1979). Supplement with E. DuBois and V. Ruiz, eds., *Unequal Sisters: A Multicultural Reader in Women's History* (1990). An indispensable fictional account of women in the African American freedom struggle is A. Walker, *Meridian* (1976). Useful studies of gender in postwar America include B. Bailey, *From Front Porch to Back Seat: Courtship in Twentieth-Century America* (1988); S. Coontz, *The Way We Never Were* (1992); S. J. Douglas; *Where the Girls Are: Growing Up Female with the Mass Media* (1994); E. T. May, *Homeward Bound: American Families in the Cold War Era* (1988); and the essays in J. Meyerowitz, ed., *Not June Cleaver: Women and Gender in Postwar America, 1945–1960* (1994). On the importance of gender as a historical subject, consult "Gender Histories and Heresies," special issue of *Radical History Review* 52 (Winter 1992). Histories of sexuality and struggles over sex are addressed in B. Bailey, *Sex in the Heartland*

(1999); J. D'Emilio and E. Freedman, *Intimate Matters: A History of Sexuality in America* (1988); L. Faderman, *Odd Girls and Twilight Lovers: A History of Lesbian Life in Twentieth-Century America* (1994); J. Heidenry, *What Wild Ecstasy: The Rise and Fall of the Sexual Revolution* (1997); J. Howard, *Men Like That: A Southern Queer History* (1999); and J. Moran, *Teaching Sex: The Shaping of Adolescence in the Twentieth Century* (2000). Works on Gay Rights movements include D. Clendinen and A. Nagourney, *Out for Good: The Struggle to Build a Gay Rights Movement in America* (1999), and M. Cruikshank, *The Gay and Lesbian Liberation Movement* (1992).

The most useful histories of the United States intervention in Vietnam are E. Bergerud, *The Dynamics of Defeat* (1991); W. Gibbons, *The U.S. Government and the Vietnam War* (1986); G. Herring's forthright *America's Longest War* (2d ed., 1986); G. Hess's compelling *Vietnam and the United States* (1990); S. Karnow, *Vietnam* (rev. ed., 1991); G. Kolko, *Anatomy of a War: Vietnam, the United States, and the Modern Historical Experience* (1986); M. Lind, *Vietnam: The Necessary War* (1999); F. Logevall, *Choosing War: The Last Chance for Peace and the Escalation of War in Vietnam* (1999); R. Schulzinger, *A Time for War: The United States and Vietnam, 1941–1975* (1997); A. Short, *The Origins of the Vietnam War* (1989); and M. Young's revisionist *The Vietnam Wars* (1991). For the origins of American involvement see D. Anderson, *Trapped by Success* (1991); J. Arnold, *The First Domino* (1991); L. Gardner's insightful *Approaching Vietnam* (1988); D. Kaiser, *American Tragedy: Kennedy, Johnson, and the Origins of the Vietnam War* (2000); and A. Rotter, *The Path to Vietnam* (1987). The escalation of the war is explained by L. Berman, *Lyndon Johnson's War* (1989); L. Cable, *Unholy Grail* (1991); D. Shapley, *Promise and Power: The Life and Times of Robert McNamara* (1993); and B. Vandemark, *Into the Quagmire* (1991). Classic analyses still worth consulting are F. Fitzgerald, *Fire in the Lake: The Vietnamese and the Americans in Vietnam* (1972), and D. Halberstam, *The Best and the Brightest* (1972), on one side, and G. Lewy, *America in Vietnam* (1978), and N. Podhoretz, *Why We Were in Vietnam* (1982), on the other. Also see C. Appey, *Working Class War* (1992); A. Krepinevich, Jr., *The Army and Vietnam* (1986); T. Schoenbaum, *Waging Peace and War* (1988); and N. Sheehan, *A Bright Shining Lie: John Paul Vann and America in Vietnam* (1988). Helpful assessments of the lessons and legacies of the conflict include L. Baritz's intriguing *Backfire: A History of How American Culture Led Us into Vietnam and Made Us Fight the Way We Did* (1985); J. Hellman, *American Myth and the Legacy of Vietnam* (1986); J. Lembcke, *The Spitting Image: Myth, Memory, and the Legacy of Vietnam* (1998); D. Levy, *The Debate over Vietnam* (1991); T. J. Lomperis, *The War Everyone Lost—and Won* (1984); M. MacPherson, *Long Time Passing: Vietnam and the Haunted Generation* (1984); J. Rowe and R. Berg, eds., *The Vietnam War and American Culture* (1991) and R. Tombes, *Apocalypse Then: American Intellectuals and the Vietnam War, 1954–1975* (1998). The behavior and policies of the presidents are analyzed in D. L. Anderson, *Shadow on the White House: Presidents and the Vietnam War, 1945–1975* (1993); J. Arnold, *The First Domino* (1991); W. J. Duiker, *U.S. Containment Policy and the Conflict in Indochina* (1994); and L. Gardner's insightful *Approaching Vietnam* (1988). The escalation of the war is covered in R. Buzzanco, *Masters of War: Military Dissent and Politics in the Vietnam Era* (1996). Opposition to the war is analyzed in C. DeBenedetti and C. Chatfield, *An American Ordeal: The Antiwar Movement of the Vietnam Era* (1990); K. Heineman, *Campus Wars* (1993); A. Hunt, *The Turning Point: A History of Vietnam Veterans against the War* (1999); R. Jeffreys-Jones, *Peace Now! American Society and the Ending of the Vietnam War* (1999); R. Moser, *The New Winter Soldiers: GI and Veteran Dissent during the Vietnam Era* (1996); A. Swerdlow, *Women Strike for Peace: Traditional Motherhood and Radical Politics in the 1960s* (1993); C. R. Wyatt, *Paper Soldiers: The American Press and the Vietnam War* (1993); T. Wells, *The War Within* (1994); and N. Zaroulis and G. Sullivan, *Who Spoke Up? American Protests against the War in Vietnam* (1984). An important study is C. G. Appy, *Working-Class War: American Combat Soldiers in Vietnam* (1989).

Important overviews of "the Sixties" include D. Farber, *The Age of Gread Dreams* (1994), and M. Isserman and M. Kazin, *America Divided: The Civil War of the 1960s* (2000). A. Marwick, *The Sixties: Social and Cultural Transformation in Britain, France, Italy, and the United States, 1958–1974* (1998), offers an international, comparative perspective. On "the Movement," see *Takin' It to the Streets: A Sixties Reader* (1996), edited by A. Bloom and W. Breines; T. H. Anderson, *The Movement and the Sixties* (1995); W. Breines, *Community and Organization in the New Left, 1962–1968* (rev. ed., 1989); T. Gitlin, *The Sixties: Years of Hope, Days of Rage* (1987); T. Hayden, *Reunion* (1988); M. Isserman, *If I Had a Hammer . . . : The Death of the Old Left and the Birth of the New Left* (1987); J. Miller, *"Democracy Is in the Streets": From Port Huron to the*

Siege of Chicago (1987); and W. J. Rorabaugh, *Berkeley at War: The 1960s* (1989). Also see D. Dellinger, *From Yale to Jail: The Life Story of a Moral Dissenter* (1993); A. Jamison and R. Eyerman, *Seeds of the Sixties* (1994); C. Levitt, *Children of Privilege: Student Revolt in the Sixties* (1984); D. Rossinow, *The Politics of Authenticity: Liberalism, Christianity, and the New Left in America* (1998); L. Spigel and M. Curtin, eds., *The Revolution Wasn't Televised: Sixties Television and Social Conflict* (1997); D. Steigerwald, *The Sixties and the End of Modern America* (1995); and the scholarly collection, D. Farber, ed., *The 1960s: From Memory to History* (1994). A scathing look at the New Left and the protest movements is P. Collier and D. Horowitz, *Destructive Generation: Second Thoughts about the Sixties* (1989); a positive interpretation is W. H. Chafe, *Never Stop Running: Allard Lowenstein and the Struggle to Save American Liberalism* (1993). Fascinating accounts of the counterculture include S. Booth, *Dance with the Devil: The Rolling Stones and Their Times* (1984); P. Braunstein and M. Doyle, eds., *Imagine Nation: The American Counterculture of the 1960s and '70s* (2001); P. Coyote, *Sleeping Where I Fall: A Chronicle* (1999); M. Dickstein, *Gates of Eden: American Culture in the Sixties* (1977); T. Miller, *The '60s Communes: Hippies and Beyond* (1999); C. Perry, *The Haight-Ashbury* (1984); J. Stevens, *Storming Heaven: LSD and the American Dream* (1987); and J. Weiner, *Come Together: John Lennon in His Time* (1984). They should be supplemented with C. Reich, *The Greening of America* (1970); T. Roszak, *The Making of a Counter Culture* (1969); and P. Slater, *The Pursuit of Loneliness* (rev. ed., 1976). The year of shocks is analyzed by D. Farber, *Chicago '68* (1988); L. Gould, *1968: The Election That Changed America* (1993); C. Kaiser, *1968 in America* (1988); and I. Unger and D. Unger, *Turning Point: 1968* (1988). The years after are traced by B. Epstein, *Political Protest and Cultural Revolution: Nonviolent Direct Action in the 1970s and 1980s* (1991), and P. Carroll, *It Seemed Like Nothing Happened: America in the 1970s* (1990).

Important studies of the Nixon presidency and Watergate include S. Ambrose, *Nixon*, 3 vols. (1987–1991); S. Kutler, *The Wars of Watergate: The Last Crisis of the Nixon Presidency* (1990); K. McQuaid, *The Anxious Years: America in the Vietnam-Watergate Era* (1989); R. Morris, *Richard Milhous Nixon* (1990); H. Parmet, *Richard Nixon and His America* (1990); J. Schell, *Observing the Nixon Years* (1989); and T. Wicker, *One of Us* (1991). The turn to the right is analyzed by W. C. Berman, *America's Right Turn: From Nixon to Bush* (1994); S. Blumenthal, *The Rise of the Counter-Establishment* (1986); T. Edsall and M. Edsall, *Chain Reaction* (1991); T. Ferguson and J. Rogers, *Right Turn: The Decline of the Democrats and the Future of American Politics* (1986); J. D. Hunter, *Culture Wars: The Struggle to Define America* (1991); and D. Reinhard, *The Republican Right since 1945* (1983). Also see J. R. Greene, *The Limits of Power: The Nixon and Ford Administrations* (1992); B. Kaufman, *The Presidency of James Earl Carter, Jr.* (1993); and A. J. Reichley, *Conservatives in an Age of Change: The Nixon and Ford Administrations* (1981). Key questions are raised by P. Arnold, *Making the Managerial Presidency* (1986), and W. Grover, *The President as Prisoner: A Structural Critique of the Carter and Reagan Years* (1990). Contemporary interpretations of the Reagan and Bush administrations are S. Blumenthal, *Our Long National Daydream* (1988); P. Boyer, ed., *Reagan as President* (1990); C. Campbell and B. A. Rockman, eds., *The Bush Presidency: First Appraisals* (1991); L. Cannon, *President Reagan: A Role of a Lifetime* (1991); M. Duffy and D. Goodgame, *Marching in Place: The Status Quo Presidency of George Bush* (1992); L. Freedman and E. Karsh, *The Gulf Conflict 1990–1991* (1993); H. Johnson, *Sleepwalking through History: America in the Reagan Years* (1991); W. Niskanen, *Reaganomics* (1988); K. Phillips, *The Politics of Rich and Poor* (1990); M. Rogin, *Ronald Reagan the Movie, and Other Episodes in Political Demonology* (1987); M. Schaller, *Reckoning with Reagan* (1992); and J. K. White, *The New Politics of Old Values* (1988). Interesting journalistic accounts of politics in the 1990s include E. J. Dionne, *Why Americans Hate Politics* (1992); W. Greider, *Who Will Tell the People* (1992); K. A. Jamieson, *Dirty Politics* (1992); K. Phillips, *Boiling Point: Republicans, Democrats, and the Decline of Middle-Class Prosperity* (1993); and R. Teixeira, *The Disappearing American Voter* (1992). A valuable guide for researchers is W. Hixson, Jr., *Search for the American Right Wing: An Analysis of the Social Science Record, 1955–1987* (1994).

Looking toward the new century, racial and immigration matters are analyzed in J. Cockcroft, *Outlaws in the Promised Land: Mexican Immigrant Workers and America's Future* (1986); S. Cornell, *The Return of the Native: American Indian Political Resurgence* (1988); R. Daniels, *Coming to America* (1990); M. Davis, *Mexican Voices, American Dreams* (1990); M. C. Garcia, *Havana USA: Cuban Exiles and Cuban Americans in South Florida, 1959–1994* (1996); R. Farley and W. Allen, *The Color Line and the Quality of Life in America* (1987); L. Fuchs, *The American Kaleidoscope: Race, Ethnicity and the Civic Culture* (1990); L. Kessler, *Stubborn*

Twig: Three Generations in the Life of a Japanese American Family (1993); N. McCall, *Make Me Wanna Holler: A Young Black Man in America* (1994); P. MacDonald with T. Schwarz, *The Last Warrior* (1993); D. Reimers, *Still the Golden Door: The Third World Comes to America* (1985); P. J. Rutledge, *The Vietnamese Experience in America* (1992); L. Sigelman and S. Welch, *Black Americans' Views of Racial Inequality* (1991); R. Takaki, *A Different Mirror: A History of Multicultural America* (1993); S. Terkel, *Race: How Blacks and Whites Think and Feel about the American Obsession* (1992); and V. Yans-McLaughlin, ed., *Immigration Reconsidered: History, Sociology, and Politics* (1990). Class and the economy are treated in D. Bartlett and J. Steele, *America: What Went Wrong* (1992); B. Bluestone and B. Harrison, *The Deindustrialization of America* (1982); D. Ellwood, *Poor Support: Poverty in the American Family* (1988); C. Jencks, *Rethinking Social Policy: Race, Poverty, and the Underclass* (1992); F. Levy, *Dollars and Dreams: The Changing American Income Distribution* (1987); K. Newman, *Falling from Grace: The Experience of Downward Mobility in the American Middle Class* (1988); G. Pappas, *The Magic City: Unemployment in a Working-Class Community* (1989); L. Thurow, *The Zero-Sum Society: Distribution and the Possibilites for Economic Change* (1980); and W. J. Wilson, *The Truly Disadvantaged: The Inner City, the Underclass, and Public Policy* (1987). M. Katz, *The Undeserving Poor: From the War on Poverty to the War on Welfare* (1989) is vital. For continuing gender issues, see S. Evans and B. Nelson, *Wage Justice: Comparable Worth and the Paradox of Technocratic Reform* (1989); S. Faludi, *Backlash: The Undeclared War against American Women* (1991); A. R. Hochschild, *The Second Shift: Working Parents and the Revolution at Home* (1989); and R. Sidel, *Women and Children Last* (1986). Further examinations of related issues are L. Gordon, *Heroes of Their Own Lives: The Politics and History of Family Violence* (1988); L. Gordon, ed., *Women, the State, and Welfare* (1990); S. A. Hewlett, *When the Bough Breaks: The Cost of Neglecting Our Children* (1991); J. Kozol, *Rachel and Her Children: Homeless Families in America* (1988); and E. F. Torrey, *Nowhere to Go: The Tragic Odyssey of the Homeless Mentally Ill* (1988).

Thoughtful approaches to some of today's vital environmental issues include B. Commoner's influential *The Closing Circle* (1971) and *Making Peace with the Planet* (rev. ed., 1990); M. D'Antonio, *Atomic Harvest* (1993); D. Day, *The Environmental Wars* (1989); D. Fisher, *Fire & Ice: The Greenhouse Effect, Ozone Depletion, and Nuclear Winter* (1990); D. Ford, *Three Mile Island* (1982); S. P. Hays, *Beauty, Health, and Perma-*

nence: Environmental Politics in the United States, 1955–1985 (1987);
C. Manes, *Green Rage: Radical Environmentalism* (1990); M. Melosi,
Garbage in the Cities: Refuse, Reform, and the Environment (1981);
R. Nash, *The Rights of Nature: A History of Environmental Ethics* (1989);
R. Paehlke, *Environmentalism and the Future of Progressive Politics*
(1989); M. Reisner, *Cadillac Desert: The American West and Its Disappearing Water* (1986); R. Vietor, *Energy Policy in America since 1945* (1984);
L. Winner, *The Whale and the Reactor: A Search for Limits in an Age of
High Technology* (1986); and D. Worster's thoughtful *Rivers of Empire:
Water, Aridity and the Growth of the American West* (1985). Also see
W. Dietrich, *Northwest Passage: The Great Columbia River* (1995);
C. A. Milner II, ed., *A New Significance: Re-envisioning the History of the
American West* (1996); K. C. Peterson, *River of Life, Channel of Death:
Fish and Dams on the Lower Snake* (1995); L. Pulido, *Environmentalism
and Economic Justice: Two Chicano Struggles in the Southwest* (1996); and
D. Worster, ed., *The Ends of the Earth: Perspectives on Modern Environmental History* (1988), as well as the perceptive speculations: J. Chace,
The Consequences of Peace (1992); O. Graham, *Losing Time: The Industrial Policy Debate* (1992); and N. Mills, *Culture in an Age of Money: The
Legacy of the 1980s in America* (1990).